ORGANIZATIONS
IN CONTEMPORARY
SOCIETY

ORGANIZATIONS IN CONTEMPORARY SOCIETY

Rhoda Lois Blumberg

Rutgers University

PRENTICE-HALL, INC., Englewood Cliffs, New Jersey 07632

Library of Congress Cataloging-in-Publication Data

Blumberg, Rhoda Goldstein.
 Organizations in contemporary society.

 Bibliography: p. 275
 Includes index.
 1. Organization. 2. Organizational effectiveness—
Case studies. I. Title.
HM131.B596 1987   302.3'5   86-91531
ISBN 0-13-641960-7

Credits: Extracts on pp. 35, 36, 82, 109, and 112 from Jeffrey Pfeffer, *Power in Organizations* (Marshfield, Mass.: Pitman, 1981). Used with permission of Pitman Publishing, Inc. Extracts on pp. 30, 96, 134, 167, 169, 185, and 186 from *Men and Women of the Corporation* by Rosabeth Moss Kanter. Copyright © 1977 by Rosabeth Moss Kanter. Reprinted by permission of Basic Books, Inc., Publishers. Extracts on pp. 201, 202, 204, 216, 217, and 218 from *Street-Level Bureaucracy* by Michael Lipsky. Copyright © 1980 by Russell Sage Foundation. Reprinted by permission of Basic Books, Inc., Publishers. Quotes by Chester I. Barnard on pp. 100, 101, 102, 103, and 133 from *Reader in Bureaucracy*, edited by Robert K. Merton, A. P. Gray, B. Hockey, and H. C. Selvin. Copyright © 1952, 1980 by The Free Press, a Division of Macmillan, Inc.

© 1987 by Prentice-Hall, Inc.
A Division of Simon & Schuster
Englewood Cliffs, New Jersey 07632

All rights reserved. No part of this book may be
reproduced, in any form or by any means,
without permission in writing from the publisher.

Printed in the United States of America
10 9 8 7 6 5 4 3 2 1

ISBN 0-13-641960-7 01

Prentice-Hall International (UK) Limited, *London*
Prentice-Hall of Australia Pty. Limited, *Sydney*
Prentice-Hall Canada, Inc., *Toronto*
Prentice-Hall Hispanoamericana, S.A., *Mexico*
Prentice-Hall of India Private Limited, *New Delhi*
Prentice-Hall of Japan, Inc., *Tokyo*
Prentice Hall of Southeast Asia Pte. Ltd., *Singapore*
Editora Prentice-Hall do Brasil, Ltda., *Rio de Janeiro*

For HELENA JO

CONTENTS

PREFACE   xiii

1 THE ORGANIZATIONAL SOCIETY   1

The Power and Prevalence of Organizations *1*
  The Problem: What Is the Role of Organizations in Modern Life? *1*
  An Approach to Learning about Organizations *2*
  Formal Organizations, Complex Organizations, and Bureaucracies *4*
The Bureaucratization of Modern Life *5*
  Bureaucratic versus Traditional Society *5*
  Characteristics of Bureaucratic Organization *11*
Nonbureaucratic Elements of Social Organization *17*
  The Omnipresence of Nonbureaucratic Elements *17*
  Major Nonbureaucratic Collectivities *17*
Mixtures of Family, Ethnicity, and Business: A Case Study *17*
Summary *22*

2 THE SOCIAL ROOTS OF ORGANIZATIONAL KNOWLEDGE   25

Science, Ideology, and Public Policy *25*
  *The Problem: How Are Science, Ideology, and Public Policy
    Related?* *25*

*The Social Factors in Scientific Knowledge Seeking and
    Dissemination 28*
Research and International Ideological Conflicts 30
The Needs of Corporations: How They Affect Research *31*
    Important Types of Knowledge Needed 31
    Hard Scientific and Technological Studies 31
    Social Science Research 32
Challenges to Traditional Perspectives *37*
    The Women's Studies Perspective 37
    Collective Behavior by Workers 40
    Social Movements and Citizen Revolt 41
    Marxist Critiques 41
Conflict of Interest: A Case Study *44*
Summary *45*

3 TYPOLOGIES

47

Classifying Organizations *47*
    The Problem: The Need to Classify Organizations 47
    Common-Sense and Intentional Typologies 48
Organizational Science's Neglect of Typologies *49*
    Decreasing Interest in Typologies 49
    Organizational Survival as a Focus 50
    Organizational Effectiveness as a Focus 51
Typologies Examined *52*
    Blau and Scott: Who Benefits? 52
    *Westrum and Samaha: Bureaucracy, Enterprise, and Voluntary
        Association 56*
    Etzioni: Types of Power and Compliance 58
    Goffman: Total Institutions 59
    Perrow: Technology 60
    McKelvey: Population and Taxonomy 63
Changing Doctor-Patient Relationships: A Case Study *65*
Summary *67*

4 ORGANIZATIONAL GOALS

71

The Nature of Organizational Goals *71*
    The Problem: How Important Are Officially Stated Goals? 71
    Officially Stated Goals 72
    Stated Goals and the Organization in Action 74
Operative Goals *76*
    Discovering Operative Goals 76
    Characteristics of Operative Goals 79
Goals and Environment *83*
    Internal and External Aspects of Goal Setting 83
    Survival in a Changing Environment 83
    Organizational Processes for Dealing with the Environment 85
The Goals of Universities: A Case Study *88*
Summary *93*

5 POWER, AUTHORITY, AND COMMUNICATION 95

The Distinction between Power and Authority *96*
  The Problem: How Can We Distinguish between Power and
    Authority? 96
  Definitions of Power 96
  Definitions of Authority 97
  The Role of Communication 99
Authority and Compliance *100*
  Orders as Communication 100
  Why People Comply with Authority 101
  The Zone of Indifference 103
  Limitations of the Concept of Authority 103
Power and Involvement *105*
  Types of Power 105
  Kinds of Involvement 106
  Sources of Power 108
  Conditions Determining the Use of Power 112
  Persistence of Power 113
Communication as a Vehicle of Power *114*
  Patterns of Communication 114
  Modes of Communication 117
  The Functions of Secrecy 119
Opposition to Organizational Authority: The Case of
    Whistle-Blowing *119*
Summary *122*

6 STATUS, ROLE, AND THE DIVISION OF LABOR 123

The Division of Labor in Society and in Organizations *124*
  The Problem: Who Should Do What? 124
  Status and Role: Units in the Division of Labor 124
  Societal Statuses and Status Sets 126
  The Earliest Bases of Division of Labor: Sex, Age, Race, and
    Ethnicity 126
  Modern Society: The Increase in Division of Labor and
    Specialization 127
  Latent Identities in Organizations 128
  How Nontraditional People Gain Entry 131
Cooperative and Conflict Perspectives on Status Systems *132*
  The Official Division of Labor in Organizations: Its Expression
    in Status and Role 132
  The Cooperative Perspective on Status Systems 133
  The Conflict Perspective on Status Systems 135
  Formal and Informal Negotiations Over Rules 136
  Additional Sources of Conflict in Role Relationships 137
The Informal Division of Labor as an Adjustive Mechanism *141*
  Adding or Eliminating Obligations 142
  Patterns of Mutual Aid: Helping Out 143
  The Sloughing Off of Dirty Work 144
  Voluntary Action Taken in Emergency Situations 145
Informal Organization in the Women's Prison: A Case Study *145*
Summary *147*

7   MANAGERS AND ORGANIZATIONAL CULTURES   149

Managing the Organization   *149*
   *The Problem: What Do Managers Do and How Do They Succeed
      at It?   149*
   The Manager as a Business Type   150
   *Managerial Counterparts in Government and Voluntary
      Associations   151*
   Levels of Management   152
The Manager as Organization Leader   *154*
   Use of Authority: Leadership and Compliance   154
   Cultural Leadership   156
   Decision Making   162
   Managerial Succession   165
Managerial Careers   *167*
   Selection   167
   Socialization   168
   Mobility   169
   The Wives of Management   170
Women as Managers: A Case Study   *171*
Summary   *173*

8   ORGANIZATION AND THE INDIVIDUAL   175

Role and the Self: Moral Careers   *175*
   The Problem: How Do Organizations Affect Individual Lives?   175
   The Self as Reflexive, as an Ongoing Creation   179
   Kinds of Careers   183
The Impact of Organizations on Participants: Workers   *186*
   Structural Determinants of Behavior in Organizations   186
   *The Creation of Occupational Types and Bureaucratic
      Personalities   192*
The Taylorization of Police Work: A Case Study in Deskilling   *195*
Summary   *196*

9   ORGANIZATION AND THE INDIVIDUAL: PUBLICS   199

The Public-in-Contact   *199*
   The Problem: What Are Publics-in-Contact?   199
   Commonalities of Public-in-Contact Experiences   200
   Variations in Status and Power Relationships   201
   Constraints on Service   202
   Openness of Organizational Boundaries   204
   Adaptations of Functionaries to People Work   205
   Adaptations of the Public-in-Contact   207
   The Revolt of the Client   208
The Public-at-Large   *209*
   Who is the Public-at-Large?   209
   *Importance of Relationships between the Organization and the
      Public-at-Large   210*

Public Opinion 210
Elements of the Public-at-Large 211
The Public's Exercise of Power 213
Controlling Clients and the Work Situation: The Case of Street-Level
    Bureaucrats *214*
Summary *218*

10 ORGANIZATIONS AND THEIR ENVIRONMENTS   221

The Nature of Organization-Environment Interaction *222*
    *The Problem: How Do Organizations and Their Environments
        Influence Each Other? 222*
    Why the Focus on Environments? 222
Interorganizational Relations *223*
    The Environment of Related Organizations 223
    Populations and Organizational Forms 223
    The Interorganizational Network 226
    Resources 226
    Bases of Power within Networks 227
    Effects of Interorganizational Power 228
    Network Environments 229
The General Environment *230*
    The Specific versus the General Environment 230
    Natural Selection Models versus the Resource Dependence Model 230
    Criticism of the Population Ecology Model 232
    Types of Environmental Conditions 232
    How Powerful Organizations Mold Their Environments 234
The Underworld *236*
    The Underworld as Part of Organizational Society 236
    What Is Organized Crime? 237
    Differences between Legal and Illegal Organizations 237
    The Borderline between Legal and Illegal Activity 238
    The Effects of Demand and Supply 240
    The Corruption of Officials 240
    The Effects of Changing Technology 241
Social Movements and Institutionalized Organizations *242*
    Voluntary Associations 242
    Social Movements 243
Corporate Fraud: A Case Study *244*
Summary *247*

11 CURRENT ISSUES IN THE ORGANIZATIONAL SOCIETY   249

Public Issues in Advanced Industrial Society *250*
    *The Problem: What Kinds of Public Issues Characterize Our
        Times? 250*
High Risk Technologies and Normal Accidents *251*
    Creating Risk 251
    Normal Accidents 252

Problems of American Business and Labor *257*
   Decline in Industry 257
   Worker Participation 258
   Community Labor-Management Committees 259
   Worker and Worker-Community Ownership 260
   The Role of Unions 261
   White-Collar Crime and Corporate Deviance 262
Issues of Equality *262*
   The Thrust for Equality 263
   Women and Labor Markets 265
   Affirmative Action and Equal Opportunity 266
   Human Service Issues 269
Bureaucracy and Democracy *269*
   The Relationship between Bureaucracy and Democracy 269
   Internal Democracy 270
   The Power of Bureaucracies 270
   The Dangers of Bureaucratic Impersonality 271
Summary *271*

REFERENCES   275

INDEX   287

PREFACE

Teaching a course called Complex Organizations at Rutgers University these many years has almost always been a pleasure. It has consisted of a mutual quest between students and myself to learn about bureaucracies by drawing on our experiences. Some examples: The impact of a major reorganization of campuses and centralization of control at the University several years back provided rich data. Semiannual course registration inevitably brings forth examples of what students refer to as "the Rutgers screw"—computer errors such as deregistration, which wipes out their enrollment in courses. Or there is the special campus bus schedule during final exam period, which eliminates many runs and adds on to waiting time and bus crowding during this generally stressful time. Most of my students also supplement their budgets by working over the summer; they return in the fall with varied job experiences to analyze. While the university offers many examples of depersonalization in a large bureaucracy, student work experiences often provide case studies of power and conflict in somewhat smaller settings.

Teaching Complex Organizations has also given me the opportunity to experiment with various combinations of texts and readers in the field. Unfortunately, the experimentation has not always been successful. A difficult, jargon-filled text does not win student enthusiasm, no matter how brilliant or erudite its author. A book that pleases one's colleagues for its up-to-date presentation of theoretical debates, ample citations, and statistical sophistication may prove unfathomable to many students. What I have always sought is a lucid, sociologically oriented text suitable for bright undergraduates, which was both critical (in its broadest sense) and relevant to the times.

As other authors know, if one complains loudly enough about existing texts, he or she is likely to be asked to write one. And so, while my most recent work has been on social movement organizations (a generally unemphasized aspect of organizational sociology), and my most central research on organizations appeared largely as a doctoral dissertation (*The Professional Nurse in the Hospital Bureaucracy*, 1954), I consented to undertake this task. It has been a valuable learning experience.

My point of view will be found to be eclectic. The main influence on how I approach organizations and occupations derives from insights gained while attending the lectures and seminars of Everett C. Hughes. Hughes was not interested in labeling things and so perhaps that is why there is no "Hughes' theory" of occupations. But this gentle scholar was an absolute master in helping his students to develop a "sociological eye," an insightful way of examining social life that would serve well through their remaining careers. Hughes taught us how to do field work. He did not suggest that we study "occupational cultures," but that is what we did.

My strong interest in race relations within professions had been stimulated by the influence of another great teacher, Louis Wirth, but I was made to understand that race relations could be studied only within its broader contexts. The resulting dissertation was a comparative study of three hospitals, which included analysis of the desegregating process that was then going on.

In addition to these early University of Chicago influences, there are others who helped with this work. Lucille Duberman and Penney Hills deserve thanks for reading all or part of it at crucial times. Their ideas and editorial expertise were valuable, as were those of Helen M. Hacker and Wendell J. Roye in a less formal way. Organizational researchers Patricia Y. Martin, Dafna Izraeli, and John S. Butler, as well as many of my own students, encouraged me to do the book. I am also grateful for the detailed commentary, criticism and suggestions of the Prentice-Hall reviewers: Howard E. Aldrich, Charles Mulford, William T. Clute, Ronald Rebore, James Wood, and Jerald Hage. While I am solely responsible for the results, I am sure that their contributions strengthened the product. Prentice-Hall editors were ever reasonable and supportive, especially Ed Stanford, who remembered my years'-old threat to write an organization text, and Bill Webber, who shepherded the manuscript through.

There are no longer young children or a mate around to be thanked for patience and forebearance. Instead, I am grateful to those friends and relatives who distracted me from the hypnosis of the computer screen and thereby helped to keep me human. Above all these include: Leah, Meyer, Helena Jo, Bess, Miriam, Lynda Glennon, and, collectively, the collegial members of the Metropolitan New York chapter of Sociologists for Women in Society.

R.L.B.

ORGANIZATIONS
IN CONTEMPORARY
SOCIETY

1

THE ORGANIZATIONAL SOCIETY

The Power and Prevalence of Organizations
   The Problem: What Is the Role of Organizations in Modern Life?
   An Approach to Learning about Organizations
   Formal Organizations, Complex Organizations, and Bureaucracies
The Bureaucratization of Modern Life
   Bureaucratic versus Traditional Society
   Characteristics of Bureaucratic Organization
Nonbureaucratic Elements of Social Organization
   The Omnipresence of Nonbureaucratic Elements
   Major Nonbureaucratic Collectivities
Mixtures of Family, Ethnicity, and Business: A Case Study
Summary

THE POWER AND PREVALENCE OF ORGANIZATIONS

The Problem: What Is the Role of Organizations in Modern Life?

Human infants are born into families, communities, and racial and ethnic groups. Their relationships with the people around them are concrete, meaningful, and fateful. To be born a white female American in Iowa is quite different than to be born a rural female of a lower caste in India. Life experiences will prove very

1

different under the two circumstances. But we are also born into a world where our very lives are deeply affected by what goes on far from the family, in the web of international power and conflict relations and in the international economy. We exist in a modern technological world where nations are linked by vast networks of speedy communication and transportation systems. More ominously, a serious nuclear accident in one country can imperil surrounding ones, as in the case of the April 1986 disaster at the Chernobyl nuclear power plant in the Soviet Union.

Perhaps nowhere are advances in technology so awesome as in the area of "defense" weapons—and offense weapons. Nations develop highly sensitive systems for detecting the approach of enemy attacks and prepare to strike back within seconds. They have a vast capacity to overkill; the fate of life, as we know it, depends on human judgment about pushing certain buttons and on error-proof operation of complex defense technologies. A space weapons competition is now underway. Proposed space-based antiballistic missile systems include space mines, electromagnetic hypervelocity rail guns, superpowerful lasers activated by chemical reactions or even nuclear explosions, and giant orbiting mirrors to direct laser beams (Union of Concerned Scientists, 1984). Those anxious about peace—and drawings of young schoolchildren indicate that fears of nuclear war are real at a very tender age—recognize the interdependence of nations that has been wrought by technological advance in communications, weaponry, and conquest of outer space. Technology is one product of a world transformed by modernization, the growth of science, urbaniza-tion, and specialization.

Large formal organizations are the major sites of today's frenetic activities. They serve as intermediate structures between the small, familiar world of family and community and that of the global universe. The web of formal organizations includes nation-states with their governments and myriad governmental agencies, multinational corporations and small businesses, international banking networks, religious organizations and sects, military organizations, entertainment and sports industries, and systems of medical care, recreation, and criminal justice, to name some of the major organizational systems. All have divisions and subdivisions within them. Your day-by-day experiences as student, worker, and consumer bring you into contact with units of many of such organizations. Personal relations and global concerns are linked by the intervening structures of modern life, and these realities are shaped by organizations.

An Approach to Learning about Organizations

Object of the book.   This book will give you a more systematic understand-ing of how organizations work and how they affect your life. It will focus on the vast array of formal (also called complex) organizations, defined most simply as social structures *consciously set up to accomplish specific purposes.* Theorists like to say that formal organizations are *ubiquitous*, which means they have the quality of existing or being everywhere at the same time. Such organizations include all the examples mentioned above as formally organized intermediate structures between the individual and the universe—corporations, banks, governmental agencies, churches, sports organizations, and numerous others. Later in the chapter these organizations will be contrasted with types of human collectivities that are *not* formal organizations, such as families and communities.

Starting with the known. It is always easier to start with what we know and then to move on to more abstract concepts. Fortunately, each of us has a vast pool of experience and insight we can draw on as we move to a more scientific study of organizations. A scientific grasp of how organizations work will enable us to transfer knowledge gained in one specific context to others. For example, as a newcomer on a job you may well have experienced an informal probationary period before you were fully accepted by fellow workers. Certain kinds of frequently used tactics test the neophyte's willingness to fit in with and protect the group rather than jeopardize it. Speeding up production or informing on employee pilfering would certainly reap retribution by peers. There are variations: Some people are never accepted, especially if they are from the "wrong" ethnic, racial, or gender group, while others, like a worker's kid brother, may be readily welcomed. Once you have endured rigorous testing as a newcomer on the job, you are probably better prepared for what to expect on your next new job. Similarly, if you started your education at one college and then transferred to another, your experience at the second college may prove easier because you already know some of "the ropes." As you encounter new ideas in this book, make an attempt to relate them to your own life experiences, for either confirmation or contradiction.

Limits of personal experience. Bear in mind, however, that it is dangerous to generalize from a few cases. Perhaps for example, you were one of the lucky few introduced into a job by a popular worker. Because you were readily accepted, you might tend to assume that new workers are *not* systematically tested. It would be important to confront the possibility that your experience may not have been typical. Nor is one person's common sense necessarily another's. Using your own common sense does help to arrive at hunches and hypotheses. A woman may consider it perfectly logical that she be allowed to become a firefighter, yet some of her male peers may believe that such a deviation from past practice borders on the absurd. Such differences in "common-sense" thinking lead thoughtful people to probe into the multiple factors operating in a situation. The approach to learning suggested here is this: Take off from your own experience with organizations, remain open-minded, and test your insights against the findings of experts; by doing so, you will arrive at a more balanced understanding of the subject.

Organization vocabularies. Every field has its own language, its own jargon, and the field of organizations is a prime example. Theorists invent concepts that will put complicated ideas into a few key words. If you learn the meaning of "the contingency approach," "open and closed systems," and "organizational environments," then you can use the phrases to represent these complicated ideas without going through the whole process of explanation again. However, excessive use of new terminology can defeat its own purpose; the newcomer to the field may be left behind. Therefore, familiar examples and everyday vocabulary will be used as much as possible in this book to supplement the new terminology considered essential.

Formal Organizations, Complex Organizations, and Bureaucracies

Formal or complex organizations?   Organizations have *degrees* of complexity and *degrees* of formal, official structure; writers (myself included) generally mean the same thing by the terms *complex organization* and *formal organization*. Organizations of most interest to theorists tend to be the larger, more complex ones, which may explain why the term *complex organization* currently enjoys more popularity than the term *formal organization*. Yet the latter term more clearly includes even small groups set up for specific purposes—a French club or a social movement organization, such as the Society for the Protection of Birdwatchers— that may not be very complex. These groups share with larger organizations, such as corporations and universities, such features as having been deliberately created at some point in time, having stated rules and regulations, and having a division of tasks among people who are supposed to play different roles. We shall use the terms *formal* and *complex* interchangeably to refer to all such organizations.

Bureaucracy.   In contrast, the term *bureaucracy* may or may not be used interchangeably with *formal organization*. It is a more colorful word, evoking all kinds of images. When a person complains about bureaucracy, he or she is usually criticizing the negative features of formal organizations: cold impersonality, a maze of channels to go through, inflexibility in dealing with special cases, inequality of statuses, or a plethora of rules and regulations. *Bureaucracy* is a handy word to use because it is already familiar—though in caricaturized form—to most of us.

Unfortunately, however, writers on complex organizations do use the term *bureaucracy* in several ways. Scott (1981) points out some of these variations:

> Some organizational theorists use the term bureaucracy as a general synonym for organization; others reserve the term to refer to public organizations or to the administrative units of the nation state; and still others, most notably, Weber, use the term to designate a particular administrative structure. (p. 23)

Max Weber, the father of the field, used *bureaucracy* to mean the kind of administrative organization most characteristic of formal organizations (Weber, 1952). Administration has to do with the art of getting things done, and the bureaucratic mode of organizing activities has its own special features. Weber's analysis of these key features is still the taking-off point for much debate about the nature of bureaucracy. Weber believed that with the rise of modern capitalism and a money economy, the bureaucratic form became the most efficient way of running large organizations. He maintained that organizations with many different kinds of purposes could be run bureaucratically:

> This [bureaucratic] type of organization is in principle applicable with equal facility to a wide variety of different fields. It may be applied in profit-making business or in charitable organizations, or in any number of other types of private enterprises serving ideal or material ends. It is equally applicable to political and to religious organizations. (1952:22)

Weber was concerned that bureaucracies might become too powerful. As he predicted, the bureaucratic way of running organizations has become extremely prevalent in the modern world. Organizations that resist any degree of bureaucratization—for example, communes that specifically reject naming formal leaders, assigning different tasks to different individuals, or recognizing status differences are in the minority. However, debureaucratizing tendencies do exist, as evidenced by a rising consumerism that places less faith in officials and experts.

A few writers distinguish government from private organizations; they call the former *bureaucracies* and consider businesses special enough to have their own term, *enterprises* (Westrum & Samaha, 1984). Without minimizing their differences, we define both businesses and governmental agencies as bureaucracies, since both employ bureaucratic principles. Similarly, voluntary associations such as churches, clubs, and social movement groups are formal organizations according to our definition. They also have the problem of bureaucratization because they are affected by growth, complexity, and the fact that they exist within the context of a bureaucratized society. For example, a newly formed club in a college will have to draw up bylaws, elect officers, regularize ways of collecting and using funds, abide by school rules, and deal with the college's official hierarchy. Thus, all formal or complex organizations will be considered to be bureaucratic to some degree.

THE BUREAUCRATIZATION OF MODERN LIFE

Bureaucratic versus Traditional Society

Bureaucracy is so pervasive and widespread that many have commented on the way it has created a drastic change in the kind of societal relationships people typically experience. Writers have depicted major differences between rural, or "folk," societies and urban societies, that is, between traditional and modern societies (Redfield, 1947). Modern societies are dominated by large, formal, complex organizations; traditional societies, by family, clan, community, and personal relations. The two types may be thought of as polar opposites, so long as we recognize that we are comparing "pure" types, called *ideal* types by Weber. In this usage, *pure* or *ideal* means that the basic characteristics, with no modifying features, have been isolated out to set up a model, for example, of "the urban society." No real society fits this model perfectly.

Small pockets of the city, such as old ethnic neighborhoods, may resemble the folk or traditional society in many respects (Gans, 1962). All real societies fall somewhere between the two theoretical types, for none is totally bureaucratized, nor is any totally unorganized. The so-called developing societies, such as India, show an interesting mixture of the two types. Modern societies are characterized by a highly complex division of labor, with tasks broken down into parts, much as they are in an automobile assembly line. But some division of labor occurs in every society, for example, between men and women or the old and the young (see chapter 6). One way of understanding the differences between the two polar types is to think of them as lying along a continuum, with relatively traditional societies at one end and relatively modern societies at the other. Most societies are mixtures of the two types, and traditions may be called on to justify changes (R. L. Blumberg, 1980a). Further, the "modernization" of various societies does not mean the inevitable copying of Western industrialized societies. Japan has combined traditional and modern structures, acknowledging, for example, the continuing importance of the family. Parents are invited to attend company "graduation" ceremonies for their adult children. Some United States firms are trying to emulate successful Japanese policies in mixing nonbureaucratic with bureaucratic principles.

With all these cautions, we take the position that analytically separating out the characteristic, extreme features of traditional and modern societies helps us to understand bureaucratization. Table 1-1 is an eclectic list—that is, one drawn from varied sources—that contrasts the two:

TABLE 1-1   Characteristics of Traditional and Bureaucratic Societies

TRADITIONAL	BUREAUCRATIC
Primary group relations	Secondary group relations
Simple division of labor	Complex division of labor
Traditional authority	Bureaucratic-legal authority
Norms	Rules
Religion, magic	Science, rationality
Particularism	Universalism
Qualities	Performances
Loyalty	Efficiency

Primary versus secondary group relations. The term *primary group* was created by sociologist Charles Cooley (1909) to describe the intimate, persisting, face-to-face groups in which we interact as whole personalities. Examples are the immediate family and inner circles of friends. Although such groups continue to exist in modern society, there are fewer enduring personal relationships than in traditional societies. Smaller in size and more isolated, the folk society is tied together by webs of kinship and traditional obligation. As in the small town, there are few places to hide: each person—and probably his or her whole family genealogy—is known to all. Through interaction, usually in a small geographic area over a long period of time, people get to know each other in a variety of roles rather than as individuals playing segmented, partial roles.

In the city, typifying modernization, people experience many more secondary-group type relationships. In these we interact with others in more transitory, specialized, less personal roles. As a consumer, I look for a store that will sell me what I want. The clerk who performs the service may be someone I will never see again; he or she does not know (or want to know) my personal problems. As a professor I come to know many students, some better than others, but frequently our relationship ends at the end of their college careers.

The *tendency* toward a lack of intimacy in modern life is so great that it brings about imitations of intimacy. Those who run complex organizations frequently recognize that many people value friendly relationships. "Your personal banker" was created as an advertising slogan to convince the potential customer that he or she would get personal, individualized service. This is an example of a phenomenon bringing about its opposite, a principle of *dialectics* (about which more will be said later.) The huge organization tries to minimize its impersonality by simulating concern and intimacy. This case also reminds us that change brings about further change, and that it does not simply go forward in one direction. Without getting morbid, we can suggest that if nations fail to curb their militarism, modern technology may reduce us all to a very simple, primitive type of existence—the same principle of dialectics again.

The tendency to romanticize traditional types of relationships and devalue bureaucratic ones occurs frequently. But note, also, the old adage that "city air makes men free." The anonymity of city life means that I can purchase what I want even if I have yelled at my grandmother or engaged in illicit sexual relations. I am not open to ostracism or censure by the clerk, who does not know or want to know me as a total person. In the city like-minded people of almost any persuasion are more likely to find others who share their points of view. The person considered deviant in a small town (e.g., a Democrat in a Republican town) can come to the city and find others who share his or her beliefs.

Simple division of labor versus complex division of labor. All that must be done to keep a society going—paid as well as unpaid work—is included in the term *labor.* In the folk society people are in immediate contact with nature through agricultural, gathering, and hunting activities. Raw materials are often converted into finished products in the home, where cooking and the fashioning of utensils and garments takes place. Skills are transmitted through the family. As societies industrialize, knowledge becomes so specialized that it is divided up into fields within fields and taught by experts in formal settings. Production is taken out of the home. It is done not for one's own family members but in exchange for wages. Job classifications grow as labor is divided into more parts. Unlike the traditional farmer, who tends a crop from seed to harvest, the worker in a plant often performs a specialized, repetitive operation day after day.

Countries such as the United States are now in an advanced industrial phase, where the production of goods is highly mechanized. The manufacturing of goods requires fewer and fewer workers, while the service-producing sector grows. Among services are transportation, public utilities such as telephone companies, wholesale and retail trade, finance and government services. Thus, the division of labor constantly shifts and the jobs available to people change; technology makes some skills obsolete while creating a demand for new kinds of expertise. As new areas of specialized knowledge are created, other areas undergo a reverse process—deskilling. That is, technological change removes some of the skill and decision-making previously required for a particular job. The so-called developing societies of the world have different mixes between agricultural and nonagricultural jobs, with a larger proportion of people still engaged in agriculture and living outside of cities.

Traditional authority versus bureaucratic-legal authority.   Authority is official power, the right to govern others made real by their belief that those exercising authority have the right to do so. Thus, Weber wrote of three types of legitimate authority—traditional, legal, and charismatic—each having different bases for their justification. According to him, "Traditional authority rests on the belief in the sacredness of the social order and its prerogatives as existing of yore. Patriarchal authority represents its pure type" (Weber, 1980:6). Patriarchal authority is passed down through the eldest male member of the family; it is considered sacred and correct because it was always thus. The traditional authority of kings can be explained in the same way.

In contrast, "legal authority rests on enactment; its pure type is best represented by bureaucracy" (Weber, 1980:4). Rules and regulations are established and can be changed by going through specified procedures, such as passing laws or drawing up contracts. These rules define and delimit positions of authority. Allegiance is not owed to the person, such as the patriarch, but to the office, such as the president, the supervisor, or the department head. The rights and duties of the office are defined by the organization and cannot be legitimately extended past the proper bounds. For example, in my position, or "office," of teacher, I can require a term paper but I cannot tell you the type of haircut you should get.

In the traditional society, of course, traditional authority prevailed. But modernization increasingly required trained specialists who had jurisdiction over particular areas, and who presumably would use science and rational judgment in pursuing objectives. While the top of a hierarchy, such as the president of the United States, is usually elected rather than appointed, he or she in turn needs to appoint qualified managers and experts to head up various departments. According to Weber (1980),

> this type of 'legal' rule comprises not only the modern structure of state and city government but likewise the power relations in private capitalist enterprise, in public corporations and voluntary associations of all sorts, provided that an extensive and hierarchically organized staff of functionaries exist. (p. 5)

The third type of authority, charismatic, is based on unusual personal qualities—those of a leader who is able to attract disciples by virtue of personal power.

"The purest types are the rule of the prophet, the warrior hero, the great demagogue" (Weber, 1980:8). Charismatic authority accounts for revolutionary change, circumstances in which followers are willing to forego tradition or prescribed duty and accept the charismatic leader's new ideas as correct. Examples of such leaders are Jesus, Martin Luther King, and Fidel Castro. One need not agree with the ideas of these leaders to understand that, for some people, they are strongly charismatic. Such leaders or prophets may arise historically under many conditions.

Postponing more thorough consideration of these concepts of power and authority for chapter 5, the crux of the argument here is that different types of authority prevail in bureaucracies than in traditional societies or folk societies. In everyday life, we in modern society continually make contracts, that is, agree to abide by the limitations of various rules and regulations as administered by office-holders.

Norms versus rules. Closely related to these ideas of authority are the concepts of norms and rules. A *norm* is a customary, usual, commonly accepted practice, whereas a *rule* is generally a written, formal statement of required behavior. The preliterate society was just what the term implies: pre-the written word. Without having a system of writing in which to put down rules, everyone in the society knew what was right and wrong—what the norms were.

Rules are necessary when tradition or common consensus cannot be called upon: People in contact may not even know each other, let alone agree with each other. In modern anonymous society, we live mostly by law, contract, written rules, related to systems of bureaucratic-legal authority. The prevalence of formal rules is such that we often seek them out in new encounters. If the rules are not unreasonable, we may automatically comply. For example, patrons may experience a moment of uncertainty when entering a new restaurant as they try to find out whether they are expected to take any available table or wait to be seated by a host or hostess. Their often unstated question is, "What is the rule?" In a restaurant of any pretensions (not your local fast-food outlet), another question arises when it is time to pay—does this particular establishment accept credit cards? If not, the patron generally accepts the rule, even if privately deciding not to return.

Loyalty versus efficiency. Efficiency, not loyalty, is a guiding principle of organizational society as a pure type. Workers are supposed to be promoted or fired not on the basis of personal loyalty to a boss but on the basis of how efficiently they perform. Describing the mixture of bureaucracy with traditions found in actual societies, Ouchi (1981) points out that obligations of loyalty have been successfully transferred from family and clan to the corporation in Japan. In the United States requiring loyalty to one's place of work is viewed by some as a management device to make workers feel sentimentally attached to the work place. After all, the corporation is unlikely to feel sentimentally attached, or loyal, to an inefficient worker. Similarly, as consumers seek service or goods from numerous organizations, they may be most concerned with getting what they want, that is, with the efficiency of those organizations. Yet advertising sometimes successfully creates a loyal following for a product by linking it with cherished values. When the manufacturers of Coca-Cola tried to substitute an "improved" formula for the familiar product, loyal customers expressed their resentment.

Religion and magic versus science and rationality.   The various characteristics listed on each side, respectively, of our dichotomy of folk and modern societies (table 1-1) are, of course, interrelated. The development of science created the need for specialists whose expertise in various areas was independent of their birth or ancestral line. In the preliterate society religion and magic were part of everyday life, a way of coping with the unknown. A hunting expedition, for example, would be preceded by a religious ceremony believed to ensure its success and the safe return of the hunters.

The features of traditional society grew up in response to human needs and fears, needs and fears that have certainly not altogether disappeared. However, in modern societies the use of science and a rational approach to technical tasks are considered essential. Possessed of modern technology, the pilot of an aircraft takes certain precautions before a flight—checking wind, weather, flight plan, instruments, and so on. This reliance on science for ensuring a safe flight will take place no matter how religious the flier may be, no matter that he or she carries a good luck charm or wears a special hat. A prayer is added as an extra measure of protection, recognizing that science is not foolproof and that accidents do happen. The elements of magic that we carry over into modern life, like the lucky charm or avoidance of bad-luck words, again illustrate that no society is completely bureaucratized. Fear of the unexpected exists in all types of societies, so all kinds of measures of protection may be called upon.

Particularism versus universalism.   Because these many-syllabled words express important ideas very concisely, they are frequently used. *Universalism* is a principle requiring that all persons be treated according to the same standards, without favoritism. It is represented in civil service rules that specify examinations to prove competence. *Particularism*, the opposing principle, favors treating people according to the special relationship we have with them. When families and clans predominated, it was expected that members of kin groups had special obligations to each other. Marriages might take place to strengthen economic relationships, uniting two families or clans by blood ties. Modern democratic societies try to limit the privilege of family position and the inefficiency of hiring unqualified relatives. Emphasis is officially placed on universalism, on selecting people according to specified standards rather than personal connections. Favoritism and patronage still exist; you undoubtedly know of many examples. But the subtle difference is the prominence of officially universalistic norms—such as your expectation that your tests will be graded fairly. A teacher suspected of showing favoritism may be called into question. Universities could not run if grades were overwhelmingly based on particularism. In the traditional society, particularism was generally not only expected but considered proper.

Qualities versus performances. This dichotomy, as well as the related one just discussed, is part of what Parsons has called "pattern variables" (1951:58–67). Qualities versus performances refers to "two institutionalized ways of defining people: on the basis of their abilities or on the basis of certain of their qualities" (Bredemeier & Stephenson, 1965). As defined in this context, the term *qualities* refers to who a person is, in terms of ascribed characteristics (e.g., male, middle-aged, of Hispanic origin) rather than *performances*—what he or she can do. While there are many situations in modern life that use qualities (such as being over twenty-one years old, or being a "senior citizen") as the basis of rules, there are numerous others that formally emphasize performances. For example, applications for jobs or college entrance are *supposed* to be treated universalistically and persons chosen according to their abilities rather than race or gender. Discrimination may be charged if this appears not to be the case. One of the ways that organizational elites get around the prescription of universalism is to maintain that women or members of racial minorities are less able than white men.

We have discussed each feature of the two contrasting ideal types of society. Tested against this framework, existing societies can be judged to be relatively bureaucratized or relatively unbureaucratized. Bureaucratization was linked to industrial development, the decline of feudalism and the rise of capitalism with its money economy. What about today's Socialist or Communist societies—are they bureaucratized? Ask anyone who has traveled or lived in industrialized countries of Eastern Europe, such as the Soviet Union. These countries also have highly developed science and technology, intricate divisions of labor, specialization, complex organizations—and bureaucracy. While the form of government influences the shape of the state's bureaucracies, modern industrial society requires large organizations, and large organizations tend to be run bureaucratically.

Moving from this consideration of societies, let us focus on organizations themselves. Bureaucratically run organizations—individual bureaucracies—are important units of modern societies, which collectively give these societies their characteristic "flavor."

Characteristics of Bureaucratic Organization

Models of bureaucracy: Weber's ideal type. Max Weber constructed an ideal type of the pure bureaucracy and believed that the bureaucratic method of administering large formal organizations was necessary and efficient (Weber, 1952:18–27). Although Weber was concerned with the power of bureaucracies, he left it to others to demonstrate the inefficiencies and negative aspects of bureaucratic systems.

These are the main features of bureaucracy as an ideal type:

1. There is a clear-cut division of labor, with organizational tasks officially designated as belonging to various positions, or statuses.
2. This division of labor is linked to specialization, and employees are hired on the basis of their technical qualifications for the positions.

3. There is a hierarchy of authority, with officials or superordinates above and subordinates below. The scope of authority of each position is clearly defined and limited.

4. There is a formally established system of rules and regulations that ensures coordination of activities and promotes stability.

5. Officials are expected to act universalistically and impersonally, and to judge others on the basis of their performances—that is, in terms of their actions rather than their personal traits.

6. Employment by an organization provides security in that persons are selected according to their qualifications and can expect to advance systematically if they perform their functions correctly. Presumably, persons gain the right to their positions after a trial period and are protected against arbitrary dismissal. The principle of job security is most typical of certain levels of civil service positions and is reflected in seniority rules and the use of tenure in educational institutions. This feature of Weber's ideal type is less characteristic of other actual work settings.

Real organizations are affected by such factors as economic cycles and changing technological needs. Some jobs and the skills attached to them become obsolete. In the United States aspiring executives tend to switch jobs in order to move up faster. Interestingly, Japan's major corporations do attempt to follow the principle of lifetime employment. This policy works well for the lucky ones chosen as employees by major corporations but not for many others. Females are not so chosen because of the assumption that they are temporary employees who will take time out for motherhood. These women may continue to have the status and get the wages of "temporary" employees until they retire (Ouchi, 1981).

The six features of the bureaucratic *organization* just described correspond rather closely to the ideal type of bureaucratic *society* characterized earlier. A society in which most activities occur in and through bureaucracies reflects them in its quality of life.

The rational systems model.   Weber's characteristics stress the formal, spelled-out, official structures of bureaucracy: designated positions, each with their specific duties, hierarchy of authority, officeholders acting impersonally, according to rules. The organization chart and formal designation of duties provides rational (reasoned) guidelines for accepted behavior, behavior according to the "book." Authority is official, hence legitimate, and since well-qualified persons are chosen for positions of authority, they govern appropriately. Those in lower positions accept the authority of the higher-ups. It is always possible to make an "organization chart" designating who manages whom in a formal organization, in terms of written rules and official responsibilities. Figure 1-1 provides a simple example.

Of course, real organizations and real people do not operate this way. Nor is the internal structure of the organization a self-contained unit, as assumed in the rational systems model. For instance, a firm might find it more efficient in the long run to hire the mayor's brother, regardless of his qualifications, if the firm is negotiating a contract with the city. This rational systems model leaves many questions

FIGURE 1-1 A Sample Organization Chart

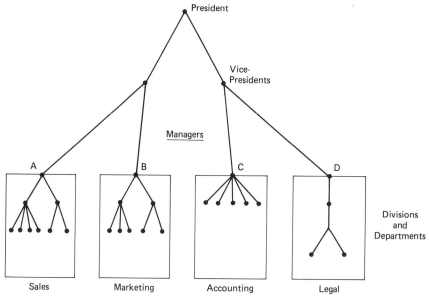

Source: *Organizations and Environments*, by Howard E. Aldrich (Englewood Cliffs, N.J.: Prentice-Hall, 1979), p. 79. Used by permission of the author.

unanswered, but it is and has been an almost universal taking-off point for further discussion, amplification, and disagreement.

The natural systems model. The rational systems model is seen by some as so far removed from reality as to distort it. For example, it makes no mention of informal structures within the formal system, yet just about every formal organization gives rise to informal structures. This is how it happens: All organizations come to life as people act out their official duties and interact with other members of their organizations, thus forming a natural system. These interactions give rise to reciprocal relationships not set out by the formal guidelines. The human beings who are fitted into organizational slots (official statuses or positions) regularly develop unofficial ways of modifying and adding to the formal structure. Formal and informal elements together form one interacting whole.

Over time, unofficial practices fall into patterns related both to the needs of people and the needs of the organization. Any organization in the abstract, as it is set up, can never perfectly anticipate everything that may happen once it comes into being. For example, unforeseen emergencies may occur, for which the official structure gives no guidelines and which require response from the organization's members. If they cannot act in the absence of such guidelines, disaster may result.

Peer groups, in almost every situation, develop their own definitions and norms to deal with the typical problems of those in their position (e.g., inmates don't squeal). A simple example of an informal communication structure is the ever-present "grapevine," used to pass along information and rumors related to crucial events such as possible plant closings or impending troop movements. Persons who depend on each other in order to perform their work or who face common dangers, such as doctors and nurses, or police officer partners, develop informal understandings about backing each other up.

In a provocative statement Selznick (1969), an advocate of the natural systems model, declares:

> they [formal structures] never succeed in conquering the non-rational dimensions of organizational behavior. The latter remain at once indispensable to the continued existence of the system of coordination and at the same time the source of friction, dilemma, doubt, and ruin. (p. 20)

Thus, the nonrational aspects (not evident in Weber's model) may be both useful and harmful to the organization.

Why is this so? The nonrational dimensions of organizational behavior derive from the fact that people are more than players of carefully circumscribed roles; they come with backgrounds, social ties, and psychological experiences. People have needs that may or may not be in line with those of the organization. If you are asked to work overtime on the evening when you have a special date, you would either decline or agree to work but resent it; yet, at another time you might be happy to have the extra pay.

People are not always guided by the official goals of an organization. In fact, as we will see in chapter 4, the officially stated goals may even mask other purposes of high-ranking officers. New goals also emerge—such as the importance of maintaining the organization over time no matter what. Certainly those in subordinate positions may lack commitment to the goals of the higher-ups. The goal of a temporary worker may be to earn extra cash with as little hassle as possible rather than to increase the employer's profits. What is rational to the organization may not seem so to the individual.

People are influenced by emotions as well as reason in seeking to make the best of situations. Rather than automatically following rules, most of us try to find out which rules may be broken and how often. At a given work site, we may want to know whether coffee breaks are limited to the stated time or are usually extended an extra five minutes. Or take the familiar example of speed limits. Enforcement is variable; the conforming driver who refuses to go over the speed limit may be breaking an informal norm of that particular road and be considered a maddeningly slow driver. Similarly, an overconformist within an organization may slow down the flow of work.

Within the formal organization, types of relationships emerge that are more usual and expected in the traditional society. Individuals are whole people and tend to interact as such rather than simply in terms of their formal roles. Thus, cliques may form on the basis of race, religion, or age, even though these characteristics are not relevant to people's positions. Note the informal groupings by race in many high school and college cafeterias. Students have not left their societal group memberships behind. People seek out warmth and connections especially in impersonal settings. They form primary groups, behave according to particularistic rather than universalistic standards, use "pull" or influence based on their available connections.

Thus the organization as an "organism," as a real-life functioning system, includes both formal and informal organization, interlinked and interrelated. The organization encompasses an ongoing human process of interaction as well as a rational structure. It only comes to life as real individuals play out their parts. And they play them out in terms of changing organizational demands, their own needs, and the limitations of the external environment. This latter point brings us to another perspective, the view of organizations as open systems.

The open systems model. "Organizations are not closed systems, sealed off from their environments, but are open to and dependent on flows of personnel and resources from outside their own system" (Scott, 1981:22).

The open system approach, described in this quotation, places much greater emphasis on the environment and sees organizations as formed just as much by forces external to them as by their internal structure. Organizations exist within a context of other related organizations, which in turn interact with still other organizations. All are tied together in regularized ways. For example, a local school district is part of a state school system that regulates and sometimes partially funds it. The local district, in turn, may consist of schools of different levels, each with its own administrator, tied together by a local board of education.

Open system theorists do not envision a single hierarchy of authority within an organization. Rather they are concerned with the power they see as residing in a coalition of shifting interest groups that are deeply affected by forces in that organization's environment. Organizations in a given society are linked to those of other societies. If a cheap supply of labor is available in Hong Kong or a country in Latin America, for example, there is pressure to move production to one of these locations and avoid a coming confrontation with union workers in the United States.[1] Various departments—production, sales, labor relations—will engage in discussions and negotiations with each other to respond to both opportunities and threats.

The different models reconciled. It is our position, and that of some others, that these different models can be reconciled. Each emphasizes different aspects of reality, but none denies the existence of elements more prominent in the other

---

[1] Fairchild Semiconductor, for example, met the competitive threat of domestic and Japanese firms by opening its first offshore (out of the United States) assembly facility in Hong Kong in 1963. Other firms followed, shifting their labor-intensive operations (those requiring repetitive, nontechnical work) first to Northeast Asia and later, when wages in that area rose, to Southeast Asia. By 1985 about half of all employment by the U.S. semiconductor manufacturers was located in offshore assembly facilities (Davis & Hatano, 1985).

models. Weber is criticized for concentrating on formal, structural elements internal to each organization. Yet his ideal type has been the backbone of a great deal of research into elements of organizational structure, such as size, centralization, complexity, and formalization (see R. Hall, 1982, chap. 3).[2]

The natural systems model accepts the existence of formal structure but questions how much of the life of any organization it describes. The open systems model criticizes earlier writing for focusing on this internal life and not paying attention to the constant interflow of elements across the borders of organizations. Current attention to the environment of organizations and interorganizational relations corrects previous ways of conceiving of organizations as isolated, closed systems. (For those interested in pursuing the comparisons further, the three models—rational, natural, and open systems—are thoroughly considered by Scott, 1981.)

In stressing the interconnectedness of organizations, we need not conclude that they have no autonomy. Theorists remind us that connections between them may be relatively controlling and extensive or relatively loose. Within an organization various parts may be highly dependent on each other and may operate relatively independently. Organizations can be described as tightly or loosely "coupled." "Loose coupling exists when structures and activities in various parts of an organization are only weakly connected to each other and therefore are free to vary independently" (Aldrich, 1979:76–77). In the extreme, at least one theorist sees organizations as so fluid that they should not be talked about as nouns, as organizations. Rather, the active verb "organizing" should be used to describe what goes on in these networks of human relationships others think of as static "organizations" (Weick, 1979).

In its own way each of the approaches discussed above contributes to a better understanding of formal organizations. Organizations vary tremendously: Some are less dependent on the environment than others; some are more stable than others; some require more decision making and less routine activity than others; some have tighter, less-open boundaries than others. By calling attention to these varying features, each of the models directs us toward important variables and provides hypotheses for research. The models discussed reflect some of the basic lines of cleavage among organizational theorists in terms of how they view their field. There are

---

[2]The study of structural factors was greatly assisted by the development of computers, the use of which was flourishing by the late 1960s. This methodological tool facilitated multivariate analysis: The influence of many variables could be studied simultaneously and their respective significance determined. Despite the popularity of this type of research in the 1970s, it soon came under criticism. Ouchi and Wilkins maintain: "All of this research on the structure of formal organizations was done in the name of Max Weber, all of it represented attempts to represent operationally the elements of bureaucratic administration that Weber had described, but in the end it was an effort dominated by a methodology and by a computer rather than by a point of view" (1985:466). Taking the same position, this author has chosen not to deal comprehensively with highly quantitative studies of organizational structure. (For a good analysis of questions examined in this area, see Hall, 1982.)

many other theoretical debates.[3] However, rather than labeling and discussing each school of thought in a chapter on theory, various perspectives will be integrated into chapters where they are most relevant.

Important as they are, formal organizations are not the only types of human collectivities that exist. It is worthwhile to look briefly at other elements of social organization and see how they interact with bureaucracies.

NONBUREAUCRATIC ELEMENTS OF SOCIAL ORGANIZATION

The Omnipresence of Nonbureaucratic Elements

Nonbureaucratic elements of social organization not only exist in the organization's environment but also enter into bureaucracies themselves. Recall that formal organizations stress impersonal relations, but people inevitably seek out and form friendships within them. Legal-rational authority may be the prevailing source of legitimacy, but personal charisma also counts in leadership positions. Nonbureaucratic elements may serve as a buffer against bureaucracies or may act as contravening structures, opposing aspects of bureaucracy. The cliques and friendship groups that exist in formal organizations may support or oppose particular rules and regulations.

Major Nonbureaucratic Collectivities

Not all collections of human beings can be technically called groups, since members of groups are oriented to and in contact with each other. The broader term *collectivity* describes people categorized together in some way. The following is a list of major nonbureaucratic collectivities:

— Families and communities
— Racial, ethnic, and gender groups

---

[3] Astley and Van de Ven maintain that six central debates on organizations "currently permeate the literature": "(1) Are organizations functionally rational, technically constrained systems, or are they socially constructed, subjectively meaningful embodiments of individual action? (2) Are changes in organizational forms explained by internal adaptation or by environmental selection? (3) Is organizational life determined by intractable environmental constraints, or is it actively created through strategic managerial choices? (4) Is the environment to be viewed as a simple aggregation of organizations governed by external economic forces, or as an integrated collectivity of organizations governed by its own internal social and political forces? (5) Is organizational behavior principally concerned with individual or collective action? (6) Are organizations neutral technical instruments engineered to achieve a goal, or are they institutionalized manifestations of the vested interests and power structure of the wider society?" (1983: 245-246). The reader is advised to return to this footnote after the rest of the book has been mastered. These controversies and the terminology used to describe them should then be more intelligible.

    —Masses
    —Social movements
    —Ecological and population changes

Families and communities. Our conception of what the family is supposed to be like differs greatly from our conception of what the formal organization is supposed to be like. Family members are supposed to love each other irrespective of individual competence, to interact with each other as whole persons rather than as segmented role players, and to engage in a wide variety of diffuse behavior together. Communities resemble families in their togetherness in space and in the variety of activities the same people share. *Community* suggests more intimacy, sense of belonging, and shared history than is expected in formal organizations. But some formally created communities are different from natural ones in that they incorporate qualities of complex organization.

Such hybrid groups are part community and part formal organization. Goffman, in his brilliant work, *Asylums* (1961), coined the phrase "total institution" to describe live-in, formal organizations—partly residential communities and partly bureaucracies, such as prisons, mental institutions, and military academies. Similarly, families may be involved in highly organized activities. As illegal entities, organized crime syndicates face special problems of loyalty and rule enforcement that encourage the concentration of power within kinship groups. Organized crime in the United States and elsewhere is made up of several "families" that, though linked by kinship, manifest extensive organization, specialization, and division of labor (Ianni, 1972). Less dramatically, some legitimate enterprises are family businesses. The case study at the end of this chapter discusses how immigrant families, of the same ethnic background, create small businesses.

Corporations that value employee loyalty may hire several members of the same family, giving them a stake in seeing that the business runs smoothly. In contrast, the nepotism rules of other companies and universities are designed to prevent the conflicts that might occur were family members working in the same place. The temptation to particularism—say, to promoting one's sister rather than a more efficient nonrelative—is thought to be great. What rules against nepotism have frequently done is to exclude the wives of men already working for an organization.

Racial, ethnic, and gender groups. Societies are stratified into racial and ethnic groups; that is, different groups occupy different positions in terms of societal prestige and privilege. Skin color is an important informal element in the United States stratification system; it is an official one in the South African system. In both countries the appropriateness of certain jobs is linked to the racial order; the result is different percentages of blacks and whites in professional and business positions, white-collar and blue-collar work. Occupational distributions can also be discovered for Asians and Latinos. Many writers maintain that the economy is divided into primary and secondary fields of employment—the first mainly reserved for native-born white men and the second, less-well paid sector utilizing minority and female workers. Periodically, the American government arranges to bring in foreign-born temporary laborers to harvest certain perishable crops. The work is hard and pay is low; hence, there is a shortage of native-born workers. Since both private and governmental organizations are employers, the composition of the labor force is important to organizational structures. Pressure groups representing agribusiness play a role in immigration legislation. In another vein, the relative success of certain immigrant groups in small business ventures is sometimes linked to their ethnic traditions. Revolving credit associations, traditional in various cultures, are transplanted to new scenes and are a mechanism by which successive group loans are made to the members—all ethnic peers (Light, 1972). Thus are formal organizations linked to nonbureaucratic collectivities.

Organizational literature to date has mostly avoided significant discussion of the ways in which race and ethnicity impinge on organizations, although the literature on minorities considers the subject of major importance. The reasons for this avoidance may become clearer in chapter 2, when we take up the issue of how knowledge gets produced. Similarly, in the past organizational literature has tended to ignore the question of gender altogether, discussing workers as if they were all men. In the indexes of many books on work the only references to women were to their roles as wives, despite the long history of such feminized occupations as teaching, nursing, and certain factory work. The woman as a major consumer is readily acknowledged in advertising directed toward her but is less visible in scientific analysis of other societal roles. In recent years the thrust of women's studies has penetrated the field of organizations and more attention is being paid to the role of gender (see, for example, Kanter, 1977, and Martin, 1980b). Federal executive orders mandating affirmative action for women and minorities have also made race, ethnicity, and gender slightly more visible in organization studies since the 1970s (Fernandez, 1981).

Masses.   A mass is a very large number of heterogenous individuals who do not necessarily know each other but who are influenced and affected by the same events or stimuli. *Mass* is very often used as an adjective to denote volume or size, as in mass communication—defined as "rapid and frequent communication of information to significantly large portions of the society" (*Society Today*, 1973:530). But it is also used to describe whole societies, and in this usage it is linked to bureaucracy.

Mass society is defined as:

> society characterized by large-scale industrialization and bureaucratization, as well as by other impersonal, specialized, and uniform organizations and activities. It is organized to deal with people in large numbers rather than individuals. (*Society Today*, 1973:530)

Being part of a huge, faceless, undifferentiated mass is quite different from being part of and playing a formally defined role in a bureaucratic enterprise. Yet paradoxically, the mass and the bureaucracy are intimately related as characteristics of modern life. Urbanization has created the concentration of huge populations who are potential voters, purchasers, audiences, decision-makers. The expense of high-technology production makes it necessary for corporations to reach the mass with their products. For example, television shows must attract a large number of viewers in order to stay on the air. Advertisers vie to gain a substantial share of the mass market. Except for specialized items directed towards elite purchasers, manufactured goods are produced in large quantity, limited to those styles that are anticipated to be more popular. Although a company that produces dresses is itself a complex organization, with its internal hierarchy, division of labor, departments, rules, statuses, and roles, its product is directed towards anonymous buyers en masse.

The huge sports industry is highly organized, with established procedures for purchasing and training players, setting up competitive schedules, enforcing rules of the game, and so forth. At the same time it is dependent on appealing to mass audiences who will pay to see the games. And, of course, attached to the sports industry is the television industry, which covers sports events and with which many contracts and agreements must be made. The educational world, with its sports teams, is also linked to the complex.

It is interesting to note the interweaving of mass and organizational behavior. Sports events depend on spontaneity as well as training, on the surprises that occur and the interaction of a small group of individuals, the team. The support of the mass of fans helps make the teams possible. Popular and well-known individual athletes, who gain fame in specialized team roles, may be selected by advertisers to create mass appeal for particular products. Thus, bureaucracies and masses are linked together in many ways. Most of us experience the anonymity of being part of a mass as we read the newspapers, watch television, or purchase a standardized product. But we also face the demands of playing specific roles in organizations where our individual abilities are called on and our performance observed.

Social movements. Social movements are collective efforts to bring about change or to prevent impending change. Often they develop over dissatisfaction with existing institutions and the hope to modify them. Movements may occur within established organizations. Religious sects arise to challenge an accepted religion that, in its present organizational form, is felt to be inauthentic in some way. New political movements arise when existing parties are thought to be too bureaucratized or inflexible. Student groups revolted in the 1960s over such issues as insensitive college administrations, large impersonal classes, and lack of university attention to social issues (Roberts & Kloss, 1979:83-93).

Social movements usually find expression in social movement organizations, such as the National Association for the Advancement of Colored People, the Natural Resources Defense Council, and the Physicians for Social Responsibility. To the extent that they are successful in drawing adherents, these organizations face the problems of bureaucratization—such as developing staffs, keeping computerized mailing lists, hiring paid workers, recruiting competent writers to put out newsletters.

Movements have as their mission the changing of certain aspects of society; as such they may target formal organizations, industries, or government. And organizations may find it necessary to respond, just as the tobacco industry has been forced by an antismoking movement to consider substitute products for their high-nicotine brands. The social movements of minorities and women have had important effects on educational institutions and work organizations. Some of the changes seemingly achieved can dissipate if the social movement declines in influence and the organizations in question have not been ideologically committed to the changes.

Ecological and population changes.   Complex organizations affect and are affected by ecological and population changes—for example, changes in sex ratios, or in the median age or educational level of the population. Migrations and other population movements affect the availability of both the labor supply and the consuming public. Factories move or shut down, and in turn affect the rate of migration into or out of a particular area.

Major organizations, such as governments, large corporations, and large universities, are relatively permanent and institutionalized compared to some of the other elements of societal life. But bureaucratic organizations must operate in the context of nonbureaucratic collectivities within and beyond their borders, an interrelationship that creates the constant possibility of change.

MIXTURES OF FAMILY, ETHNICITY, AND BUSINESS: *A CASE STUDY*

Although we described business organizations as bureaucracies, we recognized that real organizations do not conform to the "pure" type. Similarly, while families are usually thought of as nonbureaucratic entities, they sometimes play an important role in the business world. This is especially true of immigrant families that are trying to gain an economic foothold in a new society. One of the best places to observe the interconnections between families, ethnic groups, and business organizations is in the operation of small businesses.

Ethnic enterprise is a term that has been used to describe the utilization of family and ethnic ties to attain economic success (Light, 1972). Immigrants coming from countries that are less industrially advanced often bring with them a cultural orientation in which family rather than individual economic survival is a main goal. This family-oriented background serves them well in creating successful small businesses.

An article describing Hispanic business owners in the New York garment industry from 1979 to 1982 shows, however, that immigrant enterprise also needs the proper organizational environment in which to flourish (Waldinger, 1984). As manufacturing firms moved from older sites in the Northeast to low-wage areas in the South and abroad, the environment of the New York garment industry changed. In order to cope with uncertainty in costs and demand, the larger manufacturers who remained in New York limited their functions to designing and merchandising the clothing and contracted out the actual garment production.

This system of contracting proved a boon to a number of Hispanic immigrants, many of them from the Dominican Republic. Immigrant entrepreneurs discovered that as contractors, operating small factories in basements, storefronts, and apartments, they would be spared many of the costs of production. As contractors, they did not have to purchase raw materials or accumulate inventories. Their main task was to recruit labor to sew, pleat, stitch, or cut low-cost garments farmed out to them by the larger companies. Their direct ties to the labor force through family members and through the flow of new immigrants of the same ethnic background assured them a constant supply of low-cost labor. As with other immigrant groups that preceded them, these small business owners drew many recruits from their own towns or villages in the old country. Waldinger interviewed owners of ninety-six firms, of which eighty-two confined their activities to contracted work. Many of these owners had worked in similar factories when they arrived in New York and had then pooled their funds or obtained loans from relatives in order to start a small business. They combined their desire for business success with utilization of family and community loyalties. Waldinger explains:

> . . . where the size of the firm made recruitment beyond the family necessary, the employment relationship was mediated by kinship, friendship, and ethnic networks. Firms recruited through the immigrant network, thus building on the social structures that connect immigrants to settlers and reproducing them within the workplace. (p. 66)

As a footnote, it should be mentioned that the environment for small business, while sometimes favorable, can also be volatile and changeable. Pleating of clothing was a major job in the immigrant shops, and when it went out of fashion, many of these Hispanic-owned operations went out of business.

SUMMARY

Chapter 1 set the stage for the study of formal organizations by observing their power and prevalence in modern societies. The concepts of formal organization, complex organization, and bureaucracy are used relatively interchangeably, although bureaucracy more technically refers to the way that complex or formal organizations are administered. The modern industrialized, urbanized society, characterized by bureaucratic features, was compared to the traditional society by looking at an ideal, or pure, type of each. Certain kinds of human relationships were seen to be more characteristic of one or the other type of society. The characteristics compared were primary versus secondary group relations, simple division of labor versus complex division of labor, traditional authority versus bureaucratic-legal authority, religion and magic versus science and rationality, norms versus rules, particularism versus universalism, qualities versus performances, and loyalty versus efficiency.

Real societies only approximate the ideal types; they are more or less bureaucratized. Looking at organizations rather than whole societies, Max Weber's rational model of bureaucracy was compared with two other models—the natural systems and open systems models. The Weberian model stresses the formal structure of organizations: clear-cut division of labor, specialization, hiring on the basis of technical competence, hierarchy of authority, rules and regulations, expectation of universalism and impersonality, and security of employment. The natural systems model puts the people into the formal structures—and thereby brings organizations to life. Informal, unofficial patterns arise out of human interaction in response to individual and organizational needs. People are sometimes nonrational; they are whole persons rather than segmented role players. Their goals may not be the same as the organization's official goals. Organizations become oriented to persisting even if it means changing goals.

The open systems model stresses the role of the environment; it emphasizes the fact that organizations are not self-contained units but are affected by and affect whatever lies outside of their shifting borders, including other organizations and nonbureaucratic collectivities. This model views organizations as more fluid and changeable than the rational systems model does.

Each of these approaches contributes to our understanding of the world of organizations, for each emphasizes different parts of the same whole. Bureaucracies do not constitute all of society, for they exist interdependently with nonbureaucratic collectivities such as families and communities, racial, ethnic, and gender groups, masses, social movements, and population movements. These external forces are part of the environment that influences organizations and that provokes organizational change.

2

THE SOCIAL ROOTS
OF ORGANIZATIONAL
KNOWLEDGE

Science, Ideology, and Public Policy
   The Problem: How Are Science, Ideology, and Public Policy Related?
   The Social Factors in Scientific Knowledge Seeking and Dissemination
   Research and International Ideological Conflicts
The Needs of Corporations: How They Affect Research
   Important Types of Knowledge Needed
   Hard Scientific and Technological Studies
   Social Science Research
Challenges to Traditional Perspectives
   The Women's Studies Perspective
   Collective Behavior by Workers
   Social Movements and Citizen Revolt
   Marxist Critiques
Conflict of Interest: A Case Study
Summary

SCIENCE, IDEOLOGY, AND PUBLIC POLICY

The Problem: How Are Science, Ideology, and Public Policy Related?

The social roots of knowledge. It is commonly understood that the same course taught by two different professors may vary quite a bit. Each has been trained at a specific institution and at a specific time and place, each brings a store of personal experience to the classroom, and each has his or her own grasp of the course materials. Similarly, books purported to be on approximately the same subject may turn out to be rather different. Each author selects from a range of materials and interprets them from a certain perspective. Thus, all knowledge, research, and theory has social roots. No robot yet invented can eliminate the role of human beings in the knowledge-producing process.

This particular book is written from a sociological perspective. Unlike many other writers in the field of organizations, I have no formal or informal connection with schools of management.[1] This means that, after being trained in a sociology department (at the University of Chicago), my everyday intellectual interactions have tended to be with other sociologists and social scientists, such as anthropologists and economists. I have taught courses in complex organizations for over twenty years and have other long-standing specializations in sociology, notably, in the fields of minorities and gender roles. This background will inevitably be reflected in the book. Why? Because while I have made a conscious attempt to present a balanced picture of the field of organizations for the beginning student, any work is necessarily influenced by the interests of its author. Those interests will show up in the examples used, topics emphasized, criticisms of various theories, and so on. This does not mean that as an author I am any more biased than any other author. However, I strongly believe that students should be made aware of the social roots of all knowledge, and of the connections between science and politics. Current public issues stimulate thought and research, which are then reflected in scientific writings. For example, court-ordered desegregation of public schools was the result of pressure to equalize education for blacks and whites. That political event in turn led to many studies of the results of desegregation.

Science and scientific knowledge.   At the risk of oversimplifying, let us look briefly at what we mean by *scientific knowledge.* Where does any of it, including social science knowledge about the nature of organizations, come from? Any body of knowledge is developed through systematic research that is reported orally and written up and published in journals, books, and scientific reports. Reliance on science presumes that by using various accepted methods, such as observation, experimentation, interviewing, examination of records, and survey research, we can gain more precise empirical knowledge about the world. In honest scientific research, hypotheses (hunches, tentative generalizations) are subject to being proven or disproven, and then the research is exposed to further scrutiny and criticism by other experts.

Ideology.   An ideology is a system of beliefs, such as the capitalist or communist ideology. A dictionary definition is "the integrated assertions, theories, and aims that constitute a sociopolitical program" (Webster's, 1970). Every political

---

[1] As such, I am part of a minority. As of 1985 there were 600 schools of management in the United States. "These management schools now produce a good deal more organizational work than do departments of sociology, which surely must be a reversal of the situation twenty years ago" (Ouchi & Wilkins, 1985:469).

and economic system needs to justify its existence through a body of beliefs and principles that explain why it is the best possible system. Ideology is not science; it is the system of belief that supports an existing system of behavior. Or, in the case of social movements that seek change, such as the peace, environmental, or prohibition movements, an ideology is developed to explain why the aims of the movement are "correct" and how much the needed change will benefit humankind.

Those in power in a given country have an advantage over those out of power because they have much greater control of resources to support their ideologies. One of those resources is financial control over science and scientific investigation. A *Business Week* survey (July 9, 1984) of 800 major firms showed that they had spent $39.2 billion for research and development in 1983. More than half of all scientists and more than three-fourths of all engineers were employed in business and industry in 1982 (*New York Times*, July 17, 1984). Here we have a dilemma: Science is supposed to be free to pursue the truth, yet it is financially supported by businesses and governments that have their own priorities and agendas. In this chapter we will examine how that dilemma is worked out.

Public policy. Public policy refers to enacted decisions of government and generally accepted practices of government agencies. Legislation provides a most obvious example of public policy: Governments regulate organizations in many ways through various laws. To protect public health and safety, laws are enacted requiring firms to control the emission of pollutants, maintain certain safety standards in the workplaces, add seat belts to automobiles, correct misleading advertising, and so forth. Yet, in numerous documented cases firms such as airlines have been slow to correct proven hazards because of the costs involved (Perrow, 1984).

Seat belts in automobiles provide an example. It took many years of scientific testing and disputes about those tests before the evidence that seat belts would save lives became overwhelming. Even then, much social pressure was needed to counter-act the interests of the automobile companies and convince legislators that manda-tory seat belts should be a matter of official policy.

Obviously, whatever gets into public policy has important consequences for organizations, and of course, those organizations affected try to influence policy in various ways. Top business executives tend to be selected for governing and advisory boards of a variety of nonbusiness organizations, such as government and nonprofit agencies, thus playing a direct role in their governance (Useem, 1979)[2] and in how they regulate businesses.

---

[2]Useem (1969) analyzed the "business elite"—directors of the 797 largest U.S. corpora-tions in 1969, with regard to their roles in helping to run other institutions. He noted their participation in the roles of trustee, director, governor, or—in the case of economic develop-ment organizations—member in such organizations as universities, government advisory bodies, and research institutes. An inner group of influential directors—individuals who held director-ships in four or more firms—were contrasted with those who held one directorship. A positive association was found between being in this inner group and participation in the governance of other institutions. That is, persons who play a prominent role as directors of several corpora-tions are also disproportionately selected to help run nonbusiness institutions.

In fact, scientific findings do not always get translated into relevant public policy decisions; some findings may be withheld for many years. Public agencies themselves may choose to ignore facts and sacrifice safety in response to time pressures. Official investigation into the explosion of the space shuttle Challenger revealed that equipment problems had been minimized and safety possibly compromised by the National Aeronautics and Space Agency (NASA) in order to keep up with an ambitious flight schedule. Two questions highlight the interrelations between science, ideology, and public policy: How does scientific knowledge get spread or withheld? Who decides which topics will and will not be studied? Let's look at the second question first.

The Social Factors in Scientific Knowledge Seeking and Dissemination

Selection of topics for research. Knowledge is constantly being sought through research. But who is to decide what gets studied? Someone or some organization has to determine what is important to know. The selection of topics for research is one of the ways that people in power influence and control what gets studied. Research costs money; most of the scientists who engage in it must be subsidized through grants if they are located at universities or research institutes, or else they must work directly for the sponsors of the research, often major corporations or government. This is true whether the field is sociology, biology, or any other science.

There are an infinite variety of things worth knowing; some choice of research topics must be made. The question of choice is important because it means that certain subjects will gain attention and others will be relatively neglected. The case of medical research provides an illustration. There are many diseases in the world. Research is needed to discover their causes and find remedies. Which are most important: the ones that are very widespread but rarely fatal or those that are rare but almost always fatal? The answer is not given by science; it depends on one's values, what one considers most important.

Some diseases are most prevalent in or even restricted to particular population groups, as in the case of Acquired Immune Deficiency Syndrome (AIDS), a usually fatal disease that has been spreading. AIDS is found mainly among population groups that are generally accorded little public sympathy—homosexual men and drug addicts. Associations of gay people claimed that little scientific attention was being given to conquering the disease because of its prevalence among these highly stigmatized groups. An active campaign to gain more resources for research into a cure ensued and gained some success, especially after it was found that the disease could be transmitted to other population groups through contaminated blood supplies. The first prominent person to admit that he had contracted AIDS did so in the hope that more serious attention would be paid to combating it.

Most diseases are not controversial; deciding which ones should receive the most attention and research funds is a matter of judgment. People whose families have been affected by certain diseases seem to be the ones who care most. If they happen to be persons of wealth, then more money goes to those diseases. But various funds also solicit contributions from the general public, and the question may then be decided by how effectively a cause can put itself forth as worthy of receiving funds.

A historic example of an epidemic disease that gained national attention and funds was poliomyelitis. Although small children were often its victims, the late president Franklin D. Roosevelt contracted polio as an adult; he helped sponsor the polio foundation's March of Dimes, a highly successful drive for funds. This disease thus received high research priority. Vaccines were discovered, and the incidence of the disease dropped to extremely low levels in the United States.

Of course, scientists employed by industry are engaged in research that is wanted by that industry. For example, at General Motors, a major research effort is underway

> to integrate computers, software, robots, sensors and telecommunications systems into a highly automated manufacturing process that might lower the cost of producing automobiles and conceivably revolutionize the production processes in a range of other industries as well. (*New York Times*, July 17, 1984, p. C1).

Later we shall turn from these examples to the vastly more complicated arena of international ideological battles and how they affect the subjects of research.

Dissemination of research findings. In addition to choice of research topics, the question arises about how—or even whether—research findings will be disseminated. What happens if the findings seriously affect the interests of powerful groups? Will they be made public? How and when? How will the findings be written up? What will be emphasized and what omitted? One of the main safeguards against biased research is the fact that published findings are open to scrutiny. The war against slavery, for example, also consisted of an ideological battle in which the notions of natural inferiority of blacks were corroded by scientific evidence to the contrary. Questions also arise about how much sharing of research findings should take place. Countries who see each other as real or potential enemies zealously guard their scientific secrets while just as zealously trying to gain access to the other's secrets. Companies that compete with each other also protect their discoveries; some engage in industrial spying.

Sometimes a group will claim that the findings accepted by most scientists conflict with religious principles. Such is the case for the scientific concept of the biological evolution of the human species. For more than half a century fundamentalist religious groups have battled against teaching the theory of biological evolution in the public schools. The famous 1925 Scopes trial in Tennessee made front-page headlines when the lawyer Clarence Darrow brought in experts to defend the right of John T. Scopes to teach the theory in the state of Tennessee.

Sixty years later that conflict is still affecting the dissemination of scientific findings. Miriam Schlein, an author of natural science textbooks, maintains that the conflict has generated self-censorship by textbook publishers. In order to capture the major textbook market of Texas, which has a statewide adoption procedure (unless a textbook is centrally approved it cannot be purchased), publishers delete the word *evolution* and the name Charles Darwin from their textbooks. She points out that the Texas market is a crucial one for textbook publishers (*New York Times*, July 14, 1984, letter to the editor, p. 22). Publishers are also under pressure to delete material that may seem unfavorable to the United States or that might seem to support communism in any way. This results in the suppression of certain kinds of scientific and historical knowledge.

Research and International Ideological Conflicts

Research is affected by international ideological conflicts, which find expression in the policies of various nations. Since the end of World War II there has been a "cold war"—hostile rivalry—between the Soviet Union and the United States. Each country supports its allies with money, trade relations, military advice, and military weapons. Each competes for the nonaligned nations in similar ways. In a vast propaganda war, each tries to show that the other is dishonest and insincere. This is the atmosphere in which social science research operates. Each country needs scientific support for its ideology.

Where there is any academic freedom, the ideological battle is free to take place within universities as well as between countries. Although Marxist-oriented social scientists, including sociologists, face discrimination, they are able to get jobs in some educational institutions in this country. The same academic freedom is not extended to dissidents in Communist-controlled nations. Another part of American ideology consists of the belief that freedom of information will, in the long run, make a country stronger rather than weaker. The contributions of Karl Marx to social science are widely recognized even by those who disagree with his theories. In the field of organizations, Marxist-oriented critiques have stimulated much new literature. Dissent is valued as part of American life, yet many fear it. Universities are officially supposed to protect academic freedom, but some succumb to pressures and temptations in the other direction.

Basic to the politico-economic ideology of the United States is a belief in the superiority of a capitalist economy over a socialist or communist economy. How is capitalism expressed? One major way is through private enterprise; corporations are privately owned and operated, whereas in communist nations they are owned and operated through state bureaucracies. The corporation is a valued part of this country's ideological and institutional structure, supported in various ways. The dominance of large organizations, especially corporations, in American life is unquestioned. States Kanter (1977):

> Large organizations not only dominate economic and political life (one common prediction holds that 200 multinational corporations will run the world's economy by the year 2000); they also control most of the jobs. (p. 15)

How does this affect research? Those who spend money for it, including government and the corporations themselves, are most likely to support efforts that take for granted the existing distributions of power and the desirability of running society through large corporations. Research or writing that seems sympathetic to the ideology of communism is much less likely to be supported. Of course, the situation is reversed in communist countries, where the ideology of capitalism is held up to ridicule.

But ideologies are not static; each has its own development. Some of the ideologically communist nations have brought elements of private ownership and individual incentives back into their planning, integrating these developments into their ideologies. Similarly, managerial ideologies in the United States that describe the right way to manage workers have undergone change. Responses to business cycles, economic depressions, wars, new technologies, unions, and so on bring about changes, which are then explained and justified in terms of a given managerial perspective.

Given that the selection of topics and the dissemination of the findings of scientific research are not isolated from either public policy or ideology in the organizational society, we will concentrate on the reality of our type of economic system. Let us examine more closely how the needs of large organizations, especially corporations, affect the direction of research.

THE NEEDS OF CORPORATIONS: HOW THEY AFFECT RESEARCH

Important Types of Knowledge Needed

By definition, the central aim of a business organization is to make a profit. To maintain or increase profitability, corporations need many kinds of research, including:

1. "Hard" scientific and technological studies
   —to refine and improve their products, modes of production, and distribution
   —to help them adjust to the changing environment
2. Social science research
   —to ensure a productive and manageable labor force
   —to train future managers

Hard Scientific and Technological Studies

Industry's need for research in the "hard" (physical or natural) sciences is expanding as each country competes in international markets. Even during the recession of 1981–82, most large U.S. companies continued to raise their research spending. Such fields as life sciences, biotechnology, and electronics are gaining much attention; competition in microelectronics is fierce. Concomitantly, the increasing rate of industrial research has been accompanied by a surge of scientists and engineers into various industries. The needs of corporations for scientific research translate directly into jobs.

It is often presumed that the scientist in the university is free to pursue "pure" or basic research, uninfluenced by the applied needs of the society. However, scientists in universities are increasingly dependent on government and corporation grants, and questions are being raised about the extent to which these patrons influence the scientific work of the grant recipients. In some cases, professors not only receive grants but acquire financial interests in corporations.

Scientists are supposed to report their findings fairly and honestly. Does doing so represent a conflict of interest for them? Can the university researcher, subsidized by a corporation, be truly impartial? What if he or she uncovers data that has a negative impact on the desirability of the sponsor's products? A case study discussing how universities are coping with possible conflict of interest appears at the end of this chapter.

Social Science Research

The control of workers.   Were there no large organizations, a science of organizations would not exist. Were there no large corporations, questions of efficiently managing them would not arise. It was the rise of the corporation that stimulated organizational research. A great amount of industrial expansion took place between 1890 and 1910. The large corporation began to gain steam as many smaller firms merged. As industries grew and employed more and more workers, the question of how best to manage and control them gained attention. The need for professional managers arose, and professional business schools were born.

The rise of unions and collective bargaining in the early part of this century provided a challenge to the authority of owners, to their right to hire and fire at will. Owners were forced to consider the worker and what might make him or her loyal to the firm. Psychology had come into its own during World War I, when psychological testing was widely used. Industry turned to psychologists to help them understand and manipulate workers. Psychological testing was used to select both managers and lower-level employees. The applied fields of industrial psychology and industrial sociology grew, providing corporation jobs for many social scientists. Unlike those who labored in universities, the scientists who worked directly for industry had no conflict of interest with regard to their aims. In a book called, *The Servants of Power*, Baritz (1960) claims:

> Management . . . controlled the industrial social scientists in its employ. Managers did not make use of social science out of a sense of social responsibility, but out of a recognized need to attack age-old problems of costs and worker loyalty with new weapons designed to fit the needs and problems of the twentieth century. (p. 196)

Baritz claims that the scientists in industry had no conflict about the political or ethical implications of their work; they knew who their bosses were. But some scientists have banded together in organizations just to point out to the public the implications of some of their more earth-shaking research. A case in point is an association of atomic physicists who have tried to inform laypersons about the threat of nuclear war. How many scientists employed by industry or government are willing to take such public positions is a matter of question.

Scientific management and human relations studies. Two of the earliest efforts at applying science to problems of worker productivity were the *scientific management* studies of Frederick Taylor (1911) and the years-long *human relations* experiments at the Western Electric Hawthorne plant outside of Chicago, which began in 1924.[3] The writings of Taylor himself clearly reveal that he saw the interests of management and those of workers as being opposed, although later management literature would deny this (see, for example, Barnard, 1938).

Some of Taylor's studies consisted of observing workers and noting every motion that they made. The worker was to perform the tasks exactly as described by managers who, through use of the engineer's time and motion studies, possessed knowledge of the fastest way of performing necessary tasks. One of the results of his efforts was deskilling—breaking jobs down into minute elements, removing much of the thinking and judgment processes from the worker and giving them to the engineer. Taylor also recognized that this method had to compete with the normal tendency of people who work in groups to arrive at commonly accepted definitions of how much should be produced in a given time period. The amount would never be the physiological maximum amount of production; rather, it would be what the workers considered fair and unthreatening. Scientific management's careful observation of the work process drew suspicion and often resulted in worker resistance.

Working for management, Taylor tried various ways to increase production and to break the social code of the workers. He would, for example, select a specific worker to isolate and offer incentives for producing more. Although his work has been greatly criticized, it has also had tremendous influence.

Human relations school. The human relations school of management is understood to have developed out of the famous Hawthorne experiments at Western Electric (Roesthlisberger & Dickson, 1939; Baritz, 1960; Perrow, 1979). Through a process of changing the illumination and other conditions of work, these experiments succeeded in illuminating something else—the patterned, informal relationships among workers. Years of experimentation taught the researchers that these informal relations, rather than simple physical conditions, affected productivity and worker satisfaction. Of course, the desired aim was to discover ways of improving production and maintaining a quiescent work force.

[3] These have been described, explained, and criticized in numerous works and so shall not be dealt with at great length here. For critical approaches to these experiments see Perrow (1979) and Braverman (1974).

The training of future managers. One of the things that corporations must do is to recruit potential managers, and the major schools of business were established to be the training ground. As pointed out earlier, these schools arose as large corporations proliferated in the early part of this century, and many of them have remained closely allied with particular corporations. Managerial and organizational literature burgeoned to provide the theories and findings that would teach the new managers not only facts but the appropriate ideologies. Most organizational theory and research has derived from the elite business schools, and major journals are produced by these schools.

Managerial ideologies. Obviously, the future managers would be expected to believe in the system they were joining. Further, they should be socialized to be able to fit into increasingly large and complex bureaucracies. Perrow (1979) claims, in describing a series of what he calls managerial ideologies, that the thrust of research on management was related to both the changing economics of demand and supply and the actions of incipient unions. Thus, the history of managerial theory reflected an adjustment to supplies of labor, such as the labor shortages caused by major wars. In times of labor shortages, more attention is paid to ways of satisfying and maintaining one's workers. Various kinds of paternalistic programs were invented from time to time to compete with the union for the worker's loyalty.

Managerial ideologies have changed over time. Perrow (1979) has classified six types that evolved between 1870 and the 1930s; more could probably be added today. Each of these ideologies has what he calls an "explanatory doctrine," such as the principle of the survival of the fittest, which viewed the owners as superior individuals, or the principle of natural cooperation, which stressed the personality skills and statesmanship of the owners or managers. Before the advent of unions, the doctrine of survival of the fittest adapted a model of biological selection that justified those on top as being superior and those on the bottom (the workers) as being ignorant and inferior. When it became necessary to recognize the group power of workers, the human relations school came to the rescue, developing models of cooperation and loyalty.

Neglect of ideologically unpopular topics. In Chapter 1, three current theoretical models of organizations were presented, the rational, closed, and open systems models. Each was seen to select out a piece of organizational reality to emphasize; each has its own kernel of truth. Each of the theories makes an important contribution by highlighting the omissions of competing ones. However, certain omissions tend to persist—those theories that would threaten accepted ideologies.

Because there is a degree of academic freedom and because all organizational theory is not allied with business, competing viewpoints do gain a hearing. For example, the sociologist and social psychologist, Erving Goffman, was able to write his classic work on total institutions largely from the perspective of its negative impact on the individual (1961). A small number of works have been written that are sympathetic to the consumer of public services (see, for example, Lipsky, 1980).

Paul Goldman, Donald R. Van Houten, and Kenneth Benson are examples of sociologists located at universities who have been able to gain respectable hearings for their Marxist analyses of organizations and organizational theories (see, for example, Goldman & Van Houten, 1981; Benson, 1977).

Nonetheless, organizational literature continues to give much less emphasis to topics that threaten the smooth running of business enterprises. Even as new fads—popular new topics—arise, gain research funding, and are reported, they may mask certain unpleasant, threatening realities of organizational life. One of these realities is the importance of organizational power and organizational politics (Perrow, 1979; Pfeffer, 1981a). Pfeffer claims that, "under the guise of objectivity and data, the ideological bases and premises of much of the study of organizations remain systematically submerged and ignored" (Pfeffer, 1981a:17). Another overlooked issue is the possibility that conflict between workers and managers is normal, that their interests do not coincide (Braverman, 1974).

A new area that is gaining attention is organizational culture (see chapter 7). The September 1983 issue of the major journal, *Administrative Science Quarterly*, was devoted to articles on this subject. In their introduction the editors of the volume profess an ecumenical approach. Their statement addresses the general scientific benefit of a mixture of approaches rather than the circumstances under which theories arise:

> We propose that organizational analysis has been evolving . . . toward more complex, paradoxical, and even contradictory modes of understanding. Instead of monochromatic thinking, we suggest an interpretive framework more like a rainbow—a "code of many colors" that tolerates alternative assumptions. . . . For organizational analysis we need to be able to perceive and understand the complex nature of organizational phenomena, both micro and macro, organizational and individual, conservative and dynamic. We need to understand organizations in multiple ways, as having "machine-like" aspects, "organism-like" aspects, "culture-like" aspects, and others yet to be identified. We need to encourage and use the tension engendered by multiple images of our complex subject. (Jelinek, Smircich, & Hirsch, 1983:331)

> Culture is seen by these authors as a new idea redirecting attention away from

> some of the commonly accepted "important things" (such as structure or technology) and toward the (until now) less-frequently examined elements raised to importance by the new metaphor (such as shared understandings, norms, or values). (Jelinek, Smircich, & Hirsch, 1983:331)

While some of the words in the above quotations may be a bit strange to the reader, the absence of the words *power* and *conflict* is noteworthy. Thus, older paradigms—ways of viewing knowledge—may give way to new ones while still providing the same function of supporting the views of the majority. To make this a bit clearer, let us consider in some detail Pfeffer's analysis of why power is omitted in most organizational analyses.

Power and organizational politics.   In chapter 5 we will deal with power at length. Our purpose here is to follow Pfeffer's argument about why power and politics are such threatening topics in the field of organizations. He disagrees with the seemingly democratic, scientific approach that allows equal validity to various kinds of theories and chooses to emphasize the importance of power as an ever-present variable in organizations. Power has been defined in many ways, but the definition usually includes the capability of an individual or group to overcome resistance in achieving a desired result. Power exists within a given context of other individuals or groups. Pfeffer describes organizational politics, which many engage in but few acknowledge, as involved with power:

> Organizational politics involves those activities taken within organizations to acquire, develop, and use power and other resources to obtain one's pre-ferred outcomes in a situation in which there is uncertainty or dissensus about choices. (Pfeffer, 1981a:7)

We all know that power and politics are everyday realities, yet organizational politics and organizational power are frequently omitted in management and orga-nization theory literature. As pointed out earlier, this body of literature is intended to socialize would-be managers to their future occupational roles as well as to pro-vide information. Giving greater attention to power and politics could challenge taken-for-granted assumptions about the way the world is and how it should be.

Certain theories—such as the emphasis on rationality and rational choice models—are more supportive of the way things currently operate. The professional manager will most likely be working in a huge bureaucratized setting and is seen to need the kind of socialization that will

> "facilitate the manager's integration into large, formalized bureaucracies. Clearly, the acceptance of legitimate authority as implemented through a hierarchical structure is . . . important in the socialization of managers. Such authority will be more readily accepted to the extent that it is *perceived* to be legitimate. Given the social values stressing universalism and rationality, any organizational authority system and decision making apparatus that operates according to these values will appear to be more legitimate and will encourage compliance on the part of managers. (Pfeffer, 1981a:12)

The culture perspective.   Although the culture perspective, of growing inter-est in organizational studies, has room to incorporate power concepts, it may also serve to obscure them. If organizational cultures are uncritically accepted or treated as quaint anthropological finds, they are a force for stability. Unlike a society's culture—its slowly evolving way of life—an organization's culture can be consciously created and manipulated. Those in power in organizations are in a position to "shape beliefs and perceptions and to cause these realities to be accepted as social facts" (Pfeffer, 1981a:302).

Within organizations "the tendency to develop shared beliefs, world-views, or organizational cultures" serves to legitimate current practices, structures, and distributions of power (Pfeffer, 1981a:299). The culture is represented in typical stories, myths, and ceremonies passed on to generations of employees. Kanter describes the institutionalization of culture in Indsco, the corporation she studied. Many stories were told about the kindness and consideration that the firm showed employees, but all of these stories turned out to be about kindness to only one class of employees, the "exempt" category—those in the management track (1977, chap. 2). Kanter also showed that commonly held stereotypes about the traits of managers and the traits of secretaries were used as self-fulfilling prophecies to keep men in one occupational slot and women in another. Organizational culture is a topic to which we shall return in chapter 7. Analysis of organizations and organizational literature from the point of view of women is discussed in the next section as one of the challenges to traditional perspectives.

CHALLENGES TO TRADITIONAL PERSPECTIVES

This chapter has dealt at length with the strong control the powerful have over research. But power can be claimed by any group or collectivity, and this section will deal with some of the challenges to traditional perspectives made by nonmainstream critics. The challenges we choose to consider are perspectives coming out of the women's studies movement, collective behavior by workers, movements by citizens that challenge the power of organizations, and Marxist critiques.

The Women's Studies Perspective

Some readers may be familiar with the black history movement, which later spread to the other social sciences. Interest in black history, as seen from a black point of view, has been with us for a long time. However, in the 1960s, with the civil rights movement and then the black power movement, this interest burgeoned. Black scholars criticized traditional history texts, which minimized the ugly aspects of slavery and wrote of "happy darkies." The film *Black History: Lost, Strayed, or Stolen*, narrated by actor-comedian Bill Cosby, documented the omissions of black contributions and the stereotyping that occurred not only in texts but in films and other media. As black pride and awareness increased, students took up the cry for black studies programs in schools and universities (Albert, Goldstein, & Slaughter, 1974:111–160). They wanted the omissions and distortions of traditional works revealed and wanted to learn about their own past from an other-than-white point of view.

The black history movement provided the model for a similar one by women, much as the abolitionist movement served as a model for the nineteenth-century feminists. As the resurgent women's movement developed in the late 1960s and early 1970s, it took its cues from the black movement both with regard to consciousness raising and to scholarship. Womens' studies departments were instituted at major universities. The new scholarship that emerged on women, along with popular magazines and journals written from the same perspective, began to point out the distortions and omissions with regard to women.

Among the findings of the new scholarship were the pervasiveness of sexism in language and the sex-stereotyping in texts. The readers provided to young children tended to stereotype women as housewives and mothers, and men as workers—even though many women have always had to work. Boys were shown as active, girls as passive. Other traits were assigned to one or the other sex, for example, "boys don't cry." Since the rise of the women's movement, a whole new thrust has developed in materials written for children—an attempt to make them nonsexist.

Of course, works for older readers often, consciously or unconsciously, perpetuate similar sexist stereotypes. Once the "click" occurs—the rise of consciousness and ability to detect sexism when one meets it—the reader can recognize many examples. A great deal of organizational literature, unfortunately, is guilty of such sins of omission and commission. That is certainly not surprising when we realize that until the 1970s men constituted over 96 percent of all managers and administrators earning more than $15,000 yearly (Kanter, 1977:17). While the proportion of women entering managerial jobs increased in the 1970s, less than 4 percent of working women held any type of managerial job by 1982 (U.S. Department of Labor, 1983). Men were the managers and the scholars in the business schools who taught future managers. Thus, managerial ideologies were male ideologies.

Here is an interesting example of unconscious bias, striking because it is written by an author with a highly critical perspective on issues he deems important. Earlier in the chapter we quoted from a work by Baritz, who provocatively revealed the pro-business bias of industrial sociologists and psychologists. In contrast, his writing reveals a very familiar type of sexist bias. Note how he refers to the female workers chosen to participate in the Hawthorne experiments. He states (Baritz, 1960:82):

> On April 25, 1927, the relay assembly test room was opened in a corner of the regular relay assembly department. In this room were placed six *experienced women operators* whose job was to put together a little gadget called a relay, which was made up of between thirty and forty pieces. (Italics mine)

The researchers were conducting an illumination experiment to observe the effects of lighting and other working conditions on production. By the next page (p. 83), these experienced women operators have become "girls" and so they remain ever after in this book:

> The first period of the experiment lasted for about two weeks, when the *girls* selected to participate in the test room were secretly observed working in their regular department so that a base rate of their production could be established. (Italics mine)

Here is another quote to clinch the argument: "What was driving the *girls'* output up? To this question the *men* at Hawthorne, academicians and company officials alike, turned their attention" (Baritz, 1960:84, italics mine). If one wants to argue that the term *girls* is not sexist, why are the men not referred to as *boys*? The girls appear as less adult, less important. Note the context in which the term *girl* is used in figure 2-1. These examples of sexist news and advertising (sent in by readers) appear in a feature called "No Comment" in *Ms.* magazine, the only major magazine of original material that is both managed and controlled by women.

The use of the term *girl* to refer to adult women is so widespread that many women will even defend it. But one has merely to return to the area of race rela-

FIGURE 2-1

NO COMMENT®

OOPS!
We Goofed!

One of the new girls sorting the wheaties accidentally dumped several bags of mint-marked and new penny rolls from 1916 up to 1940 into a bucket originally used in our newsstand ads for wheaties. Well, what could we say to the crying little thing except to make her let us print this little episode and give her credit for the next deal, you will receive. All lots guaranteed unsearched.

Chattanooga Stamp & Coin

Chattanooga, Tenn. 37411

advertisement appearing in the *Coin Wholesaler*, submitted by Jay Leisner, Eugene, Oreg.

BECKER CPA REVIEW

HELPING ACCOUNTANTS BECOME PROFESSIONALS SINCE 1957

To: The wives of my students:

This printed bit of encouragement is being sent to each of my students' wives as an appeal for understanding and help.

Your husband is presently involved with one of the most difficult endeavors of his accounting career; that of preparing for the CPA examination to be given next November or May.

His success depends to a large degree on you. You have sacrificed a great deal to enable your husband to get this far in life. Probably you are the one who encouraged him to take the CPA examination. In the future, you will miss your husband while he is in class. For some of you, it will mean that you will have to put the children to bed by yourself. For each of you, it will mean that you will be badly neglected as a wife.

Please be aware that your understanding and help is important to the professional success of your husband. The sacrifice you make today will reap the rewards of financial security tomorrow.

The next three or four months are the most important to your husband's success on the CPA examination. To be assured of success on the examination, he should invest time outside of class doing homework. This time should be from 50% to 100% of his time in class. Please make it as easy as you can for him to do a conscientious job on his homework.

In three or four months this will all be over and every hour of study lost to your husband between now and the examination will have been irretrievably lost.

Please be kind and especially understanding until after the examination.

Years later, you'll be able to look back at this period of mutual sacrifice with the warm feeling of having conquered together the most difficult of professional examinations.

form letter given to members of a coed accounting course, submitted by Ann Halpin. Rancho Palos Verdes, Calif.

material in a three-drawer alphabetic file cabinet. An item has to be filed under the letter "S." To do this sequentially, the girl opens the first file drawer, starts at the beginning, and looks for the letter S. When she does not find it, she goes to the second drawer and repeats the process. Since it is not in the second drawer, she must now go to the third drawer, where she finds the folder and files the item away (see Figure 1-11).

This obviously is not the fastest way to solve the problem. However, under sequential filing, it is the only way that the item can be filed.

from a computer textbook, submitted by Joanne Dennis, Whitefish Bay, Wis.

Source: *Ms.* Magazine, August 1980, September 1982, and December 1982. Used with permission.

tions to gain some insight on why this term is objectionable. Before the civil rights movement, black adults in the South (and sometimes in other regions) were referred to as "girls" and "boys." This was accompanied by other practices, such as never according them the titles of Mr. or Mrs. It was a demeaning symbolization, recognized universally by black people as such. The terminology treated them as children, not as full adults entitled to respect. Referring to one set of people as adults and the others as children immediately set up an unequal relationship. In the case of the Western Electric study its use reinforced the lowly position of the female workers compared to the male executives and academicians—who it must be assumed were all male. After all, the author says "the men" at Hawthorne turned their attention to the question at hand.

That such language is less likely to be used in the future by respectable publishers can now be assumed. Many now routinely advise their writers to avoid sexist language. But this is only one aspect of change that reflects feminist perspectives. The presence of sex bias in managerial ideologies and of tokenism in the employment of women managers was raised definitively in Kanter's 1977 book, *Men and Women of the Corporation.* Since that time more female sociologists have entered the field of organizational research; one of the most important research fields in women's studies is the related one of women and work.

Collective Behavior by Workers

Another important area of resistance to official doctrines lies in the responses of workers. Time and motion studies, embraced actively by industrial firms, were usually rejected by workers. Their assumption was that the benefits of increased production would not be permanently passed on to them but would simply add to profits. People low in hierarchies have their own perceptions of the powerful. When able, they respond to perceived threats with informal and formal tactics, ranging from slowdown and sabotage of machinery to the collective action of joining unions. In times of labor shortage, workers may be able to force management towards techniques of persuasion rather than coercion. Management may also resort to such ameliorative techniques to stem union organizing. In the 1930s, as human relations approaches became more prominent, psychological counseling was offered to workers. According to Baritz (1960:104): "Counseling, as the management of Western Electric conceived of it, was a method of helping people think in such a way that they would be happier with their jobs." While this may be a gentler approach than coercion, unions tend to be wary of such approaches, considering them paternalistic. And so the interaction and interplay of management-worker relations go on; management policy begets worker response, worker response begets management rethinking (sometimes), and practices get modified.

The case of the illegal workers' union, Solidarity, in Poland indicates that even where labor is tightly controlled, workers may defy the authorities. Although the situation is too complex to analyze thoroughly here, it appears that the very ideology Polish workers have absorbed stresses the dignity and importance of workers and therefore serves to strengthen their defiance. They may be told that the state is benevolent, but this does not mean they believe it. Similarly, it may be claimed that bureaucracy and complex organization are functional, useful for all members, and based on rational principles. However, particular members of particular organizations, by their actions, can demonstrate their disagreement with the theory. Persons in relatively low positions such as workers, or consumers, sometimes create a need for new theories that will incorporate recognition of natural conflicts.

Social Movements and Citizen Revolt

While formal organizations dominate much of modern life, it was suggested in chapter 1 that nonbureaucratic collectivities—communities, racial, ethnic, and gender groups, and social movements—may counter the power of bureaucracies. Groups within American society's heterogenous population are beginning to demand better representation at various levels of its organizations. The influence of the feminist movement on rules against sex stereotyping in publishing has already illustrated this point.

Citizens who interact with public bureaucracies have increasingly come to question the expertise and humanitarian motives of their functionaries, a point we shall expand on in chapter 9. Out of the social movements of the 1960s came demands for participation of the poor and for citizen representation on local boards of education, as well as on the boards of such community-serving organizations as universities and hospitals. A rise in consumer knowledge, fostered by consumer interest groups and a generally increased level of education, led to challenges to both government and industry. One result was decreased public confidence in government and corporations (Smith & Taylor, 1979; Vogel, 1978). Vogel has noted that organized citizen groups, recognizing the power of corporations, are now pressuring them directly. One example is the demand that they reduce their investments in apartheid South Africa; another is the case of internal corporation battles brought about by shareholders unwilling to go along with all the recommendations of management. How effective these pressures are is a separate question worthy of study. The final challenge to traditional perspectives that we will examine is the Marxist critique of organizational research and theory.

Marxist Critiques

No one familiar with the historical development of organizational research and theory questions the fact that they have been strongly influenced by the needs of corporations. This observation is a matter of historical fact and is not confined to those who hold a Marxist perspective. Only in recent decades have Marxist social scientists seriously focused their attention on complex organizations. In doing so, they are attempting to examine organizational writing and theory from a class perspective.

That is, Marxists are trying to bring together two fairly separate intellectual traditions: (1) the analysis of the organizational society in terms of formal organizations, and (2) the analysis of the free enterprise society in terms of class inequalities. In the process of doing so, they raise new questions and force the reexamination of previously taken-for-granted assumptions. For example, the class perspective maintains that unequal classes develop under capitalism, and thus the translation of this inequality into the organizational world is not a mistake, not simple discrimination, but an essential element of organizational structure.

Class and organization as separate scientific paradigms.   At least one theorist, Kenneth Westhues, has tried to describe class and organization as two separate scientific paradigms rather than as a battle of ideologies. A paradigm is a framework of major concepts through which the scientist views the world. These concepts form the bases for testable hypotheses in research. A paradigm is not immutable; it refers to the initial systematic basis for generating hypotheses and may be replaced if too many of these hypotheses are proven wrong.

Westhues (1980:74) provides the following example: "A scientific revolution occurs when one such paradigm is rejected for another, as in the shift from Ptolemaic to Copernican astronomy or from Newtonian to Einsteinian physics."

According to Westhues, sociological paradigms are determined largely by what the sociologist considers the "most critical decision-making unit" in a society, the unit most responsible for what happens. A social-psychological perspective would take the individual as the key unit. A *social class perspective* "defines as the basic decision-making unit a collectivity of individuals who share a common relationship to the means of production—for example, a capitalist bourgeoisie, a proletariat, or a peasantry" (Westhues, 1980:76).

In contrast, an *organization perspective* considers the basic unit of analysis to be an organization, such as a corporation, government bureaucracy, or church. Karl Marx and Max Weber are acknowledged as the major social scientists who gave rise to these two separate systems of concepts. Weber viewed bureaucracy as the central feature of the modern world. He was concerned with the possible threat bureaucratic domination posed to democracy, even though he described the bureaucratic model as efficient and rational. Marx had earlier maintained that classes were the major decision-making units of society, and that the domination of the capitalist class is oppressive. Marxists have focused on the dynamics and contradictions of capitalist society, seeing struggle, not stability, as normal.

The deficiencies of organizational analysis.   Although these two different paradigms have led to different research directions, they are increasingly coming together in the Marxist critique of organizational theory. For example, Goldman and Van Houten (1981a) describe five of what they consider serious deficiencies in organizational analysis:

1.   The field has been ahistorical with little attention given the ways in which a particular organization (or type of organization) has evolved or changed.

2. The sociology of organizations has been isolated from issues of social class, social stratification, and social conflict.
3. The field has emphasized microanalysis with either the work group or the single organization serving as the primary unit of analysis. Thus there is little discussion of how the economy, the political context, or the community affects day-to-day organizational life.
4. The field is elitist in the interests of capital and management rather than those of workers and in assuming that managerial behavior is more important, more variable, and more worthy of study than that of workers.
5. The discipline, with the exception of the now unfashionable study of bureaucratic "dysfunctions," is undialectical, seldom seeing the roots of tomorrow in the reality of today. (p. 92)

Let us examine these criticisms. The first point is relatively self-explanatory. Except for brief reviews of the history of organizational theory in some texts, most organizational research focuses on relatively brief time periods. The lack of attention to class and conflict, the second criticism, is being remedied by the new Marxist research into organizations and by other works such as those of Pfeffer (1981) and his colleages and Perrow (1979). The tendency to deal with the individual organization as the unit of analysis, the third criticism, has been greatly diminished by recent attention to organizational environments and interorganizational relationships (see chapter 10). Whether or not these new foci are linked to the "day-to-day" operations of organizations is a subject for discovery. Certainly, it is recognized that the international competition for markets, and the import/export balance are issues which have sparked changes in American firms.

Regarding the fourth criticism, the assumption that the organization field is "elitist," operates in the interests of management, and assumes that managerial behavior is more worthy of study than that of workers, my view is mixed. We have already seen the strong corporate influence on theory and research in the field, and indeed, the descriptive case concluding the chapter illustrates this issue. However, class theorists in sociology are now able to have their works published in mainstream journals, alongside those of organization theorists, as well as in radical journals such as the *Monthly Review*. Organization theorists tend to dominate the prestigious *Administrative Science Quarterly*, based at the Cornell Graduate School of Business and Public Administration, and other business schools journals. Serious sociological work on unions is extremely rare, although the interests *of managers* have given rise to numerous studies of workers. Given the social roots of knowledge, it is not surprising that many more resources are available to support work that does not challenge the existing institutional structure. Extra effort and persistence are needed to overcome resistance to unpopular points of view so that dissenting paradigms can get their hearing and be published, and occasionally this occurs.

The fifth criticism, that organization studies tend to be undialectical, requires clarification of the term *dialectics*. Although the dialectical perspective has many aspects, its central emphasis is on *process*. It maintains that societies, organizations, and other aspects of social reality are continually in the process of becoming; what seems fixed and permanent at one time may change. Dialectics focuses on the transformations through which a particular set of arrangements gives way to another. As an illustration, once the omission of dialectics in organizational theory had been observed, writers began to fill in the void. Benson wrote an article called, "Organizations: A Dialectical View," and it did get published in the *Administrative Science Quarterly* (1977:1-21).

In contrast to those who describe organizations as rational, integrated, and coherent, the dialectical point of view insists that they are characterized by contradictions—ruptures, breaks, or inconsistencies that will bring about change (Benson, 1977). Within the broader Marxist framework, dialectics is a major principle that explains how transitions from one type of economic system to another occur. The emphasis on change, transition, and disruption by class theorists challenges theories that stress order, stability, and the maintenance of existing power hierarchies. Within sociology, order and conflict theorists have long debated and the Marxist challenge surely enlivens organizational research.

These examples of how traditional perspectives are challenged by diverse sources show that formal organizations are not insulated from either intellectual or grass-roots movements for change. This consideration has naturally been quite general; how effective these challenges are will require intensive study of specific issues.

CONFLICT OF INTEREST: *A CASE STUDY*

The publicly expressed concerns of universities about the kinds of choices made by professors with strong financial ties to corporations was the topic of an article appearing on February 8, 1983, in the *New York Times*. The article, "Coast Teachers Warned on Ties to Corporations," dealt with the possible conflicts in interest that exist between observing the canons of scientific research and being financially tied to corporations. Universities are now concerned about the matter, even as they reward academicians who are big grant-getters.

The article reported that the University of California had issued written warnings to more than a dozen professors with substantial financial ties to corporations that also sponsor their academic research. They were told that they were risking violations of the school's conflict of interests policy and "should be extremely wary of allowing corporate sponsors to influence their research or limit publication of their findings."

According to the *Times*: (February 8, 1983)

The university's action, the first of its kind to be made public, comes at a time of heightened concern that professors who act as corporate consultants, officers or stockholders may skew their research toward studies profitable to the companies. The debate has been especially strong at Stanford, Harvard and Yale, where many faculty members are involved in the competitive and profitable fields of bioengineering and computer electronics. (p. A16)

Under a recent reinterpretation of a 1974 California law, professors are considered public officials who must disclose personal financial information if they receive research funds from a company in which they have a financial interest. The University of California took a census and received 2,569 disclosure statements. Of these, 113 indicated potential conflicts of interest. In some cases the professors received research funds from companies or corporate-owned foundations from which they also received thousands of dollars in salary or consulting fees each year or in which they held substantial stock.

Each of the disclosure statements was reviewed by faculty committees that decided, in each case, that the financial interest would not necessarily compromise academic principles.

Unsurprisingly, some professors oppose financial disclosures. The *Times*, referring to opposition to the disclosure statements by important faculty groups, such as the California Faculty Senate, indicated that questions had been raised about whether faculty review committees would be willing to modify or terminate contracts that pose a conflict of interest. In fact, no research was disapproved and no conditions were attached to any research application. That the concern of the university was at least partly genuine was supposedly shown by the following action:

> In at least one case completed since the review, a professor at the university's Riverside campus whose entire salary and research were financed, directly or indirectly, by Southern California Edison was required to find alternative sources of funds. The professor was told he could not continue as the sole principal investigator in research the utility sponsored. (p. A16)

The professor in question was rather miffed, claiming that the utility had never tried to influence the choice of research topics or prevent the publication of findings.

The article adds:

> Concerns about corporate influence are rising on several campuses. Already some graduate students at Stanford and Harvard report cases in which they are discouraged from sharing their findings with colleagues doing research sponsored by competing companies. (p. A16)

Thus closely linked are the university and the corporation. Nor does it seem likely that this can change, for universities are increasingly dependent on outside grants for their financing. Hence, the lion's share of rewards—in the form of tenure, promotions, and honors—are accorded to faculty members who obtain large research grants, perpetuating the process.

SUMMARY

This chapter began by analyzing the social roots of organizational knowledge—showing that knowledge arises out of the needs of particular groups in a society. Science, ideology, and social policy are related. Every political and economic system has an ideology, justifying its central premises. Those who represent each system have at their command the greatest amount of power and economic resources in order to maintain it. For our purposes, this translates into a high degree of control over the directions of scientific research, the choice of topics, and the use or repression of its results. Public policy is often dependent on the findings of science, and organizations are very concerned with how public policy will affect them. The findings of scientific research are sometimes rejected by those who base their beliefs on other systems of knowing, such as religion. As one example of the ways in which the dissemination of knowledge is controlled, religious influence on what textbooks will publish was cited. The ideological battle between capitalism and communism finds both systems seeking scientific support. While most published analyses of formal organizations serve to support the United States' free enterprise system, the right to dissent has enabled Marxist-oriented social scientists to raise interesting challenges to mainstream formulations.

The second part of the chapter dealt in greater detail with how the needs of corporations affect research. Industry's need for research in the "hard" (physical or natural) sciences is expanding, and they are sponsoring more and more such research. Management also supports studies in the social sciences both to control workers and to train future managers. Industrial psychologists and sociologists are employed in large numbers by industries. And many who labor in universities are also generously subsidized by corporations, thus raising the issue of possible conflict of interest and forcing universities to examine the ties between professors and their sponsors.

Scientific management and human relations studies are two well-known examples of management-oriented research. Despite the wide diversity in organizational theories and research, some contend that more controversial topics are ignored. The importance of power, the conflict between workers and management, and the role of unions are often neglected or played down as areas of research. New fields of interest, such as the current rediscovery of organizational culture, may consciously or unconsciously continue to obscure ideologically unpopular topics.

The chapter's final section considers some of the current challenges to traditional perspectives by both nonbureaucratic forces within the society and Marxist critics within sociology. The women's studies perspective has attacked sex bias in scientific and popular writing, and feminist thinkers have questioned sexual inequality in the world of work. Collective behavior by workers and critical postures by citizen groups have challenged and continue to challenge the legitimacy of the authority of public and private bureaucracies. Finally, some of the major points of the Marxist critique of traditional organizational theory and ideology were presented.

We concluded with a case study on how universities are trying to cope with possible conflicts of interest between the pursuit of free and honest science and the indebtedness of researchers to the largesse of big corporations.

3

TYPOLOGIES

Classifying Organizations
     The Problem: The Need to Classify Organizations
     Common-Sense and Intentional Typologies
Organizational Science's Neglect of Typologies
     Decreasing Interest in Typologies
     Organizational Survival as a Focus
     Organizational Effectiveness as a Focus
Typologies Examined
     Blau and Scott: Who Benefits?
     Westrum and Samaha: Bureaucracy, Enterprise, and Voluntary Association
     Etzioni: Types of Power and Compliance
     Goffman: Total Institutions
     Perrow: Technology
     McKelvey: Population and Taxonomy
Changing Doctor–Patient Relationships: A Case Study
Summary

CLASSIFYING ORGANIZATIONS

The Problem: The Need to Classify Organizations

It was useful to initiate our study of organizations by separating them out from other major social collectivities (see chapter 1). To go beyond that, we need to recognize that the great variety of organizations cannot be treated as if they were all alike, nor can each organization be viewed as totally unique. We therefore classify organizations into scientifically useful groupings or types.[1] Such types should "indicate a meaningful difference between the types or classes identified" (R. Hall, 1982).

Chapter 1 introduced the reader to three perspectives, or models, of organizations: rational, natural, and open systems. These are broad approaches or outlooks that guide more specific studies; they are frameworks for viewing or approaching the field. Typologies tend to reflect these points of view implicitly or explicitly. But a typology is not a perspective as such; it is an attempt to organize or classify similar organizations into groups and set them apart from those that differ in significant ways.

The creation of typologies is related to our need to make the world less chaotic, to organize experience and put it into categories. Human perception constantly sorts out and tries to make sense of experience. Indeed, stereotypes arise out of this tendency to try to simplify and group people and things. The stereotype is an overgeneralization based on a perceived cue—such as color, sex, or ethnicity. But there is a positive side to this tendency to classify. Past experience enables us to react to new people, places, experiences, organizations, and happenings without investigating each thoroughly. On the basis of similarities, and despite varying details, the new people, places, and things can be grouped in a common-sense way. A man with black hair, brown hair, or no hair who is wearing a wedding ring will be recognized as a married man. This recognition often influences the way in which unmarried females relate to him. (The man with no ring cannot be similarly classified and may have to be puzzled over.)

The world of science is also faced with the problem of classification. In order for the vast field of organizations to become intelligible, we have to begin to divide them up into ones that have crucial similarities. But how are we to do so? Which similarities are important? Which are predictive of organizational survival or change or structure? Each of the sample of typologies to be discussed takes its own point of departure about which organizational features are most significant.

Common-Sense and Intentional Typologies

In everyday life, organizations are classified in a common-sense way, often expressed in their names, titles, or descriptions. Suppose you were seeking a bachelor's degree: It would be essential to know which schools are two-year and which are four-year colleges, two different types. Such a simple classification would not tell you all that you needed to know about these schools, but it would be useful since a bachelor's degree can be earned at one type of school but not at the other.

---

[1] Such terms as *classification*, *typology*, and *taxonomy* are used in different ways by different authors. While semantic arguments may be important to theorists in the field, they are omitted here as of less interest to the student. For those who do wish a brief review of how various authors use these terms see McKelvey (1975:509–510).

Some typologies proposed by organizational scientists are also based on "common sense," such as classifying organizations by whether they are profit or nonprofit. Westrum and Samaha's (1984) typology of bureaucracies, enterprises, and voluntary associations, mentioned in chapter 1 and discussed below, is a common-sense typology. However, critics claim that simply because people usually think of organizations as different does not mean that they differ in significant ways.

Another kind of classification, which Richard Hall (1982) calls "intentional typologies," sorts organizations according to one particular set of elements deemed basic, such as power, technology, or nature of participants. Well-known examples of this genre, the typologies of Etzioni (1980), Blau and Scott (1962), and Perrow (1967) are discussed below. Etzioni's model, for example, centers around concepts of power and compliance. More recently, McKelvey has proposed scrapping most of these typologies in favor of a "population" model, which borrows extensively from biology (1982; McKelvey & Aldrich, 1983). This, too, will be examined.

ORGANIZATIONAL SCIENCE'S NEGLECT OF TYPOLOGIES

Decreasing Interest in Typologies

Writing in 1975, McKelvey claimed that little progress had been made in developing methods of classifying organizations during the previous fifteen years. He later published his own approach to taxonomy, *Organizational Systematics* (1982).

After attempts at constructing typologies in the 1960s, swings in attention drew research efforts to such previously neglected topics as the environment, population ecology, and organizational cultures—to be discussed in succeeding chapters. Possibly because of fascination with these new areas, interest in typology building (a form of theory building) declined. Nonetheless, some of the concepts and ideas introduced in various typologies became part of organizational vocabulary. For example, Woodward's (1965) three contrasting terms for the kind of technology employed in production—unit and small-batch production, large-batch and mass production, and process production—have been utilized in subsequent studies; her work gave great impetus to theories emphasizing technology.

Perhaps more important as a factor accounting for the decline of interest in creating typologies was the burgeoning growth in quantitative research that occurred, some of it testing these typologies. A 1980 collection of selected studies (Katz, Kahn, & Adams) is prefaced by the observation that the major growth of such empirical research developed in the previous fifteen years. It occurred in a variety of organizational settings, tended to be well funded, and often utilized

sophisticated statistical techniques. The editors of the collection view the development as one advancing the state of organizational study as a science. Nonetheless,
the tests of typologies often came up with conflicting results.

A somewhat contrasting point of view is taken by Zey-Ferrell and Aiken, who
also edited a volume of studies (1981). Speculating about the theoretical impetus
for sociological work over roughly the same time period, they include as influencing
factors "the coalescence of the interests of students of management techniques
with those of quantitatively oriented organizational researchers" (p. 228).

Not as happy as Katz, Kahn, and Adams about this development, Zey-Ferrell
and Aiken observe:

> This coalescence of interests may have run its course by now. A bifurcation
> seems to be occurring among researchers, dividing those essentially interested
> in better management from those wanting to ask broader questions about or-
> ganizations in society. . . . The outcome of this process is likely to be an
> increasing polarization in the kinds of studies that are conducted—managerial-
> oriented research versus critical societal analyses that examine the role of
> organizations as agents of social change, agents of social control in society,
> and agents of domination for the ruling classes. (p. 228).

Their collection of articles exemplifying "critical perspectives" deals mainly
with the societally oriented questions. Diversity in points of view and interests
within a field, as reflected in the comments of the two sets of editors quoted, is
certainly a healthy sign. Another kind of diversity arises because the study of organizations is relevant to many different academic disciplines.

It is harder to develop theory and build models when a field is interdisciplinary and draws on subject areas with their own traditions, such as sociology,
psychology, administrative science, business management, and others (Katz, Kahn,
& Adams, 1980:1).[2]

Organizational Survival as a Focus

The managerial interest in organizations often takes the form of concern with
success and survival. More societally oriented typologies, such as those of Blau and
Scott (1962), and Etzioni (1961, 1980), deal with a wide spectrum of organizations,
including governmental agencies, prisons and mental institutions, and voluntary
associations such as nonprofit charities. After the 1960s, when social problems and
governmental response to them were highly topical, the problems of inflation and
of business survival became more widely discussed in popular literature. Many
theorists who turned their attention to organizational survival dealt explicitly or

---

[2] These disciplines do converge in some of the organizational research that is being done
(Katz, Kahn, & Adams, 1980:1).

implicitly with *business* survival. They seemed to ignore the desirability of phasing out or eliminating certain types of organizations—prisons, for example, or super-fluous governmental agencies. The tremendous interest in organizational survival supports Zey-Ferrell and Aiken's (1981) comments about the influence of mana-gerial-oriented research. Growth and survival of all types of organizations is a sign of neither their success nor societal health. Would anyone contend that the flourish-ing criminal justice industry is a preferred state of affairs, despite the jobs it provides?

Organizational Effectiveness as a Focus

Survival is one possible measure of organizational effectiveness, or more broadly, of how well an organization is performing—doing its job—and how well it is functioning in general. Interest in effectiveness has a long history, but researchers disagree on how best to measure it. In addition to survival, other main criteria used have been the organization's attainment of basic goals or the extent to which it has obtained critical resources (Kimberly, Norling, & Weiss, 1983:249).[3]

Steers identified seventeen different models of organizational effectiveness, most of which are multivariate (see Figure 3-1). Effectiveness tends to be measured "in terms of the sum of a set of relevant criteria" (Steers, 1975:546). For example, Yuchtman and Seashore (1967) combine two main elements in their system resource approach: the successful acquisition of scarce and valued resources plus control over the environment. E. Schein (1970) focuses on micro (organization–individual) issues: open communication, flexibility, creativity, and psychological commitment.

Figure 3-1 lists the criteria of effectiveness used in the seventeen models studied by Steers.

Just as we cautioned that survival may not be desirable under all circumstances, so it can be pointed out that long-run effectiveness may not result from any one factor such as constant growth or a high level of productivity (Kimberly, Norling, & Weiss, 1983:259).

Having briefly discussed models of organizational effectiveness, we now turn to the central task of this chapter: the examination of selected typologies of organi-zations. While some models suggest how different types of organizations succeed or survive, the central aim of models is to classify organizations on the basis of "mean-ingful differences" between the types.

Despite their flaws, major and frequently discussed early typologies are worth examining for what they contribute and for an understanding of what they try to do. Our selection is a sampling of typologies, which partly overlaps with and partly differs from those of others (see, for example, Eldridge & Crombie, 1975, chap. 3; R. Hall, 1982:40-48; Perrow, 1979:160-164; and Scott, 1981, chap. 2).

---

[3] One way of gaining an understanding of the elusive idea of effectiveness is to note how researchers have operationalized and measured it (Steers, 1975:546).

FIGURE 3-1   Evaluation Criteria in Multivariate Models of Organizational Effectiveness

Georgopoulos and Tannenbaum (1957)
Productivity, Flexibility, Absence of
    organizational strain

Bennis (1962)
Adaptability, Sense of identity, Capacity
    to test reality

Blake and Mouton (1964)
Simultaneous achievement of high pro-
    duction-centered and high people-
    centered enterprise

Caplow (1964)
Stability, Integration, Voluntarism,
    Achievement

Katz and Kahn (1966)
Growth, Storage, Survival, Control over
    environment

Lawrence and Lorsch (1967)
Optimal balance of integration and dif-
    ferentiation

Yuchtman and Seashore (1967)
Successful acquisition of scarce and
    valued resources,
Control over environment

Friedlander and Pickle (1968)
Profitability, Employee satisfaction,
    Societal value

Price (1968)
Productivity, Conformity, Morale,
Adaptiveness, Institutionalization

Mahoney and Weitzel (1969)
General business model
    Productivity-support-utilization, Plan-
        ning,
    Reliability, Initiative
R and D Model
    Reliability, Cooperation, Development

Schein (1970)
Open communication, Flexibility,
    Creativity
Psychological commitment

Mott (1972)
Productivity, Flexibility, Adaptability

Duncan (1973)
Goal attainment, Integration, Adaptation

Gibson et al. (1973)
Short-run
    Production, Efficiency, Satisfaction
Intermediate
    Adaptiveness, Development
Long-run
    Survival

Negandhi and Reimann (1973)
Behavioral index
    Manpower acquisition, Employee satis-
        faction,
    Manpower retention, Interpersonal
        relations,
    Interdepartmental relations, Manpower
        utilization
Economic index
    Growth in sales, Net profit

Child (1974, 1975)
Profitability, Growth

Webb (1974)
Cohesion, Efficiency, Adaptability,
    Support

Source: Reprinted from "Problems in the Measurement of Organizational Effectiveness," by Richard M. Steers, published in *Administrative Science Quarterly* 20 (1975): 546-558. Used by permission of *Administrative Science Quarterly*.

TYPOLOGIES EXAMINED

Blau and Scott: Who Benefits?

In 1962 Peter Blau and W. Richard Scott developed a typology that became widely discussed. Scott included his own work in his more recent review of various typologies (1981). This typology is based on the question, "*cui bono*—who benefits?" That is, who among the different types of participants in an organization is the prime beneficiary? Who is supposed to benefit the most? Four types of organizations are distinguished, each of which has a different prime beneficiary.

The Blau and Scott typology (along with Etzioni's) is one of the few that takes as an important variable the nature of one's participation, one's role, in an organization. The differences in experience of, for example, boss and worker or professional and client are recognized. It is understood that members of these categories often have varying interests. The authors define four basic categories of persons in relation to any given formal organization. They are:

(1) the members or rank-and-file participants; (2) the owners or managers of the organization; (3) the clients or, more generally, the "public-in-contact," which means the people who are technically "outside" the organization yet have regular contact with it, under whatever label—patient, customer, law violator, prisoner, enemy soldier, student; and (4) the public-at-large, that is, the members of the society in which the organization operates. (Blau & Scott, 1962:42)

After defining these four categories (which many other typologies ignore, implicitly taking the owner's or manager's point of view), Blau and Scott classify organizations on the basis of *cui bono*—who benefits: "Which of these four categories is the prime beneficiary of their operations?" (p. 42). The word "prime" is essential because the authors acknowledge that each type of participant tends to receive some benefits. In a business firm, the owners, employees, and customers each get something for their contributions or they would not participate. Even the public-at-large—the general public—benefits from that firm's contribution to the production and distribution of needed goods and services.

Although all parties benefit, "the benefits to one party furnish the reason for the organization's existing while the benefits to others are essentially a cost" (p. 43). A business is expected to operate for a profit and to liquidate if it shows a continuing loss. In contrast, "the city is not expected to close its police department or the community hospital because it fails to show a profit, but to operate it in the interest of the public even at a financial loss" (p. 43). In these examples, as well as others, the issue under discussion is, who is *expected* to benefit rather than who *actually* benefits. Later, criticizing his own work, Scott admits that a clear distinction was not made between the two questions (1975:45). One positive aspect of this typology is that it does not take one outcome—organizational survival—as the desired aim of all organizations. Rather, it maintains that different types of organizations have different central problems.

Applying the *cui bono* criterion, Blau and Scott arrive at a classification of four types of organizations, each with a different prime beneficiary and a distinctive central problem or tension (see table 3-1).

Mutual benefit associations. The prime beneficiary of mutual benefit associations is the membership, that is, the rank-and-file members. The crucial problem of such organizations as trade unions and clubs is maintaining internal democratic

TABLE 3-1   Blau and Scott's Typology Based on Prime Beneficiary

PRIME BENEFICIARY	ORGANIZATIONAL TYPE	CONCRETE EXAMPLES
Rank-and-file members	Mutual benefit associations	Political parties, unions, fraternal associations, clubs, professional associations, religious sects
Owners and managers	Business concerns	Industrial firms, wholesale and retail stores, banks, for-profit service agencies
Public-in-contact (clients)	Service organizations	Social work agencies, hospitals schools, mental health clinics
Public-at-large	Commonweal organizations	State bureaus, military establishment, police and fire departments, research firms, custodial prisons

Source: W. Richard Scott, *Organizations: Rational, Natural, and Open Systems* (Englewood Cliffs, N.J: Prentice-Hall, 1981), p. 42.© 1981. Reprinted by permission of Prentice-Hall, Inc., Englewood Cliffs, N.J.

processes, combating the tendency toward oligarchy—the tendency for power to reside in the hands of an elite minority—made famous by Michels (1949, first published in 1915). The student who belongs to a club or fraternity may be familiar with the complaint that "a few people do all the work" and the consequent tendency for a small clique to run the group.

Business concerns.   The owners are the prime beneficiary of a business concern. The key problem is that of maximizing operating efficiency in a competitive situation—making a profit.

Service organizations.   The clients, or public-in-contact, are the prime beneficiaries of service organizations. The chief problem is keeping the welfare of the client above the administrative needs of the organization or the self-interest of the professional providing service. When Blau and Scott wrote, they accepted the dictum that the professional person is a better judge of clients' needs than clients themselves. Although professionals and expert-service providers would tend to agree, clients may feel otherwise, especially if they are displeased with professionals' judgments (see e.g., Haug & Sussman, 1969). The case study of doctor-patient relationships at the end of this chapter suggests clients are increasingly wary of supposedly expert judgment. Further, service providers are not always professionals; they may be the various kinds of clerks at the motor vehicle bureau, the welfare office, and the passport office who we would hope have knowledge of their specific tasks but no training in professional ethics. The service sector in our economy is growing, meaning more and more workers come face-to-face with those seeking their attention for health or beautification needs, meals, government services, and the like.

The term *public-in-contact* can be applied to a wide variety of situations in which an outsider regularly interacts with an organization but is not really considered part of its structure. It has the virtue of showing that the boundaries of organizations are continually being crossed and hence being influenced by role players who may have ideas other than those the organization intended for them. Much of the criticism of bureaucracy flows from the problems encountered in the interaction between bureaucrats and clients, and the clients' complaints that they are not receiving adequate or timely service. The "buck" for such complaints is now frequently passed on to "the computer," and the impersonal machine rather than the service giver is blamed for delays and mistakes. Chapter 9 deals at greater length with organizations and their publics.

Commonweal organizations. The prime beneficiary of commonweal organizations is the public-at-large. Certain organizations, such as armies, police, and fire departments are supposed to serve the general public, the citizenry rather than specific role players. Blau and Scott see the central issue as maintaining external democratic control—for example, preventing an army from taking over the government in a coup (a not unusual occurrence in certain countries). The danger is that the military will be used to dominate the society that produced it. Another problem of the commonweal organization is that of "promoting extraordinary performances" (Blau & Scott, 1962:55), such as the bravery required of police and firemen or of the armed forces during wartime. Military training is guided by this need. A third problem of commonweal organizations such as prisons and mental institutions is that of dealing with society's outcasts. If the aim of a prison is protection of the public, it is a commonweal organization. The need to reduce recidivism (return to crime after release) fits in with this goal. Such aims are often mixed with the at least professed goal of rehabilitation, in which case the institution could be considered partly a service organization.

Criticism of the Blau and Scott typology. As indicated, one of the authors of this typology agrees with critics that it does not make a clear distinction between the question of who actually benefits most and who should or is supposed to benefit the most. Yet the typical problems sketched out for each type do refer to situations in which the good of the supposed beneficiary has been subordinated to that of other participants. The term *should* is normative; it contains a moral judgment or a basic premise. Professional ethics are normative—regardless of whether they are adhered to. The doctor or social worker is supposed to put the patient or client's interest above his or her own. A society that builds up its armed forces nevertheless does not want or expect the military to take over national decision making. The deviation from the normal, expected prime beneficiary constitutes a problem for the organization and the society.

Another criticism of the Blau and Scott formulation is that many organizations are "mixed" types, which points to the need to refine the typology further, should anyone be inclined to do so (Blau and Scott do not seem so inclined). Scott agrees that he and his coauthor failed "to spell out a set of rules for applying the typology to complex and multifaceted real-world organizations" (1981:45). Some such examples were given above, one being commonweal organizations such as prisons that not only intend to protect and thereby benefit the general public but also aim at some service to their public-in-contact, such as inmates. Most organizations are mixed by virtue of the fact that, whatever else they purport to do, they are also places of work for their staff or employees, who have normal desires for payment and personal satisfaction—which of course are benefits.

While some see the problem of classifying mixed organizations as a flaw in this typology, its insights can help explain some of the conflicts found among varied participants. Despite the presence of multiple beneficiaries, organizations are subject to criticism and control if they primarily benefit the wrong participants for their type. Prisons are faulted for "coddling" their prisoners, charitable organizations for paying their executives too much.

Westrum and Samaha: Bureaucracy, Enterprise, and Voluntary Association

Westrum and Samaha use two principles to classify organizations: "(1) Organizations whose members are full time differ from those whose members are mostly part time and (2) Organizations that are supposed to earn a profit are different from those that aren't" (1984:5). From those premises they derive three types of organization: *bureaucracy*, defined as a full-time, nonprofit organization; *enterprise*, defined as a full-time profit-oriented organization; and *voluntary association*, a part-time organization. The voluntary association is also considered basically nonprofit.

Bureaucracy.   A bureaucracy is designed to

> carry out a specific mission: deliver the mail, clean the streets, arrest criminals, or catch stray dogs. These functions are specified by national, state, or local laws, and they are supposed to be carried out in compliance with the laws. The funds that support these agencies come from public monies and are largely collected through taxes and fees. (1984:6)

Enterprise.   An enterprise is set up to make money by producing goods or services or by investing in other organizations. "The managers of a business enterprise are primarily responsible to the owners" (p. 6). This formulation differs only slightly from the Blau and Scott typology discussed above: obviously the enterprise is supposed to benefit primarily the owners by making profit.

Voluntary association.   Most voluntary associations differ from the above in that their members do not have a full-time commitment (defined in terms of an approximately 40-hour work week) to the organization. Churches, unions, political parties, and clubs fall into this grouping. Westrum and Samaha say that the primary beneficiaries of many voluntary associations are their members, partially agreeing with Blau and Scott, but that this is not supposed to be true for charitable or public service organizations. Thus, if one does volunteer work for the Heart Association or joins a group that provides readers for the blind, one is supposed to be primarily service oriented. These organizations are not supposed to be mutual benefit associations, even though the activity is unpaid.

Criticism of the Westrum and Samaha typology. Certainly, Westrum and Samaha's common-sense typology points up important differences among its three groupings. The most immediate problem is its selection of the term *bureaucracy* to represent only organizations in the governmental or public sector. Bureaucratic features abound in most large complex organizations, including firms. The study of organizational form, so popular in research on business, examines such bureaucratic elements as hierarchy, status, and span of control. Apart from the unfortunate selection of terminology, separating out public-sector, nonprofit organizations from private, profit-oriented ones is useful, and the two types deserve more careful comparison. Countries have different mixes of private and public sectors; that is, they have a smaller or larger proportion of societal life run by government, and such countries provide natural laboratories for comparative study. For example, one can hypothesize that the preference for public or private sector work will differ, depending on the strength and prestige of the public sector. In doing research on women and work in India, I found that government jobs, more permanent and prestigious, were often preferred to jobs in the private sector. In the United States, the reverse is often true; jobs in private industry are generally more prestigious and better paid than similar ones in government. The United States creates many of its public sector jobs to fill gaps left by private industry or to help solve social problems; it thus differs from a country where a degree of socialization of industry is deemed desirable.

Bureaucracies, enterprises, and voluntary associations are viewed as differing along several dimensions: the way in which they originate, the nature of their internal conflicts, how they control individuals participating in them, and their interaction with their relevant environments (organizational ecology). Accepting an open systems approach, Westrum and Samaha suggest that each of these types faces a different kind of relevant environment. Bureaucracies need to get funds and grants of power from voters and legislators, they need support from those people directly affected by their actions (their constituency), they compete with other agencies claiming similar jurisdictions. Enterprises are concerned with customers and competitors and are forced to be more efficient than government agencies, which do not need to make a profit. While that may be true for small business, the discussion overlooks the close links between big business and government in a "free-enterprise" economy and government's tendency to rescue ailing corporations important to the national economy.

Voluntary associations seek members from the public and must deal with cooperators and competitors. However, organizational growth through amassing more members is not always the central organization-environment issue, as Westrum and Samaha claim. Successful solicitation of financial resources and/or effective lobbying may be equally important. Some associations are deliberately exclusive, basing their prestige on how difficult it is to gain entry. While membership issues are basic in the life of a voluntary association, success is more complicated than just increasing numbers (see R. L. Blumberg, 1984:167–177 for analysis of the relations between social movement organizations and their environments).

Westrum and Samaha correctly observe that "Many bureaucracies and voluntary associations may use each other as resources for information or political pressure" (p. 11). One of the best analyses of this interplay is Freeman's study of the interaction between women in government and those in organizations of the nascent women's movement (1975). Certainly this common-sense typology points up important distinctions between its three kinds of organizations.

Etzioni: Types of Power and Compliance

Amitai Etzioni's carefully elaborated and frequently criticized typology (1961, rev. 1975) centers around two concepts: power and compliance. *Power*, as Etzioni defines it, is the ability to induce or influence another role player to carry out one's directives or any other norms he or she supports. *Compliance* is an element in the relationship between those who have power and those over whom they exercise it. It refers "both to a relation in which an actor behaves in accordance with a directive supported by another actor's power, and to the orientation of the subordinated actor to the power applied" (1961:3). That is, the subordinated person in the relationship accepts or follows orders; orientation to the power applied involves a mental state accompanying the behavior. This orientation is considered the actor's or person's involvement in the organization.

Three types of power—coercive, remunerative, and normative—tend to be correlated with three kinds of involvement—alienative, calculative, and moral. Coercive power is based on the threat or application of physical sanctions, such as pain or punishment. Remunerative power is based on control over material resources such as money or services, and normative power is based on the giving of symbolic rewards such as prestige and acceptance. Certain types of power are congruent—that is, they fit best—with certain types of involvement, but theoretically the power and involvement may be matched in varying ways. Thus, a coercive institution such as a prison tends to engender alienative, negative involvement, but a few prisoners may become so well-adjusted to life behind the walls that they cannot function on the "outside." In that case they are probably not alienatively involved.

Criticism of Etzioni's typology. A main criticism of Etzioni's typology is related to the assumption of a tendency toward congruence. If particular types of power tend to generate particular types of compliance, these two dimensions are not independent, and hence should be treated as a single variable rather than two different variables (Scott, 1981:45). Or, in Perrow's words, the typology is tautological (redundant). "Prisoners are coerced in coercive organizations by coercive power and do not like it" (Perrow, 1979:161). Their alienative involvement is automatic in a coercive institution. Proponents of the model would counter that while certain types of involvement tend to be correlated with certain types of power, that is not always the case. The deviant cases are instructive. For example, the alienative involvement of some students in their schools, which are supposed to use predominantly normative power, suggests that something is amiss.

Because power is a central concept in this typology, we reserve further discussion of it for chapter 5, where we consider power, authority, and communication.

Goffman: Total Institutions

Erving Goffman's (1961) "total institution" concept contains an implicit typology (Eldridge & Crombie, 1975:52). A total institution may be thought of as an ideal or polar type, based on its all-encompassing control over the individual. Such institutions can be contrasted with those that have temporary or transitory contacts with publics and that can affect them only in segmentary, partial ways.[4] Even the college experience can vary tremendously, depending on whether a student is confined to a sleep-away college located in isolated countryside or takes the subway to attend a city, sleep-at-home college.

In a total institution the public-in-contact may consist of such persons as inmates of mental institutions or prisons, or it may consist of cloistered religious personnel or students in military academies. What is similar is that the individual does not have a separation of place for sleep, play, and work but engages in all of these on the same premises. A small administrative staff surveys and controls the larger number of inmates. The resocialization that occurs in these people-processing institutions tends to be harsh, reducing previous identities through a leveling process and deprivation of former comforts and privileges.

Goffman's interest is in the organization's effect on the individual, its attempts at resocialization, and the individual's manner of coping with assaults on the self. While total institutions differ widely in the functions they serve, Goffman has selected out the common features that create a similar kind of experience for the individual. He is concerned with the effects of involvement itself, independent of the institution's aims or the kinds of power it exerts, in Etzioni's sense.

Criticism of Goffman's typology. Note that the concept of total institutions ignores Etzioni's distinction between whether one is bound to an organization in an alienative or committed way. While both the prisoner and the military cadet are

---

[4]Lefton and Rosengren suggest there is variation in both the time and space dimensions of an organization's contact with a particular client (1966:802–810). Such situations as hospital emergency-room contacts involve a very short time span while long-term psychiatric placement may involve an indeterminate time span. Time span is referred to as the "longitudinal interest" in clients' biographical careers. Biographical space, called "lateral interest," refers to how much of the total individual is the organization's concern. Organizations may be interested in limited aspects of a client, such as removing a diseased gall bladder, or in the total individual, for example, producing an educated, well-rounded person, the goal of liberal arts colleges.

subject to coercive power, the cadet's possible alienation is tempered by future prospects. Like the religious novice, the cadet endures humiliations in the hopes of achieving a goal that will bring higher status. Both have voluntarily entered a total institution of their own choice, unlike persons committed involuntarily. The prisoner's alienation is permanent, and the derogatory label of ex-con will probably stick. Although Goffman provides many examples of degradation occurring in total organizations other than negatively valued ones such as prisons and mental institutions, he does not consider the possible difference in meaning these experiences have to individuals expecting an ultimate rise in status.

Among the contributions Eldridge and Crombie consider Goffman to have made is the following: "By taking an organisation in which extreme deprivation of things that are taken for granted in many situations occurs, it can teach us something about life and the mechanisms which operate in all formal organizations" (p. 55). We can make a typology of Goffman's ideal type by looking at the impacts on individuals of organizations that are either more or less encompassing and at the variations in needed adjustments to each.

Perrow: Technology

A number of theorists have created typologies based on variations in technology—defined as the kind of tasks or techniques through which different kinds of organizations produce their outputs. As mentioned earlier in this chapter, Woodward (1965) classified the technologies of the English business firms she studied into three basic types: unit and small-batch production, large-batch and mass production, and continuous process production. The simplest type is unit and small-batch production, such as producing a designer dress. Technical complexity increases when numerous similar items (e.g., autos) are mass produced. Process production, which consists of continuous production of such products as oil and chemicals, is considered the most technologically complex.

Woodward claimed that technical methods were the most important factor in determining organizational structure and in setting the tone of human relationships inside the firms. Thus, instead of starting with different structures—that is, different combinations of such items as hierarchy, size, and executives' span of control (the number of people who report to them)—she took the nature of technology as the independent variable. She found that structure and human relations were dependent on the nature of the technology employed. Attempts to replicate her work have both supported and been in conflict with it, but there is no question that her approach influenced that of many others and gave rise to what is known as contingency theory. The basic idea of this theory is that "the best organizational structure for a given task is *contingent* (depends on) the nature of the task" (Westrum & Samaha, 1984:18). Here we deal with Perrow's attempt to build on her insights.

At the time he proposed his typology, Perrow (who tends to revise his work) considered technology—"the work done in organizations"—as their defining characteristic (1967:194–195). Like Woodward, he treats technology as an independent variable and structure (the arrangements among people for getting work done) as a dependent variable. Technology is further described as "the actions that an individual performs upon an object, with or without the aid of tools or mechanical devices, in order to make a change in that object" (1967:195). For example, variations in the nature of technology will influence such things as the numbers of skilled and unskilled workers required, how many workers a supervisor can oversee, and whether supervision will be extensive or minimal. The concepts of the technological approach are extended in order to include the study of nonindustrial, people-processing organizations in Perrow's version. He identifies two independent dimensions: the number of exceptional cases encountered in the work, and the nature of the search process that is undertaken by the individual when exceptions occur.

Number of exceptional cases encountered. The term *exceptional cases* refers to the degree to which the material encountered, whether physical objects or people, is routinely understood or perceived as unfamiliar. Organizations try to standardize their material rather than deal with many exceptions. Thus, a professor may announce that no make-up tests will be offered in order to avoid dealing with the variety of excuses students proffer for missing an exam. In some cases, such as the relatively new scientific endeavor of sending people into space, the technology is not amenable to this manipulation.

Nature of the search process. When exceptional cases are encountered two types of search processes occur. The first is one that can be conducted on a logical, analytical basis. Even though nonroutine, a search can be "logical, systematic, and analytical." The example given by Perrow is that of programmers writing individual programs for slow readers in a special school. The programs may be individualized, but the solution is based on a given number of factors involved in reading difficulties.

The second type of search process occurs

> when the problem is so vague and poorly conceptualized as to make it virtually unanalyzable. In this case, no "formal search" is undertaken, but instead one draws upon the residue of unanalyzed experience or intuition, or relies upon chance and guesswork. (Perrow, 1967:196)

Examples given are work with exotic metals or nuclear fuels and psychiatric casework. A fourfold table is created by combining these two aspects of technology (see figure 3–2).

Looking at figure 3–2, the lower left-hand quadrant, cell 4, illustrates the routine extreme in which there are also analytic techniques for handling the few exceptions that occur. In contrast, the upper right-hand quadrant, cell 2, has many exceptional cases and few analytical techniques for dealing with them. Whether workers have repetitive, readily supervised tasks or whether they need to use discretion and lack specific routines determine how work is organized. Parts of the same

FIGURE 3-2   Model of Technology Variables

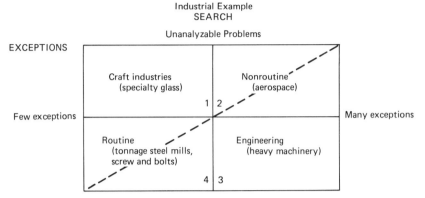

Industrial Example
SEARCH

Source: Charles Perrow, "A Framework for the Comparative Analysis of Organizations," *American Sociological Review* 32 (1967):196. Used with permission.

organization may differ in these characteristics and hence have to be organized differently. And organizations seemingly similar in purpose may differ greatly if they perceive their task as either more or less routine. For example, public mental hospitals, poorly financed and staffed, may classify patients into a few major categories and routinize their care. In contrast, an expensive private mental clinic may perceive the patient as an individual who can be helped through intensive study and treatment and engage in a search for solutions through individualized psychiatric care.

It is interesting to note that the importance of technology and its effect on the human relations of work is also a basic tenet of Marxism, though stated differently. This is how Benson presents the Marxist version of social construction-production:

> Social arrangements are created from the basically concrete, mundane tasks confronting people in their everyday life. Relationships are formed, roles are constructed, institutions are built from the encounters and confrontations of people in their daily round of life. Their production of social structure is itself guided and constrained by the context. (Benson 1977:3)

One's relationship to the tools of production determines one's class position and also the social relations of production.

Criticism of Perrow's typology. "Task, or technology, prove to be important variables, but not of the overriding importance we first claimed for them. The new wave-gathering force appears to be the environment" (Perrow, 1979:200). Technology is not abandoned, but technological determinism is now avoided by some of its proponents. This modified approach is exemplified in a major contribution, Perrow's *Normal Accidents* (1984), in which he analyzes high-risk technologies such as those of nuclear and chemical plants (about which more will be said in chapter 11). The complexity of certain technologies and the ways in which components of them are linked together make accidents a "normal," likely occurrence. Perrow suggests that we might consider abandoning certain life-threatening technologies.

Technology is treated as an important variable by many researchers, but "empirical studies of the relation between technology and structure show mixed and often conflicting results" (Scott, 1981:233). Structure includes such interacting elements as division of labor, hierarchy, and statuses or positions—all the ways in which people are distributed into various positions and how this distribution affects their interaction (R. Hall, 1982, chap. 3). Marxian dialectics would propose that connections between technology and such structural elements as power be studied historically to see how the relationships have been produced and maintained. According to this view, technology and structure are linked, but in continuously developing ways.

McKelvey: Population and Taxonomy

McKelvey's *Organizational Systematics* (1982) is an extremely scholarly attempt to develop a system of identifying and classifying specific organizational populations according to principles developed in biology. A less technical article, coauthored with Aldrich (1983), champions the usefulness of this approach in applications of organizational science and forms the basis for the following discussion.

According to McKelvey and Aldrich (1983):

> The population perspective presented de-emphasizes the all-alike and all-unique approaches, placing emphasis instead on research methods that improve the description and classification of organizational forms, define more homogeneous groupings, and specify the limited conditions under which predictions may be expected to hold true. (p. 101)

The population perspective proposed includes four related areas of investigation: taxonomy, classification, evolution, and population ecology. This is how these terms are defined:

> *Taxonomy* focuses on activities pertaining principally to developing a theory of organizational differences and a theory of classification. *Classification* procedures allow identification and description of organizational populations and their relation to other more or less similar populations. *Evolutionary* inquiry supports taxonomic and classificatory activities by providing an underlying theoretical framework explaining how different kinds of organizations come to be different, why they remain different, and what taxonomic characters might be evolutionarily significant. Evolutionarily significant characters are attributes that enhance an organization's ability to survive; they may persist even though the specific environmental condition for which they were favorable no longer exists. (pp. 107–108)

This model clearly parallels biology's emphasis on evolution and survival and also reflects very current practical concern with organizational survival in a turbulent world. Say the authors, "Fundamental to the successful application of findings from organizational science is an understanding of why organizations succeed or fail" (p. 117). During the 1970s and 1980s some major firms suffered setbacks and possible demise while others flourished. Along with the more theoretical attempts to study these questions, a number of popular books were published that examined the creation and development of more and less successful business firms (see chapter 7). In their own way, these books proposed theories to explain what went wrong in some and what worked in others. Although some tended to highlight individual managers and individual organizations, the sum total of such efforts revealed populations of successful and unsuccessful organizations (see, for example, Deal & Kennedy, 1982; Lawrence & Dyer, 1983; Peters & Waterman, 1982).

An important point of departure of the McKelvey-Aldrich perspective is that *populations* of organizations, not individual organizations, should be units of study.

Populations of organizations consist of organizations that are highly similar, though not similar in all details, and that have been discovered to have the same organizational forms. Part of the task of researchers is to describe different kinds of organizational forms, starting, for example, with measurable attributes that significantly discriminate one form from another. Organizations with the same organizational form belong to the same population group. Organizations "are neither all-alike nor all-unique, but rather appear to be a moderate number of different populations composed of similar forms" (McKelvey & Aldrich, 1983:110).[5] As with typologies, the question arises as to which similarities and differences are crucial.

Rather than proposing a theoretical typology of populations, this approach requires research that will identify existing populations and classify them in relation to each other. In doing so it utilizes, modified when necessary, the biological theory of natural selection, as expressed in the basic principles of variation, natural selection, retention and diffusion, and struggle for existence (McKelvey & Aldrich, 1983:113-115). But it also incorporates and integrates quite different strands of organizational theory.

McKelvey and Aldrich have not provided a finished typology: their contribution is to specify the principles by which a taxonomy can be created, through extensive study and classification of the variety of existing organizations. This brief introduction to McKelvey's elaborate work should suffice for present purposes; interested students can consult the original sources mentioned for further elaboration.

It is worth noting that the typologies described above are both deductive and inductive. Deductive theories are derived through reasoning or conceptualization, as in the case of the types proposed by Blau and Scott and by Etzioni. Inductive

---

[5]Organizational form is a complex concept, which McKelvey (1982:458) defines as: "the internal structure and process of an organization and the interrelation of its subunits which contribute to the unity of the whole of the organization and to the maintenance of its characteristic activities, function or nature."

theories are empirically based; that is, the theory is derived from research findings. Thus, theory may emerge from the data rather than being imposed on it. Woodward's studies of technology and Goffman's concept of total institution are examples. In any discipline, research is needed to find out if seemingly good ideas and hunches are borne out in reality. Organizational research is flourishing because complex organizations are so crucial to modern society.

Our survey of typologies may leave the student somewhat puzzled by both the variety of approaches and the discontent on the part of writers with even their own past theories. But this is part of the process of building a new scientific field, and as you become more familiar with the materials, you will see that useful ideas embodied in these typologies have found their way into the accepted knowledge about organizations. Some of the topics in later chapters have also been debated, and this whole book could be written about various studies—who agrees with whom, and who has produced conflicting evidence. In general, this practice will be avoided for two reasons: The debates are of most interest to scholars, and it is more important for the beginning student to get a general grasp of the central features of organizations.

CHANGING DOCTOR-PATIENT RELATIONSHIPS: *A CASE STUDY*

The authors of "Changing Doctor–Patient Relationships and the Rise in Concern for Accountability" consider as still problematic the question of *who benefits the most* in relations between professionals and their clients, reflecting the central focus of the Blau and Scott typology published some twenty years earlier (Betz & O'Connell, 1983; all quotes in the case study are from this article).

Professional practice now frequently occurs as group practice. In the case of medicine, it is linked in a complex system that includes public and private hospitals, health insurance plans, government agencies, Medicare and Medicaid, and medical research. Technological advances contribute to the rising costs of medical care.

Surveys have found that people in the United States are increasingly distrustful of professionals. "The public is asking whose interests the professionals are serving and who is benefiting most from those services—the professional or the client" (p. 84). Using doctor–patient relationships to illustrate, professionals and clients are said to have become separated into

> two communities: (1) producers of services, who are oriented toward technical performance standards enforced by their occupational association; and (2) consumers, who often have little power. While clients respect the professionals' expertise, they do not assume that "expert" decisions are made always with the clients' best interests in mind. (pp. 84-85)

Fully 72 percent of the public expressed confidence in doctors in 1966; only 43 percent did in 1975. Betz and O'Connell propose that the changing nature of medical practice has produced this dissatisfaction and has also led to a call for accountability. Physicians must now justify and explain their actions to patients; their pronouncements are no longer taken on faith. Medicine used to be community-based with more frequent home visits than today. The community could sanction and support the medical exchange. But medicine is increasingly practiced in bureaucratic settings. "Specialists in the 1980s see patients only for the duration of a specific illness, make few housecalls, and spend little time with a patient per visit" (p. 86).

As the doctor–patient relationship becomes more specialized, impersonal, and short-lived, the patient's sense of trust is lessened. Population mobility, professionalization, bureaucratization, and specialization have all had an impact. Short-term transactions with strangers become more common, and community influence over behavior tends to be reduced when people make frequent geographic moves. Professionalization fosters peer group control over its members, with physicians becoming more accountable to their professional associations than to the client. The legal authority of the American Medical Association (AMA) replaces the authority of the community.

Doctors have also become more oriented to technical treatment of illness rather than to emotional or personal aspects of care. A much higher proportion of them are in group practice than in earlier days, so that health care more often takes place in the office of a group practice, a clinic, or a hospital. Specialization among doctors increased greatly in the twenty years between 1948 and 1968; the client's long-term relationship with one practitioner was replaced by short-term relationships with several specialists.

The result is that physicians and patients have come to look at their relationships from different vantage points. The medical profession's ideology "contends that doctors can be trusted because they pursue a calling for the sake of service to the patient, unlike merchants, who pursue profit" (p. 91). Given its ideology, the medical profession claims that its interests and those of patients are identical. The profession claims to police itself through a code of ethics and licensing. But those also promote the monopolization of medical practice and increased power.

In the view of patients who demand accountability, "doctors are self-interested vendors of a service, and as unworthy of trust as merchants" (p. 91). Patients who are part of the accountability movement now demand more active participation in consultation and treatment. They believe, for example, that patients are entitled to more information about alternative therapies and costs and should be able to gain redress of grievances when a transaction is deemed unfair. The patient ideology holds that doctors and patients may have different interests. According to Betz and O'Connell, trust between doctors and patients depends on more than "personal demeanor"; it depends on the existence of third parties—the community—who serve as agents of control. The nature of the interaction between doctor and patient has changed; the accountability movement is the patients' response both to the changed relationship and to the increased power of the doctors.

Medical care tends to be considered as much businesslike as service-oriented by patients, a transition from the situation of community-based medicine. Doctors and patients seem not to agree about where the current practice of the profession should be placed in Blau and Scott's typology of organizations. Perhaps mixed types of organizations, and conflicting perspectives among role players, are more prevalent than Blau and Scott's theory implied. Nonetheless, the theory's focal issues continue to provide a useful take-off point for other theories and research.

SUMMARY

The need to classify or type organizations, rather than to treat them as all alike or all unique, is obvious. The principle is the same as that we use in everyday life as we organize our perceptions and understand new experiences based on past ones. In the field of organizations, varied typologies have been created based on features considered to be most crucial or significant. Common-sense typologies, based on such familiar distinctions as whether an organization is profit or nonprofit, have sometimes been used, and many theorists set businesses apart as a special type. Intentional typologies categorize organizations according to one particular feature, deemed the independent variable, such as power or technology. Other aspects of the organization, the dependent variables, are affected by—dependent on—the characteristics of the independent variable.

Since the 1960s interest in creating typologies has lessened as managerial-oriented quantitative research flourished. A critical perspective also arose challenging the assumptions of some of this research. An edited volume of research by Katz, Kahn, and Adams lauds the proliferation of empirical studies, while one by Zey-Ferrell and Aiken presents critical perspectives. In addition, organizational science draws from many disciplines, each with its own traditions, which makes building theories and typologies more difficult.

Concern with changing business fortunes has made organizational survival a major focus of some typologies; it is reflected in new work utilizing biological evolutionary concepts. Organizational effectiveness, a related but broader concept, has also been an implicit or explicit part of some typologies as well as an independent topic of research.

Several major typologies were examined: those of Blau and Scott, Westrum and Samaha, Etzioni, Goffman, Perrow, and McKelvey. (Major discussion of Etzioni's model is, however, reserved for a later chapter.)

Blau and Scott's typology is based on the question, *"cui bono"*—who among the different participants in an organization is supposed to benefit the most? Four types of participants are identified: members or rank-and-file participants, owners or managers, clients or public-in-contact, and the public at large. According to the answer to who benefits, organizations are divided into four types, each of which has a different kind of central problem to solve: mutual benefit associations, business concerns, service organizations, and commonweal organizations. Criticisms of this typology center around its use of *"cui bono"* in two different ways and its inadequacy in dealing with mixed types of organizations.

Westrum and Samaha use a common-sense typology that distinguishes organizations on the basis of two principles, whether or not they are supposed to be profit-making, or whether their members' commitment is primarily full- or part-time. They arrive at three types: bureaucracies, enterprises, and voluntary associations. To reserve the term *bureaucracy* for governmental organizations, as these authors do, is criticized as confusing. Many others, including Max Weber, consider the term equally applicable to businesses and voluntary associations.

Etzioni's typology uses power and compliance as the two most important variables. Three types of power—coercive, remunerative, and normative—are described as characterizing different types of organizations. The bases of compliance, that is, the orientation of the actor or role player to the power employed, can be alienative, calculative, or moral. Main critics of Etzioni's typology have claimed that it does not tell us much more than we already know and that the two major dimensions are not independent.

Goffman's concept of total institutions contains an implicit typology, with total institutions representing a polar type. The total institution is one that attempts to control individuals in all their sleeping and waking hours and does this through various assaults on the self. Other organizations involve their publics-in-contact in more partial ways, which is significant for people's ability to retain their sense of self. Goffman's insights about organization–individual relationships are widely applicable. However, he does not appear to have considered the differences in effect of organizations entered voluntarily, such as military academies and monasteries, from those entered involuntarily, such as prisons and mental institutions.

Perrow's typology is one of many that have focused on technology as a crucial independent variable. Technology refers to the tasks or techniques utilized in the organization. Variations in technology are claimed to influence such structural elements as the number of skilled and unskilled workers required, and how many workers a supervisor can oversee. Perrow identifies two independent dimensions: the number of exceptional cases encountered in the work, and the nature of the search process that is undertaken by the individual when exceptions occur. The number of exceptional cases encountered—or perceived—determines whether or not tasks will be handled routinely. The nature of the search process to find ways of handling exceptional cases may follow a logical, analytical procedure or may rely on such factors as chance, guesswork, and intuition.

While technology is still a subject of great interest to organizational researchers, Perrow and others view it as less determining or causative of organizational structure than was previously assumed. Elements of organizational structure have not been found to vary consistently with particular kinds of technology, as had been hypothesized; environmental influence is now a focal point of attention.

McKelvey's intent is to define an approach that will systematically identify and classify specific populations of organizations. Populations consist of organizations which are highly similar. The classification of populations, like the classification of biological species, comes as an end result of considerable empirical research. Despite its attempt to model itself after a more precise science, this approach reflects the preoccupation of many organizations with their goal of survival and leaves other features of organizations unexamined.

We presented a variety of approaches to the classification of organizations, along with critiques of them, not to confuse the student but to illustrate the process of building a new scientific field. Despite the criticisms, you will find that many of the ideas contained in these typologies have contributed to our knowledge of organizations. The case study of changing doctor-patient relationships illustrated how one such typology, that based on "who benefits," is still stimulating thinking.

4

ORGANIZATIONAL GOALS

The Nature of Organizational Goals
    The Problem: How Important Are Officially Stated Goals?
    Officially Stated Goals
    Stated Goals and the Organization in Action
Operative Goals
    Discovering Operative Goals
    Characteristics of Operative Goals
Goals and Environment
    Internal and External Aspects of Goal Setting
    Survival in a Changing Environment
    Organizational Processes for Dealing with the Environment
The Goals of Universities: A Case Study
Summary

THE NATURE OF ORGANIZATIONAL GOALS

The Problem: How Important Are Officially Stated Goals?

How important are officially stated goals in directing the life of an organization? The concept of organizational goals, once a fairly simple, taken-for-granted aspect of the study of organizations, has been subjected to considerable examination. Its usefulness as a key to understanding organizations has been debated, and other concepts (e.g., organizational environments, organizational cultures) have been elevated in significance. Many of the questions about the importance of goals derive from earlier attempts to measure organizational "effectiveness" using a "goal model" to determine whether or not the professed goals of an organization were being achieved. This is probably the way many ordinary people do judge an organization: Does it do what it says it will do? Does the baseball team win games, the college educate, the bridge club play bridge? Theorists who represent the "systems resource" approach believe that an organization's success in gaining needed resources from its external environment, such as labor, raw materials, or financing, is a better measure of its effectiveness (see, e.g., Yuchtman & Seashore, 1967). Regardless of this one issue—how organizational effectiveness should be measured— goals are an important part of organizational life and worthy of our consideration.

In this chapter we look at the some of the many issues that have been raised about organizational goals:

- —Are official goals always the actual operative goals?
- —If not, how does one discover the actual goals?
- —What factors internal to the organization help determine goals?
- —How does the environment help determine goals?
- —How stable are organizational goals?
- —How are these characteristics of goals expressed: goal multiplicity, conflict, succession, and displacement?

Officially Stated Goals

A goal is an intent to achieve some outcome, some result. Formal organizations have stated goals that tend to be narrower and more specific than those of collectivities such as families, ethnic groups, and communities, which serve a wider range of purposes for their members. Most formal organizations have a charter or statement of purpose when they start out, so *officially stated goals* are not hard to find. They are claimed objectives, desired states of affairs to be realized, such as to sell products for profit, to raise money for research on a particular disease, to provide an education for the students of a given state, to represent the interests of a particular group, or to create recreational activities for members.

Instrumental and expressive goals. One way of classifying the stated goals of particular organizations is to divide them into instrumental and expressive types. *Instrumentally oriented* organizations say they will produce some desired result, such as products manufactured and sold or services provided to the public. These goals include a necessary interaction with other groups and individuals in the environment. *Expressively oriented* organizations consider their activities to be of intrinsic value to their own members. That is, interpersonal interaction in one or more activities is an end in itself in groups such as social or hobby clubs, bridge clubs, and some athletic clubs.

Often organizations engage in both instrumental and expressive activities (Gordon & Babchuk, 1959). A fraternity's goal is to promote mutual fellowship, but it also seeks to enhance its own image; hence, it may sponsor some worthy, noncontroversial community service project. Clubs and fraternities are known to be important sources of business connections, thereby providing for the instrumental as well as the expressive needs of their members. Some firms hold picnics or have athletic teams in order to add positive interpersonal experiences to the work situation. These examples begin to show that organizational goals are not limited to the official stated ones, but develop, multiply, and may change.

Organizations as goal-oriented. For Parsons and many others, *"primacy of orientation to the attainment of a specific goal* is used as the defining characteristic of an organization which distinguishes it from other types of social systems" (Parsons, 1981:98).

In other words, organizations—more than other social structures—are known by their striving to reach particular, formalized goals. A similar emphasis on goals appears in this definition: *"an organization is a collectivity oriented to the pursuit of relatively specific goals and exhibiting a relatively highly formalized social structure"* (Scott, 1981:21).

For others these definitions lack an important element—recognition of the role of the organization's external environment in the very setting of goals. The intent of the organization is not sufficient to enable it to pursue its goals. Organizations must present their goals in such a way as to receive needed support and resources; hence, the environment is involved in determining official objectives. Thompson and McEwen (1969:188) see the problem of setting goals as "determining a relationship of the organization to the larger society, which in turn becomes a question of what the society (or elements within it) wants done or can be persuaded to support."

To illustrate, governments are one part of the environment that limit and define such aspects of organizations as:

- Their very legality; businesses that sell marijuana are illegal but pharmacies can dispense prescribed addictive drugs.
- How they should be taxed; some are tax exempt, others are granted important tax shelters, others are heavily taxed.
- What protections for employees are required; protective clothing may be required in certain industries while health hazards in others may remain unregulated.

Organizations are dependent on many other forces in the environment besides government. Looking at just some of them, factories need sources of raw materials and workers; businesses need credit and customers; colleges need to recruit students and professors and to get research grants. (As an exercise you might try to name all the forces in the environment with which your college interacts.)

Obviously, governmental organizations also need support. The public votes on bond issues for the building of schools, hospitals, and prisons as well as on candidates for office whose policies they approve; it is taxed to provide the funds to keep governments going. Thus officially stated instrumental and expressive goals must be ones that will gain the needed resources and support for the environment.

Stated Goals and the Organization in Action

The need to discover goals.   While few would question the fact that organizations have goals, many have questioned the extent to which *officially stated* goals really guide organizations. Research has demonstrated that goals are not stable over time, that new ones emerge, and that proclaimed goals are not always nor permanently the actual goals of an organization in action. It becomes necessary to discover them rather than assume they are set by the intentions of organizational founders.

Transitive and reflexive goals.   Transitive goals are "output" ones, reflected in a product or service that will affect society outside the organization. However, if those running an organization want it to continue to exist, they must pay attention to its maintenance needs—that is, they must support goals that ensure system survival. This means that some goals are reflexive, or internally oriented, such as the aims of staying in business, gaining honor, or keeping harmony among employees (Mohr, 1973). The dichotomy between transitive, or output, goals and reflexive, or maintenance, goals has been widely recognized and referred to by many different terms.

Public relations nature of stated goals.   Organizations proclaim to the public acceptable, appropriate, and even noble goals. Yet many organizations have "hidden agendas," less worthy objectives, either from the beginning or as a response to the pressures around them. For example, a corporation would never say its aim is to swindle the public—yet many fly-by-night mail order companies, which send out shoddy merchandise or none at all, are prosecuted each year. Nor does a slumlord announce that he or she is buying up properties in the hopes of selling them at much higher prices and has no plan to spend money on necessary repairs. These cases suggest that, for some organizations, acceptable goals are proclaimed mainly for public relations purposes. Figure 4-1 depicts a familiar way of thinly concealing illegal activities behind a facade of legitimacy.

The masking of real goals.   The masking of real goals may help in achieving those the organization actually pursues. Educational and nonprofit organizations are not taxed, for example. "Thus an organization whose real goal is to make a profit might benefit if it can pass as an educational, non-profit organization" (Etzioni, 1964:7). Let's take another example that may seem strange. Suppose a

FIGURE 4-1   Facades of Legitimacy

These stores bear signs naming legitimate services or commodities but hint that they might be fronts for illegal ones such as the sale of drugs or prostitution.

business firm shows a deficit year after year, but continues to exist. How can this happen if businesses are supposed to make profits? Easily—if the firm is a front for unreported illicit activities or a tax write-off for an individual making a high profit elsewhere. While these examples may seem extreme, they encourage a healthy cynicism about accepting goal statements at face value.

Real goals. More generally speaking, and despite the honest intentions of those who create it, an organization in action must be adaptive and cope with three interrelated sets of realities:

1. The varied needs and interests of its members and their conceptions of organizational purpose.
2. The maintenance needs of the organization.
3. The opportunities and limitations—constraints—imposed by its environment, such as the ability to obtain needed resources.

These elements mutually influence each other. They will, in interaction, shape and reshape an organization's real goals, which can be defined as follows:

> The *real goals* of the organization (are) those future states toward which a majority of the organization's means and the major organizational commitments of the participants are directed, and which, in cases of conflict with goals which are *stated* but command few resources, have clear priority. (Etzioni, 1964:7).

Thus, real goals have priority and are the ones towards which specific activities are geared, towards which time and resources are allocated. Changes in goals that emerge over time may not be acknowledged as real goals or, in contrast, they may be rationalized, justified, and treated as if they had been consciously planned.

OPERATIVE GOALS

Discovering Operative Goals

The concept of *operative goals* is similar to that of real goals and is defined by Perrow as "the ends sought through the actual operating policies of the organization" (1961:855). He suggests the need for empirical assessment of the objectives that determine the main course of organizational behavior. Operative goals must be discovered.

As a little bit of life's true disorder is acknowledged in analyzing organizations, the subject matter becomes complex, troublesome, and infinitely more interesting. That is what has happened in the study of goals, as researchers have probed behind officially stated goals. Many of us like to see life as orderly and rational, and we try to make it so even when it is not. Take the example of seeking information—presumably an intelligent, scientific way of gaining the data necessary to make a decision. But one study shows that seeking information may serve symbolic rather than real purposes. The information may come in after the decision has been made or may simply not be used, but few know this. The seeking of it has given notice of the legitimacy of the decision. "The gathering of information provides a ritualistic assurance that appropriate attitudes about decision making exist" (Feldman & March 1981:177). Stated goals, too, may be symbolic.

Indicators of operative goals. Since it is now obvious that goals are not always what they appear to be, how does one determine which desired ends guide the activities of an organization at any given time and place? Obviously, research is needed. One approach is to interview a representative sample of those within the organization. A useful example of this approach is the case study at the end of this chapter, which compares the perceived goals of public and private universities (Gross, 1968).

The detective work starts with a series of questions, many of them suggested by Etzioni (1964, chap. 2): How are resources being spent? What does the organization's budget look like? How much money and effort goes into maintaining the organization itself rather than achieving its stated instrumental goals? What topics are talked about at board meetings, occur and reoccur in organizational minutes, documents, and papers? Which programs receive the most time and attention? How do the organization's functionaries behave in concrete situations? The output—the amount of various goods or services that are produced—is another measure of the organization's true goals.

If an organization's financial records are available, they provide a rich source of data. The budget tells how various activities rate and also how much money and effort go into maintaining the organization—into items such as fancy offices or weekend retreats for executives. The facts and figures show what activities and what products are valued and the degree to which stated goals are being pursued. In the case of a university, certain departments may receive more lines for personnel than others, indicating their importance. If a university suddenly expands its evening program and includes more subjects of interest to adults, a modification of goals is probably underway. The goals are revealed in the behavior of the organization as it responds to its environment. Declining youth enrollments have forced many institutions of higher learning to readjust their goals in order to tap the potential market of adult students.

Millions of dollars are given to charitable causes. The wary public wants to know what proportion of its contributions provides high salaries for executives and promotion campaigns. On their part, charities compete for qualified personnel and for funds that people might wish to spend elsewhere. They often find it necessary to utilize the latest, most successful type of appeal, such as high-powered direct mail campaigns. If most of the money given to a charity ends up in the pursuit of more of it, maintaining the organization has supplanted the original cause. This is one form of what is known as goal displacement. Means have become ends. Figure 4-2 provides an extreme—and newsworthy—example of a tax-exempt organization that "made no charitable contributions of any sort."

Goals revealed in behavior. The behavior of an organization's functionaries, its role players, provides a concrete guide to its operating goals. Agencies that offer services to the poor may reflect conflicting purposes in the way these services are meted out. While the provision of food stamps and unemployment benefits are

FIGURE 4-2

Tax-Exempt Group Made No Gifts to Charity

By Tamar Lewin

The Preservation of American Free Enterprise Inc., a tax-exempt organization with which two men involved in a Securities and Exchange Commission investigation have been connected, used all its money to hold social events and made no charitable contributions of any sort, according to New York State records.

One of the men involved is David W. C. Clark, a Manhattan laywer who is the named subject of the S.E.C. investigation. The commission is examining a pattern of stock trading that may be related to the release of information before its publication in The Wall Street Journal's "Heard on the Street" column. The other man is Peter N. Brant, who was Mr. Clark's stockbroker. Mr. Brant resigned yesterday from

his position at Kidder, Peabody & Company.

The Journal said yesterday that Mr. Clark and Mr. Brant were active in the foundation, whose stated purpose, reported in its registration forms, is "to disseminate knowledge in reference to the manner, forms and benefits of the American free enterprise system." But the group's sole function seems to have been giving parties for paying guests.

According to the state's Office of Charities Registration in Albany, the foundation took in $52,000 in 1982, and reported using $26,000 of that to hold a cocktail party and a dinner party each month that year. Another $27,000 went to fund-raising costs and $10,000 to management.

Source: *New York Times*, April 10, 1984. p. D13. Copyright © 1984 by The New York Times Company. Reprinted by permission.

accepted as a government obligation, there are also clear efforts to distinguish between the "worthy" or "true" poor and others who only seem to qualify, or worse, are "cheats."

Services and goods such as food stamps may be provided slowly, in a surly manner, or only after much bureaucratic entanglement in rules. This serves to discourage some applicants, or to make the experience so unpleasant that it is endured only when in extreme need (Lipsky, 1980; also see chapter 9). Obviously, the agency's aim is not to increase the number of clients but to keep it at a manageable level. Contrast the behavior of many employees of public agencies with the behavior of those salespeople whose jobs depend on pleasing customers (especially when the salespeople are being watched by supervisors or are on commission).

Goal displacement. When goal displacement takes place, the original output goals are subordinated to maintenance goals. That is, in the process of trying to keep itself going, the organization becomes overly preoccupied with its internal needs. In the case of individuals, goal displacement is thought by some to be a characteristic malady of the bureaucratic personality (Merton, 1952). This type of role player becomes ritualistically involved in doing things right, following every rule to the letter, and filling out every form—dotting each *i* and crossing every *t*. In the process the original intention of the action, such as providing service to a client is lost. Means have become ends. Anyone who has been shunted from one window to the next when seeking a government service has experienced an over-conformity to bureaucratic specialization and division of labor which puts the needs of clerk and office on a much higher priority than the needs of those waiting to be served. Such behavior is not necessarily due to the personal inclinations of the bureaucrats but to the rules, regulations, and specialization of role that constrict them. In fact, a survey of over 3,000 male workers found that those who worked in bureaucratic firms valued self-direction rather than conformity and were more open-minded and receptive to change than those who worked in non-bureaucratic settings (Kohn, 1971:465).

Perrow has questioned the assumption that goal displacement is always unconscious or unplanned. He maintains, "What some sociologists like to see as 'goal displacement' may refer only to goals never entertained by the leaders. The output of the organization may be just what they planned" (1979:190). This is illustrated in the behavior of those public service functionaries who understand that part of their goal is to conserve public funds rather than to service clients fully.

Accountability to goals. Organizations are accountable to their members, stockholders, and the public in varying degrees. Whether goals are changed consciously or unconsciously, organizations are open to criticism if data prove that they are spending most of their resources in ways other than those publicly proclaimed. They are also subject to sanctions if they fail to abide by governmentally mandated goals, such as that of providing equal opportunity. A public school, which is supposed to serve both sexes equally, can now be called into account if the boys' athletic teams receive more money than the girls' teams, a frequent occurrence that formerly went unregulated.

These varied examples have demonstrated some of the main characteristics of an organization's actual operative goals, which can now be spelled out.

Characteristics of Operative Goals

Actual goals are:

— Emergent, changeable, and adaptive
— Multiple and sometimes conflicting
— Negotiated
— Rationalizations of past decisions

Goals are emergent, changeable, and adaptive. The reappraisal of goals is a constant problem in an unstable environment, less so in a relatively stable one. This early insight of Thompson and McEwen (1969) has been translated into research on the environmental influence on organizations.

Small businesses are highly vulnerable to "not making it." Many survive by finding something special to offer that larger ones do not. Small neighborhood food stores, for example, survive in many ways: by giving credit unavailable through supermarkets, by keeping long daily and weekend hours, by offering ethnic products that cannot be obtained elsewhere, and of course, by using unpaid family labor. But conditions can change. Supermarkets rebound by extending their hours and creating sections for ethnic foods. In some cities a recent immigrant group, Koreans, appears to be succeeding well in the fresh fruit and produce business. By specializing in very high quality fruits and vegetables, they capture the market of affluent city dwellers who appreciate and can afford the quality produce. But, if the supermarkets respond by upgrading their produce and opening salad bars, the small stores will have to find some other unique service to offer.

The population ecology model considers the nature and distribution of resources in an organization's environment as crucial to its survival. Accordingly, the types of organizations that can meet environmental needs and pressures are selected to survive; goals are modified when necessary. The parts of an organization's environment most critical to its success are the ones that modify and shape its goals. Borrowing from biological models of natural selection, the environment is seen as selecting certain types of organizations for survival and rejecting others (Aldrich, 1979:29). Take, for example, a potent new element in our society—the computer. The burgeoning growth of computer technology has affected many institutions, and many organizations act as if their survival is dependent on computerizing their operations.

The use of computers in education has expanded tremendously, requiring revisions of budget and curriculum goals to accommodate the purchase of expensive computers and the hiring of computer experts. Teachers find themselves catching up with computer-wise children; teacher education will undoubtedly have to address this new area of expertise. School budgets will have to reflect these changes. Private schools have the resources to obtain the computers and the experts, but so widely accepted is the value of computer literacy that many public schools are able to justify the expenditures necessary to bring children into the new technological world.

Computer expertise has also created some new hazards. Amateurs as well as crooks are breaking into the computer systems of major corporations, hospitals, and banks. The potential for criminal use of information is great, and the possibility of accidental or not-so-accidental damage to records is tremendous. The changing technological environment requires that organizations be able to deal with these hazards. A new industry will have to be built around trying to protect computer systems; chastising offenders is hardly likely to solve the problem.

Recognizing that goals are modifiable, one must admit that a *degree* of stability also exists. The traditional values of the organization, its sense of mission, and its customary budgetary allocations set patterns that tend to persist (Perrow, 1979:159). The accountability mentioned earlier has its effects. Constituencies, to different degrees, are able to monitor the organization and criticize it if it is not fulfilling its mission, particularly if the organization is dependent on public support, as we saw in the example of charities. The degree of stable power the organization wields may also enable it to shape the environment, making it more favorable. Lobbies of many kinds of groups are headquartered in Washington, D.C., pressuring Congress to pass or repeal laws that affect their operations.

Goals are multiple and sometimes conflicting. Both individual and group goals exist within organizations. Individuals have both personal goals, related to their own motivations and interests, and organizational ones, based on their relationship to the organization. Compare the personal goals of summer workers, for whom a particular job is a temporary stop-gap, with those of permanent workers who must accept the job as a life career. College students, on their way up, sometimes work alongside older persons who are supporting families. The significance of the job to each type of role player may bring about a very different stance toward it. Many organizations have a mix of persons who exhibit varied degrees of loyalty or commitment and for whom the particular job is more or less fateful.

The individual's goal may differ from what the organization intended it to be. A story I know to be true concerns the interaction of a teacher and a crying kindergarten child, then at the beginning of his school career. The child was told that if he didn't stop, he would not be allowed back in school—whereupon he cried all the harder. Goffman (1961) has shown how inmates in prisons and mental institutions learn to "make out," to use spaces and the meager physical objects available to them for their own purposes. Workers frequently need to find hiding places where they can smoke, rest, or chat away from the eyes of supervisors. The organization has not created hiding places, but individual and group needs make people inventive.

Those in different departments or divisions of a firm and at different hierarchical levels tend to view organizational purpose from their own vantage points. A salesperson is likely to desire a quality product that will create satisfied customers; someone in production may be more concerned with finding a cheap substitute for raw material that is in short supply. Whose views predominate? The possibility of conflict over organizational priorities is ever-present in all but the simplest of organizations. A publishing company, for instance, may have both trade and textbook divisions, which compete for resources and access to publicity.

Sometimes very different values are expressed in the conflicting aims of particular types of organizations. When an organization serves multiple functions—such as a hospital that provides medical care, teaches students, and engages in research—decisions about priorities must constantly be made. In a hospital with a strong research orientation, those with less interesting diseases get less attention, to the chagrin of health care professionals who put the patients' needs first.

Is the purpose of various welfare provisions altruistic—to help those in need—or is it to forestall urban disorders? Or both (see Piven & Cloward, 1971)? Do funding levels decrease and rules tighten during times of relative community calm? That might indicate some priorities. The humanitarian value in American life decrees that government should provide for its neediest, most helpless citizens. At the same time there is a strong work ethic and a disdain for "chiselers." This conflict is expressed in the actual, operative goals of our public agencies, as mentioned earlier. The operations of such agencies are monitored by those wary of how public services are used. The result, as suggested above, is that public service bureaucrats have to operate with limited funds and limited time, ensuring that people will be discouraged from easy access to public largesse (see Lipsky, 1980).

Similarly, in criminal justice there is a conflict between rehabilitative and punitive goals. Prison reformers stress the long-term value of rehabilitation, but the public tends to be more concerned with its own protection and with retribution. The high cost of operating procedures—courts and juries—sets other, economic time/cost goals that lead to plea bargaining.

Finally, among the multiple goals of organizations are the almost ever-present maintenance goals. Time and other resources must be expended taking care of internal business. All organizations, as they grow, must deal with problems such as hiring and firing, promotion reviews, labor demands, coordination of various departments, and morale.

There are also physical tasks involved in maintaining the organization and its participants. In the case of total institutions, inmates have to be fed and housed, be provided with medical care and recreation, and so forth. Many other organizations must engage in functions that are not necessarily part of their primary reasons for existence. Residential colleges must supply food, housing, and recreation for their students, as well as education, in order to keep the system going. Academic departments may have to entice potential majors through social activities unrelated to their discipline, such as holding department picnics or teas.

Goals are negotiated. Contrasting perspectives on organizational goals are presented by Pfeffer (1981b:228-247), as follows. Management literature tends to accept as given that organizations have unified goals, and accordingly, "the problem of management is to recruit, train, control, and motivate organizational participants so as to achieve the organization's goal (or goals)" (p. 231). A more conflict-oriented perspective, projected by some sociologists, political scientists, and social reformers, views organizations "as coalitions, composed of varying groups and individuals with different demands" (p. 231). Coalitions are temporary alliances for joint action. At any one time there tends to be a dominant coalition, a key group of influential decision makers (Beer, 1980:78).

According to this perspective, the organization's operative goals emerge out of internal bargaining and struggle between its various parts as it and they are constrained by environmental pressures. The process may involve various coalitions of groups and individuals; these can shift. And of course, persons in different positions within the organization have varying power to push their objectives (Pfeffer, 1981b:231; Pfeffer & Salancik, 1974:135-151). Groups within the organization may call on others outside the formal organizational boundaries to support their positions. Pfeffer (1981a) gives the following illustration:

> In some sense, the use of the outside expert can be viewed as a coalition formation strategy with an external party. In that case, the inside subunit or groups form a coalition with an outside expert or set of experts to advocate their position on a set of decision issues (p. 154).

Thus, a research firm may be hired to support the conclusions already arrived at.

Goals are rationalizations of past decisions. There is a tendency to believe that attitudes—predispositions to act—come before behavior. That is not always true. People, and organizations, may behave in certain ways because of the circumstances in which they find themselves, rather than because of prior attitudes or intent. Much of human behavior takes place without plan. Even important career decisions may emerge unexpectedly. Afterwards, when asked about a particular decision, the individual is often able to explain quite rationally how it came about. In studying a group of white civil rights activists, I found that most of them had thought about the origins of their involvement in the movement and could describe the crucial events or experiences that had influenced them. The reflection was done retrospectively and made great sense (R. Blumberg, 1980a). So, as pointed out by Weick (1969), the meaning of action is often inferred afterwards. That also applies to the emergent goals of the organization in action. Although the goals may be the product of internal negotiation or adaptation to the environment, the organization is able to explain them as perfectly logical, rational, and intentional. Because of the importance of words and images, purposes will tend to be described in the most positive of terms.

Now let us turn specifically to the important question of the relationship between goals and environment, a subject that has inevitably crept into much of our previous discussion.

GOALS AND ENVIRONMENT

Internal and External Aspects of Goal Setting

It has been necessary to separate out analytically the internal processes that go on within the organization and the relationship of the organization to its external environment. Of course, whatever is going on within the organization is taking place at the same time that the organization is dealing with its surroundings—other organizations, government, and public, and national and international events that affect it.

Suppose that, through processes of decision making, negotiation, and compromise, those within the organization are prepared to arrive at agreement about goals. What will guarantee an environmental climate favorable to their pursuit? To what extent can even the more powerful role players within the organization actually determine goals? To what extent will environmental factors, such as changing demand and supply, competition, population movements, war, or depression, force organizations to modify goals? How does one discover the combination of internal and external forces operating in a given case? Systems models of organizations incorporate all of the above factors in attempting to describe the dynamic interrelationships of various parts of the organization as it interacts with its environment (Beer, 1980:76). Organizations are seen as ongoing systems of interaction rather than just goal-seeking collectivities.

A related question is how powerful organizations try to modify the factors beyond their boundaries that most affect them. Certainly, many have money and influence with which to do so. Since government and its regulations are one of the major environmental forces affecting organizations, they are frequently the object of pressure groups. Legislation, the repeal of legislation, the administration of various agencies are all of concern to major corporations. On the local level organizations may be in an even better position to influence government. For example, a firm may seek special favors because of what it has to offer in return. A town dependent on a major firm tends to make concessions, perhaps providing zoning exceptions or tax advantages, to prevent the firm from moving elsewhere. Similarly, many organizations are deeply involved in public relations functions, seeking the support of the general public and potential clients for their goals, especially if there is a threat to the organization's existence.

Survival in a Changing Environment

The Tylenol case: trying to overcome environmental threat. A case in which a firm almost overcame potential threat occurred when Johnson & Johnson withdrew its product Tylenol from the market in fall 1982. An unknown individual or individuals had tampered with this over-the-counter pain reliever and placed poison in a number of bottles, leading to a number of deaths. Other over-the-counter medications were also potential booby-traps because they used similar types of bottles. However, for reasons not yet officially established, Tylenol was the product selected for contamination. Johnson & Johnson's prompt action in publicizing the threat and calling in supplies, reimbursing losses, and inventing a tamper-proof bottle restored public confidence in a relatively short time. The crisis caused by the deaths influenced the firm to put all its energies into developing a new, safe container and then getting the product back into the market. Television commercials showed loyal customers who expressed their long-term confidence in Tylenol. At that time the campaign succeeded in regaining much of Tylenol's lost market. By December of the same year Johnson & Johnson's stock had made a speedy recovery, but Tylenol's profits decreased somewhat because of increased marketing and advertising expenses (*New York Times*, January 31, 1984, p. D8).

For a while it appeared that the firm's response had successfully overcome the public's fears of recurrence. But Johnson & Johnson's nightmare returned. In early 1986 another death occurred by cyanide that had been placed in a Tylenol capsule. This time Johnson & Johnson decided to withdraw the capsule form of the medication from the market.

The population ecology model.   Not all cases are as obvious or dramatic as the Tylenol case. But organizational survival is deemed so important that it is central to a recently developed organizational framework, the population ecology model. Using this model, investigators shift from the language of goal-setting to the issue of how organizations are selected to survive. The environment is said to select certain types of organizations for survival and to reject other, maladapted ones. According to Aldrich (1979):

> The population ecology model . . . explains organizational change by examining the nature and distribution of resources in organizations' environments. Environmental pressures make competition for resources the central force in organizational activities, and the resource dependence perspective focuses on tactics and strategies used by authorities in seeking to manage their environments as well as their organizations. (pp. 27–28)

> Selection of new or changed organizational forms occurs as a result of environmental constraints. Organizations fitting environmental criteria are positively selected and survive, while others either fail or change to match environmental requirements. (p. 29)

The model deals with groupings of organizations rather than individual ones. So, for example, a bureaucratically organized group might be able to survive where a participatory democracy type could not. A student group that tried to operate with no assigned leaders or officials (characteristic of participatory democracy) might have difficulty in negotiating with the university for a meeting room or faculty advisor and might have to either appoint a chairperson or go off campus.

As mentioned earlier in the chapter, small retail food stores may be pushed out of operation by the presence of large chains. Indeed, there is a rather low survival rate for newly established small businesses. A chain can support a new operation through its more established branches and can effect economies that the independent entrepreneur cannot.

In dealing with goals and environment we have necessarily entered into a major area of interest to organizational researchers—organization–environment relations. This topic is the focus of chapter 10.

Organizational Processes for Dealing with the Environment

Two older and still useful systematic analyses of the processes by which organizations deal with their changing environments are those centered on (1) the concepts of goal succession, and (2) the four processes of competition, bargaining, co-optation, and coalition.

Goal succession. Succession of goals is one of the ways that organizations have to adapt to changing environments. That is, an organization consciously decides to substitute a new goal for an older one. Some well-known examples are drawn from the field of voluntary organizations that had very specific stated purposes. For example, Sills' classic study, *The Volunteers* (1957), explained how the foundation established to combat polyeomelitis maintained itself even after its primary goal was achieved. As mentioned in a previous chapter, the foundation had achieved large-scale grass-roots participation and was endorsed by President Franklin D. Roosevelt, himself a victim of the disease. A vaccine was developed that virtually eradicated polio in the United States. Rather than disband a working structure, the organization transformed its goal to the conquest of other diseases. Although its new goal, the elimination of birth defects, was close to its original purpose, the organization had to convince the public that the choice of target was a good one.

Some other voluntary organizations did not adapt as well and here the frequently cited example is Gusfield's study of the Women's Christian Temperance Union (WCTU) (Gusfield, 1955). The WCTU was originally composed of middle- and upper-middle-class women who wanted to combat the evil of drink among the working class. Later, its membership included fewer high-status persons, and the groups changed its target to the drinking habits of the middle class. Changes in American drinking habits over the years had made the rule of complete abstinence unpopular. The WCTU did not shift its goals but made them more limited, and underwent changes in its membership patterns. It dwindled in numbers and influence. The fact that it remained a woman's organization probably contributed to its relative powerlessness, since the societal devaluation of women carries over to the causes they espouse. Also, the Prohibition Amendment did get passed, was tried, and ended up in so much illicit use of liquor that it was overturned. The goal of reducing alcohol consumption remains with us.

In the case of the voluntary organizations described, goal succession was a relatively conscious process in which the organizations sought to survive by adapting. The first organization described had a noncontroversial purpose—to eradicate a disease. The second one, aimed at reducing the drinking of alcohol, was opposed by the alcohol industry.

It is instructive to study organizations that did not survive, as Aldrich suggests, and to see what environmental forces they could not overcome or adjust to. For example, the Student Nonviolent Coordinating Committee (SNCC) was extremely important in the civil rights movement of the early 1960s but, out of its own historical experiences, became a black power group in the last half of that decade. It changed its ideology and goals and met with increased hostility from the government (see Carson, 1981). Factionalism, infiltration by government agents, and loss of financial resources all contributed to its demise. The organization was not willing to change its new goals in order to gain funds or support from the general public. As we shall see, Thompson and McEwen (1969) dealt with the issue of how organizations compromise, but few theorists discuss how far organizations will go in compromising their principles in order to exist. SNCC, a social movement organization that was intent on societal change, would not compromise in order to survive.

The concept of goal displacement, discussed earlier, is sometimes confused with goal succession. *Goal displacement* describes a response to internal pressures; *goal succession* refers to changes in goals necessitated by a changed environment or the achievement of original goals.

Four ways in which organizations cope with and relate to other organizations in their environment are delineated by Thompson and McEwen (1969):

Competition. *Competition* is a form of rivalry between two or more organizations that is mediated by a third party, such as the public. The prevalence of competition among businesses is taken for granted. Less obvious is the fact that organizations, both alike and unalike, compete for a share of society's resources in the form of funding or purchases, good will, legitimacy, or right to a domain. Thus, universities compete for the more highly qualified students, stores compete for customers, churches compete with commercial recreational facilities for attendance, and so on. New types of competitors may emerge as the environment changes. As an example, the women's movement has criticized the domination by doctors of the birth process and has created new interest in and demand for nurse-midwives. The obstetrician now has a new (really old) competitor reentering the field. Competition forces organizations to readjust and modify their aims and procedures.

The many charitable and political organizations in society today compete for the funds of the general public. Many adopt the high-pressure public relations techniques of groups they might even oppose. They bombard the potential giver with reams of unreadable material put out in a glossy form that seem to violate the spirit of, for example, helping poor people or famine victims. Yet in adapting to the competitive environment, they would probably insist that they are forced to utilize the most up-to-date, proven appeals. Market research has taught them that they will receive a percentage of returns from X number of direct mail appeals, even though their approach may offend some.

Bargaining. *Bargaining* "refers to the negotiation of an agreement for the exchange of goods or services between two or more organizations" (Thompson & McEwen, 1969:193). Just as internal bargaining goes on between powerful role players, so organizations negotiate with each other to readjust their relationships and find a solution satisfactory to all parties. Perhaps the best known case of institutionalized bargaining occurs in labor relations. Unions and management arrive at a contract that is a result of their position, relative strength, current labor laws, and such other factors as are operative in the situation. A strike signifies the breakdown of the bargaining process. Union and management have to go back to the "bargaining table."

Plea bargaining is another well-known use of this process. With courts overloaded, prosecutors and defense attorneys get together to convince the accused to plead guilty to lesser charges than the ones for which they had been arrested. The judge agrees to the routine processing of these pleas, saving the court and lawyers a good amount of time and effort. Whether or not or to what extent the individual is guilty is not relevant, leading to widespread cynicism and the charge that defendants are coerced into giving up their rights to trial too readily. It has been suggested that plea bargaining serves the interests of efficiency and routinization rather than justice (Perrow, 1979:181). Much bargaining is not as formalized as in these two cases. But, for example, two social agencies may divide up the kinds of cases they will process rather than competing for the same ones. Similarly, social movement organizations concerned with the same general issue may agree about a division of labor among them.

Co-optation. *Co-optation* is defined by Thompson and McEwen "as the process of absorbing new elements into the leadership or policy-determining structure of an organization as a means of averting threats to its stability or existence" (1969:194). The term is often used in a derogatory sense when one party is accused of selling out to another in exchange for certain advantages. With its "poverty programs" following waves of urban disorders in the late 1960s, the government was seen as attempting to co-opt minority leaders. Once on the payroll of a government agency, it was felt that job security, a role in dispensing government funds to their constituencies, and an understanding of the inner workings of the government would pacify these leaders and help prevent further outbreaks. Thus many dissident elements were absorbed into poverty boards and agencies. A certain amount of disorder did continue, bureaucratic practices were often not followed, and some protests occurred—but these were managed protests, tolerable without causing a breakdown of the society or any further urban rioting (Piven & Cloward, 1971).

Co-opting works in other ways. An organization may seek the support of important outsiders by giving them positions within the organization, for example, on its board. Memberships of organizations frequently overlap, which can lead to a sharing or overlapping of goals, defusing competition.

Coalition. *Coalition*, the fourth process, refers to "a combination of two or more organizations for a common purpose" (Thompson & McEwen, 1969:195). Two or more organizations act in unity with respect to certain goals, although they do not give up their individual identities. We have already discussed the role of internal coalitions in goal setting. Coalitions are a familiar process in politics, creating some strange bedfellows. The late President Lyndon Johnson was said to be a master at forging the most unlikely coalitions.

In some cases organizations that are supposed to maintain independence are found to be too closely associated with certain others. This is recognized as "conflict of interest," a vaguely bounded area. Conflict of interest means that certain alliances put together persons or organizations who should operate independently, such as a government agency and the corporations it regulates. Persons taking important government positions are often required to give up their stock in corporations that might come under the jurisdiction of their department or agency. These examples only skim the surface of describing interorganizational networks within which coalitions abound. Coalitions are one way of avoiding the negative aspects of the valued competition.

As the emphasis on organizational environments has grown, so has interest in interorganizational networks. This topic is discussed in more detail in chapter 10.

THE GOALS OF UNIVERSITIES: *A CASE STUDY*

INTRODUCTION: THE STUDY

This case study is based on an article by Edward Gross (1968) that appeared in the *American Sociological Review* (all page references are to this article). Although it was written in 1968, and universities have changed since that time, it remains one of the most careful and theoretically based analyses of the goals of a specific type of organization—universities.

Gross took as given the fact that universities have multiple goals. Administrators and faculty members in sixty-eight major universities in the United States were surveyed by means of a long questionnaire (Gross, 1968:518–540). They were asked to rank lists of goals according to how important they felt each was, and how important it should be, at their universities (see Figure 4–3). Gross tried to discover what variables were responsible for differences in goals among the universities.

The goals were divided into five types: output goals, adaptation goals, management goals, motivation goals, and positional goals.

OUTPUT GOALS

Output goals are "those goals of the university which are reflected, immediately or in the future, in some product, service, skill or orientation which

FIGURE 4-3 Sample Goal Question and Instructions

One of the great issues in American education has to do with the proper aims or goals of the university. The question is: What are we trying to accomplish? Are we trying to prepare people for jobs, to broaden them intellectually, or what? Below we have listed a large number of the more commonly claimed aims, intentions or goals of a university. We would like you to react to each of these in two different ways:

(1) How important *is* each aim at this university?
(2) How important *should* the aim be at this university?

Example: to serve as substitute parents	of absolutely top impor- tance	of great impor- tance	of medium impor- tance	of little impor- tance	of no impor- tance	don't know or can't say
Is	☐	☐	☒	☐	☐	☐
Should Be	☐	☐	☐	☐	☒	☐

A person who had marked the alternatives in the manner shown above would be expressing his perception that the aim, intention or goal, "to serve as substitute parents," *is* of medium importance at his university but that he believes it should be of no importance as an aim, intention, or goal of his university.

NOTE: "of absolutely top importance" should only be checked if the aim is *so* important that, if it were to be removed, the university would be shaken to its very roots and its character changed in a fundamental way.

Source: Edward Gross, "Universities as Organizations: A Research Approach," *American Sociological Review* 33 (1968):523, table 1. Reprinted by permission of the author.

will affect (and is intended to affect) society" (Gross, 1968:524). Among output goals, Gross includes student-expressive, student-instrumental, research, and direct service goals. *Student-expressive* goals are attempts to change the student's identity or character in some fundamental way, such as producing a student who has had his or her intellect cultivated to the maximum. *Student-instrumental goals* are expressed in attempts to equip the student to do something specific for the society, such as preparing students for useful careers or to be good consumers. *Research goals* are ones directed toward producing new knowledge or solving problems. *Direct service goals* aim at providing services to the population outside the university, such as assisting citizens through extension programs or providing cultural leadership for the community.

The other four categories of goals are not subdivided.

ADAPTATION GOALS

The organization's need to adapt to the environment is reflected in goals that "revolve about the need to attract students and staff, to finance the enterprise, secure needed resources, and validate the activities of the university with those persons or agencies in a position to affect them" (p. 524). In this category are included such items as the need to ensure the continued confidence of those who provide funds and the favorable appraisal of those who accredit the university's programs. State universities tend to be highly dependent on state legislatures for funds; private universities on donors, grants, and endowments. All are supported by government research programs.

MANAGEMENT GOALS

Management goals include many of what we have called maintenance goals. They "reflect decisions on who should run the university, the need to handle conflict, and the establishment of priorities on which output goals are to be given maximum attention" (p. 524). Under this heading Gross includes such specific goals as involving faculty in the government of the university, making sure that salaries, teaching assignments, and such reflect the contribution that the person involved is making to the university, and making sure those selected to run the university are the ones who can best attain the goals of the university efficiently. The goals included under this heading have to do with the smooth internal functioning of the university as an ongoing unit.

MOTIVATION GOALS

Motivation goals are centered on ensuring the motivation of the people involved in the university, "ensuring a high level of satisfaction on the part of staff and students" (p. 525). They emphasize loyalty to the university as a whole. Included are such specific goals as protecting the faculty's right to academic freedom and providing a full round of student activities.

Although the right to academic freedom is buried in the middle of the author's long list of goals, it turns out to be the most important for private universities, as we shall see when we examine Gross's results further.

POSITIONAL GOALS

Finally, the last category of goals are those that help maintain the university's position in its relative standing among other universities, despite changes in the environment. Included are maintaining top quality in all programs, keeping up-to-date and responsive, and maintaining the character of the particular institution as it likes to see itself.

A total of forty-seven goal statements were included. The administrators and faculty members surveyed were asked to score them in order of importance.

RESULTS: WHICH GOALS ARE MOST IMPORTANT TO UNIVERSITIES?

First Gross attempted to determine the relative importance of various goals among all the universities, then to find out if dividing the universities into types produced different hierarchies. Table 4–1 shows the composite ranking of goals of the sixty-eight institutions studied.

The ranking indicates the goals respondents considered to be the most important operative ones, not what they thought the goals *should* be. But the

TABLE 4-1   Ranking of the Goals of American Universities

"IS"	GOAL	"SHOULD"	"IS"	GOAL	"SHOULD"
1	Acad Freedom	1	25	Fac U Govt	19
2	U Prestige	11	26	Reward Prof	21
3	Top Qual Imp	7	27	Stud Activities	43
4	Ensur Confidence	26	28	Stud Success	33
5	Keep up to Date	6	29	Run U Demo	22
6	Train Scholarship	2	30	Affect Stud Perm	15
7	Pure Research	16	31	Assist Citizens	36
8	Top Qual All	4	32	Just Rewd Inst	13
9	Mntn Fav Apprsl	34	33	Devlp Pride Univ	23
10	Ensure U Goals	9	34	Sat Area Needs	42
11	Dissem Ideas	5	35	Mntn Bal Qualty	31
12	Applied Research	30	36	Will of Fac	24
13	Stud Careers	32	37	Special Training	38
14	Stud Intellect	3	38	Stud Character	12
15	Hold Our Staff	18	39	Educ to Utmost	37
16	Comm Cult Ldshp	28	40	Accp Good Stud Only	39
17	Stud Inquire	10	41	Stud Pol Rights	40
18	Encour Grad Wk	27	42	Devlp Fac Lylty	29
19	Preserve Heritage	20	43	Keep Harmony	41
20	Stud Good Citzn	14	44	Undrgrad Inst	44
21	Well Round Stud	17	45	Stud Univ Govt	46
22	Max Opprtunity	25	46	Pres Character	47
23	Stud Objectivity	8	47	Stud Taste	45
24	Keep Costs Down	35			

Source: Edward Gross, "Universities as Organizations: A Research Approach," *American Sociological Review* (1968) 33:529, table 3. Reprinted by permission of the author.

top goal, protecting academic freedom, is not only ranked as the top operative goal but is also believed to be the most important one, ideally. Note that it was included under motivation goals and is not an output goal. If, as Gross points out, the list of goals had been limited to usual output goals such as teaching, research, and service, the importance of academic freedom would have been overlooked. Academic freedom refers to such rights as the instructor's right to present material without fear of censorship or political repercussion and to gain or be denied promotion on the basis of merit rather than personal political views.

Support or adaptation goals top the list. Most of the top goals turned out to be support goals, not output goals. In addition to protecting academic freedom, the top group included increasing the prestige of the university, maintaining top quality in programs felt to be especially important, and insuring the continued support of those who contribute material resources to the university. Ranking sixth was the first one mentioning students, namely, "train students in methods of scholarship and/or scientific research and/or creative endeavor" (p. 530). It is striking that goals involving students rank so low, especially since eighteen out of the forty-seven goals listed refer to students in some way. In fact, three out of the four lowest-ranking goals have to do with students, namely,

44. emphasize undergraduate instruction even at the expense of the graduate program
45. involve students in the government of the university
47. make a good consumer of the student. (p. 530)

However, it should be noted that the second ranking goal at the top, while not mentioning students, is probably important to them. It, university prestige, weighs heavily in the choices that students make among colleges. That is, most students who do well academically would prefer to attend a prestigious university. Whether or not a student does well, the name of the institution counts for something in the job world.

Do you wonder how this ranking of goals might have differed had students been asked their opinions? Academic freedom, of such importance to their professors, may have been a poorly understood or little valued issue to many students. Since the university's clients, its students, have little power, their preferences would probably carry little weight at major universities.

WHICH VARIABLES AFFECT GOALS?

Goals differed between state and private colleges (where type of environmental control is different) and by the relative prestige of the institution. Protecting academic freedom receives more emphasis in private than in state universities. Also in private universities the more important goals are student-expressive ones, such as permanently affecting the student with great ideas or training the student in scholarship. State universities tended to emphasize what Gross calls "student-instrumental goals," such as preparing the students for useful careers.

In line with those who stress environmental factors, Gross found that the biggest difference in goal structures arose when legislatures and state governments were perceived as having greater power relative to administrators and faculty.

Gross's unstated assumption (since he did not include them in his sample) that students would have little to say about the determination of long-range goals may have been correct. However, there is also a weakness in simply asking top role players which goals they consider important. Students do exercise a choice over goals in that those who are better college material are sought-after resources. Students also influence curriculum by the courses they select, having relatively more or less choice depending on the market situation. In the 1980s when college enrollments were down, many less prestigious colleges vied to offer courses and programs that would entice students (computer science was "in").

In another kind of market students had less choice. At least temporarily, the demand for places in state universities grew as the costs of private universities became prohibitive for all but the wealthy or those on scholarships. Here students, content to be accepted at good state institutions, ones with high prestige, seemed little concerned with their relative power. I asked one class why they so passively accepted each year's tuition raise. The students pointed out that they were glad to be accepted at a highly regarded university and were so used to inflation that the raises seemed routine.

Gross had some other conclusions, which will not be pursued here. However, his study is a good example of how the once taken-for-granted subject of goals yields interesting and unexpected discoveries.

SUMMARY

Early theorists of bureaucracy provided an image of formal organizations set up to fulfill a particular goal or set of goals. But it was found that stated goals are not always actual operative goals. Actual goals are emergent, changeable and adaptive; multiple and sometimes conflicting; negotiated; and often serve as rationalizations of past decisions. Uncertainty has been added: the power of decision makers within an organization to determine its choice of goals has been thrown into question. The environment has been given increased emphasis, selecting certain types of organizations for survival and rejecting others. But powerful organizations attempt to and do influence their environments. Organizations interact with their environments and each other in a number of ways in the modification of goals: goal succession, competition, bargaining, co-optation, and coalition. The chapter concluded with a report on a careful case study of organizational goals—those of universities.

5

POWER, AUTHORITY, AND COMMUNICATION

The Distinction between Power and Authority
    The Problem: How Can We Distinguish between Power and Authority?
    Definitions of Power
    Definitions of Authority
    The Role of Communication
Authority and Compliance
    Orders as Communication
    Why People Comply with Authority
    The Zone of Indifference
    Limitations of the Concept of Authority
Power and Involvement
    Types of Power
    Kinds of Involvement
    Sources of Power
    Conditions Determining the Use of Power
    Persistence of Power
Communication as a Vehicle of Power
    Patterns of Communication
    Modes of Communication
    The Functions of Secrecy
Opposition to Organizational Authority: The Case of Whistle-Blowing
Summary

THE DISTINCTION BETWEEN POWER AND AUTHORITY

The Problem: How Can We Distinguish between Power and Authority?

We sense a certain similarity of meaning in the terms *power* and *authority* as they are used in everyday life, but for many people *authority* has pleasanter connotations than *power*. Both concepts are central to the study of organizations, yet many theorists emphasize one over the other. Because of their importance it has been necessary to touch on power and authority in earlier chapters.

A preference for viewing organizations as orderly and rational would lead us to emphasize authority—official, institutionalized power. In contrast, a conflict perspective would stress the dynamic interplay of power and political behavior in organizational decision making. Moving from what we already know about power in society and from brief discussions of authority in chapter 1, power in chapter 2, and the typology based on power in chapter 3, let us become more precise about their interconnections. In the process, power will emerge as a broader, more inclusive concept than authority. The crucial role of *communication* in authority and power relations will also be demonstrated.

Definitions of Power

Chapter 2 pointed out that most definitions of *power* include the capability of an individual or group to overcome resistance in achieving a desired result. Here is a classic definition by Max Weber (1958):

> In general, we understand by "power" the chance of a man or a number of men to realize their own will in a communal action even against the resistance of others who are participating in the action. (p. 180)

This and similar definitions specify a relationship between at least two persons, and two persons who are not in total agreement. (We hope that Weber, writing today, might have substituted nonsexist language). The person with power is able to get his or her way in a joint action. The one without power or with less power feels compelled, for a variety of different reasons ranging from a gun at his or her back to a moral obligation, to do as the other wishes. But power is relative and is used in a specific social context. If a third person, in the form of a police officer or an ally of the victim, enters the scene where someone is being held up at gunpoint, the power situation changes.

Other definitions of power seem a bit more benign, in that they place less stress on the coercive aspects of power. Distinguishing power from hierarchical domination, Kanter (1977) proposes:

> Power is the ability to get things done, to mobilize resources, to get and use whatever it is that a person needs for the goals he or she is attempting to meet. (p. 166)

Kanter's definition is influenced by her belief that the total amount of power in an organization need not be restricted to the few at the top of the hierarchy; that persons lower down in the scale can be empowered by giving them more autonomy, more access to resources, and more participation in decision making. However, should a less powerful person's goals come into conflict with those of a more powerful one, who is most likely to win? The person with more power obviously has the advantage.

Nonetheless, the answer is not as easy as it first seems, for those in top positions may find it necessary to share their power for many reasons. The response of the less powerful to those who are more powerful brings into discussion the issue of *compliance*. Not only does the more powerful person initiate action in the form of demands or orders or even suggestions, but the less powerful person in the interaction also plays a role, consciously and unconsciously, deliberately or unthinkingly, in responding.

By responding poorly, with little enthusiasm, or incorrectly to an order, the lower participant (person in a low-ranking position) is exerting a degree of power. As we shall see later, persons in low statuses often have a measure of power, especially when they act in concert. To gain more positive compliance and decrease possible conflict, persons with high power may have to defer to the desires of others, especially in unimportant matters. Nonetheless, to define power as an ideal concept, it necessarily includes, ultimately, the ability to overcome resistance in gaining a desired result.

Definitions of Authority

In chapter 1 we defined authority as official power, as the right to govern others made real by their belief that those exercising authority have the right to do so. We looked briefly at Weber's three types of legitimate authority—patriarchal, bureaucratic-legal, and charismatic. Bureaucratic-legal authority is the one that justifies the rights of official power holders in formal organizations. What does this mean? According to Weber (1958):

> The legitimacy of the power-holder to give commands rests upon rules that are rationally established by enactment, by agreement, or by imposition. Orders are given in the name of the impersonal norm, rather than in the name of a personal authority; and even the giving of a command constitutes obedience toward a norm rather than an arbitary freedom, favor, or privilege. (p. 294–295)

That is what is generally meant by rule by law. Laws, whether in society or in such organizational forms as official university or corporate rules, set down relationships among persons in different positions or statuses. All of the persons who accept these positions, the role players, are supposed to abide by the laws. Thus, the honest police officer is supposed to make an arrest when he sees a criminal act; he is not supposed to turn his head. The supervisor is supposed to direct the workers, whether or not she feels uncomfortable in doing so. In turn, the workers are expected to abide by the rules and accept the authority of the supervisor. A hierarchical authority system defines a chain of command, determines who one's superiors and subordinates are. A middle-level manager or supervisor both takes orders and gives orders.

What is "supposed to" happen is thus defined by official, formal rules. However, organizations in action do not always operate in accordance with the formal authority system. The nature of compliance—the acceptance of orders or communications, and the abidance or nonabidance by rules—will require examination.

Is the system of authority, the official power hierarchy, thereby unimportant? We would agree with Weber that it *is* important. It sets a structure that must be attended to and that can be referred back to in time of conflict. Using a professor's authority as a familiar example, if I ask a student to mow my lawn, he or she is perfectly entitled to refuse. It was not in our original contract; I do not have the authority to make such a request, even though I have power over the student's grade. In contrast, if I require that the student write a term paper, that student will most likely comply, because I am exercising my power legitimately. However, if I inform the student today that I want a fifteen-page term paper by next Monday, he or she may be unwilling and probably unable to produce the work in such a short time. These examples derive from Barnard's (1952) brief but interesting analysis of compliance, to which we shall return.

The organization may be understood to have a legal order paralleling that of a society. That is, it has an organized system of rules and regulations that are supposed to govern it. Voluntary organizations, such as the Boy Scouts or parent-teachers' associations, have their constitutions and bylaws, their definitions of officers' rights and duties, and the stated obligations of members.

Weber (1958) stresses the importance of law and legal authority:

> Law exists when there is a probability that an order will be upheld by a specific staff of men who will use physical or psychical compulsion with the intention of obtaining conformity with the order, or of inflicting sanctions for infringement of it. The structure of every legal order directly influences the distribution of power, economic or otherwise, within its respective community. This is true of all legal orders and not only that of the state. (p. 180)

The organization can be thought of as such a legal order, a minisociety or ministate. Although organizations operate within the larger legal order of their countries, they are bureaucratic-legal entities. The individual participant in the organization is obliged to abide by its rules. The official authority system lays out the statuses—positions in the structure—indicating who must take and receive orders. Note that the concept of authority is based on the assumption that people recognize those in official positions as officially entitled to exert power, within defined limits. Authority is power that is considered legitimate and legal. So authority is a certain type of power, but surely a basic type. A key element in the exercise of authority, as in other types of power, is communication.

The Role of Communication

Communication is so important that people sometimes assume that every problem can be solved by better communication. But all problems are not due to misunderstandings; real conflicts of interest cannot be solved by better communication. In fact, concealing such conflicts is a fairly common way of dealing with them. Rather than advocating "better communication," it would be wise to consider a number of specific issues such as the nature of communication patterns, both formal and informal, between various role players; the extent or lack of communication between those in various positions; the varied forms communication takes; special organizational languages; and the uses of secrecy and withholding of communication. These topics will be considered in a later section of this chapter.

For the present, here are some simple examples of what is meant by communication patterns. The authority system designates positions that are superordinate and subordinate, and according to Weber's formal scheme, orders are given and accepted. This would be one way of describing the communication patterns between various role players. It seems like a one-way street, with those in higher positions passing on orders to those lower down. And indeed, to understand an authority structure it is helpful to observe who usually initiates communications and who rarely initiates them.

Patterned communication also involves customary, accepted language prescribed for interaction with those who have greater or lesser authority. Thus, a special language is developed to approach superiors whose mistakes or potential mistakes must be corrected. This is tricky because the underling does not want to be accused of undermining authority. For example, a nurse may receive orders from a doctor but she cannot give him or her any. Nonetheless, in real life, she may be in the position of trying to prevent a doctor from making a serious mistake, of having to tell him or her to stop doing what is being done. This must be communicated without violating the customary norms of the interaction. So, a nurse, seeing an obvious incorrect dosage prescribed for a patient, will say, "Did you mean this, Doctor?" At other times she may wordlessly hand an inexperienced intern the proper instrument for a particular procedure, saving the intern the embarassment of asking her for information. Another way of correcting is to refer back to a previous action of the superior, such as "But Professor, you said there would be no midterm." The manners of address used in communication are symbolic: who may use first names and who must be addressed by titles provides a key to authority and status.

Official communication patterns are only the tip of the iceberg. Most organizations have a vast and varied communication system, including unofficial grapevines, informal patterns between peers, and a range of techniques for giving or withholding strategic information to superiors. The power of crucial information can be great, within and between organizations. Elsewhere we refer to the need of companies to hoard their secrets and their attempts to restrict their scientists and engineers from defecting to competitors. Real power within an organization often depends on "being in the know." Those who are peripheral, not part of the central cliques, often complain that they are the last to know what is going on. They probably are. Lower participants gain in power if they possess crucial information needed by higher-ups or are located in a physically strategic place in the structure (see Mechanic, 1962).

In the next section, we examine a theory that explains authority in terms of official communication.

AUTHORITY AND COMPLIANCE

Orders as Communications

Communication is central to Barnard's (1952) definition of authority:

> Authority is the character of a communication (order) in a formal organization by virtue of which it is accepted by a contributor to or "member" of the organization as governing the action he contributes. . . .
>
> If a directive communication is accepted by one to whom it is addressed, its authority for him is confirmed or established. It is admitted as the basis of action. Disobedience of such a communication is a denial of its authority for him. Therefore, under this definition the decision as to whether an order has authority or not lies with the persons to whom it is addressed, and does not reside in "persons of authority" or those who issue these orders. (p. 180)

Here the act of *compliance*, of following an order or (more euphemistically) of accepting a communication, is not taken for granted just because of where people are in the formal structure. The act of compliance legitimizes the directive, indicates that it is proper and acceptable.

In Barnard's view, a person does not *have* authority; he or she achieves it in the process of having the order or communication accepted. The tendency for subordinates to accept directives from superiors, however, is not denied. With an additional concept, "the zone of indifference," Barnard is able to explain why most routine communications are accepted and are therefore authoritative.

Barnard was a corporate executive interested in promoting a view of the organization as a cooperative system. Hence, rather than use the term *order*, he preferred *communication* to describe the same phenomenon. Still, he analyzed communications as part of a hierarchical system. The superordinate initiated the communication, much as Weber's man initiated the order. But where Weber took compliance with the order of a qualified superior for granted, Barnard examined the conditions under which a communication would be accepted or rejected.

The contribution he makes here is that obeying orders, compliance with directives, is not as simple as the rational systems model suggests. To take for granted that role players will comply because they are morally, legally, or contractually bound to obey persons in authority leaves out the many human elements that intervene between obligation and action. Here Selznick's concept of recalcitrance comes in. People do not always do what they are officially supposed to do; there may be pulls in other directions. Take, for example, the college athlete who must choose between spending an afternoon writing a paper or attending practice. Both the athlete's teacher and coach have communicated their expectations; both have legitimate positions in the authority structure. Their communications or orders are conflicting; one will have to be disregarded. The dutiful student-athlete experiences role conflict; one or the other of his or her superiors experiences rejection of an order. It is also conceivable that the student could decide to go to the movies rather than do either of the above. People have many motivations.

Why People Comply with Authority

Can we specify conditions under which people will comply with orders, directives, or communications? According to Barnard (1952):

> A person can and will accept a communication as authoritative only when four conditions simultaneously obtain: (a) he can and does understand the communication; (b) *at the time of his decision* he believes that it is not inconsistent with the purpose of the organization; (c) *at the time of his decision*, he believes it to be compatible with his personal interest as a whole, and (d) he is able mentally and physically to comply with it. (p. 180)

These are broad and inclusive conditions that appear to cover every contingency. They are useful because they start us off on the path of trying to comprehend the acceptance or rejection of specific orders. Let us examine each.

The person can and does understand the communication. This point seems obvious, but in actuality many orders are unclear and confusing. They may be phrased in language that the recipient does not understand. When peer group members are available, people often turn to them to discuss and clarify the meaning of a particular order. Here the power of the peer group enters: Its acceptance may be essential in order to gain this clarification and perform one's duties. Too, the person in authority has the power to discourage disliked subordinates by providing inadequate or unclear directions and thereby ensuring failure.

The person believes that it is not inconsistent with the purpose of the organization. To illustrate this point Barnard provides the example of conflicts of orders. In the extreme case he believes individuals would be unable to comply: "for example, an employee of a water system ordered to blow up an essential pump, or soldiers ordered to shoot their own comrades" (1952:181–182). Executives are advised to explain why the appearance of a conflict is an illusion when they give orders that seem to be contrary to the main purposes of the organization.

However, the extent to which individuals are really willing to judge their superior's orders in terms of organizational objectives is another issue. Barnard admits that lower participants are reticent to question a superior's orders in terms of the good of the organization. He asserts that most people are reluctant to take responsibility for their own actions and are even less willing to take it on for the organization. Hence, those with little authority usually assume that the higher-ups know what is good for the organization. Even if they question the ability or honesty of their bosses, they may rightfully fear the consequences of challenging them publicly. (See the case study of attempted "whistle-blowing," exposure of the weaknesses of superiors, which concludes this chapter.)

In chapter 8, we point out the tendency for individual role players in a bureaucracy to become involved in their day-to-day procedures and to sometimes lose sight of larger objectives. The example is given of the highly bureaucratized and efficient system of mass murder in Nazi Germany, wherein many functionaries claimed they were not responsible for their own behavior but were merely following orders.

Too, some categories of individuals may not wish to serve the purposes of the organization. Take the case of prison inmates, who are incarcerated against their will. They can hardly be expected to be in sympathy with the purposes of the prison. Such resistance is seen as deviance by Barnard, although he was concentrating on corporations. Says he, "To fail in an obligation intentionally is an act of hostility. This no organization can permit; and it must respond with punitive action if it can, even to the point of incarcerating or executing the culprit" (1952:185). But what if the culprit is already incarcerated?

Here is where the concept of authority, considered outside of its broader context, is limited. Discussions of authority tend to treat only peripherally the fact that people must sometimes be coerced into obeying orders; discussions of power treat this issue as central.

Too, Barnard's harsh criticism of those who "fail in an obligation intentionally" ignores the fact that conflicting authority systems may exist within the same organization, creating the need to choose between them. Earlier in this chapter we gave the example of college athletes who might receive conflicting orders from their teachers and coaches. They then have to decide whom to obey and whom to disobey. Bureaucratic systems are often the context in which professionals operate; bureaucratic norms of processing large numbers of people as rapidly as possible conflict with professional norms that emphasize well-informed, personalized attention. The dilemmas of legal services lawyers intended to aid the indigent serve to illustrate; high case loads prevent them from providing service that conforms with professional norms.

The person believes it to be compatible with his or her personal interest as a whole, and the person is able mentally and physically to comply. These are the two other conditions Barnard says are required for compliance. The first suggests that individuals tend to act in their own best interests, but the second allows that individuals are not always mentally and physically able to do so. That final condition saves the analysis from the false implication that people always behave rationally. Emotion, sentiment, and will power come in by the back door, as part of people's mental or physical condition. Smokers continue to smoke, even though they may be damaging their health; drug addicts continue to take drugs because they cannot stop, despite adverse affects. And some people act, not out of narrow self-interest, but out of altruistic motives. Barnard does not take all of this into account explicitly, but his categories are broad enough to include almost everything.

The Zone of Indifference

The four simultaneous conditions that must apply in order for a communication to be accepted are useful in showing that compliance is not automatic. But does constant decision making and questioning actually take place?

Much behavior involves automatic compliance—especially when orders clearly fall within the realm of normal expectations. Hence, a secretary is not surprised that she is expected to arrive at work at a specified time, take only a given number of breaks, answer the telephone, and produce reasonably correct finished copies of correspondence.[1] Being asked to type a letter during regular working hours will unquestionably be accepted, as it is a normal part of her job. Unquestionably acceptable orders are said to lie within the "zone of indifference." "Such an order lies within the range that in a general way was anticipated at the time of undertaking the connection with the organization" (Barnard, 1952:183).

Two other types of orders contrast with the ones that lie in the zone of indifference: orders that are clearly unacceptable to the person affected and that will certainly not be obeyed, and orders that are on the borderline, barely acceptable or barely unacceptable. The range of orders that will be accepted will be more limited among those who, in Barnard's words, "are barely induced to contribute to the system" (1952:184), that is, who are less attached to the organization. In recognizing a distinction between various degrees of willingness to comply, Barnard has introduced an additional factor: the degree of attachment and involvement individuals have to particular organizations. This factor receives much more thorough treatment in Etzioni's typology of compliance (1980:87-100), as first pointed out in chapter 3. Presumably, it is in the borderline range of cases where highly committed subordinates will accept even dubious orders while the more alienated will reject orders that are not clearly within the authorized bounds.

The issue of compliance highlights the deficiency of concentrating only on authority, or official power, and makes more obvious the need to consider unofficial power as well, power in its various manifestations.

Limitations of the Concept of Authority

Inattention to force and economic incentives. Etzioni (1980:93-94) criticizes studies conducted in the tradition of Weber, which focus only on authority and minimize other sources of power—mainly force and economic incentives. The use

---

[1] Use of the female pronoun here is deliberate, since almost all secretaries are women. This job remains sex-linked (see Kanter, 1977, chaps. 1 and 4).

of force may be legitimate, as in the case of a soldier in wartime, or illegitimate, as in the case of the stick-up artist. Economic incentives may be legitimate, as in the case of wages, or illegitimate, as in the case of bribes. The point is, there are other sources of legitimate power in addition to bureaucratic authority, and there are also sources of illegitimate power.

Inattention to individual needs. The focus on authority also tends to stress the legitimacy of orders and directives, as determining compliance. It gives less recognition to the role of what Etzioni calls the subordinate's "need-dispositions." He maintains:

> Commitment is generated not merely by directives which are considered legitimate but also by those which are in line with internalized needs of the subordinate. Involvement is positive if the line of action directed is conceived by the subordinate as both legitimate and gratifying. (1980:94)

Although Barnard alludes to individual needs and capabilities, Etzioni goes further. As you recall, he balances a typology of kinds of power with a typology of the ways in which individuals relate to organizations, the nature of their involvement.

Inattention to the relative power of subgroups and organizations. Many of the definitions of authority specify person-to-person relations, and the orders, communications, or directives directed downward in the hierarchy by managers, owners, and bosses. However, power resides not only in individuals but also differentially among the various subgroups within an organization. Pfeffer and Salancik (1974) studied the relative power of different academic departments within a university. While each department had its official place alongside others as an academic unit, certain departments proved to be much more powerful than others. Similarly in corporations, one department or function will be found, through empirical study, to be more powerful than another. Organizational politics is a concept that recognizes that there may be struggles for power within an organization, just as political parties struggle for power in a more open way.

Dominant coalitions arise through such internal struggles; certain subunits of the organization together form its power center at any particular time. The degree of centralization, which refers to how formal power is distributed within the organization, may itself become a subject of struggle and dispute.[2]

The concept of authority is inadequate to deal with the relative power of organizations in their environments, including other organizations and the world. Each country has authority as a sovereign nation and as an official member of various international groups, but this in no way explains a country's degree of power in the international scene. One country does not officially have authority over

---

[2]Various researchers have studied the relationship of centralization to such factors as size (Blau, 1973) or technology (Child, 1973). See the discussion of typologies based on technology in chapter 3.

another (unless the other is a colony), but the more powerful ones can certainly influence the less powerful ones, politically, economically, and culturally.

Inattention to the power of subordinates and peers. Barnard's examination of the conditions under which communications are accepted hints at the power of subordinates, but only in a limited way. When orders or communications do not fall within the zone of indifference, they may not be accepted as authoritative and hence may not be obeyed. But the power of subordinates is not limited to refusing orders.

As we have already suggested, the sources of power in organizations are not bounded by a person's official position. Individuals with little formal authority but who carry important organizational knowledge in their heads may be fairly irreplaceable. Such individuals have considerable power—the power of the expert. It becomes apparent that knowledge is a source of power when new managers or supervisors are brought in over seasoned workers. These workers have detailed information about daily operations; they can make it extremely difficult for the new manager to perform by withholding vital information or assistance. Power also exists within groups of peers. Natural leaders arise. Informal norms develop, the violation of which can get an individual into trouble. In order to be accepted by the peer group, a person may engage in actions that are against his or her own desires. For example, students may engage in cheating—not without guilt, but because it seems necessary to gain peer group acceptance in certain schools. Despite the universal school and college rule against cheating, the practice persists, due in part to the power of peer groups.

POWER AND INVOLVEMENT

Types of Power

In this section we go back to Etzioni's analysis of compliance, which appears both in books (1961, rev. 1975) and a summarizing article (1980), and which we introduced as a typology. Etzioni bases his analysis of power on the relationships between two main types of role players: higher ranked people in power positions, who also may be seen as organizational representatives or elites, and those in subject positions, lower in rank, called lower participants. Bosses and workers, guards and prisoners, teachers and students are examples of these two complementary, unequal interacting categories.

Types of power are classified in terms of the means used to make the subjects comply. Three types are defined: coercive, remunerative, and normative.

Coercive power uses physical means, such as the application of force, infliction of pain or threat of it, or the withholding of food and other things needed by human beings.

Remunerative power uses financial or other material rewards, such as wages, fringe benefits, commissions, or services.

Normative power relies on the giving or withholding of symbolic rewards and deprivations, the power of persuasion, of making people feel right and good. It is the kind of power stressed in Weber's formulations about legitimate authority. Etzioni refers to two types of normative power, that between highers and lowers (pure normative power) and that between peers (social power). Those in higher positions may give those in lower positions such rewards as gold stars, compliments, certificates of merit, and so forth. Peer group power is the group's informal power to give its members acceptance and positive response, as we have discussed.

Organizations tend to emphasize one type of power over others, although all may be present. According to Etzioni, one type of power may neutralize another. For example, the application of force creates such a high degree of alienation that "it becomes impossible to apply normative power successfully" (1980:89). Also, certain types of power are considered more appropriate in given organizational contexts. Members of social movement organizations, such as civil rights or environmental groups, are supposed to be dedicated and participate because of their moral beliefs, not for financial gain. In contrast, accepting employment legitimately creates an expectation that one will be paid, that one is working for financial rewards, whether or not there are moral rewards in the job.

Kinds of Involvement

Organizations seek positive attachment to their power or authority, although they may not always get it. While business organizations hope for employee loyalty, they must also provide remuneration for work and sometimes threaten to fire people. The fact is that there are different degrees of loyalty, of involvement in the various organizations in which we all participate.

Etzioni presents a continuum of involvement, of "cathective-evaluative" orientation of the individual to the organization, including both intensity and direction. *Cathective* refers to emotional orientation, while *evaluative* refers to judgmental orientation. In other words, we approach our role in organizations both from a feeling and a reasoning perspective. Intensity is either high or low; direction is either positive or negative. I might feel quite positive about being a member of the Sociologists for Women in Society, yet my involvement might be of minor importance to me. I might have an intensely negative or intensely positive orientation toward the way in which my college is run.

Positive involvement is referred to as commitment or moral involvement, while negative involvement is alienation. For less intense involvements, Etzioni uses the word *calculative*.

Alienative involvement, as the term implies, is an intense negative orientation, and it is characteristic of enforced participation in organizations, such as that of people in concentration camps or mental institutions. Calculative involvement is considered a positive or negative orientation of low intensity, sort of the attitude of "I'll see what I can get out of this situation." A person might feel this way about a temporary job: "I don't like the supervisor, but I'm earning what I need and will soon be able to quit." Moral involvement is a positive orientation of high intensity, such as is true of a devoted church member or an active fraternity participant.

Etzioni then puts together the three possible kinds of power enumerated above with the three possible kinds of involvement to form a table (see table 5-1) of compliance relations.

As noted in chapter 3, certain types of power are considered congruent with certain types of involvement, such as the moral involvement of the devoted church member. Still, a person's sense of relationship to an organization is affected by many factors, including personal history, socialization, and membership in other groups. Some church members attend services perfunctorily, to please others rather than because of a moral involvement. Some minors probably attend church because they are forced to do so. People can also become disaffected with an organization to which they once felt great allegiance.

Congruent involvement is considered more effective. For example, it is unnecessary to pay highly committed persons because they would perform well without remuneration. Paying alienated persons does not always succeed in gaining their maximum cooperation. Interesting hypotheses that Etzioni (1980) develops are the following:

> To the degree that the environment of the organization allows, *organizations tend to shift their compliance structure from incongruent to congruent types* and *organizations which have congruent compliance structures tend to resist factors pushing them toward incongruent compliance structures.* (p. 93)

Take the example of volunteer police and fire departments in rural areas, which tend to be made up of persons who get moral rewards from their service, gaining esteem within their communities. In an urban, more impersonal setting, it becomes necessary to have paid fire and police departments. Volunteers can no longer be depended upon; material rewards are necessary to recruit workers. An interesting dilemma occurs when certain types of workers, such as hospital employees, threaten to strike. Their focus on their economic needs is taken as somehow unfair; it is as if they should be more concerned with patients' needs. During a 1984 strike in an American city, hospital management sponsored radio commer-

TABLE 5-1   A Typology of Compliance Relations

KINDS OF POWER	KINDS OF INVOLVEMENT		
	Alienative	*Calculative*	*Moral*
Coercive	1	2	3
Remunerative	4	5	6
Normative	7	8	9

Source: *A Sociological Reader on Complex Organizations*, 3rd ed. by Amitai Etzioni and Edward W. Lehman. Copyright © 1961, 1969 by Holt, Rinehart & Winston, Inc. Copyright © 1980 by Holt, Rinehart & Winston. Reprinted by permission of CBS College Publishing.

cials suggesting the workers were callous about their patients. The criticism implied that hospital workers, for their patients' sakes, should have a moral involvement, not a calculative involvement, toward the hospitals that employed them. Yet many people are denied doctors' services if they do not have the money to pay; doctors are not expected to work for low fees. Interestingly enough, the medical profession has, until recently, been able to convince the public of its humanitarian motives. With the rise of a consumer movement, that is less true.

Perrow's (1979) criticism of the self-evident nature of Etzioni's congruent types has already been discussed (see chapter 3). Cases in which types of power are joined with *incongruent* types of involvement are illuminating, however, in that they draw attention to problems and changed conditions in the organization. A high school that needs armed police in its corridors makes us terribly uneasy. Prisoners who like prison appear somewhat abnormal, as if they have a deficiency in their personality or socialization. But most important, Etzioni's typologies demonstrate the need to go past formal authority structures and deal with various forms of power in organizations and to take into account different kinds of involvement in organizations. Of course, organizations may employ more than one type of power.

Sources of Power

The power of organizations in the world.   Much of our discussion of power has dealt with intraorganizational power and the relationships between the individual and the organization. Most organization books, including this one, start out by emphasizing the prevalence of large formal organizations in the modern world. However, organizational researchers have generally left it to other specialists to study power on a grand scale.

Sociologists and political scientists interested in communities have done research on community power structures (see, for example, Hunter, 1953; Dahl, 1961). C. Wright Mills, in *The Power Elite* (1956) maintained that the top leaders of government, industry, and military organizations constituted an interlocked, unified power elite. Others, such as Dahl, claim that societal power is more dispersed, shared by various interest groups.

Dahl studied community power structure in New Haven by focusing on specific issues, such as community welfare or public education. He found that the group having the most power varied according to the issue involved. Different constellations of groups attempted to influence different political decisions.

The debate between those who advocate the power elite theory and those who depict power as pluralistically distributed continues. The fact is, the networks of power in any community or nation are not simply open to inspection. Official officeholders do not always represent the pinnacles of power. Others behind the scenes may be highly influential, especially if they possess ample financial resources. For example, a major firm's threat to move its corporate headquarters elsewhere may be sufficient to help bring about a citywide renewal project.

An area of study that touches on the power of organizations internationally is that of development. Countries are economically developed in various degrees, and patterns of mutual dependence are created. Multinational corporations take the world as their field, sometimes using the international labor supply as their pool of workers. The effects of these corporations on local industries and local economies can be great. And, of course, the availability of certain jobs at home is affected by those that are relocated abroad. Trade and commerce are regulated by governments, sometimes restricting and sometimes serving the interests of different industries. Major corporations are not idle in trying to direct such government involvement.

Within the United States mergers and takeovers of firms fill the pages of business news; sometimes the underlying struggles they represent are brought to the surface. In recent years, some organizational theorists have been willing to tackle the complex subject of interorganizational relations that such events reflect. In doing so, they necessarily deal in some degree with power relations.

The study of power is, of course, a very vast subject and the central issue of political science. Research is required to discover sources of power and how power operates. Organizational power is worldwide and we have only suggested some of its manifestations here. The topic will reappear in other chapters.

For now, let us return to what has been discovered about sources of power within organizations. Just as in the community, national, and international scenes, these sources need to be ferreted out through careful research. Power and conflicts of power are not as obvious as the openly stated authority structure of an organization.

Power within organizations. Pfeffer maintains that the power of organizational actors "is fundamentally determined by two things, the importance of what they do in the organization and their skill in doing it" (1981a:98). Given the usual division of labor, certain activities are recognized as being more important than others in accomplishing organizational objectives and ensuring survival. The organizational structure determines which functions are most crucial. Thus, the word-processing and personnel functions, while necessary, are supportive of other usually more important ones such as production and sales. The head of the word-processing department is unlikely to be influential in organizational decision making. In this discussion we follow closely Pfeffer's arguments in his important book, *Power in Organizations* (1981a).

Pfeffer's second point is that having an important and critical function is not enough. The organizational actor must have the skill needed both to perform well and to convince others of the importance of his or her work and how well he or she does it. The latter is a political rather than a technical skill.

There are a number of ways in which a function becomes important and a source of power for the clever role player. Among those that Pfeffer discusses are dependence, having needed resources, and being able to cope with uncertainty. The power-seeking organizational actor finds ways of creating some of these sources.

If others are dependent on a person and have no alternative way to get what they need, the dependency creates power. A person seeking a promotion may need the recommendation of his or her immediate supervisor. The only way the supervisor's power is lessened is if the person no longer values the promotion, has some alternative source of mobility, or can provide the supervisor with something of equivalent value. Cases of sexual harassment on the job illustrate nicely. Employees are sometimes propositioned, offered rewards for providing sexual services. With the outlawing of sexual harassment and newly created avenues to protest it, the use of such exchanges may still occur, but on a less coercive basis. Organizational units that provide something essential and unavailable through other means are obviously important and a source of power.

Resource dependence.   This perspective has been used to study organizational power and the successes and failures of social movement organizations. Basically an open systems approach, it emphasizes most organizations' dependence on resources in the environment—such as funds, legitimacy, workers and customers, materials. In chapter 2 we discussed the concern of universities with the power of corporations to affect research, since corporations are a main source of research funding. Top university officials often have as one of their main duties the seeking of donations, budget allocations if they are state universities, and the approval of important publics. The high priority accorded this resource seeking is evidenced by the exalted positions of the seekers. Not all university presidents are excellent administrators, but if they are successful in garnering outside resources, they are unlikely to be dismissed. Money can, of course, be manipulated to gain power. Government can provide funds, subject to specified conditions of accountability. Or a foundation can offer funds for certain kinds of projects, thereby influencing numbers of people and organizations in the direction of their interests.

Ability to cope with uncertainty.   Power also derives from the ability to cope with uncertainty. Organizations prefer to decrease uncertainty in their operations. In the music business, producers of records used to keep artists on contract. But given a growing uncertainty about who would achieve hits, they changed to purchasing the services of artists on a royalty basis, with no longstanding mutual obligations (Hirsch, 1972). They reduced the possibility of being tied to less successful artists. Uncertainty can take many forms. Production may become dependent on a particular piece of complex technology that very few understand, such as an elaborate computer. If only one specialist is able to fix it, he or she thereby gains importance and power. As mentioned earlier, people with special knowledge often like to keep it in their heads in an attempt to become indispensable. If they cannot easily be replaced, their irreplaceability provides them with power. However, this irreplaceability must be recognized and accepted as such. If such a person bargains for extremely high rewards, more serious attempts may be made to replace him or her.

Two examples from the same university come to mind. A noted professor indicated to the president that he had good offers of more lucrative employment at other major universities. While his salary could not be officially raised at the time, he was offered and accepted a very low interest loan from the university for the purchase of a home. Meanwhile, an exceptionally promising junior faculty member who had important quantitative skills informed his department head that he would have to go elsewhere if certain conditions were not met. In this case the department was unwilling to admit his relative indispensability, he did leave, and the department probably suffered.

The power of numbers. Power often derives from numbers. Those in low positions, relatively dispensable as individuals, gain in clout when they band together. When a whole work force walks off the job, they are trying to demonstrate their power. What they hope is that the employer will be forced to bargain with them over their demands.

Resistance to unionization on the part of employers reflects recognition of the potential power shift that it would probably entail. In a book entitled (with refreshing honesty), *Making Unions Unnecessary*, Charles Hughes (1976:31) suggests using employee committees that are appointed by management, rather than elected, in order to forestall union-creating tendencies. In a similar vein, these committees are to be clearly told that their role is advisory so that they do not get the impression that they can make demands.

The right of workers to engage in collective petitioning for higher wages and better working conditions was won through social movement activity. That is, the labor movement developed out of conflict with employers over the right of workers to have their needs taken into account. This was, and often still is, a power struggle— the power of the individual employer against the power of numbers. The employer usually does not need an individual worker, but he or she does need the group of workers. In a strike great efforts may be made to minimize this need, by using supervisory personnel to take over or by bringing in nonunionized workers (scabs). The film *Huelga* shows how striking Mexican-American farmworkers were able to win over scabs by appealing to their loyalty to their own ethnic group. Because of the possibility that strikers may win over nonunionized workers, the groups brought in to replace strikers are most often chosen from other racial or ethnic groups. Black workers have often been used in this way. Racial or ethnic group loyalty, then, can be another source of cohesiveness and power.

Collective bargaining came about when workers began to rebel against the arbitrary and often harsh power of owners. People in very low power positions may feel driven to strike, as did the highly underpaid women textile workers, many of whom were foreign-born, in Lowell, Massachusetts, in 1812 (Rowbotham, 1973). Social movements arise when a group cannot use existing channels of authority successfully to satisfy its needs or demands. The group must feel, at that time, that there is some possibility of success. Group demonstrations, though decried, may force authorities to move faster or make compromises.

The threat of unrest or low morale. Very much related to the power of numbers is the power caused by unrest or threats of it. In society, urban unrest reduces safety, may result in property damage, and in general is bad for business. Concessions may be made to moderate representatives of a movement if its more radical members take to the streets. Organizations are concerned if their participants are unusually dissatisfied or agitated, or if they show low morale. Such individual states can lead to absenteeism, poor workmanship, alienation, and possibly even group action.

The power of lower participants. The power or potential power of lower participants has been referred to earlier. Throughout the book mention has been made of the informal norms that tend to develop among peers: workers, students, fellow inmates. Chapter 6, which focuses on division of labor, status, and role, will again deal with aspects of informal organization. All of these discussions should reveal that those *without* formal power often try to develop it informally. Subjugated racial groups and women, the subordinate gender group, develop techniques for appealing to the better instincts of their superiors. Role playing, acting dumb, coquetry, and manipulation are some of these techniques. Within organizations special strategies may similarly be developed by individuals or groups of lower participants.

More open direct action by lower participants in opposing superiors can be dangerous, especially if taken individually or in small numbers. For official actions, one has to go through channels; attempts to bypass them even for good cause may backfire (Weinstein, 1979). Here is where the official authority system is used to protect the superiors, who can righteously accuse the lower participant of insubordination and dodge any real issue that has been brought up. If corruption has infected a system, it may be present at many levels. Honest police officers, for example, must be wary in reporting the misconduct of others to their superiors, not knowing whether or not they are involved in what has transpired. The same is true of lower participants who observe some variety of white-collar crime taking place in their offices, since very high and powerful officials may be implicated.

Conditions Determining the Use of Power

Power is not exerted at all times. Its potential to be activated is greater when conflicts exist and choices have to be made. Conflicts require resolution and hence the exercise of power. How do conflicts arise? There are several conditions:

> Conflict is produced to the extent that there exists interdependence among organizational subunits, a condition of resource scarcity, and disagreements concerning goals, preferences, the technology of the organization, or the connections between actions and consequences. These conditions produce decision situations in which the use of power and politics is more likely. For power to be employed, it is necessary that the decision involve a critical or important issue. (Pfeffer, 1981a:96)

Interdependence among organizational subunits means that what one does affects the others. Take the battle that goes on between two people working or sleeping in the same room who prefer different room temperatures. One opens the window, the other closes it. If they worked or slept in different rooms, such actions would not be interdependent. The condition of resource scarcity is such that there is only one room to share, and hence they cannot both be satisfied.

Individuals or subunits who hold heterogeneous or inconsistent goals provide another potential scenario for the display of power. Pfeffer maintains that there is a lesser potential for conflict in business organizations than in nonprofit or public agencies, largely because in the former the goal of profit maximization is clear and agreed upon. As is suggested in various contexts, goal ambivalence in public agencies derives from the clash between the goal of providing services and that of conserving governmental monies. In businesses as elsewhere, the subunits or departments created by a division of labor are often preoccupied with their own special needs and purposes.

Here is an example: The marketing department of a firm wants to increase sales by minimizing delivery time and maximizing product variety; at the same time, its production department wants to restrict costs by minimizing product variety and holding as little inventory as possible (Pfeffer, 1981a:72). This sets the stage for a struggle over which goals will predominate. Such conflict is not always harmful to the firm, for it may help to insure a successful balancing of the needs of the different departments.

Further, while the goal of profit maximization may be agreed upon by those in the management hierarchy, it is precisely this goal that is frequently questioned by workers. They often feel that excessive profits should be transformed into higher wages or more benefits rather than increased dividends for stockholders.

Persistence of Power

It is an old adage that power is never relinquished without a struggle. This is seemingly contradicted by the instances in which colonial nations have given freedom to their colonies. But such actions tend to occur in the wake of nationalist revolutions elsewhere and sensitivity to the "writing on the wall." By relinquishing political power the colonial nation is generally able to maintain a large degree of economic power over its former colony.

Those in power are in a position to gain and retain resources that enable them to perpetuate their power. Take an incumbent president who is running for political office. He has numerous opportunities to make public appearances, to grant privileges and offer positions to strategic groups and individuals. He has a private aircraft, numerous salaried aides, and many other perquisites of office to facilitate his activities, including his political campaign. Activities that others dub political he may classify as official duties. His rival has only promises to offer and must spend much more private funds on the campaign.

Power tends to become institutionalized. Usual ways of doing things become normative and customary; change is resisted. Once a decision has been made, people tend to be bound by that decision and attempt to remain consistent. Even policies instituted only a short while previously can take on the aura of permanence.

Students entering Rutgers University after a major reorganization had taken place were unfamiliar with its previous structure. They accepted the inconveniences caused by reorganization philosophically because it appeared to them that things had always been this way. In contrast, many students who had experienced both the old and the new system were highly critical of the changes that had been made because they remembered the preexisting structure.

Pfeffer cites cases in which "failing" courses of action are maintained because of a belief in consistency and perseverance. Policies that were successful in the early years of an organization may be held onto even after their usefulness has declined. For example, the power of a founder may be so strong and accepted that he or she is able to continue policies that have become detrimental to the organization.

Yet there are other cases in which seemingly successful courses of action are abandoned for newer schemes. Introducing innovations may be a way of maintaining or increasing power, for example, by reclassifying jobs into smaller units, centralizing or decentralizing operations, or relocating plants to cheaper labor areas.

In a rapidly changing world, especially technologically, an emphasis on the value of innovation balances the tendency for persistence. Note how advertising of products specifies that they are "new and improved." Well-known manufacturers are able to maintain their dominance by stressing that they are "state of the art" (totally up to date with the latest innovations). The fashion industry is built on this premise. Major fashion houses must continually create new demand, and they do so by changing styles every year. The successful ones become fashion leaders and fight to hold this place. Given a changing environment, organizational leaders may retain and increase power by being responsive to new environmental developments.

Organizational power distributions themselves tend to become consolidated and institutionalized, even if those in power introduce some innovations. Within the organization a culture develops that provides common norms, common perspectives, and a common language. Existing power distributions become accepted as normal. Institutionalized, they take on the qualities of authority systems. That is, they become recognized and legitimatized, which makes them more difficult to challenge. An important part of culture consists of the special language, formal and informal communication patterns within an organization, that tends to reinforce status and power differences.

COMMUNICATION AS A VEHICLE OF POWER

Patterns of Communication

We return now to a more careful examination of the role of communication as a vehicle of power, mentioned earlier in this chapter and related to the topics of status and role considered in the next one. The formal, official structure of an organization defines statuses that are related to each other and between which communications are expected to take place.

Communication lines consist of downward, upward, and lateral patterns that can be both formal and informal. The term *pattern* means that communication does not occur randomly but has discoverable uniformities regarding how and between whom it takes place. The topic of communication is frequently neglected in sociologically oriented organization texts, less so in management-oriented ones. Practitioners tend to recognize that human interaction is mediated by symbols and that communication occurs by way of symbols. Hence, books intended to train managers, following Barnard's lead, frequently advise on how best to communicate (see, e.g., Hodgetts & Altman, 1979; C. Hughes, 1976).

Formal communication patterns. The official hierarchy of an organization provides a blueprint of its authority structure, expressed often in a pyramid of unequal statuses. Recall that much discussion of authority and power focuses on communication downward, from bosses and managers to lower participants. Such communication may be verbal or may take the form of memos, reports, handbooks, or newspapers. Upward communication is seen by management as a way of gaining feedback from subordinates (Hodgetts & Altman, 1979:297), but is often difficult to obtain. Suggestion programs, grievance procedures, and group meetings are avenues that may be made available, but lower participants sometimes view them with suspicion. Such management-initiated avenues may have specific purposes.

To achieve the purpose of making unions unnecessary, Hughes advises repetition of the message that the firm's policy is to remain nonunion. He urges management to present a strong case to employees for why it is more beneficial to them not to have a union than to have one. Directed audience response is recommended, by throwing out such questions as, "Did the union get you your job? Has a union gotten you the pay increases that you've had in the past?" Tested techniques for effective speechmaking are also suggested:

> Arguments presented at the beginning or at the end of the communication will be remembered better than the arguments presented in the middle. Therefore, management should present its case first, give the union side in the middle, then draw its conclusion at the end, thus creating a more indelible image in the minds of employees. Facts and information alone almost never change attitudes. It is necessary to draw conclusions and state the position that you wish people to follow. (C. Hughes, 1976:16)

In this excerpt the purpose of management is to prevent the formation of unions, an event that would restrict its power. In other cases the purposes of downward communication may not be as obvious, either by design or error.

The possibility that lower participants will draw their own conclusions or not get the message that superiors intend to convey is strengthened by their different backgrounds and different interests. Managers may perceive themselves as better communicators than they actually are. In one study, personnel were asked if superiors make use of the ideas and opinions of their subordinates in the solution of job problems. People at different levels of the official hierarchy expressed very different perceptions, each level rating themselves better than did their subordinates (see table 5-2). For example, 73 percent of supervisors responded that they "always or nearly always get subordinates' ideas and opinions," yet only 16 percent of workers believed that was true.

Horizontal or lateral communication.   Horizontal communication takes place between people at the same level of the hierarchy and, except for official meetings, is usually informal rather than formal. In many cases management attempts to restrict such communication. However, Henri Fayol, sometimes called the father of management theory, recommended the gangplank principle, that individuals at the same level of the hierarchy

> be allowed to communicate directly, provided they have permission from their supervisors to do so and they tell their respective chiefs afterward what they have agreed to do. In this way, while the integrity of the hierarchy is never threatened, it is possible to avoid following the formal chain of command by having to send messages up one part of the organization and down the other. (Hodgetts & Altman, 1979:298)

At upper levels it is sometimes understood that peers need to coordinate their activities through such devices as, for example, a meeting of vice-presidents or an academic department meeting. The same may be true for those lower down in the hierarchy, but as can be seen from the above quote, such peer group interaction, unsupervised, is often suspected.

TABLE 5-2   Views of Supervisor Behavior

	DO SUPERIORS USE SUBORDINATES' IDEAS AND OPINIONS IN THE SOLUTION OF JOB PROBLEMS?*			
	Top Staff's View of Their Own Behavior	*Supervisors' View of Top Staff's Behavior*	*Supervisors' View of Their Own Behavior*	*Workers' View of Supervisors' Behavior*
Always or nearly always get subordinates' ideas and opinions	70%	52%	73%	16%
Often get subordinates' ideas and opinions	25%	17%	23%	23%
Sometimes or seldom get these ideas and opinions	5%	31%	4%	61%

*Adapted from Rensis Likert, *New Patterns of Management* (New York: McGraw-Hill Book Company, 1961), p. 53. Copyright © 1961 by McGraw-Hill. Reproduced with permission.

A great deal of informal interaction does take place, nevertheless, between persons at the same level. Such communication is not necessarily harmful to the organization and may help it to run smoothly. Suppose one waiter passes on to another the information that the special plate of the day has run out. This saves the latter from unnecessary trips to the kitchen and from having to ask customers for substitute orders. Work group members have many ways of helping each other—and also impeding each other, should someone break the informal code. However, concern over the potential power of unified subordinates, as well as the possibility that they are using company time for private matters, makes management want to limit and control their communications. Frederick Taylor himself observed what he called "soldiering," the restriction of production developed by work groups, in which they created their own norms about what constituted a proper day's work. Separating workers from each other is one way of preventing the growth of strong informal codes. Yet, in highly restrictive situations, such as total institutions or closely monitored tests, peer groups develop innovative methods for communicating.

Modes of Communication

Official symbolism. The difference between formal and public language and that used with intimates can be striking. For example, racial and religious stereotypes and sexual jokes abound in private conversations, yet the public official who inadvertently lets such language slip out tends to create a furor. Image making is important to organizations and their intentions must always be phrased in the most moral terms. Jargon also tends to develop at every level. Within Indsco, the corporation studied by Kanter (1977), upward mobility was so important that numerous terms were invented to describe those who seemed destined for it: water-walkers, fast trackers, high fliers, superstars, one performers, and boy or girl wonders. Stories, myths, and ceremonies are invented to reinforce loyalty to the organization and a shared culture. A student reporting on the colorful if somewhat coarse language used in military training indicated that it was a highly unifying common bond among future officers. However, in the classroom he was stymied by inhibitions and sought in vain for mild examples to illustrate his point. The highly pornographic words just could not be spoken in a different public setting. We return to discussion of symbols in chapter 7.

The grapevine. The grapevine is an informal communication network that arises spontaneously between people in contact with each other. Especially where a degree of secrecy is enforced, the grapevine flourishes. In times of war, troops may know in advance their intended destination, despite every effort to prevent it. Rumors, accurate and inaccurate, are circulated and various bits of information are put together. Secretaries and aides are privy to the desks of their superiors; the loading of supplies can be observed; besides, someone has access to inventories (winter clothing would hardly be ordered for troops going to a tropical climate). Every organization has contact with elements from the environment, people who come and go bringing their news with them. It is not surprising that prisoners know when there are uprisings in other prisons even if prison officials attempt to with-hold this information.

Efforts at informal communication are intensified when formal channels are limited and information is scarce. Particularly when people face common problems, they need to support each other with available tips. Superiors are often talked *about* in rather familiar terms; when talking *directly* to them the language is care-fully controlled. Those who have access to news and impart it to others gain in importance. These are just some of the reasons why informal communication arises—supplementing, expanding, and adding human interest to the impersonal formal sources. While everything that gets reported on the grapevine is not instru-mentally useful, the more information individuals have, the greater their chance of using it to their own advantage.

Several patterns have been observed in grapevine communication (see figure 5-1 below). In the *cluster chain*, a selective informal pattern, messages are passed

FIGURE 5-1   Grapevine Communication Networks

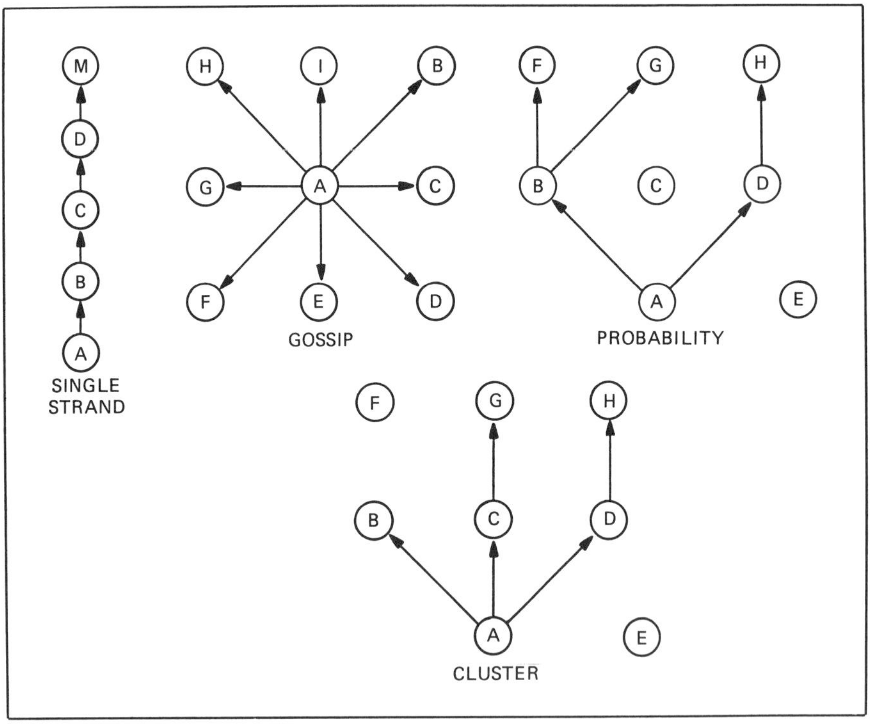

Source: Reprinted by permission of the *Harvard Business Review*. An exhibit from "Manage-ment Communication and the Grapevine," by Keith Davis (September/October 1963). Copy-right © 1963 by the President and Fellows of Harvard College; all rights reserved.

on to some people and other people are deliberately bypassed. This occurs where there are cliques. In the *single strand* pattern, information is passed from one person to another along a line of people. This might occur in a prison, where individual movements are restricted and a human chain must be made. The *gossip channel* is one in which one person will tell all of the others what he or she has found out. Finally, and conveniently, there is the *probability channel*, which encompasses communication that takes place on a random basis, for example, someone happens to be at the right place at the right time to hear something.

This typology is suggestive rather than comprehensive. Though grapevines are difficult to observe and study unless one is an insider, they can tell us much about human interaction in an organization.

The Functions of Secrecy

Just as inside knowledge is useful, so secrecy can serve to enhance power. Secrecy, the withholding of knowledge, can be simply saying no more or no less than is officially required. This deprives the person receiving the communication of important informal knowledge. A worker or student picks up valuable information about the location of needed resources, hiding places, particular teachers or supervisors, which rules can be broken and which must be followed. The information can be shared or withheld from others. Feedback can be withheld from superiors, keeping them in ignorance of dissatisfaction and possible job actions.

Lower participants who are favored and thereby sponsored by their superiors may be fed useful information unavailable to others in their position, privileged information. Graduate students have to form faculty committees to supervise their dissertations. Where faculty factions exist, the students need to find out which professors are apt to get along on a committee and which may engage in combat through the students. If they have developed informal relations with particular professors, this information may be imparted.

Elsewhere we have mentioned the importance of secrecy to firms that are in close competition in developing scientific fields. The competitive edge may be lost if other firms gain access to recently discovered improvements. Since deviance arises when temptations are great, we can be sure that a great deal of industrial spying takes place between organizations nationally and internationally.

OPPOSITION TO ORGANIZATIONAL AUTHORITY: *THE CASE OF WHISTLE-BLOWING*

Bureaucracies, private and public, are small societies or states, microcosms of the world in which they exist. Opportunities for inefficiency, mistakes, and deviance are plentiful. And just as street crime is more visible than white-collar crime, so the deviant acts of lower participants may be more observable and less protected than those of higher-ups within organizations. Power persists for many reasons, not least of which is because it often includes the power to protect itself from exposure. The many cases in which public officials and businessmen have actually been prosecuted for white-collar crimes may seem to give the lie to this statement; however, we also find that their illegal activities often persisted for quite some time before exposure. In the society at large, political parties serve a function by ferreting out the misdeeds of their opponents. Within an organization, there is less likely to be a clear-cut system of semiequal factions; there is also the desire to save the public image of the organization by keeping conflict internal.

Nonetheless, opposition to organizational authority sometimes surfaces. Studies have recently been made of professionals employed in private organizations and public agencies who go outside of them "to expose what they feel are illegal, inefficient, immoral or unethical practices of their employing organizations" (Perrucci et al., 1980:149).

Opposition usually starts internally; attempts are made to report superiors by going over their heads to higher authorities. This tactic may prove so unsuccessful that the persistent critic takes the case to the public—a tactic called whistle-blowing. Of course, we do not know how many individuals are willing to take this dangerous step. The fate of whistle-blowers is often unfortunate, as we can see by examining a few real cases.

Consider the case of three engineers who were fired from the San Francisco Bay Area Rapid Transit District (BART) in 1973. They were concerned that the automatic train control system was not safe and expressed their concerns to management in oral and written form over an extended period of time. Despite a tacit acknowledgment that their concern had some basis in fact, it seemed evident that little was going to be done to correct the problems. That condition appears to be an essential one in the progression toward whistle-blowing (Perrucci et al., 1980:158). The engineers gradually took bolder and bolder steps, eventually hiring a private engineering consultant who provided them with a written report supporting their claims. This they took to a new member of BART's board of directors.

As they got bolder, the engineers felt that management was getting more intransigent. Management came to view them not as troublesome employees but as a dangerous element in the organization. The progression of events was such that:

> With each action and reaction, the chance of turning back declined; the conflicting parties had "burned their bridges" behind them. The question was no longer whether or not the three engineers would go public, but when they would do it, and with whom they would seek to form a coalition. (Perrucci et al., 1980:161)

According to the social scientists who studied this case, the new board member used the issue for his own political purposes, going public with it before trying to work with other members of the board. Soon the names of the three engineers were known, and they were fired. Although the situation then got a great deal of publicity, it did little to help the whistle-blowers. They remained unemployed for extended periods, had difficulty getting suitable jobs, and experienced financial and personal problems.

Another case of a whistle-blower, Karen Silkwood, had a tragic outcome. A worker who had exposed lax health and safety procedures at the Kerr-

McGee Cimarron River plutonium plant, Silkwood died in an unexplained automobile crash on her way to present her information to a newspaper (Weinstein, 1979).

Returning to the research on the three BART engineers, the authors conclude:

> Whistle-blowers receive little protection from the external powers that they originally contact for help, resulting either in their being fired by their organization or, if not fired, experiencing reductions in organizational status and power. (Perrucci et al., 1980:162)

The next case concerns employees of the Human Resources Administration of New York City, a superagency a little less than twenty years old when the problem surfaced in 1984. The agency was intended to unify the services of several others that have more or less the same clients: the Department of Welfare, the Youth Board, and other employment and antipoverty programs. Originally focused largely on employment and job training, the Human Resources Administration was faced with attending to serious new social problems such as housing the homeless and investigating child abuse.

The number of child abuse cases investigated yearly had climbed to the unbelievable figure of 40,000 by 1984. An employee, Irwin Levin, alleged that some cases had been handled negligently, resulting in the deaths of a number of children. He was subsequently suspended and demoted. Meanwhile, another employee, Joan Stake, wrote a report confirming Levin's allegations. Finally, a city investigation in spring 1984 found that social workers in Brooklyn had indeed been seriously negligent in child abuse cases, which resulted in the deaths of nine children.

Levin was subsequently reinstated by Mayor Edward Koch, but Stake was fired. Stake told the newspapers and city officials confirmed that she had been fired because "she was too emotional and lacked the necessary investigative skills" (*New York Times*, August 5, 1984, p. E7). The mayor defended her firing.

The Human Resources Administration also figured in publicized allegations of sexual molestation at HRA-funded day-care centers in the summer of 1984. The mayor publicly and emotionally decried the role of the press in publicizing these cases of alleged child sexual molestation, including rape. To the regret of the mayor, the head of the agency, James A. Krauskopf, felt impelled to resign because he felt his effectiveness had been impaired. Joan Stake was still out of a job, too.

Apparently the press had been effective in arousing the public. In a memorandum dated August 15, 1984, and circulated widely, Mayor Koch explained that he had taken action to have Stake reinstated in her position. He cited the public's perception of her as a whistle-blower as an important factor in his decision. Explaining the reasons for the reinstatement, he wrote:

> First, although I have confidence in the Department of Investigation's findings that whatever personnel action taken regarding Ms. Stake is not as a result of 'whistleblowing,' it is apparent that the public perception of her situation does not draw such a distinction.

The public interest in having a clear and certain policy to protect whistleblowers is of such importance, in my judgment, that I believe we should dispel any confusion and where there is a doubt err if we must on the side of more, rather than less protection.

Second, as you know, it is not my policy to tell a commissioner who can be hired or who should be fired, but I make an exception here. While it is understandable that prior years of service or human decency might require a reasonable period of notice when dismissing an employee, it doesn't make sense to me that Ms. Stake would have been retained for over a year if she were incapable of performing her duties and carrying out her responsibilities.

SUMMARY

This chapter has examined the distinctions between power and authority, two very important concepts. Power involves the capability of an individual or group to overcome resistance in achieving a desired result. Authority is formal power. Communication is an important vehicle of power and authority; it occurs both formally and informally, horizontally, vertically, and laterally. Authors such as Weber who stress authority tend to take compliance much for granted. Barnard and Etzioni both examine, in different ways, conditions under which lower participants comply with orders. Barnard stresses the nature of the communication—whether it can be understood, whether it appears to be in line with the purpose of the organization, whether it appears to be compatible with the receiver's personal interest, and whether that person is mentally and physically able to comply.

For Etzioni, three congruent types of compliance—moral, calculative, and alienative—are related, respectively, to three types of power—normative, remunerative, and coercive. Etzioni's focus on power highlights the fact that formal authority, while important, is only one type of power. The concept of authority, as used in organization studies, often overlooks force and economic incentives, individual needs, the power of subgroups and organizations, and the power of subordinates and peers.

Many sources of power were discussed that overlooked or omitted the elements just mentioned in considerations of authority. Conditions determining power and its tendency to persist were also explained. Finally, aspects of communication such as official symbolism and the informal grapevine were seen as, at least partly, tools of power. Secrecy is complementary to communication, for the selective withholding and passing on of information can also be used as a mechanism of power.

Finally, a case study of opposition to organizational authority—the case of whistle-blowing—illustrated how difficult it really is to go over the head of an ineffective or dishonest superior.

6

STATUS, ROLE, AND
THE DIVISION OF LABOR

The Division of Labor in Society and in Organizations
    The Problem: Who Should Do What?
    Status and Role: Units in the Division of Labor
    Societal Statuses and Status Sets
    The Earliest Bases of Division of Labor: Sex, Age, Race, and Ethnicity
    Modern Society: The Increase in Division of Labor and Specialization
    Latent Identities in Organizations
    How Nontraditional People Gain Entry
Cooperative and Conflict Perspectives on Status Systems
    The Official Division of Labor in Organizations: Its Expression in Status and
      Role
    The Cooperative Perspective on Status Systems
    The Conflict Perspective on Status Systems
    Formal and Informal Negotiations Over Rules
    Additional Sources of Conflict in Role Relationships
The Informal Division of Labor as an Adjustive Mechanism
    Adding or Eliminating Obligations
    Patterns of Mutual Aid: Helping Out
    The Sloughing Off of Dirty Work
    Voluntary Action Taken in Emergency Situations
Informal Organization in the Women's Prison: A Case Study
Summary

THE DIVISION OF LABOR IN SOCIETY AND IN ORGANIZATIONS

The Problem: Who Should Do What?

The division of labor in society and in organizations is often perceived as a "cooperative system." As Bredemeier and Stephenson state: "Instead of meeting the survival problems of nourishment and protection individually, as for example bears and turtles do, termites and people meet them cooperatively through a division of labor" (1965:28).

Consequently, according to these authors, each society must solve the question of: "how is the labor to be divided, and which members are to do what in the division of labor?" (1965:28).

Whether group living is considered a cooperative venture or a constant war for survival, the group must be able to count on someone to perform such basic tasks as growing food or hunting, creating a means of shelter, or caring for and teaching the young. Each society that survives develops a regularized system for dividing up among its members all the tasks that have to be done to maintain it.

Similarly, but even more deliberately, organizations lay out their necessary tasks and assign them to different types of participants. However, since each organization exists within a larger society, each mirrors that society to some degree, just as we tried to show in chapter 1 that the bureaucratized society reflects its organizational structures. By examining the division of labor in societies we gain insights into the same process in its component parts (R. Hall, 1972: 49-53).

First let us review the meaning of two basic concepts, status and role, which link individuals to organizations.

Status and Role: Units in the Division of Labor

The division of labor in organizations finds expression in its official system of statuses and roles.[1] The status label, such as manager, technician, nurse, student, or client, symbolizes to others a relative position within the total system. Line positions, those involved in production, are ranked within the hierarchy. There is a line of command from the boss down to the worker. Staff positions, those that provide advisory or specialist functions, are not usually in this formal chain of command.

In addition to specific duties or obligations, a given degree of official power, prestige, and material reward is attached to each status. Formal statuses conveniently provide individuals with the official version of their positions in the division of labor. Thus they offer a guideline against which the relative standing of each can be assessed. For the organization, division of labor and status systems provide an official structure, a prescribed framework for operation.

Role is a concept closely related to that of status. Consider how *role* is used

---

[1] Much of the discussion of status and role will be familiar to the reader who has taken sociology courses. It is included in order to familiarize others with these concepts basic to the study of organizations.

in drama, as the playing out of a part. Obviously different actors may play the same role differently.

In real life we do not have written scripts, but we are expected to behave "properly," that is, in ways appropriate to our particular statuses. Because each person has statuses in many groups, he or she has many expected roles attached to these statuses. What do we mean by expected roles? Children expect a parent to provide for them economically, to be loving and caring, and yet to insist on good behavior. Students expect a teacher to teach, to test them as necessary, and to treat them fairly. These examples also demonstrate that certain roles are recurrently linked to others in reciprocal interaction. Role players that are so linked are called *role partners*. The things that different role partners expect include both instrumental (task-oriented) and affective (emotional) components. The teacher who is a parent switches roles in different times and places, just as we all do. In every case acting human beings bring their own life experiences and cultural backgrounds to bear in interpreting and fulfilling role expectations (Reissman, 1949).

To summarize, for every status we have in particular groups, such as worker at a plant, student at a college, son or daughter, we have role partners and a range of correct behaviors. Some roles are more limited and constrained than others; some provide more leeway for individual variation. As Etzioni's compliance model suggests (see chapters 3 and 5), it is easier to "get into" certain roles than others and normal to resist low-status or stigmatized roles that have been forced upon us.

FIGURE 6-1 A Status Set

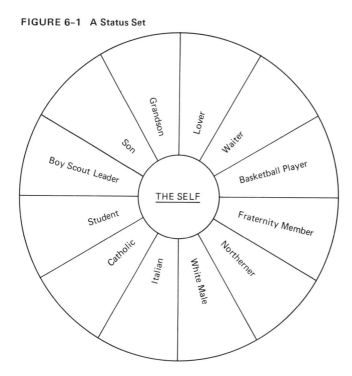

Societal Statuses and Status Sets

In addition to *achieved* statuses, such as those described above, individuals also have certain societal statuses based on *ascribed characteristics*, such as sex, age, race, and physical appearance (note figure 6-1). Human beings are taught to act as males or females, as children or adults, and to behave towards others in terms of *their* ascribed characteristics. The admonition to a boy, "You're acting like a girl!" suggests deviance.

An individual's *status set* includes all of his or her statuses at a particular time in personal history. When acting in a given setting the status relevant to that setting is supposed to dominate; the others, to remain *latent* or in the background. The student who has just broken off a love relationship is *supposed* to put out of mind the lost role partner and be attentive in class. Obviously, latent statuses are not always easily ignored either by ourselves or by others. Indeed, *role performance*, how one actually plays out a role, frequently differs from the way others think we should perform in the role. Informal patterns and variations inevitably develop out of the interaction among human beings, the various pressures they face, and changing organizational needs. The informal patterns that center around an organization's division of labor and official designations of status and role will be examined more closely later in this chapter.

The Earliest Bases of Division of Labor: Sex, Age, Race, and Ethnicity

Anthropologists have uncovered great variations in the ways in which societies decide "who is to do what." Both internal developments such as new inventions and external factors such as culture contact enter into the evolution of each society's practices.

Ascribed statuses such as sex and age are the most primitive bases for differentiating roles. Sexual divisions of labor vary tremendously, but each society tends to develop conventions about "men's work" and "women's work" (Rosaldo, 1974: 18). These conventions gradually become normative and take on the value of being "right" and "natural" (Boserup, 1970:15).

However, patterns considered desirable in one society at one point in history are not only *not* natural for all classes of that society but are subject to change. The once strong norm that middle-class mothers should not work outside the home has weakened in contemporary America in response to rapid inflation and an increased need for workers in the service sector. By 1980 almost two-thirds of women with children between the ages of six and eighteen were employed, and half of the women with children under age six were in the labor force (Fox & Hesse-Biber, 1984, chap. 5).

In many African nations women were essential participants in labor, as the primary agriculturalists (Boserup, 1970, chap. 1). However, one of the effects of "development," the exporting of Western technology and values to less developed nations, has been a diffusion of norms about "men's" and "women's" work.

Women's participation in agriculture in such countries has been reduced (Boserup, 1970).

Age has been another important basis for division of labor. The elderly in various societies have often had such special roles as repositories of wisdom, maintainers of oral history, and caretakers of children. Many traditional societies are clearly age-graded and have ceremonies to celebrate the individual's passage from one age group into another. Such *rites de passage* signify the taking on of new rights and duties related to the new age status (E. Hughes, 1958:13).

Age grades are less clearly defined in contemporary American society, but the recognition of differing social tasks for different age groups is familiar. The education-oriented parent tells his or her child, "Your job is to study," and may indeed monitor, judge, reward, and punish the child's job performance. Informally, "ageism" operates in both the work and social spheres, with the cards especially stacked against older women.

Another historic division of labor grew out of war and conquest when persons from defeated nations became a subordinate or even slave class, differentiated from the dominants by race or culture. In modern days similar racial and ethnic stratification of the labor force results when foreign workers are imported to fill particular labor needs. Certain types of jobs become unofficially linked to certain groups. As Shibutani and Kwan put it: "In many communities people in different ethnic categories perform different tasks, have different property rights, and get unequal shares of the rewards" (1965:169).

Ascribed characteristics such as those discussed above still affect the ways people are placed in societies. Persons of a "certain kind" are expected to do fixed kinds of work (paid or unpaid) and are not expected to do other kinds. Different degrees of prestige, power, and material benefits are distributed accordingly.

Modern Society: The Increase in Division of Labor and Specialization

The growth of modern societies is marked by increasing division of labor and specialization (Durkheim, 1933). Tasks once done within the home, such as weaving cloth or educating the young, are now the work of paid specialists. Another trend, related to money economies, is the tendency to think of "work" as only whatever is *paid for* as work, and to exclude household or unpaid family labor. Certain theorists challenge this view as biased and inaccurate (e.g., G. Miller, 1980; Benston, 1977). They stress the importance of household labor as "socially necessary production" that supplements the efforts of the family's paid workers (Benston, 1977:218). Volunteer work is another form of unpaid labor that contributes essential services to societies.

It is useful, then, to consider as "labor" all that has to be done to keep society operating, whether it is paid or unpaid. Similarly, labor in organizations includes everything that has to be done to keep it going, whether or not the task appears in a job description. This definition makes it possible to look past the formal allocation of jobs in organizations and to observe the ways in which divisions of work actually develop among role players. In the occupation of waiting on tables there are many tasks that may or may not be made explicit, such as sweeping up or using interpersonal skill in rebuffing disorderly customers without angering them.

Taking the student status as an example, it was noted earlier that this status involves such obligations as paying attention—or at least appearing to do so—and handing in assignments. The classroom could not exist without students, and so they have a part in the division of labor in the school. A student receives rewards other than money for proper role behavior. Students may end up doing more than their own "work." For example, an informal student type sometimes known as a "brown-noser" takes pride in assisting teachers, happily doing such tasks as grading papers or taking attendance in the hopes of being rewarded with an A.

Latent Identities in Organizations

Ascribed status as part of latent identity.   How are society-wide ascribed statuses (age, sex, ethnicity) related to statuses in particular organizations? A closed system approach (see chapter 1) presents the view that organizational status is based on ability and qualifications—on achievement alone. Role players are sought who can fulfill the requirements of each position, which is clearly delineated on the organization chart. All statuses are tied together through authority and communication patterns.

Others believe that a society's system of ascribed status enters the picture in significant ways. Such statuses form part of the latent identities of various role players, accompanying them even when not relevant to performance.

More than twenty-five years ago an organizational sociologist admonished against the curious tendency to ignore this reality:

> At the present time, little systematic attention is given to the functioning of either latent identities or roles. It is too easy to focus on the more evident manifest identities and roles in a group. As a result, even in a world on which Freudian theory has made its impact, many sociologists give little indication of the fact that the people they study in offices, factories, schools, or hospitals are also males and females. The sociologists' assumption often seems to be that the latent identities and roles are as irrelevant as the people whom they are studying conventionally pretend. The fact seems to be, however, that these do affect group behavior. (Gouldner, 1957:285)

How latent identities operate in selection.   An important way in which latent identities affect organizational life is by influencing the selection of people into organizational slots. Although selection is supposedly based on rational criteria and universalism, such as having a high school diploma or passing a certain test, it often reflects traditional factors (Alvarez, 1979:8–9). Sometimes these are readily acknowledged; for example, colleges openly prefer to admit the children of alumni. A bond of mutual loyalty and support serves to create advantage for the children of the college-educated. In contrast, members of racial minorities frequently claim that they are overselected for prisons. That is, they claim that courts are more prone to judge them guilty and sentence them to prison than they do the white and middle class. Accumulated evidence supports their position (Brown 1979:355–374).

Latent identities are taken into account in determining preferred types for particular organizational positions in less obvious ways. In the sifting and selecting of applicants there are tacit notions of what kind of person best fits, belongs, or would feel comfortable in a particular position. This process was brilliantly illuminated by Everett Hughes a number of decades ago (1945). What some call latent identities may actually be so salient that they are unofficial requirements tacked on to the formal ones. They are master status-determining traits. A master status-determining trait is one that "tends to overpower, in most crucial situations, any other characteristics which might run counter to it" (E. Hughes, 1945:357). Figure 6-2 illustrates the probable saliency of race to a real estate broker, despite his

FIGURE 6–2   Race—A Latent Status or a Master Status?

'Checkers' Visiting Brokers
Spot Exclusionary Practices

Source: *New York Times*, July 21, 1979, p. D1. Copyright © 1979 by The New York Times Company. Reprinted by permission.

outward facade. To detect housing discrimination, white "checkers" have sometimes been used to apply for apartments or houses recently refused to black clients (see figure 6-2).

In the United States the concept of secretary includes a person who not only has specific skills but who is also a woman. In the 1980s, 99 percent of secretarial positions continued to be held by females. Our case study in chapter 7 cites the fact that the proportion of women holding managerial jobs has remained at a nearly constant level since 1947, and that only 1 percent of positions as high as vice-president are held by women. Women executives in business account for less than 2 percent of all top officers of major companies (Hess, Markson, & Stein, 1985:202; see chap. 7).

Handicapped persons are another category who have a master status-determining trait that tends to overpower their technical qualifications. They have followed the example of racial minorities and women in actively trying to combat the discrimination they face.

To summarize, individuals selected into organizations have to meet the informal as well as the formal expectations for positions. Racially and sexually stratified work forces are frequently found. Thus the organization expresses and reflects the understood ascribed status system of the society, while claiming to honor achieved status as "the rule" for hiring and upgrading.

Black people and women in the United States, through their social movement efforts, have challenged the discriminatory patterns based on ascribed status. The federal government has acknowledged the operation of the master status-determining traits of race and sex by requiring organizations to provide equal opportunity and, through affirmative action measures, to reverse the usual preference for white males in desirable positions. Those who advocate a "color blind" or "sex blind" approach to hiring and promotion ignore the fact that, without intervention, the usual racial and sexual biases will probably persist.

Latent identities and informal groups.   The latent identities of individuals help to shape their response to official statuses. A wide variety of background characteristics in addition to sex, age, and race may prove relevant. James D. Thompson (1976) notes:

> Each individual recruited into an organization brings to it not only the particular skills, beliefs, dispositions, and the like that are appropriate but also talents, beliefs or attitudes that are irrelevant to the technology. Individuals may distinguish among themselves on a great many criteria, separating old from young, Yankees from rebels, Republicans from Democrats, friendly drinkers from abstainers. Racial and ethnic origin, family lineage, socioeconomic class and religious beliefs are frequently applied. (p. 25)

The particular identities most relevant for interaction may vary from one organizational setting to another. Informal cliques tend to develop based on one or more of these differentiating factors. For example, research on female prisoners (to which we return later in this chapter), disclosed very strong ties among women who came from the same home town. Once having located each other, "homeys" developed patterns of mutual aid and obligation (Giallombardo, 1966). Such closeness insured that an inmate's reputation in her home town would be protected.

Mention was made earlier of the sharp division that sometimes appears between those who are regular workers and those who are summer or temporary ones. A status distinction is similarly made between "direct" employees and "job-shoppers," those recruited by an agency rather than a specific employer, and farmed out as needed.

It is frequently believed that diversity in latent status characteristics creates a potential for conflict or uncertainty (J. Thompson, 1976; Kanter, 1977:58). According to Thompson, "This is particularly true of organizations which have ideological objectives, such as those with a reform mission which require strong commitment to organizational values" (1976:28). Thompson suggests: "This organization can exercise care in preadmission screening, with emphasis less on technical abilities than on latent-role factors such as 'character' " (1976:29)—that is, it will choose someone who is likely to be loyal to the group.

A local enterprise, such as a community hospital or a community college, tends to be restricted in clientele or market to the same territory that supplies the labor force. This is another situation in which latent characteristics are so important that technical requirements for position become downgraded. In a well-known study, management in a gypsum plant showed preference in choosing personnel to local, respected community people over "city" people (Gouldner, 1954a). Here one's community background was used as an auxiliary status requirement.

How Nontraditional People Gain Entry

We pointed out that various groups in the United States have challenged as discriminatory the operation of such master status-determining traits as race, sex, age, or physical handicap. They have tried to minimize the operation of these factors in job selection and promotion. The government's affirmative action mandates (now being revised) have, in the recent past, placed its official support against traditional use of these characteristics (see chapter 11). Positive rather than negative evaluation of such traits as being a women or being an Hispanic is officially required. Consequently, many organizations are faced with pressure to modify previously accepted unofficial practices to which they have been accustomed (R. Hall, 1977: 306). Laws are important external constraints on organizations, but legal efforts do not always bring about immediate or lasting change. There are many ways to circumvent laws. "New types" of status occupants are faced with longstanding expectations and assumptions based on their social identities. Though qualified according to universalistic standards, people continue to meet resistance for being too old, too young, members of racial or religious minorities, or handicapped.[2]

Change sometimes comes about through the operation of impersonal factors

---

[2] This issue is probably given more emphasis in our book than in a number of others dealing with complex organizations. In U.S. society every major work and educational institution has had to come to terms with the impact of equal opportunity policies; we find their relevance undeniable.

rather than through new laws. War causes labor shortages, and formerly excluded but qualified individuals are welcomed, even if only temporarily. Changes in the demand for and supply of labor also have their effects. Consider, for example, the current use of foreign-trained interns in American hospitals. Their acceptance has been sparked by the shortage of American-trained interns (Schaefer, 1979:117), although their credentials are questioned periodically. In times of shortage, auxiliary status characteristics are discarded, and all persons who can actually perform the job are employed. In time the new source of labor may even come to be considered the proper or expected type for the particular position. The "feminization" of certain occupations refers to such a transition. However, the earliest pioneers from a group encounter problems related to their differentness (see Kanter, 1977, chap. 8).

The notions of latent status and preferred types are also applicable to customers and clients. While many organizations profess to treat all customers and clients alike, their preferences may be thinly disguised. When I made telephone inquiries about a professional photograph I was told quite directly by a firm specializing in executive photography that they only photographed men.

Pricing is one way to assure a "desirable" (high-status) clientele, but more subtle devices are also used to welcome or discourage certain classes of customers. The professional–client or salesperson–customer relation is easily affected by the social identities of the two individuals in the transaction. The welfare client probably does not expect deferential or even polite treatment from the government social worker; the wife of the hospital board member would be surprised if hospital workers did not treat her extremely well. Some interesting variations occur. One case in which welfare clients tended to receive better treatment occurred when civil rights activists had a pipeline into jobs in the welfare agency (personal interview).

Now let us turn to an examination of the internal status and role systems of organizations.

COOPERATIVE AND CONFLICT PERSPECTIVES ON STATUS SYSTEMS

The Official Division of Labor in Organizations: Its Expression in Status and Role

Hierarchies and inequalities of power, prestige, and reward in formal organizations appear to be inevitable. It is also obvious and has been verified empirically (Pugh et al., 1968) that they vary in different types of organizations.

In reaction to the prevalence of these inequalities some communes and social movement groups, experimenting with new organizational forms, have made extraordinary efforts to minimize status and power distinctions among members (J. Hall, 1978). We shall concentrate not on these variations but on the general characteristics of official systems.

The desire for expertise and efficiency makes specialization and the division of labor necessary in large groups. Official duties are divided among a number of positions rather than having each person do everything. In other words, the status and role system represents the division of labor as it is supposed to be. Of course, the specific ways in which duties can be divided up may be more or less flexible. Those who emphasize the importance of an organization's technology maintain that it provides limitations on the organization of work and division of labor.

Status and role systems are of great interest to sociologists but do not always receive specific attention from organizational theorists. An exception is Chester Barnard who, as President of the New Jersey Bell Telephone Company, wrote at length on the functions and pathologies of status systems in formal organizations. Viewing organizations as cooperative systems, Barnard (1946) described status systems as a needed mechanism for coordinating efforts, positive for both the organization and the individual. He admitted that sometimes they got out of hand and became dysfunctional. Some of his positions are debatable in today's society, but they are worth examining.

The Cooperative Perspective on Status Systems

Status is a way of making three things clear: the importance of various kinds of work, the difficulty of various kinds of work, and the differences in the ability of the workers.

Some statuses and roles are seen as more demanding and as requiring persons of greater ability. Greater mental ability is here implied: "The importance of the work . . . establishes the importance of the position that 'seeks' those of exceptional ability" (Barnard, 1946:56). Ideally, there is a good fit between the importance and difficulty of the work and the qualifications of the person selected to fill it.

Barnard claims that lower participants in a structure prefer to believe that those giving orders are highly qualified. The status system makes it easier for them to assume this. A person is generally much more willing to obey "doctor's orders" than those of a layperson giving the same advice, although in more recent years skepticism about the motivations of experts has increased (Haug & Sussman, 1969: 153-161).

Status is publicized and reinforced in many familiar ways, such as ceremonies of induction and appointment, insignia, and titles of office. To use some examples from the military, the new recruit is sworn in, wears a uniform designating his or her lowly status, may add symbols of better status if he or she should get promoted, and will at that time be elevated to the title of "private first class."

In the case of management people, the symbols of status are also very concrete:

> The use or nonuse of restricted quarters, automobiles, chauffeurs, private offices, private secretaries and other perquisites in various combinations, time clocks, etc., provide a complex code that describes the system of status in effect, thoroughly understood by the initiated and fairly easily sensed by the outside observer. (Barnard, 1946:51)

The meaning of perquisites, referred to some time ago by Barnard in the excerpt above, has not changed much in succeeding years, although some new "perks" have been created. When government tries to limit certain executive perks, in the interest of tax reform, others seem to replace them. For example, one proposal in 1985 was to limit the tax deduction for business lunches to twenty-five dollars plus half the cost of anything above that. A *Fortune* article advised its readers not to worry, reassuring them: "Consultants on benefits are confident that most perks will survive" (Kessler, 1985:26). Noncash benefits ranging from paid club memberships to free personal computers and free financial counseling are some of the present rewards provided high-status executives. Company cars are still a most favored perk. As *Fortune* points out, such executives can readily afford to purchase expensive cars, but that is not the issue. Rather, the "benefit" symbolizes how valuable the person is to the firm.

One need not be an executive to understand status symbols. A former cleaning woman in the sociology department was an apt student of status differentials. Although she had no private secretaries or chauffeurs to dispense, she always advised younger faculty members when it was their turn to move to larger or better-situated offices and made sure that desks and other equipment were suitably distributed according to academic rank. (Obviously her title of cleaning woman did not cover her informal functions.)

Insignia, uniforms, and offices are symbols and they are functional just as is the division of labor, according to Barnard. Symbols have the effect of credentials, creating expectations about the skills, ability, and relative power an individual has. Should you call someone by his or her first name, or by title? Should you say hello first or wait for the other to do so? Knowledge of another's status cues us into proper role behavior. Cases of mistaken identity occur when symbols are not clear, and they can prove embarrassing. A customer may be mistaken for a salesclerk, a teacher for a student. Physical or social segregation of people of unequal status may prevent such mistakes. Fewer cases of mistaken identity can be anticipated in the informal milieu of a restroom if one knows that the higher ranks have their own facilities. The usual status barriers are temporarily removed in the Mardi Gras and in the democratizing atmosphere of the once-a-year Christmas party.

What are some of the dysfunctions or pathologies that occur when status systems are entrenched? An official who has become closely identified with the organization may be difficult to remove, even if incompetent. Flexibility and adaptability are reduced by a rigid status system, such as one that produces bureaucratic personalities (Merton, 1952). Status systems may be of such concern that they become means, not ends, as in the following case:

> Some jobs . . . lost their meaning and became, instead, stepping-stones on the path to upper management. Sales was the prime example of a management supply function, much to the annoyance of those who wanted to create a 'professional sales force' and pride in the sales job. (Kanter, 1977:130)

Kanter reports that a sales manager said, "People think they have to move, to progress to gain respect, so even if they love selling, they think they're going to have to move on" (1977:130).

The whole system may seem undemocratic if status distinctions are too rigid. Many persons would not agree with Barnard that those of exceptional ability always have the opportunity to rise.

Negative tendencies may be inevitable, but some organizational theorists are certain that they can be overcome since organizations and people can be changed. This point of view is aptly described by Tausky (1978):

> For theorists grounded in the cooperative perspective, organizations are potentially capable of obtaining members' commitment and high levels of work effort as a result of "proper" organizational and task design. Workers would then exercise self-control on behalf of collective ends, rather than self-interest on behalf of personal advantage. (p. 91)

One way suggested to accomplish this is to add greater opportunities for decision making to the worker's role (Bennis, 1970; Whyte et al., 1983). Flattening hierarchies would help to do this by eliminating some levels of supervision (Kanter, 1977). Another hope is to find ways of transforming individuals and their values to make them consistent with those of the organization (Scott & Hart, 1979:50–80).

The Conflict Perspective on Status Systems

A contrasting viewpoint emphasizes the normality of actual and potential conflict in organizations. How are status and role systems seen from this vantage point? Here is a succinct statement of the position:

> From the conflict perspective, discord—particularly between hierarchical levels—is seen to arise from the different and divergent material interests of organization members. Bargaining, negotiation, and power come into play on the tension-producing issue of who gets what. (Tausky, 1978:91)

The unequal reward aspect of status systems is viewed as problematic. Why should one worker advance and another not? Why should supervisors be paid more than workers? Quite often the answer is based on another recurrent source of conflict: the differing interests of persons located at various places in the hierarchy. It is generally assumed that human beings want to have some control over their pace of work and that they have their own ideas about what is "fair" (Crozier, 1964, chap. 6). Management, too, will have its ideas about the quantity and quality of output; rewarding those who meet the organization's standards is a way of responding to these conflicting interests.

A popular viewpoint about work systems is that evaluation and reward of some kind are necessary under both capitalism and socialism (Tausky, 1978:92). There is a division of labor in both economic systems; hence, differing perspectives arise. On a trip to Bulgaria in 1980, I visited several factories and at one asked about the role of the trade union. The reply was that the trade union encourages worker productivity. The anecdote confirms the well-known fact that in socialist countries as elsewhere individuals do not necessarily work up to officially required standards (see also Haug & Dofny, 1977).

Marxist theory, of course, makes a sharp distinction between the owners of the means of production and those who have only their own labor to sell. Under capitalism, workers and management are expected to be natural adversaries. Owners try to maximize profit by extracting as much labor as possible at a given cost. Workers respond by developing peer group solidarity and by creating informal tactics to control the amount produced and pace of work (Roy, 1952). The pressure to do this is great when tasks are routine and monotonous:

> Workers who have been restricted by scientific work organization to a completely stereotyped task use every available means to regain enough unpredictability in their behavior to enhance their low bargaining power. Also, their struggle for making out is one of the essential elements of their strategy. (Crozier, 1964:162)

"Making out" is a way workers have of regulating their pace. They produce very rapidly to accomplish a fair day's work in order then to have time to loaf or take care of personal matters. Despite the hard effort required, they can show that they have retained some control.

Isolation or segregation of various strata from each other leads to the development of strong informal peer groups. The greater the barriers between statuses, the more need there seems to be for internal solidarity among those of the same status (Coser, 1956:87). The "staff–inmate split" of total institutions, where sharp official power and status difference exist between such categories as prisoners and inmates, provides the best example (Goffman, 1961:7-9). Powerful informal systems with clear-cut informal roles develop among the inmates (Leger & Stratton, 1977), who are thus able to regain some degree of control over their daily lives.

The prison tries to motivate conformity through a privilege system. Since some of the taken-for-granted comforts of daily life, such as the ability to brew a cup of coffee or have a cigarette, are restricted, access to such things becomes a privilege doled out to the worthy. Prison employees lose their monopoly over such rewards when certain members of the peer group manage to become a source of contraband supplies. It should be no surprise that informal peer groups are universally found in all types of organizations (R. Hall, 1977:113).

Formal and Informal Negotiations Over Rules

The trade union is a more formal device for the expression of conflicting interests in capitalist societies. Regularized ways of mediating conflict are provided through the bargaining process. Accommodation between the claims of management and workers is created and re-created through the formulation of new agreements and rules. Once reached, these agreements become part of the formal structure, serve as a reference point for both parties, are binding on both, and hence constrain both.

In fact, just as agreements made in collective bargaining are used by all sides, so can other rules be used. Here is one description of the way that supervisors and workers relate to rules:

> Officially, each supports the rules, and puts as much pressure as possible on the other side to oblige the latter to obey these rules, while it is fighting to preserve its own area of freedom and making covert deals in defiance of the same rules it is promoting. (Crozier, 1964:161)

This quotation illustrates two additional points. First, negotiation and bargaining between members of different status categories is an ongoing process used to resolve conflicts in interest. Second, it shows the interplay and mutual dependence of formal and informal modes of behavior. One cannot bargain and exchange if there is nothing about which to bargain.

Additional Sources of Conflict in Role Relationships

Potential conflicts in organizations are, of course, not limited to persons facing each other across different hierarchical levels. Conflicts and misunderstandings can occur between any two people in interaction. However, our interest is not in what is sometimes labeled personality conflict, but rather in the tension-producing aspects of certain typical role relationships. Role strain occurs when performing one's roles produces stress that cannot be fully relieved through legitimate means (Grusky, 1963:26). Four types of conflict will be discussed, the last somewhat different than the first three. They are:

1. Conflict due to the interdependence of workers, including those due to the sharing of work places or responsibilities
2. Role conflict, where the demands on people in particular organizational positions are diverse and conflicting, or where there is such role overload that the individual cannot meet obligations
3. Conflict deriving from the differing perspectives of role partners
4. Organization–community conflict that spills over into the organization internally

Conflict due to interdependence. One aspect of interdependence that is often neglected is the potential for conflict between persons who must share the same equipment and facilities. If they are in face-to-face interaction, there is a good chance that informal norms will be developed between the positions. However, the persons involved may operate independently of each other in time.

Shift workers are a case in point. Each person on a shift must clean up after himself or herself, keep equipment and supplies available and in good order, and pass on any important information acquired during the shift. If they do not, the people on the next shift are affected in their capacity to perform.

Last-minute emergencies create extra work for members of one shift which, if left, add to the work of the next group. This is particularly odious if it happens to be "dirty work," such as cleaning up a spill or dealing with soiled linen. If an inordinate amount of supplies are used up on one shift, the next shift suffers. Supplies may be hoarded or hidden if they disappear too rapidly. Sharing relationships can often be developed with one's peers at other work stations, so that borrowing and lending tides over situations of shortage. Or the provision of supplies may become more formalized, requiring individuals to sign for each item.

Greater attention has been paid to situations in which different role players depend on each other in the performance of their work. If the role players have different perspectives, the scene is ripe for conflict. Hospitals provide a rich context for observations of this phenomenon. At least four important perspectives are in operation: those of the patient, the nonprofessional aide, the professional nurse, and the physician in charge (Freidson, 1980). Latent statuses of each may further complicate the picture, for a gamut of social identities will be found among these role players.

The weight of conflicting perspectives falls most heavily on certain roles, for example, the nurse. She must

> balance the individual physician's orders for the care of individual patients against the independent demands of the patients as such and against the need to manage an aggregate of cases in an administratively acceptable way. It is because . . . the nurse serves as an adjunct of both medical and administrative authority that she seems to be the intense focus of conflicting perspectives. (Friedson, 1980:185)

The professions emphasize personal judgment and individualized care. Bureaucratic administration substitutes rules and a sharp division of labor for the use of discretion. Bureaucratic efficiency requires processing large numbers of cases rather than giving people individualized attention. As student nurses move from school to hospital they find bureaucratic principles running counter to abstract professional ideals (Goldstein, 1954; Corwin, 1961). Nurses must make constant decisions about whose needs and demands should be met first. They can minimize conflict by developing a system of priorities. Characteristic stances taken by nurses lead to informal role types, such as the administrative nurse, who is oriented mostly to paperwork, or the Florence Nightingale type, dedicated to patients; or the "professionalizer," most oriented to the profession (Corwin, 1961; Goldstein, 1954; Habenstein & Christ, 1955). One way of easing potential conflict with physician role partners is to develop informal agreements and to set up mutual helping arrangements.

Another mediator role is that of waiters and waitresses. According to a study of waitresses, they are the conduit between individual customers and the cook, dependent on both sets of role partners (Whyte, 1948). Each customer has certain standards about food and the time needed to get service. Cooks have the administrative problem of getting out batches of digestible orders in a limited amount of time. They may use any number of ways, such as bawling out the waitress or drinking, to ease *their* tension. The waitress necessarily develops tactics to deal with both customers and cooks. Size of restaurant undoubtedly enters into the complexity or impersonality of these relationships. Changing the physical arrangements between waitresses and cooks, to minimize the appearance that the waitress is ordering the cook around, has been found helpful (Whyte, 1948).

Role conflict and role overload.   Middlewoman or middleman roles are prime ones for experiencing role conflict. But there are others. In the last chapter we referred to the dilemmas of persons subject to conflicting sources of authority. Such conflict often occurs in field placements or internships of various sorts where a trainee must please the theoretician (such as a teacher) and the practitioner (such as a supervisor) on the working scene. Taught to perform in an ideal way in the classroom, the student who applies the same standards in the real world may be unable to function. Inability to adapt to less than perfect conditions may result in personal stress or unfinished work. The frustrations of ambitious young teachers in urban classrooms are a case in point (Kozol, 1967). Teacher "burnout" is ever with us.

The potential for role conflict is great when an organization member has strong loyalties to other groups in the task environment. *Task environment* refers to that part of the total community or society that is "not indifferent to the organization" (J. Thompson, 1976), or in other words, affects or is affected by the organization.

The demands or expectations of other membership groups often run counter to those of the organization. Their effects are related to at least three factors: the degree of simultaneous exposure an individual has to both, the degree of identity he or she has with each, and the intensity of pressure from each. Police–community relations provide a vivid illustration.

Relationships between minority groups and the police are notoriously tense in American cities. Black people and Hispanic minorities have urged the hiring of minority group officers. They believe such officers are more likely to understand minority cultures and less likely to resort to lethal violence. However, their very tendency to understand their own community creates conflict for minority police officers. Sympathetic to the problems of their own group, they are bound also by the strong peer group norms of police forces (Bayley & Mendelsohn, 1969). Race, supposedly a latent characteristic, is a master status-determining trait, and situations of confrontation between minorities and the police make race even more conspicuous. The inclination to act on the basis of race surfaces for both racial groups. Minority officers are caught between the loyalty demands of their own racial group and those of their occupational peers. Neither group is likely to trust the minority officer fully. He or she experiences, sometimes very acutely, the problems of the "token," a person from a previously barred group who has been selected to represent it in a new role.

Role overload is closely related to role conflict in its effects on the individual. It is experienced by people who have too much to do to perform well. A poignant film, *The Coming Asunder of Jimmy Bright*, depicts all too graphically the breakdown of a public case worker among whose problems was an impossible case load.

Alienation or withdrawal are among the personal responses brought on by overload (see chapter 9).

Conflict due to the differing perspectives of role partners. The conflicting perspectives of functionaries and those they serve has entered into earlier discussion. The hospital context can be used again, but this time let us move into the Emergency Room for our examples.

Ordinarily, patients enter the Emergency Room in what is for them an unusual state. A sudden medical problem requires immediate attention. But what the patient sees as an emergency is actually part of the Emergency Room's daily routine (E. Hughes, 1958:54). Unless the case is spectacular, it will have to take its place in line with other emergencies. The nursing staff makes quick judgments about which emergencies should be treated first—the others have to wait. Bound by legal rules and the economic needs of the hospital, the functionaries bring out their official forms—questions to be answered and requests for payment. Such behavior seems harsh and unfeeling to the family of a bleeding patient, but it is part of the organization's business. In turn, Emergency Room personnel get irked by the many nonemergency patients who come to their doors seeking treatment.

Similar but less dramatic conflicts in perspective occur between nursing staff and patients on the hospital floor. Patients are concerned with their own unique conditions. Being hospitalized signifies inability to function normally and the need to define oneself as sick. But hospital workers are confronted with many patients, some sicker than others, who again form their routine. Caring for all cannot take place simultaneously, and waiting becomes a fact of life. Patients want more deference, personal service, and emotional support than may be available (Freidson, 1980:183). The very concept of serious illness is defined differently in the hospital culture than in everyday life. Hospital personnel may see terminal illness frequently; the recuperating patient is viewed as relatively well. The patient may consider professional "cool" to be hardness and inhumanity (Katz & Danet, 1973, intro.).

Are these conflicts in perspective totally unfortunate? Not necessarily, for they check and balance each other. The patient's self-interest can prevent serious mistakes.

Professsional nurses were asked to depict their version of the ideal patient. That ideal was described as one who is not overly demanding but who speaks up in his or her own interests. The totally noncomplaining patient was viewed as a source of danger because he or she might not report serious problems or mistakes (Goldstein, 1954). Those who never speak up for themselves require more careful monitoring.

Organization-community conflicts. The role conflict experienced by minority police officers was related to organization–community conflict. Consumer or citizen groups provide another source of conflict and pressures for the organization (R. Hall, 1977:306–307). Advocates of environmental protection urge the government to set strict standards in order to limit pollution and conserve natural resources. Required modifications of equipment, technology, or even the workplace site increase a firm's costs considerably, reduce its profits, and lead it to resist regulation. One of the many indications of this conflict are the number of lawsuits alleging that company or governmental negligence—such as the use of Agent Orange in Vietnam—has caused serious health problems. Citizens exposed to contamination by harmful chemical or nuclear wastes can hardly be sympathetic to the needs of the organizations producing them. Such controversies tend to spill over into the organization when some of its members are closely identified with the community. Homeowners in the deceptively named Love Canal area of Niagara Falls, New York, found that mysterious illnesses were cropping up. In helping to relocate those affected, the government eventually acknowledged that the health problems were probably the result of chemical wastes dumped in the area in the 1940s and 1950s (*New York Times*, August 6, 1980, p. B2). For a number of years conflicts had swirled as to who was actually responsible for the unusual rate of illnesses and of genetic mutations found among residents of the area. The federal and state governments, the chemical firm involved, and citizens' groups all entered into the conflict.

How organizations, communities, and government work out solutions to their disputes is a major subject, which best belongs in the discussion of interorganizational relations (see chapter 10). How organizations work out solutions to internal conflicts will be partially answered as we next consider the informal division of labor as an adjustive mechanism.

THE INFORMAL DIVISION OF LABOR
AS AN ADJUSTIVE MECHANISM

Decision makers and those who advise them use what they know about organizations to help minimize frictions. Administrative discretion (J. Thompson, 1976) can be exercised, within limits, to modify problematic aspects of hierarchy. Physical space can be redesigned to minimize troublesome interactions. Human relations specialists can be called in to do training or evaluation. But an organization breeds its own response in the form of constantly developing informal patterns.[3]

The unwritten informal system is highly responsive to formal inflexibility, to change, and to recurring contingencies—periodic and problematic events that create stress for particular role players.

Take the question of the tests and exams faced by every college student. That they occur with frightening regularity is not a subject of debate. They are problematic because they help determine the fate of the individual's career. Except in the case of superhuman role players, they create stress. The result is that systems of mutual aid are developed, whether they be legitimate devices such as joint study sessions or illegitimate ones such as cheating.

Another well-known informal pattern was referred to earlier—the regulation of work output by a peer group. Those employed in a particular job come to understand what a decent day's work should be and convey this information to newcomers.

[3]Informal organization is such a pervasive aspect of organizational life that it recurs as a topic in a number of chapters.

Thus, informal norms governing role behavior develop as group defenses against the recurrent problems tied to particular positions. Those who violate them are considered disloyal and are subject to reprisals. The power of informal rules is reflected in the familiar term *peer pressure*. Such norms are intended to reduce competition within the stratum, provide mutual assistance, and help defend against the demands of superordinates, subordinates, and other frequent role partners.

Regularly operating informal norms are not confined to peer groups, however, nor do the people involved need to be personal friends. Situations of potential conflict, such as those between superiors and subordinates, may be moderated by informal understandings. Bargaining and negotiating enable the involved role players to work out solutions that can satisfy both.

When such mutual understanding creates informal shifts in the division of labor, it may even help the organization. In the real world the flow of work is not as even, continuous, and predictable as official guidelines suggest. Need for modifications in the actual division of work may be created by changes in technology, variations in demand and supply, busy periods and slow periods, unexpected or emergency situations, unclear borderlines between the work assigned to various positions, and personal indispositions of role players.

Once official divisions of labor are recognized, specific departures from them frequently occur. The symbolic differences among role players are based on what each is supposed to do—yet these very distinctions can be manipulated to modify the actual division of tasks. This point will become clearer as some of the typical variations around official tasks are examined. Some of these variations are:

1. Adding or eliminating one or more of the obligations usually attached to the position
2. Patterns of mutual aid between role partners that involve sharing work, performing extra tasks for and providing vital information to the other
3. The sloughing off of dirty work—unwanted, low-status tasks—to new types of employees or to persons who are not officially members of the work force, such as customers, clients, visitors, or research workers
4. Voluntary action taken in emergency situations when leadership is needed and action is not covered by previous rules

Let us look at each of these, recognizing that there is some overlap among them.

Adding or Eliminating Obligations

Persons are often asked and sometimes volunteer to take on extra duties. Why would anyone agree to do more work than was bargained for?

One must question what options are open to persons in that particular status. There may be no other choice but to resign—hardly a desirable alternative. Group resistance is possible, should there be others placed in a similar bind. A student who feels that a teacher's additional assignments are outrageous would do well to band with others rather than protest alone. In the paid work world, unions protect workers from inappropriate changes in workload or work assignments.

Many role players take on tasks that appear to have higher social honor attached to them because these tasks normally belong to those above them in the status hierarchy. Even in total institutions such as mental hospitals and prisons where the staff–inmate split is wide, inmates may gain the privilege of closer association with the higher-status group through work assignments. The highly trusted prisoner is the one allowed to provide personal services to prison officials.

Being allowed to do part of the job of a superior is often taken as an expression of confidence and approval. Indeed, doing it can provide valuable training or an opportunity to meet others higher up in the status system. Self-interest or imagined self-interest certainly provides a needed incentive to accept additional work.

When are duties removed from positions? A particular status occupant is sometimes found to be, or becomes, less competent than was earlier supposed. In other cases, a new and less-trusted type of person, such as a woman or a black person, has gained entry into high status. The position entails more power than the organization is willing to allow its present occupant, but replacing that person would cause trouble. In such cases the organization may formally or informally remove certain key responsibilities. The role occupant is left with the more obvious status symbols and their accompanying material rewards, and may settle for these (see Phillips & Blumberg, 1982).

Patterns of Mutual Aid: Helping Out

"Helping out" is a widespread practice that modifies existing divisions of labor. The very terminology suggests that someone is performing a task voluntarily, not officially. Role players take on the work of others for many reasons: out of peer solidarity, for their own self-interest, as a matter of bargaining, and sometimes out of dedication to the organization. The last reason operates especially in voluntary and social movement organizations. Close identification with the purposes of the organization is expected, tasks are relatively less standardized, and rewards are not measured in money.

A second characteristic of "helping out" is that it focuses on the cementing of personal relationships rather than on particular activities. Of high priority is the idea that the present helper-outer expects, some day, to be the recipient of equivalent aid.

Official power broadens the influence of a supervisor or other superordinate, when used judiciously:

> One function of formal rules and status prerogatives in organizations . . . is that they bestow powers upon the supervisor that enable him to obligate subordinates and win their good will simply by refraining from using these powers. (Blau & Scott, 1962:142)

The supervisor or boss builds up good will by bending certain rules, such as allowing the worker extra time on breaks or granting permission to leave early. The subordinate is expected to reciprocate by performing beyond the point of official duty when necessary. Thus strategic leniency does accomplish its purpose (Blau & Meyer, 1971:62).

There is a give-and-take in such relationships that profits both parties. A somewhat different but nonetheless interesting tendency is the "reciprocities mul tiplier." According to this informal norm, an additional piece of work, consistently performed, gradually becomes part of the official workload. Waiters and waitresses will readily recount the assorted duties that such statuses can entail. Houseworkers, given the vague and general nature of their occupation, may take pains to specify at the time of hiring the specific things that they will *not* do, such as washing windows or walking the dog. They thus act to inhibit the addition of duties considered inappropriate.

Special kinds of cooperative arrangements tend to arise between persons in close physical contact. Given the opportunity to learn parts of the other's work, people may judiciously fill in under particular circumstances. In a study of three hospitals, I found that nurses did favors for certain doctors, those they knew could be relied upon to back them up. A nurse would perform a minor medical function without calling the house doctor to the floor. The reliable doctor gratefully wrote up an order later on. Because of legal liability, such actions entail risk and will not be performed for unproven physicians nor by all nurses (Goldstein, 1954). Hospital pharmacists can help doctors by preventing mistakes—tactfully questioning inaccurately written prescriptions.

In the absence of readily available nursing personnel, patients (and even patients' visitors) have many opportunities to help one another, for example, by handing things to other patients, summoning a nurse, or answering phone calls for those not able to do so. Taking on such duties in no way changes the clear split in identity between patient and hospital worker, but over time the staff may come to rely on this unpaid labor. At the same time the mutual support accorded one hospital patient by another confirms the solidarity of a group more than usually dependent on paid functionaries. It displays a degree of power and self-sufficiency greater than each patient would have alone.

Another form of helping out occurs when a person of superordinate status helps those of lower status. Food market managers who pick up a broom do not demean themselves thereby, but publicly demonstrate their support of the work force and their democratic outlook. Nonetheless, the extraordinary quality of such an act would be diminished if it were done on a regular basis. Supervisors in skilled lines of work achieve the same good will by helping out and in doing so also show that they have not lost their original skills.

The Sloughing Off of Dirty Work

Most jobs contain not simply one but a bundle of activities, some more pleasant than others. The least desirable ones are the dirty work (E. Hughes, 1958:49). Dirty work may be physical, as in carting out garbage. But dirty work may also be "a symbol of degradation, something that wounds one's dignity," or work that in "some way goes counter to the more heroic of our moral conceptions" (E. Hughes, 1958:49-50).

People tend to slough off their dirty work onto various others. In the professions, technical aides can be introduced to perform the less important, repetitive, or unwanted tasks. Such auxiliary positions are frequently filled by persons lower in social identity, for whom such tasks may represent greater social honor than they previously had. At times customers and clients are induced to perform services for themselves that would otherwise be done by paid personnel. Those who prepare income taxes professionally probably encounter vast differences in the amount of preparatory work done by each client.

Another example is the supermarket customer who finds a lone cashier, working without a packer. Customers are not required to pack their own groceries but may do so either out of self-interest or sympathy for the bogged-down cashier. The customer is usually thanked for taking on this dirty work task. However, customers who offer to provide the prices of various items are less often thanked. Here assistance may be disregarded as unreliable, related to self-interest.

The retail clothing store is another place where the division of work between buyer and seller shows many interesting variations. The potential buyer in a shop selling expensive clothing is assisted by a sales person who brings and takes away clothing after it has been tried on. In those stores where less expensive clothing is sold, the customer makes his or her own choice and is expected to return unwanted clothing to the racks (dirty work). The share of the customer in the division of labor is really remarkably different in these situations, although it is not labeled as such.

Voluntary Action Taken in Emergency Situations

Emergencies are situations in which strict status lines are neglected because something has to be done quickly. In the absence of trained medical personnel, a civilian pitches in to do a resuscitation procedure. Or someone volunteers to direct traffic at the scene of an accident. A student is called upon to proctor an examination for an ailing teacher. In these cases, no change in official status is entailed. The work is done by someone willing to do it and available on a temporary basis. In a variation, the author found that white patients in a southern city willingly used the services of a black dentist in times of emergency, although they would normally have opted for a white one (Goldstein, 1952). Before the 1960s, when the study was done, the status characteristic of race ordinarily would have operated to disqualify the black dentist. In times of emergency certain usual norms are suspended.

INFORMAL ORGANIZATION IN THE WOMEN'S PRISON: *A CASE STUDY*

We have touched on the need for group unity among people who share similar life contingencies, especially those set off in low-status categories such as students or production workers. The prison is an even more fertile field for the study of informal peer groups. The sharp divergence of outlook between prisoners and those who guard them is verified by harsh treatment prisoners mete out to traitors, or "squealers," especially in men's prisons.

Since inmates are the "raw material" being processed by the prison, they have little official power. They take some control over their own lives and those of other inmates through elaborate informal systems. Both official and unofficial aspects of social organization help determine behavior in prisons, but "it is likely . . . that unofficial arrangements are of most significance to inmates, and, at least, to lower level employees, for most of their time is spent in them" (Cressey, 1961:3).

Unofficial arrangements deal with more than power. They create a culture to substitute for the one out in the real world. The inmate role types that develop reflect response not only to their unnatural situation but also to their prior socialization (Giallombardo, 1966; Sykes & Messinger, 1960; Wheeler, 1961).

Giallombardo spent a year doing fieldwork in a women's prison. She held long interviews with inmates and found that "although the deprivations of imprisonment were present and keenly felt by the female prisoners, the female argot roles differ in structural form and the sentiment attached to them from the roles assumed by male prisoners" (1966:394).

Male prisoners enter the prison with an orientation to manliness; female prisoners with an orientation to their family roles (Leger and Stratton, 1977). What female prisoners tend to do is to create a substitute family system within the prison. Giallombardo found six clusters of role types (see figure 6-3).

What do these clusters of role types represent? Snitchers are female counterparts to the "rats" found in the male prison—inmates who break the rule that one should never give information to staff. Group punishment occurs, but it is generally less severe than that found in the male prison. Inmate cops or lieutenants are those who are in a position of authority over other inmates, who can issue orders to them or report infractions of work rules.

Squares are the pariahs—inmates who are considered to be accidental criminals. They are disliked because of their orientation to the prison administration and anticriminal loyalties. The jive bitch is another disliked type—a troublemaker who cannot be trusted and distorts facts.

Rap buddies are special friends, ones who can talk easily to each other. They are friends, not homosexual companions. Homeys are another type, referred to earlier in the chapter, between whom there is a special bond. Homeys seek out other inmates from their home towns or nearby communities, even though they may not have known each other previously, and develop

FIGURE 6-3   Social Roles in a Prison for Women

- Snitchers and inmate cops or lieutenants
- Squares and jive bitches
- Rap buddies and homeys
- Connects and boosters
- Pinners
- The homosexual cluster:
    Penitentiary turnouts, lesbians, femmes, studs, broads, tricks, commissary hustlers, chippies, kick partners, cherries, punks and turnabouts.

Source: Rose Giallombardo, "Social Roles in a Prison for Women," *Social Problems* 13 (Winter 1966):268–288.

mutual obligations. An unspoken assumption is that they will not bring back tales of the prisoner's behavior to the home community.

A connect is an inmate with a good job who will cooperate in obtaining scarce goods or information. A booster is a successful stealer of fairly large quantities of goods from official sources. She carries on a business enterprise within the prison. A pinner is a lookout who prevents surprise attacks, whether by staff or inmates, on others who are engaging in illicit activities. This role is important since it prevents detection and disciplinary action.

Finally, the homosexual cluster contains a large variety of types. The absence of heterosexual relations in prison is a severe deprivation. Only the lesbian role type actually prefers homosexual relations in a free community, resembling the fag in male prisons. Most prisoners prefer male partners if given a choice. Homosexual relationships in the prison take on family styles rather than serving for sex alone. The femme or mommy, for example, is a highly sought-after role because it simulates that played outside the prison. The stud broad or daddy role carries prestige because it is a male role and is thought to be difficult to take on. Other refinements of particular homosexual roles are suggested by some of the labels in figure 6–3.

Although these descriptions are derived from one particular study and role types may change, they illustrate the informal means of coping with difficult life in a total institution and the carryover of latent roles into the organization. It would be interesting to see if the women's movement has been reflected in today's prison types and how today's role types compare to those Giallombardo found in her 1966 study.

SUMMARY

Chapter 6 has dealt with a pervasive fact of societal and organizational life—division of labor and specialization as they are expressed in status systems. Most known societies have used sex, age, and race or ethnicity (ascribed characteristics) as bases for assigning statuses and roles. Consequently, persons with these and other ascribed status characteristics tend to be identified with particular kinds of work, paid and unpaid, in society. Differing amounts of prestige, power, and material rewards are considered appropriate for them.

Although organizations emphasize achieved characteristics, they are greatly influenced by traditional practices in a given society. Ascribed statuses are supposed to remain latent in organizations, but they are often master status-determining traits—crucial aspects of social identity, according to Gouldner and Hughes. Certain kinds of people are associated with particular roles, such as women as secretaries and men as corporate executives. Ascribed characteristics are formally or informally tacked on as requirements for position.

In recent decades the United States government has challenged such unofficial requirements as discriminatory and instituted what are known as affirmative action measures. Government rulings meet resistance and do not bring immediate change; impersonal economic and political factors frequently do. In times of shortage or emergency, anyone who can do a particular job is sought regardless of personal characteristics. However, the first section of this chapter emphasized the point that organizations express and reflect the understood status systems of their societies.

The second part of the chapter examined the operation of status systems in organizations and the relationships between formal and informal status interaction. Cooperative and conflict perspectives on the nature of organizational status systems were contrasted. Some theorists, such as Barnard, believe that status hierarchies are necessary for coordination and are basically helpful to interaction. Status symbols are said to provide credibility and belief in the competence of those who hold superordinate positions. Further, it is believed that dysfunctions or pathologies that arise can be overcome by administrative discretion or modification of human behavior.

The opposite perspective views conflict between different hierarchical levels as a natural consequence of economic inequality and of differences in interest. However, conflict is not limited to role partners who are superordinates and subordinates. Typical situations of organizational conflict also occur between functionaries and the clients they serve. Nurses or waiters and waitresses, for example, often take care of large numbers of patients or customers, all of whom would like more individualized attention than they receive. Conflict between role players may be useful in seeing that all interests are represented and that serious mistakes are prevented.

The chapter's third section examined informal division of labor as an adjustive mechanism. Formal rules provide the framework for negotiation and bargaining between different role players. Patterns of mutual aid develop, especially among those on the same hierarchical level but also between persons dependent on each other for the performance of their own duties. Such cooperation minimizes potential friction.

Informal patterns frequently reflect people's social identities. They provide lower participants in an organization with a measure of control over their own situations. The chapter concluded with a case study of informal role types within a women's prison. Informal types develop in both men's and women's prisons, but these types only partially coincide. The varied types that arise reflect prior male and female role identities as well as reponse to the deprivations of imprisonment. Here again organizational roles are affected by societal roles.

7

MANAGERS AND ORGANIZATIONAL CULTURES

Managing the Organization
    The Problem: What Do Managers Do and How Do They Succeed at It?
    The Manager as a Business Type
    Managerial Counterparts in Government and Voluntary Associations
    Levels of Management
The Manager as Organization Leader
    Use of Authority: Leadership and Compliance
    Cultural Leadership
    Decision Making
    Managerial Succession
Managerial Careers
    Selection
    Socialization
    Mobility
    The Wives of Management
Women as Managers: A Case Study
Summary

MANAGING THE ORGANIZATION

The Problem: What Do Managers Do and How Do They Succeed At It?

Managers lead the organization and make decisions for it. They direct and evaluate other organizational participants. They represent the organization to the public and the world. By definition they have official power (authority or position power) over those below them. The higher up they are in the managerial hierarchy, the greater is their official power. Chapter 5 pointed out that compliance with authority is more problematic than Weber's model suggests. The question of how organizational managers could best utilize their positions of power to attain willing and motivated compliance became a central issue almost as soon as size and complexity created a need for this class of professionals. Research on successful and unsuccessful styles of supervising others has been plentiful, but not always convincing.

In addition to supervising and directing others, powerful managers make major decisions for the organization. Here questions revolve around the issue of the degree of choice that organizational leaders have. Are the qualities and judgment of top managers crucial, or are these individuals constrained by such factors as organizational structure, power coalitions, and environmental conditions (as R. Hall asserts, 1982:158)?

Top managers are among the most highly paid and influential role players in modern societies. They are the prototype of the Horatio Alger vision of American success—the poor boy who works himself to the top of a major business, making a lot of money on the way. Little wonder then that much interest has developed in how managers get ahead, how young managers are socialized to their roles, and what their career mobility entails for themselves and their families.

These issues will be addressed in this chapter, which is a bridge between our considerations of authority, power, and status and the succeeding chapters that deal with the relationship between the individual and the organization.

The Manager as a Business Type

Westrum and Samaha make a sharp distinction between the enterprise, the bureaucracy, and the voluntary association (1984). While we have objected to their *terminology* as confusing (see chapter 3), we find the *distinction* between these three types of organizations useful. The issue of managing *does* differ among business enterprises, government bureaucracies, and voluntary organizations. What constitutes a test of good management is less problematic for the business organization, since its goals are clearer—increasing profits and maintaining financial health.

Concern with successful management comes mainly from the business world and the schools of business, rather than from organizations in the public sector or voluntary associations.[1] Competition, changing world conditions, and changing

---

[1] As we suggest later, there is ambivalence about the objectives of public agencies; what constitutes successful management may be debatable if there is no agreement about their mission. And even a well-functioning agency or commission may be abolished for reasons unrelated to its management. Viewing public organizations from a political economy perspective, Wamsley and Zald observe: "Public agencies are nested in a set of political and economic structures and relations that determine and shape their long-run directions of change and their short-run interactions and concerns. Sooner or later, in any political system . . . changes in the sentiment distributions of the general public and the public in-contact flow through in-contact influentials to effect basic agency goals and legitimacy. At the same time the ability of agencies to accomplish their tasks is affected by the costs of the factors of production and the pattern of industry structure and competition originating in the larger societal economy" (1973:55).

technology all demand adaptability. Corporations have high stakes in developing effective executives who can make the right decisions and manage others. As both Kanter (1977) and Perrow (1986) showed, the many mergers that led to the rise of large corporations at the turn of the twentieth century created the demand for schools of management that would train a new managerial class. Interest in successful management intensified when major American industries experienced financial difficulties in the 1970s and 1980s. Several best-selling books contrasted various management practices and compared the foibles of faltering American industries with their more achieving international competitors (Deal & Kennedy, 1982; Lawrence & Dyer, 1983; Peters & Waterman, 1982).

Managerial Counterparts in Government and Voluntary Associations

Government bureaucracies do have heads, but the issue of what constitutes successful management in the public sector is complicated. Above the career government bureaucrats are heads of departments, chosen with many considerations in mind—such as party affiliation and loyalty to the chief executive. Frequently they are drawn from the top levels of corporation management, bringing their own industry's interests as well as their professional expertise to the job.

Chief executives differ in their commitment to the missions of the different government agencies they have inherited. Changing levels of funding reflect such partiality as well as the power of various constituencies that support or oppose that agency's function. Elsewhere in this book we have used the Environmental Protection Agency as an example of changing priorities between different administrations. The United States Civil Rights Commission is another agency reconstituted by President Ronald Reagan to more accurately reflect his own opposition to previously accepted civil rights policies. The agency has now entered legal cases on the opposite side of issues it once favored—for example, school desegregation. In this instance what constitutes successful administration is now a matter of opinion; weakening the original mission of the agency might be considered success. A governmental agency may even be dismantled because it has been too energetic rather than the reverse.

On the other hand, a president's commitment to national defense and technological advance in space can be tempered by public outcries against military spending and overwhelming national deficits. If budget reductions were to take place, it would not signify poor management but changing national priorities.

In chapter 9 we will see that agencies serving the public, especially the poor, are not expected to perform excellently. In many cases their mediocrity and bureaucratic nature truly reflect public ambivalence about using taxpayers' money for humanitarian purposes. In a free enterprise society, government professionals tend to be paid less than their equivalents in the private sector, so that the "cream" of professionals or management types opt for jobs in industry. It is not surprising that less upwardly mobile types are drawn to government posts. Management that is obviously questionable leads to outcries against "waste" or "corruption," but excellence seems less expected in the public sector.

Voluntary associations and social movement organizations are concerned with leadership but less with administrative ability than with other traits. Central issues for voluntary groups, such as trade unions and professional associations, have been whether leaders truly represent the needs of the rank-and-file and run the organization democratically (see Blau and Scott's typology [1962], discussed in chapter 3). Social movement organizations need most to attract committed followers and resources from the public and to be responsive to changes in the environment. Leadership, especially in the early stages of movements, requires inspirational qualities rather than good organizational practices. Nor can efficiency be judged the same way for beleaguered organizations that are encountering opposition as for stable, institutionalized groups. For example, by seeming to act erratically, not keeping careful records, and changing plans frequently, certain civil rights organizations eluded information-seeking attempts of hostile groups.

Measuring the success of voluntary organizations is especially difficult when their purpose is the enjoyment or edification of members. Numbers of members alone do not necessarily prove success or lack of it. Further, the mobility of lower-level leaders to more encompassing roles requires its own study in such settings, entailing varied mixtures of charismatic, traditional, and rational-legal power.

Research literature on successful management and managerial mobility in organizations has been heavily geared to the business enterprise setting; this chapter has the same focus.

Levels of Management

Harry Cunningham is the president of K-Mart and is called a manager. He is responsible for supervising thousands of employees and the operations of over 1500 K-Mart Stores. Don Bolger is the manager of five waitresses at the local Dairy Queen. Both are managers, but their jobs are not the same. Managerial jobs differ according to how high the manager is in the organization. (Hellriegel & Slocum, 1982:6)

In a business enterprise, the managerial ladder consists of first-line managers at the bottom, who hold such titles as section chief or supervisor; then one or more levels of middle management, depending on the size and complexity of the firm; and finally the appropriately labeled top management group at the peak of the hierarchy. Table 7-1 compares the titles for similar levels of managers in seven types of organizations (see table 7-1).

Studies show that the time spent in various activities differs depending on level. First-line managers are in charge of those who actually produce the goods and services and tend to spend much of their time with these workers. Middle managers serve as coordinators, receiving policy directives from top managers and transmitting these to the first-line managers. A buffer group between those above and below, middle managers tend to be highly involved in the process of communica-

TABLE 7-1   Comparison of Titles for Similar Positions at Various Managerial Levels
in Seven Types of Organizations

MANAGEMENT LEVEL	INDUSTRY	LARGE OFFICE OR DEPARTMENT STORE	UNIVERSITY
Top	President	President	President
Middle	Plant manager	General manager	Dean
First line	Foreman	Supervisor or department manager	Department head

MANAGEMENT LEVEL	LARGE PUBLIC SCHOOL SYSTEM	HOSPITAL	GOVERNMENT AGENCY	CHURCH
Top	Superintendent	Administrator	Administrator	Bishop
Middle	Principal	Chief of medical staff	Division chief	Dean
Top	Department head	Nursing supervisor	Section head	Rector

Source: From p. 318 in *Industrial Sociology: Work in Organizational Life*, 3rd ed., by Delbert C. Miller and William H. Form. Copyright © 1980 by Delbert C. Miller and William H. Form. Reprinted by permission of Harper & Row, Publishers, Inc.

tion: using the telephone, writing and reading reports, sitting in committee meetings. Top managers—presidents, chairpersons, executive officers—establish policies and determine the organization's strategies for interacting with its task environment, often spending a good part of their time negotiating with government and making business deals. They are the spokespersons who represent the organization to the community and the world, most noticeably in situations of public crisis, such as a crash of one of their airplanes or a dangerous gas leak. While such crises may not occur often, they highlight what is considered a central feature of managerial work—coping with uncertainty, being ready to deal with the unexpected.

In addition to relating to persons, groups, and events outside the business organization, top executives have been forced to refocus on the internal problems of bolstering efficiency and commitment. Loss of leadership to Japan and certain European countries in industries such as radios, cameras, stereo equipment, steel, and autos has engendered debate within American industry. The lower productivity of American workers and their relative inefficiency compared to the Japanese has been deplored, and questions have been raised about how American industry can be renewed and revitalized. Top organizational leaders are charged with inspiring higher levels of commitment and more efficient service from workers. Successful ventures are credited as being due to good management:

The importance of good management can be seen everywhere. Look at the success of McDonald's, K-Mart, Radio Shack, Seven-up, Miller Brewing Company, and W. R. Grace and Company, to name a few. On the other hand, look at the management failures of W. T. Grant, World Football League, Chrysler Corporation, Lockheed Aircraft Corporation, and Amtrak, among others. Good management is the difference between success and failure of an organization. (Hellriegel & Slocum, 1982:6)

One of the problems with naming names of organizations reflecting "good" and "bad" management is that they can easily get outdated. When the U.S. government has intervened to bail out ailing corporations, such as Chrysler, the comebacks have occasionally been astonishing. Some organizational analysts have gone further than naming names, making efforts to ferret out (after the fact, of course) the poor or good management decisions made by these firms. In addition to some popular impressionistic accounts, serious attempts are being made to discover the types of internal structures that best enable organizations to cope with relevant environmental factors (see Lawrence & Dyer, 1983).

Those concerned with such internal aspects of the firm as worker loyalty and commitment often view top managers not just as task-oriented, scientific management types but as culture leaders. Key executives are expected to create strong company cultures that breed the desired sentiments of loyalty and commitment. As such they are and must be exemplars of these virtues, putting the corporation first above any other demands or inclinations. The aspiring junior manager is shown by example that loyalty requires sacrifice of family obligations to the needs of the firm, such as long evening hours, weekly traveling, and frequent transfers (Margolis, 1979).

Managerial careers progress from the lower levels up to the highest ones, and in major corporations mobility up the ladder is an overriding concern for the young manager.

We now turn to consideration of the manager as organizational leader.

THE MANAGER AS ORGANIZATION LEADER

Use of Authority: Leadership and Compliance

Leadership is considered part of the manager's job, defined as "*the process of influencing people to direct their efforts toward the achievement of some particular goal(s)*" (Hodgetts & Altman, 1979:182). The vast amount of research on leadership exists because it has been needed, because official power does not, in itself, create compliance.

A useful distinction is made between power and influence. Influence involves a *change of preferences* to that of the leader: The individual wants to do what the leader proposes (R. Hall, 1982). The exercise of power, in contrast, may involve compliance even against the wishes of the one complying. Leadership, despite the problems in defining it precisely, exists at many levels.

In chapter 5 we showed that power does not reside solely in the hands of those who have official authority but that *legitimate* power does tend to draw a degree of compliance, especially if the order (communication) falls within the subordinate's zone of indifference. Thus, the person in authority has a certain amount of position-based influence. Another type, knowledge-based influence, is defined as:

> the ability of certain persons *as persons* to influence the commitment of organization resources and to influence the behavior of others, based on the relevance of the information available to them, the soundness of their reasoning, and their reputation for being right in the past. (Lawrence & Lorsch, 1969:173)

Managers, by definition, have official power over those they manage. They tend to have a certain amount of influence based on their official, position power. They may have more or less knowledge-based influence. The effectiveness of managerial leadership is seen to derive from a combination of official power and influence. Great reams of material are written, training programs are developed and pursued, and tales of heroic corporation leaders circulated to teach and illustrate such successful leadership (see, for example, Deal & Kennedy, 1982). The study of managerial succession, that is, of new managers replacing old ones, illuminates the process whereby a person given position power goes about trying to make that power work (see Gouldner, 1954a; Izraeli, 1977).

Theories about effective management–worker relations have been based largely on studies of first-line supervisors or managers, as R. Hall points out (1982, chap. 8). The authoritarian type of leader, as exemplified in McGregor's Theory X has often been negatively contrasted with his Theory Y type, who provides workers with direction but more autonomy and respect (McGregor, 1960). It is simplistic, however, to assume that all organizations can be run in one "best" way. Not only do the tasks of firms and of departments within firms differ, but their environments also differ.

That is a central premise of the *contingency approach*, which suggests that

> the effectiveness of various managerial styles, guidelines, techniques, or approaches will vary according to the situation. . . . the essence of the contingency approach is that management practices generally should be consistent with the tasks being performed by the individuals, the external environment, and the relative needs of the employees. (Hellriegel & Slocum, 1982:26)

Another way of conceptualizing polar systems of management is the contrast between mechanistic and organic systems. Mechanistic organizations tend to be centralized, have little employee participation, and rely quite strictly on rules and regulations. Organic types are more decentralized, less hierarchical, involve more flexible jobs and more teamwork. Lawrence and Lorsch, who have a well-deserved reputation for their contributions to contingency theory, list the multitude of management techniques created since World War II (1969:160). Summarizing, they state:

Each of these techniques seems to carry with it a thrust in one of two directions—either toward greater order, systematization, routinization, and pre-
dictability, or toward greater openness, sharing, creativity, and individual
initiative. One thrust is to tighten the organization; the other, to loosen it up.
(p. 161)

Through their own research on high-performing and low-performing organizations and an analysis of other major studies using the contingency approach (see
Lawrence & Lorsch, 1969, chap. 8), these authors come up with the reason for this
split in prescribed directions. Managerial practices must be fitted to both internal
and external contingencies, which require a variety of management styles. Some
departments may have relatively routine work, in which a relatively bureaucratic
organization will work efficiently. Others, such as research and development, may
contain a great deal of uncertainty and thrive on minimal supervision and innovative team effort. Different environmental conditions—situations of greater and
lesser uncertainty, for example—require different types of adaptation and different
organizational structures. A changing environment requires correct decision making
by those in charge. So, for example, in the late 1960s Detroit auto makers were
proven to have chosen wrongly in manufacturing "overpowered and oversized
vehicles with a growing reputation for low quality" (Lawrence & Dyer, 1983:46).

Choice of the wrong type of car to produce was not due to leadership in
supervision, but to making wrong decisions. Low quality and productivity may
have been due to such factors as high levels of absenteeism and turnover and dis-
gruntled workers.

"G.M. [General Motors] became the first of the Big Three to apply the
remedies of 'tribal organization' to the blue-collar blues," maintain Lawrence and
Dyer (1983:49). Starting in 1968 G.M. began experimenting with job improvement
and enrichment programs and was more successful than its rivals in readapting its
organization. The issue of motivating workers is linked to expressive, socioemotional
qualities of managers, reflected in their cultural leadership.

Cultural Leadership

The manager's role as culture leader is being spelled out forcefully in organizational literature. Top management is said to set the tone and direction for what is
now called company culture, sometimes referred to as company climate. But what
is meant by culture?

The concept of culture.   Culture, an old and respected term in both anthropology and sociology, consists of all learned behavior, all that is not instinctive and
automatic. It includes material objects and artifacts created by people and nonmaterial inventions such as religion and philosophy. Among culture's most important elements are language and other symbolic meaning systems, norms, taboos,
rites, and rituals.

Rites and rituals are symbolic, repetitive acts that infuse important occurrences with religious or magical meanings, and which become part of the society's repertoire for dealing with these events. For example, the ritual rain dance is engaged in to gain supernatural help in bringing needed water. Marriage ceremonies tend to be elaborate rites, signifying the important act of joining two families in the eyes of the deity as well as humans. In modern times such rites and rituals as graduation ceremonies, annual dinners and awards, and the office Christmas party are intended to serve status-conferring and unifying functions.

Nonmaterial culture consists of patterned ways of life that are gradually established, through trial and error, and that come to be believed in as right and normal. For instance, dress customs in each society prescribe "correct attire" for various times and places. Beliefs are linked to the material objects of culture, which acquire not only utilitarian but symbolic meanings. Hence the clothes that are worn may be regulated by the society in terms of the status of the wearer. Uniforms are a case in point: They symbolize such things as rank, occupation or profession, or school. Culture has commonly been thought of as patterns of life that grow up slowly, often unconsciously.

Culture's influence on individual and group behavior is accepted. The reverse, the individual's role in *creating* culture, is sometimes overlooked, since the very essence of culture is its gradual, cumulative nature, its expression of group values, and its resistance to change. Individual action in modifying culture is demonstrated through the influence of great leaders who facilitate changes appropriate to their times. Max Weber drew attention to the charismatic individual who draws on existent beliefs in a given culture to dramatize its flaws and contradictions and to suggest new pathways.

The manager's role. In one of organizational theory's popular applied usages, managers are viewed as leaders who can shape corporate cultures. Accordingly, corporate culture is understood as a system of meanings created by management to further such sentiments as loyalty, pride in the organization, and strong motivation. Early leaders of American business, according to Deal and Kennedy, saw their role "as creating an environment—in effect, a culture—in their companies in which employees could be secure and thereby do the work necessary to make the business a success" (1982:5). The Japanese example is brought in as illustration of how a strong and cohesive culture throughout that nation contributed to successful businesses. Such qualities as loyalty and respect, revered in Japanese culture, have been translated into corporate life (Ouchi, 1981).

Culture substituted for subculture. The last chapter showed that the division of labor in organizations reflects that of their society. As in Japan, the culture of organizations mirrors society's values, but from a particular perspective. In a sense, each specific organization develops a "subculture" of its own. It was once understood that societies have many subcultures. The concept of subculture captures the notion that *variations* in general cultural themes appear within tightly-knit, relatively isolated groups. Because *sub* also implies subordinate or less worthy, the term has fallen into disuse and been replaced by terms describing such subcultures as racial and ethnic ones, for example, black culture, Italian-American culture. Actually, black Americans and Italian-Americans share much of the general American culture, such as language and laws, but also exhibit variations based on their history and special experiences. The term *youth culture* rather than *youth subculture* is used today, although the youth culture consists of patterns shaped by the position of youth within the broader national scene.

Similarly, *organizational cultures* are not formed totally new but grow out of the societies in which they originate and reproduce these societies in some manner. The special place of that organization in the world, the things it does, and the interaction that goes on within it produces variations. So, for example, variant language usages are created out of a common language by groups sharing a special group situation. Certain examples of these special vocabularies have been mentioned in the previous chapter, such as the numerous terms invented to describe the upwardly mobile person in a corporation—"fast trackers," "high fliers," "superstars" (Kanter, 1977). Minority groups find special words for other groups ("redneck," "honky," "Anglo"), just as they are named derogatively by outsiders. When society's official norms change, as in the affirmative action era, public expressions of racial bias need to be camouflaged, hence are coded into more subtle terms.

The culture concept in different guises.   Descriptions of organizational culture have appeared under such headings as "informal organization" or "underlife" long before the language of culture gained currency. What is new is the emphasis on culture created from the top of the organization to suit management's purposes.[2] In a departure from anthropological tradition the role of key individuals in conscious culture production is emphasized. Partly through its cultural role, management is seen as an art as well as a science.

Cultural creation as a legitimate concern of management brings back into formal organizations elements that the emphasis on bureaucratic rationality had minimized—such noninstrumental activities as rituals, parties, awards, games, jokes, folk tales, and the feelings they evoke. (Deal and Kennedy's book, *Corporate Cultures*, 1982, is subtitled *The Rites and Rituals of Corporate Life*.) These cultural elements are intended to foster such sentiments as loyalty and pride, which are important to unity, morale, and performance. As with the emphasis on loyalty, the term *clan*—originally designating an anthropological kin group—has gained currency as a positive, nonbureaucratic tie within complex organizations (see Ouchi, 1981).

Emphasis on culture, loyalty, and clan highlight the current distrust of organi-

---

[2] The concept "organizational climate" has included the idea that top management can influence the internal mood of an organization. It refers to "a set of properties of the work environment perceived by individuals who work there and which serve as a major force in influencing their job behavior. Illustrations include structure, job descriptions, performance standards, rewards, leadership style, challenge, supportiveness and work values" (Hodgetts & Altman, 1979:344).

zation based purely on bureaucratic principles. However, some critics suspect that culture creation by management is another form of controlling workers (Heydebrand, 1984).

The totality of organizational culture. Organizational culture consists of vastly more than the creations of top management. It is a continually evolving set of practices, meanings, and adaptations. So, for example, influential older works describe the world of lower participants from an anthropological perspective, showing the rich "underlife" that develops among such restricted groups as mental institution inmates (Goffman, 1961). Goffman used the term "secondary adjustments" to reveal the innovative ways in which individuals use even meager resources to retain individuality and satisfy personal needs, such as having toilet paper serve as writing paper or a shoe as a pillow. That is, individuals find, through trial and error, available cultural objects to meet their everyday needs. It is not only top managers who can innovate.

The terms *formal organization* and *informal organization*, as discussed in the previous chapter, contrast two aspects of organizational life: the official, formal structures and rules and the unofficial, unstated patterns and norms. Despite its usefulness, this dichotomy easily becomes conceptually problematic. Informal norms do grow up as adaptations to group and individual needs, but they can become so permanent and regular that they are recognized and accepted even by superiors. Does this acceptance make them part of the formal structure, even if they did not originate there? The line between formal and informal patterns becomes hazy. Difficulties are somewhat overcome by seeing them both as related parts of a whole, of organizational culture, and by recognizing the process of transition from informal to formal. Informal work breaks may become formalized by management into official breaks. Workers in various industries formalize their negotiations for better pay and working conditions by establishing unions and formal collective bargaining agreements.

Strong company cultures? The concept of informal organization—created by management—is linked to that of culture in the following statement: "A strong culture is a system of informal rules that spells out how people are to behave most of the time" (Deal & Kennedy, 1982:15).

These rules as they are described, are *ways* of behaving in general, rather than the detailed prescriptions found in written rules. Thus, Deal and Kennedy describe one type of business culture as: "the work hard/play hard culture. Fun and action are the rule here, and employees take few risks, all with quick feedback. To succeed, the culture encourages them to maintain a high level of relatively low-risk activity" (p. 208). This type characterizes sales organizations such as computer companies, automotive distributors, almost any door-to-door sales operation, and most retail stores.

Dalton's concept of unofficial rewards, in research done a number of years ago, implied use of the same working definition as that proposed by Deal and Kennedy—a system of informal rules that spells out how people should behave, but that is sometimes understood and accepted by management or even created by it. In Dalton's study (1959) employees who made especially valuable contributions were rewarded by the firm's practice of overlooking the fact that they took home valuable materials. Had the issue come up for formal discussion, the practice might have had to cease. It was an understood deviation from formal rules to compensate positive behavior, in which the agent of control tacitly allowed the deviation to take place; this differentiated it from theft. The reward existed only because there was a rule in the first place and leniency could be shown. In this case, the formal rule is kept so that a meaningful deviation from it is possible.

Deal and Kennedy's definition of culture can apply broadly to unwritten rules developed by management, by lower participants, or by combinations of role partners of different ranks. Frederick Taylor's scientific management schemes took into account the attempts by workers to regulate their pace of production. He struggled against such peer group norms, hoping to provide incentives to individual workers so that they would disregard accepted informal rates.

The concept of informal organization is also included in Selznick's notion of the organization as an organism (1969), as an adaptive social structure. He states:

> Deviations from the formal system tend to become institutionalized, so that "unwritten laws" and informal associations are established.... These institutionalized rules and modes of informal cooperation are normally attempts by participants in the formal organization to control the group relations which form the environment of organizational decisions. The informal patterns (such as cliques) arise spontaneously, are based on personal relationships, and are usually directed to the control of some specific situation. (1969:22–23)

Many descriptions of informal organizations show how they help peer groups gain control over a problematic situation (e.g., work speed-ups or strict supervision), while others demonstrate their expressive functions for individuals. Games created on the work site help dispel the boredom of repetitive work, as demonstrated in Roy's classic study, "The Banana Game" (1959–1960)—a ritualized joking byplay involving real bananas that took place daily in a small work group. Informal organization, then, has most often been seen as emergent culture, created by people interacting with each other, forming patterns, repeating them, and infusing them with meaning. Seen this way, the concept of culture is broadly inclusive and not limited to the typical modes of organizational behavior modeled by management.

An annual award dinner created by top executives may indeed be a successful ceremony, expected and anticipated, and serving the organization's goal of increasing motivation and morale. But employees or inmates also create adaptive patterns and relationships and provide punishments and rewards (see the case study in chapter 6). The initiation ritual, formalized in some fraternities, whereby new pledgees have to endure various dangers and embarrassments before being accepted, occurs in myriad forms. Cohesive groups find ways of testing new entrants on the scene before sharing needed informal knowledge or providing help. Margolis observes that top bosses may put aspiring managers through an extended initiation period, seeking to test their commitment to the firm (1979). Thus, the manager may be transferred frequently with little regard to the problems encountered by continually uprooted wives and children. Refusing the transfer would mean failing the test. This testing is part of organizational culture, not written out but part of the informal code of management. The manifest function of transferring a manager because he or she is needed elsewhere also serves the latent function of testing commitment.

One of the most systematic listings of elements of informal organization is provided by Miller and Form (1980:360–361, see fig. 7-1). They include such items as myths, ceremonies, rites, and communication systems, which others now see as elements of organizational culture. Miller and Form emphasize the existence of informal organization among workers, who are linked together by such features as age, sex, marital status, social background, length of service, race, and ethnic identity as well as position in the work structure. They also claim that management has an informal organization, which is harder to discern by simple observation; that managers are involved in social activities not prescribed by the job, and fall into cliques. Here they refer to the fact that peer group ties develop at upper as well as lower levels. This formulation is more complex than Deal and Kennedy's concept of an official culture directed from the very top to those below.

"A strong culture enables people to feel better about what they do, so they are more likely to work harder," assert Deal and Kennedy (1982:16). This, of course, refers to the strong culture created by management. A strong culture created by lower participants for themselves may also enable them to feel better; it may or may not make them work harder or comply with authority.

Further, a strong management-created culture may not make everyone feel

FIGURE 7-1 Interrelated Segments of Informal Organization

1. Congeniality groups, such as gangs, friendships, and cliques.
2. An organization and structure which define the relations between these groups, in terms of rights, obligations, prestige, and influence.
3. Codes of conduct for group members, including customs and norms. These may be arbitrarily divided into two sections:
   a. *Internal* codes, which regulate activities within the informal social organization.
   b. *External* codes, which regulate activities toward formal organization (management and union) and other formally or informally organized out-groups.
4. Scheme of ideas, beliefs, and values which underlie and support the code of conduct and group activities, such as "folk" knowledge, prejudices, stereotypes, myths, and ideologies which give meaning to occurrences.
5. Informal group activities, related to or independent of formal work behavior. Ceremonies, rites, gambling, recreation, swearing, and joking are examples.
6. Communication systems which inform members of ideas, sentiments, and occurrences vital to group solidarity and action.

Source: From pp. 360–61 in *Industrial Sociology: Work in Organizational Life,* 3rd ed., by Delbert C. Miller and William H. Form. Copyright © 1980 by Delbert C. Miller and William H. Form. Reprinted by permission of Harper & Row, Publishers, Inc.

better. The "tough-guy, macho culture," for example, of police departments, may push out women or more sensitive men. Regardless of how they feel, individuals must learn the informal culture of management and abide by its general terms in order to get ahead in an organization with a strongly defined culture. In some cases it may be necessary to adapt for survival, as in the tough-guy macho culture of the male prison.

The suggestion that certain types of cultures typify certain types of businesses is vaguely congruent with the contingency approach to management. That is, it recognizes in general that different types of organization and styles of supervision may be required according to the nature of the technology or task.

Decision Making

The top manager's role as culture leader has been increasingly highlighted; the manager as decision maker is a traditionally taken-for-granted role. Participation in decision making is influenced by the manager's level in the hierarchy, of course, but other factors such as the turbulence or peacefulness of the environment and the nature of the tasks performed limit or extend this role.

Decisional roles.   A major management text lists four decisional roles, those of entrepreneur, disturbance-handler, resource allocator, and negotiator (Hellriegel & Slocum, 1982). The entrepreneurial role involves such tasks as choosing new projects or deciding on a merger that could change the directions of the organization. Top management deals with such nonroutine occurrences or disturbances as a coal mine explosion, loss of a supply source due to international politics, or a wildcat strike.

Depending on their level, managers have varying amounts of resources at their command, which they are empowered to divide up and distribute. The choice of workers for particular assignments, newly opened positions, or merit awards must be made. Funds have to be allocated to different departments. Personnel have to be distributed at various work stations and on various shifts. Ability to acquire needed resources—personnel, materials, customers—is essential for the manager to do his or her job; the right to distribute these to others is a source of power.

The negotiator role involves bargaining with many role partners: suppliers, customers, other heads of departments. A form of bargaining takes place with subordinates as the manager develops obligations through use of strategic leniency and other tactics. The manager uses discretion in allowing time off for personal needs, overlooking minor errors or deviance, and backing up workers. In return he or she may expect extra effort in times of crisis or overload. Other kinds of give and take occur with the manager's other role partners.

How decisions are made.   The specifics of how decisions are actually made have been dissected and debated. Are they made rationally, based on information, or intuitively, based on insight? Are they determined by power relations, or environmental constraints, or because ready-made solutions beckon? All points of view have their adherents (see, e.g., Child, 1972; Cohen, March, & Olsen, 1972; Pfeffer & Salancik, 1974).

Analysis of decision making leads to related questions about information seeking and use. Because decisions are supposed to be based on available facts, "rules for gathering, storing, communicating, and using information are essential elements of organizational operating procedures" (Feldman & March, 1981:171). Nonetheless, the way information is interpreted and used may bear little resemblance to such rules. Of interest are the mental processes by which individuals filter information. Information processing refers to this cognitive action whereby cues are selected, combined, weighted, and altered (Ungson, Braunstein, & Hall, 1981).

Despite the issues raised about information selection and use, information is being collected and computerized at an increasing pace. One popular article asserts that there is a new "information-electronics" economy, in which "successful companies must acknowledge that their primary resource is information and their primary assets are their employees" (Naisbitt, 1984)—the employees presumably needed to process that information.

Information use and information complexity. What could be simpler than systematically gathering information and using it to make decisions? Feldman and March reply that the link between gathering information and using it is not that clear (1981). They make six observations based on an analysis of relevant research literature:

> (1) Much of the information that is gathered and communicated by individuals and organizations has little decision relevance. (2) Much of the information that is used to justify a decision is collected and interpreted after the decision has been made. (3) Much of the information gathered in response to requests for information is not considered in the making of decisions for which it was requested. (4) Regardless of the information available at the time a decision is first considered, more information is requested. (5) Complaints that an organization does not have enough information to make a decision occur while available information is ignored. (6) The relevance of the information provided in the decision-making process to the decision being made is less conspicuous than is the insistence on information. In short, most organizations and individuals often collect more information than they use or can reasonably expect to use in the making of decisions. At the same time, they appear to be constantly needing or requesting more information, or complaining about inadequacies in information. (1981:174)

Rather than ascribing malicious intent to this weak connection between information gathering and its use, Feldman and March find many reasons for it. For example, organizations provide incentives for gathering more information than is necessary, for "it is better from the decision maker's point of view to have information that is not needed than not to have information that might be needed" (Feldman & March, 1981:176). Some information may be unreliable or even a misrepresentation. Those who recognize the political aspects of organizations consider bargaining and negotiation to be "the primary decision making modes," with analysis used as a tool in the power struggle (Pfeffer, 1981a:354). Information is not neutral; it may be used politically. Nowhere is this more evident than in the careful managing of information provided to the public by their governments.

Possibly even more important, information gathering has symbolic functions. The idea of intelligent choice is a highly held value in modern Western civilization and especially in bureaucracies. So, "the gathering of information provides a ritualistic assurance that appropriate attitudes about decision-making exist" (Feldman & March, 1981:177).

Even from a managerial perspective that presupposes a certain degree of rationality in decision making, problems still revolve around the role of information in organizations. One issue is information complexity: Lawrence and Dyer use it as one of two key variables in their approach to revitalizing American industry. Information complexity is defined as:

> the degree of competitive product, market, technological, and regulatory variations in a firm's relevant environment. These variations represent the critical information uncertainties that must be analyzed by a firm trying to make rational choices about its environmental transactions. (1983:300)

These authors claim there can be too much or too little "information complexity" (IC) to induce innovation or member involvement, both of which are considered vital to an organization's adaptability. IC is lower under monopoly conditions where there are no competitors to take into account. IC is higher when a large number of competitors, using different strategies, offer competing goods and services. Lawrence and Dyer's theories have been touched on only briefly here to illustrate the centrality of information concepts in the analysis of organizational decision making. Those interested in learning how they propose to "renew American industry" are urged to read the original source.

Constraints on decision making.   Despite the great man theory of history and those who tend to consider a change in leadership as the solution to all problems, management is constrained in what it can actually do. Organizational theorists point out the limitations on decision making. For example, research has shown that organizational structure is much affected by the nature of its technology and cannot arbitrarily be determined by management (R. Hall, 1982:167). Thus, a highly routinized mass production operation limits the kind of worker participation that can be introduced. Similarly, a mechanical type of organization could probably not be successfully imposed on a work unit engaged in unstructured, basic research. Hall maintains that leadership behavior has a larger impact in organizations with relatively loose structures, but leadership succession in such highly structured situations as the American presidency does not create as much change as some people suppose is possible.

Since Hall made this point, a subsequent federal election again demonstrated the limits of the presidency. While Walter Mondale's presidential campaign projected the national deficit as the major problem facing the nation, President Reagan evaded the issue. Yet right after his reelection, Reagan and his relevant subordinates immediately turned their attention to the deficit—about which Mondale had so conveniently educated the public.

In December 1984 Union Carbide faced a major crisis when a dangerous chemical escaped at their Bhopal, India, plant. More than two thousand people were killed and half a city fled its homes. What happened could not be undone, nor was it immediately clear what the responsibility of the parent firm was. Major decisions by management revolved around the kind of public statements to be made, relationships with the Indian plant, and the legal and financial impact of the accident. Union Carbide could choose to disassociate its American plants and their safety practices from the Bhopal subsidiary. This option became less viable when an accident, a lesser one to be sure, occurred at its Institute, West Virginia, plant in August 1985.

In spite of the limits on individual managers, when something goes wrong, a change in management is often demanded. In the field of sports the manager is blamed for poor organizational performance; he becomes a scapegoat for the team's miserable showing, even when factors beyond his control are largely responsible. Hall provides an interesting review of the literature on this subject, some of which tries to determine whether or not changing managers actually improves team performance (see Grusky, 1963; R. Hall, 1982:170–172). The act of replacing managers (managerial succession) is not confined to the sports arena; it occurs under many circumstances.

Managerial Succession

Managerial succession provides an experimental situation for estimating the impact of a change of managers on performance and on informal arrangements. Alvin Gouldner's (1954a) classic example was so convincing and well presented that his findings might easily be overgeneralized. A man named Peele was promoted to manager of a gypsum plant, replacing Old Doug, who had recently died. Over the years Doug had become "indulgent" and loose in his practices and production had slumped. Peele, who was given the specific mandate to increase production, would be carefully observed by upper management.

Anxious to tighten things up and please his superiors, Peele faced a number of problems. First, he had been brought in from the outside, from a smaller plant, and was a stranger. He faced a workforce accustomed to long-standing informal practices. They had expected one of their own group to succeed to his position. Over the years the previous manager had developed a corps of loyal lieutenants who were tied to him in a system of mutual obligations. Peele felt he had no need to attend to the obligations engendered by his predecessor. As a result he faced resentment and resistance. For example, the office manager, Cook, was in a strategic position to either aid or sabotage him. When the main office telephoned the plant, Cook often took the call in Peele's absence. Cook would appear to make some effort to find him and then report that he couldn't be found, implying that Peele had not left information about his whereabouts. It would have been just as easy to "cover up" for him, as he had for Old Doug. Other old lieutenants were in similarly strategic positions where they could do Peele damage.

Given his newness and anxiety to please, Peele depended on higher management more than the men under him thought desirable. Another source of resistance lay in what Gouldner called the "Rebecca Myth," taken from a novel by Daphne Du Maurier. The workers remembered an idealized version of Old Doug that maximized his virtues and minimized his faults. They contrasted such traits as his leniency and friendliness with Peele's strictness and close supervision.

Gouldner goes on to deal with "the successor's defenses," such as replacing strategic personnel and, before establishing his own informal ties, relying on and enforcing the formal rules. Other research on managerial succession suggests that new managers may not encounter as much resistance as Peele did, especially if they replace a more production-oriented manager, are promoted from the inside, or enter situations in which managerial replacement is relatively frequent. Nonetheless, a period in which the new manager tries to gain compliance, in which established informal relations are disturbed and others gradually created, appears to be a common occurrence.

Izraeli suggests that this "settling in" period is best understood through a model that stresses process as well as structure (1977). Becoming a manager is viewed as a political process in which negotiation takes place between various role players. The new manager actively tries to shape his or her role rather than merely being "socialized" to the new position or firm. Support must be won, opposition neutralized, and compliance gained. At the top management level the political nature of replacement is understood. Struggles over leadership and dramatic takeovers gain headlines in the business press, but these have not been studied as scientifically as the replacement of lower level managers.

Grusky studied the relationship between effectiveness and managerial succession in the field of baseball. The baseball manager is held responsible for results, even though he is dependent on such factors as a strong farm system and advantageous trades (Grusky, 1963:27). The successes and failures of his team are public knowledge, mercilessly evaluated by informed fans. Many aspects of his role produce strain and stimulate efforts to replace him.

Grusky (1963) explains:

> If a team is ineffective, clientele support and profitability decline. Accordingly, strong external pressures for managerial change are set in motion and, concomitantly, the magnitude of managerial role strain increases. . . . The greater the managerial role strain, the higher the rate of succession. Moreover, the higher the rates of succession, the stronger the expectations of replacement when team performance declines. (p. 30)

MANAGERIAL CAREERS

Management-oriented texts abound with the success stories of such figures as J. Peter Grace, head of W. R. Grace and Co., Mary Kay of Mary Kay Cosmetics, and Ray A. Kroc of McDonald's. They are praised for their innovations and their dedication to their jobs, as exemplified by the eighty-hour work week. They are the role models presented to aspiring managers.

Mobility is the theme for managers: to be successful, they must be promoted, which often involves transfers within the firm. In universities, instructors generally must move up or out. Very promising persons in both settings may be able to transfer out to a higher position in another firm or university. How do the lower-level contenders move from their initial positions up the managerial ladder? Some are born into the right families, most are from preferred racial, ethnic, and gender groups, and others learn how to apply their talents through a combination of ability, being at the right place at the right time, understanding the unwritten rules, and acquiring sponsorship, the support and guidance of a higher-up. The first step is to be selected as a candidate.

Selection

When growing size and complexity made the simple, family-run business an inadequate structure, schools of management were created. As pointed out earlier, a new class, the managerial class, had to be developed. The schools would initiate the socialization of appropriate candidates to their new role. But who were selected to be the new managers? For one thing, the qualities determined to be managerial were sex-linked—male, just as secretarial qualities gradually came to be defined as female. Managers were to be tough-minded, analytical, unemotional.

We have seen that the managerial position involves decision making and flexibility. The higher up managers are in the structure, the more uncertainty they face and the greater the need for judgment. "The lack of structure in top jobs makes it very important for decision-makers to work together closely in at least the harmony of shared understanding and a degree of mutual trust" (Kanter, 1977:53). The manager's judgment and loyalty to the firm would be crucial qualities. One way of assuring the selection of persons who could be trusted was to pick them from persons of familiar backgrounds, who had been in the same fraternities and the same clubs. Potential managers who were chosen were socially similar and therefore could be trusted. Thus:

> In one industrial organization, managers who moved ahead needed to be members of the Masonic Order and the local yacht club, not Roman Catholic; Anglo-Saxon or Germanic in origin; and Republican.
> At Indsco [the firm studied] until ten years ago, top executives in the corporation were traceable to the founders of the company or its subsidiaries—people who held stock or were married to people who did. . . . The social homogeneity of corporate executives was duly noted by other managers. One asked a consultant, "Do all companies have an ethnic flavor? Our top men all seem to be Scotch-Irish." (Kanter, 1977:54).

The performance pressures on new types of people in managerial slots—such as women or minorities—can be great in such companies. They are usually tokens, persons so rare as to stand out because of their difference. They serve as public symbols of a supposedly enlightened policy, but the policy itself may be quite limited and not intended to create real change. Because tokens are different, they are trusted less and are less able to become part of informal networks (see Kanter, 1977, chap. 8).

A seeming trend away from reliance on ethnicity was observed by Kanter in the firm she studied, though few women were as yet making it to management. But prescriptions for American industry that suggest the value of clanlike structures, that stress emotional ties in place of bureaucratic ones, would seem to favor the return of the less universalistic ethnic criteria. While foreseeing great organizational change and the creation of international "multi-organizations" with a broad range of functions and tasks, Lawrence and Lorsch also bring in as a legitimate concern the fit of cultures to division of labor. They state:

> Basic cultural values are among the slowest-changing aspects of human life. These values prepare people to play some occupational roles better than others. Perhaps our multi-organizations will be able to build on these differences, to design a division of labor around them, and to reduce the present strong trend toward a universal culture of industrialized man. (1969:242)

Somewhat protective of variations in culture in intent, this formulation presents certain dangers. Decisions about division of labor based on culture could maintain ethnically stratified hierarchies, with homosocial industrialized men on top. The use of young Asian women to do repetitive, eye-straining delicate work in the computer industry is often justified by their patience, dexterity, and docility—cultural and gender traits. In fact, they do provide a cheap, meek labor supply in American plants transplanted abroad.

However, while nonhomogeneous types rarely make it to top management, middle managers and certainly first-line supervisors may come from more diverse class origins. Margolis interviewed eighty-one middle managers and wives of managers, who were, "for the most part, sons or daughters of farmers, miners, factory workers, or semi-skilled craftsmen; a few had fathers who were professionals or businessmen" (1979:9). They were located at a firm listed as one of the country's 100 largest industrial corporations. All of the managers were men; their race or religion were not considered in the study. The key issues discussed by Margolis were the quest for upward mobility, corporate socialization, and its impact on family and community life.

Socialization

From our discussion of company culture, it would seem that managers have a lot to learn, both formally and informally. Formal socialization may begin in business school and continue later in training sessions. Informal learning takes place as well. The material culture is obvious, the nonmaterial slightly less so. For example, in Indsco, as elsewhere, corporation managers are expected to have a tailored, conservative appearance. But other types of conformity pressures abound. It is important to get along well with peers and also to gain an important sponsor who can pass along know-how and see that the young person is invited to the right meetings.

Loyalty to the corporation is a prime virtue, since only the loyal can be trusted. One way that loyalty is tested is by the sacrifices the manager is willing to make on his way up. It is made clear to the male manager that family comes second, in such ways as giving him an assignment late in the day that is needed the next morning, transferring him to another city at a time inconvenient for the family, expecting him to work or attend company functions on evenings and weekends. Those with other values will drop out or not get ahead.

Women in managerial jobs, discussed more fully at the end of this chapter, face problems even more intense than their male counterparts (see, e.g., Farley, 1983). Women's obligations to family have always been rated higher than men's; they are judged by themselves and others on how well they balance their double day and act as superwomen. The bind is that if women are given special treatment based on their marital or parental status, they will automatically be omitted from moving up in management. Such special treatment would indicate that total loyalty cannot be expected from members of their sex.

Mobility

The testing period for managerial mobility may be long and drawn out. Managers who get ahead learn to sacrifice all other interests to the needs of the firm. This issue of loyalty and devotion is seen as crucial in Margolis's study. But given these virtues, the young manager must demonstrate ability to get things done. Simply being nice to subordinates does not gain their support; the manager earns it, at least partially, by demonstrating ability to impress his superiors and get what he or she needs in the way of resources (Kanter, 1977, chap. 3).

Structural effects of high and low mobility. Individual behavior is always evolving; what happens to us in crucial group settings is bound to have an impact. Just as being a managerial replacement, or a token, call forth certain responses, so high and low mobility tend to affect how people perform. Individual personalities have to respond to thwarted aspirations and disappointments as well as success. Here is what Kanter (1977) found in her study of Indsco:

> Those people set on high-mobility tracks tend to develop attitudes and values that impel them further along the track: work commitment, high aspirations, and upward orientations. Those set on low-mobility tracks tend to become indifferent, to give up, and thus to "prove" that their initial placement was correct. They develop low-risk, conservative attitudes, or become complaining critics, demonstrating how right the organization was not to let them go further. (p. 158)

Peer group culture in low-opportunity situations tends to develop an antihierarchy, antisuccess orientation. People look for recognition outside of the firm in other activities, such as community causes. Margolis found that aspiring managers had another reason for not getting involved in community work: the frequent transfers of those who were making it prevented them from gaining roots in a particular town (1979). The next two chapters are devoted to a more extended consideration of the individual–organization relationship.

The Wives of Management

Having a proper, well-behaving wife has long been understood as a sign of the manager's general conformity to societal expectations. In the husband's early career stages the wife's role is not highly visible but is nonetheless important. She quietly helps him build relationships through her correct behavior in social situations. As he moves up the ladder her role may become more public, involving a vast amount of business entertaining and community good works. Because the aspiring manager must put in long hours and often travel, the wife is left to cope with varied emergencies and with the largest burden of child care and household management. She becomes an important career resource by providing not only such material comforts as a clean house, good food, and quiet children, but also emotional support. If she wants her husband to succeed, she will recognize the primacy of the corporation, sublimate other needs, and demand less from the husband and father role. "The wife-as-resource argument presumes that because he is married, the male employee has additional resources to invest in his career and job" (Pfeffer & Ross, 1982:69).

So far it sounds like a traditional, stay-at-home wife is needed. A study that explored the effects of marriage and the effects of a working wife on the husband's occupational status and wage attainment seems to bear this out (Pfeffer & Ross, 1982). The authors found, in a national random sample, that the positive effects of being married and the negative effects of having a wife employed outside the home were greater for managers and professionals than for blue-collar workers. Married managers did better in their careers than the unmarried; those with nonworking wives did better than ones with working wives. It can readily be surmised that having a job outside the home might easily lessen the resources available for supporting the husband's managerial career. Some of the wifely functions described above are presumably less necessary for the blue-collar worker, since his salary does not vary accordingly.[3] From a purely economic point of view (and without regard to womens' career aspirations), it might be argued that the benefits of a two-salary household can outweigh the career advantages to a manager of having a nonworking wife. A literature is growing that examines the varied issues that face two-career families such as how to manage household location, site transfers, travel, child care, and division of family labor (see, e.g., Voydanoff, 1984).

---

[3] However, the radical feminist position holds that wifely and motherly functions constitute the *social reproduction* of the labor force, without which capitalist enterprise could not survive.

WOMEN AS MANAGERS: *A CASE STUDY*

In a book entitled *Women and Work,* the position of women in management is presented as stark:

> In management, as in the professions, we find that women are conspicuous by their absence. Although women are 42 percent of all workers, they are only 25 percent of the country's managers and administrators. And among all employed women, only 6 percent work in managerial positions. . . .
>
> As in the professions, the women are concentrated in the low-ranking, low-paying, and less powerful positions within management. Only 1 percent of the positions as high as vice president, and just 6 percent of the nation's middle-management positions are held by women. Rather, women are concentrated in the first-level and supervisory ranks in low-level positions, such as buyer, restaurant manager, general office manager, or department head in retail trade. This concentration of women at the low ranks reflects, in part, their recent entry into business and industry after years of being excluded altogether. Yet even when women do have high-ranking titles, their positions seldom lead to top management, but rather are on ancillary, dead-end routes. (Fox & Hesse-Biber, 1984:135–136).

The authors of this summary explain women's position in terms of three factors: cultural attitudes and ensuing sex-role conflicts, occupational demands for career continuity and commitment, and the male culture of organizations. The last factor is one we have emphasized frequently. The discussion to follow relies heavily on *Women and Work.*

Occupations are sex-linked; women's occupations have often served as extensions of family and sex roles. Thus, nursing, teaching, and social work have been predominantly female occupations. Specialties within professions also show this link. Women tend to find acceptance in occupations that call upon the so-called female traits—nurturance, empathy, and support. They are often considered unfit for those that require so-called male traits—agressiveness, competitiveness, and opportunism. However, fields or specialties considered natural for women often also turn out to be those with lower prestige and remuneration. As pointed out earlier, the ideal manager is based on the supposed male traits.

This generalization is supported by a study that asked male middle managers of insurance companies to rate women in general, men in general, and successful managers on ninety-two descriptive terms. There was a significant resemblance between ratings of men and managers and no resemblance between ratings of women and managers (Schein, 1975). Female managers also perceived successful managers as possessing the male traits. In addition, the effect of sex role stereotyping may cause subordinates (male and female) to resent female managers when they actually behave in ways that male managers do. Another study indicates that male managers are not always preferred to female ones (Fernandez, 1981, pp. 167–168), also due to gender-related traits. A large number of managers interviewed by Fernandez felt that female bosses were better communicators and gave them better feedback on their own performance than did males.

From all that has been said in this chapter, it is obvious that managerial work is time- and energy-consuming. The organizational timetable expects successful managers to make their mark and start their climb early. Performance is expected to be single-minded and continuous. Since men have been judged mainly in their roles as providers, devotion to work has in the past been deemed in the family's interest. Not so with the managerial woman, whose family duties center on what she does in the home. Withdrawal from employment for childbearing or child care, even though it may now be done for shorter periods than in the past, creates career discontinuity. In some cases, the option has been opened for fathers to take time off for child care, but there is little evidence that this is widely chosen. Fathers who do take such time off are liable to experience career problems similar to those of women.

Professional or managerial women who are married to men in similar positions face the problem of their husbands' transfers or relocations. Some couples experiment with dual residences, so that one partner does not have to give up a good job if the other transfers, but pressure on the woman to give up her job for her husband's tends to be greater. It is reported that some large firms have agreed to become part of a spouse employment network. When one of their members hires a professional, they agree to give more than cursory attention to the resume of that person's spouse (Byrnes, 1983:50).

Women also have difficulty gaining access to the traditionally male settings in which informal work connections are made. In corporations or the professions, certain young people are selected by sponsors who coach and aid them and prevent them from making mistakes. Young men are more likely to be favored. In addition, the female faces the possibility of sexual harassment by would-be sponsors, a situation that has been found to be rather widespread in some graduate schools. Lack of these sponsorship and collegial ties with men means limited access to informal networks of information. Womens' professional and managerial associations try to create "old girls' networks" and to pass on professional know-how, but they cannot provide the immediate help that isolated women may need to cope with particular problems encountered in the work setting.

Moreover, women may simply not be able to learn the rules for success. As an example, many women cannot specify whether they have staff or line jobs. This puts them at a disadvantage because, "Line jobs are where the action is, where the money is, where the power is. A rule of thumb to identify line jobs: those are the jobs for which women are deemed to be 'unqualified,'" asserts Harragan (1983). In private industry, line jobs tend to be in sales-marketing, production, or high-level finance departments that make money on money. Typical staff departments are ones that do not have policy decision-making authority, such as accounting, personnel, and customer relations. These departments, most vulnerable to job cuts in times of recession, are where most managerial women are found (Harragan, 1983:17).

If an organization has very few women executives, they face special performance pressures. Token women tend to be extremely self-conscious because they are continually being judged, from above and below. From the top they are often viewed as test cases representing their sex. Women beneath them in position may consider themselves a constituency and expect gains for the group. Or alternately, they may themselves stereotype the woman manager.

Various solutions have been proposed for remedying the disadvantages of women in management. Fox and Hess-Biber (1983) emphasize two general principles:

> Improvement in women's status within professions and management will require, along with their increasing numbers, certain changes in the organization of their work—namely, (1) greater flexibility in the structure and design of work and careers, and (2) greater access to the key positions, critical functions, and supportive alliances that enable advancement. (p. 150)

As a footnote, but nonetheless an important one, several of the points about women hold true also for members of minority groups previously barred from managerial positions (see Phillips and Blumberg, 1982). Managers who are minority females experience the effects of double discrimination. One advantage many black women have had is early socialization to the expectation that they will one day work and support themselves. But minority managers as a whole often encounter problems similar to those faced by women: of needing to fit into white male culture, of being stereotyped, and of experiencing the difficult situation of being tokens.

SUMMARY

The role of manager, a key figure in organizations, and the concept of organizational culture, were examined. Businesses and the business schools have been most concerned with issues of management, and the relevant organizational literature is strongly focused on the business firm. Managers vary by level, from first-line supervisors heavily involved in directing their subordinates, to middle managers, to top managers who spend much time negotiating forces in the environment. Two central roles, cultural leadership and decision making, were discussed. Recent concern with the weakened position of American industry in relation to its international competition has brought forth a number of works hoping to remedy the situation. The promotion of strong corporation cultures, with the manager as culture leader, has been recommended. Such leadership would pay attention to the nonrational elements of organizational life, to the need for loyalty and commitment. The concept of culture, borrowed from anthropology and sociology, is used in a special way to refer to informal norms as well as formal ceremonies, rites, and rituals created by management. However, the concept of culture is broader and includes informal patterns that develop at all levels of organizational structure. Related terms, such as subculture, informal organization, and secondary adjustments, were used to analyze culture in earlier organizational writings.

That making decisions is a major function of management is less disputed than the question of how these decisions are actually made. One issue is how information is perceived, sifted and used in decision making, with some asserting that the connection between information seeking and its use is weak. One reason is that choice is a political act and is not based merely on information. People have vested interests in various outcomes. Constraints on decision making exist and need to be studied; some organizations are more fluid and loose, others more bureaucratic. What a given individual in a position of power can do depends on a number of factors, such as organizational structure, technology, and the environment.

The replacement of one manager by another—managerial succession—provides a means of noting the impact of individuals on the organization. New managers experience a process of "settling in," which they must accomplish successfully. A new manager may be a stranger to the group, unfamiliar with the informal system and hence tending to rely on formal rules. He or she may be scrutinized by superiors and expected to perform better than his or her predecessor. New managers often replace subordinates loyal to the previous manager and gradually negotiate new informal agreements.

Individuals are selected for managerial careers on the basis of formal and informal qualifications, such as education (formal) and family ties (informal). Because of the large amount of uncertainty and decision making that must occur on top levels, those selected to be managers are often very similar to those already there, making it difficult for "new" types to break in.

Mobility is expected in the large corporation, as in the university, and is achieved through birth, connections, sponsorship, peer group support, getting into the right networks, and negotiating the structure.

The aspiring manager learns the necessity of being devoted to the firm, giving it priority over family or community demands. Success breeds success; those on the "fast track" maintain high aspirations and commitment and good contacts. The less successful tend to be more oriented to their peers, sometimes antiauthority, and seek satisfactions in outside activities.

Managers' wives, while not part of the structure, perform important functions in helping their husbands get ahead. A wife who is not employed outside the home appears to be an asset because she has time to attend to the many tasks her busy husband is unable to perform at home as well as to listen to him and support him emotionally. The increased number of working women has given rise to studies of the problems faced by dual-career families. In the concluding case study we examined the special circumstances of women managers, a relatively new but aspiring group, whose marital status appears to work against their upward mobility in the corporation.

In looking at managers we have begun our study of the individual–organization relationship, the central topic of the next two chapters.

8

ORGANIZATION
AND THE INDIVIDUAL

Roles and the Self: Moral Careers
    The Problem: How Do Organizations Affect Individual Lives?
    The Self as Reflexive, as an Ongoing Creation
    Kinds of Careers
The Impact of Organizations on Participants: Workers
    Structural Determinants of Behavior in Organizations
    The Creation of Occupational Types and Bureaucratic Personalities
The Taylorization of Police Work: A Case Study in Deskilling
Summary

ROLES AND THE SELF: MORAL CAREERS

The Problem: How Do Organizations Affect Individual Lives?

Depersonalization, dehumanization, deskilling—these terms have all been used to portray the effect of huge impersonal organizations on individual human beings. Organizations are said to treat people as numbers, to be rigid, and to reduce skilled tasks to monotonous, repetitive ones.

To be able to address such specific charges we need to consider the more general question: How do varying *organizational roles* impact on the self? The concept of role is the bridge, the connection between individuals and organizations.

We have seen that the division of labor in society and in organizations results in numerous statuses with associated roles. Much of the discussion in chapter 6 centered on statuses and roles in terms of the organization, its needs and tendencies. Now let us look at the other side of the coin: the impact of organizations on individuals and the individual self.

Role as the bridge between individual and group.   According to Gerth and Mills (1953):

> Man as a *person* . . . is composed of the specific roles which he enacts and of the effects of enacting these roles upon his self. And society as a *social structure* is composed of roles as segments variously combined in its total circle of institutions. The organization of roles is important in building up a particular social structure; it also has psychological implications for the persons who act out the social structure. (p. 14)

This excerpt presents a balanced picture of: (1) the human being as a composite or combination of the roles that he or she plays, affected by the playing of these roles, and (2) the human being as acting individual who, through acting, helps form the social world.

Sometimes it seems that the individual is dwarfed by the huge organization, yet as we examine specific organizations and specific role players we begin to see that individually and collectively acting human beings do make a difference—some more than others. Individuals high in power, such as owners, managers, or officials, usually exert more power individually, although they too are constrained by numerous conditions. Political upsets and power plays bring about the replacement of key individuals and the modification of programs in both government and private organizations. But less grandly, most roles involve some flexibility in interpretation, and individual role players play them out differently, creating variety and change. As an illustration, consider the fact that two employees in the same job classification, such as receptionist, may act quite differently to persons coming to them for information. Such gatekeeper roles may be low in status but high in power.

As new types of people are brought into an organization through co-optation or mergers, or as the result of labor shortages or social movements (to name a few mechanisms of such change), collectively, they influence the organization in distinctive ways. For example, handicapped people as a pressure group in their own interest have challenged the building of inaccessible public structures or transportation systems that make no provision for the disabled. Facilities are slowly being modified in the needed direction, although there is no assurance that the process will continue. And of course, trade unions were initiated in order to give groups of lower participants greater clout in determining the conditions of their work.

Ways in which individuals relate to groups.   Using Blau and Scott's terminology (1962), people are involved in organizations in four general ways: as owners or managers, as members or rank and file (lower) participants, as public-in-contact, and as the public-at-large (see chapter 3). These relationships take form in the following roles:

1. A proportion of us are, or aspire to be, *owners* or *managers*—persons high up in the authority structure. We have explored the managerial role in chapter 7. Managers often do not own their own enterprises but, especially at the higher levels, tend to be high-salaried decision makers, acting in the interests of the organization. For heads of major corporations, this activity includes attempts to influence public policy in such ways as lobbying and supporting particular candidates or political parties (R. Hall, 1983:296).
2. As *members* or *rank-and-file participants* we play roles in diverse groups such as families, work and educational organizations, and voluntary associations (e.g., fraternities, clubs, civic groups). We are workers, teachers, church members.
3. As *public-in-contact* we are technically outside of specific organizations but have regular direct contact with them as customers, clients, patients.
4. As part of the *public-at-large* we are members of the broader society in which organizations operate.

Following up on our discussion of managers, each of the other types of roles will be examined briefly here. (Table 8-1 provides examples for each of the types.) The remainder of the chapter will deal more extensively with rank-and-file participants, especially workers. Chapter 9 examines public-in-contact and public-at-large roles in more detail.

TABLE 8-1 Types of Roles

CATEGORY OF ROLE	EXAMPLES
Owner or manager	Bank president, army general, head of a department
Member or rank-and-file participant	Maintenance worker, post office clerk, fraternity member
Public-in-contact	Patient, inmate, welfare recipient, customer
Public-at-large	All members of the society not in direct contact with the organization

Classifying types of organizations by prime beneficiary (see chapter 3) Blau and Scott (1962) separated owners and managers from members or rank-and-file participants (lower participants). The more familiar terminology, *management* and *labor*, used in collective bargaining and discussions of labor issues also sets the two groups apart as role players who have differing and sometimes opposing vantage points. Those who write from a Marxist perspective often attempt to uncover the ways in which management seeks to control labor and limit its power (see, e.g., Zimbalist, 1979). As indicated earlier, the mutual interaction of management and workers has been explored from a managerial perspective in research on various managerial styles and how they affect worker satisfaction and productivity. Organizational sociologists and psychologists have sought the magic key to successful management. Another way of looking at the managerial and lower-participant roles is to contrast the structure of opportunities available in each. Kanter (1977) emphasizes the stark differences in the possibility of job mobility between two such groupings, managers and secretaries.

Increased interest in publics-in-contact (clients, students, customers, and so on), has developed out of several sources. The 1960s, "the social movement decade," was a time of revolt against existing institutions that seemed harsh, exclusive, and powerful. Among the movements was one for citizen control over community organizations, such as the effort to empower the clients of various government agencies (see, e.g., Haug and Sussman 1969).

Such agencies, in direct contact with the public, provide services that are paid for out of national, state, and local budgets. Many are what Lipsky has called "street-corner bureaucracies," the special dilemmas of which are noted in chapter 9. Out of the many proposals and demands of the 1960s and early 1970s came some degree of community control of schools, poverty agencies, and other public service organizations.

The interest in client discontent and informed consumerism has continued at a lesser pace, gaining a new focus in the 1980s. Concern with environmental hazards has brought many formerly inactive citizens into confrontation with government and corporations. Besides its role in direct contact with clients, government acts as a third party to modify, regulate, and control the relationships of organizations to publics-in-contact and the general public. Such issues as environmental protection or public safety are so broad that they affect the general public.

Another strand of interest in how organizations impact on their publics-in-contact derives from the work of social psychologists who look at the impact of total institutions on their "clients." The public-in-contact in a total institution is in intensive contact with the organization, having their total activities monitored and controlled by it. The people who are this public-in-contact are the raw material being handled and processed by the lower participants. They are quite separate symbolically and socially from wardens, nurses, guards, and other keepers and overseers. Using some of the most oppressive of organizations for his examples, Goffman (1961) has vividly described how individuals in total institutions relate to their roles, what they make of them, and how these roles are handled by the self. His analyses are widely valid, although most organizations are only partially inclusive of the self.

The general public, or public-at-large, is of course greatly affected by the actions of huge organizations and in turn attempts to affect them. Public opinion and voting behavior are ways of doing so; corporations, government, and social and religious movement organizations all court public approval.

Many of us interact with different organizations in a variety of different roles. These contacts with organizations constitute much of our daily experience and have consequences for how we view ourselves. So before dealing with organizational roles more specifically, it is worth examining the psychological meaning of roles to the individual self.

The Self as Reflexive, as an Ongoing Creation

Roles and identity. Roles have been described as expected behaviors that individuals are channeled into as they play out given statuses, whether ascribed or achieved. In chapter 6, the term *status set* was defined as including all of one's statuses at a particular time in personal history. Most of the types that have been described above appear in the status sets of average persons, who are sometimes participants, sometimes clients or customers (publics-in-contact), and often part of the general public.

Each status has with it associated roles, and each role that an individual has is tied to a role set. *Role set* has been defined as "All the role relations that a person in a particular status has with people in other statuses" (Bredemeier & Stephenson, 1965:38).[1] Figure 8-1 illustrates the role set of a hypothetical college student. A father relates as father to his son, daughter, their mother, their schoolteachers, their principal, and so on. This constitutes his role set for the status of father. A supervisor, in that status, relates to her boss, those she supervises, other supervisors, and other persons in the organization and outside of it. One individual holds many statuses and plays many, sometimes conflicting, roles. As people relate to a particular status they tend to emphasize the parts they like—that is, the most satisfactory or rewarding roles. One supervisor may play up to the boss, another may be oriented to the workers.

Roles become part of the self in varying degrees, part of the inner core of the individual. Social psychologists, following the path-breaking work of Mead (1934), have shown us that babies are not born with a sense of self, an identity. It is something they must learn. And they learn it reflexively—by reacting to how the most intimate persons in their environment behave toward them. In the first role—new baby, son or daughter, the infant begins to get a sense of how others feel about him or her as object, and to respond back. The child learns that certain behaviors elicit certain results and starts to repeat the ones that work. Over the first few years of life the child's self, and image of self, is being produced in interaction with the important other people of his or her immediate family environment. Called "bad boy" or "bad girl" often enough, the child internalizes this image.

Later, as the child enters into play with peers another element is added, a new set of standards: father or mother may have disapproved of certain behavior that now finds favor with peers. Different standards require the individual to modify his or her behavior in terms of various audiences. The child learns to role-play, that is, to respond to the expectations of his or her various membership groups.

[1] For an alternate definition of the concept of role-set, see Pfeffer and Salancik, 1980.

FIGURE 8-1   A Hypothetical College Student and the Role Set Attached to His Status as Student

Each major role becomes incorporated into the self, becomes a part of the person. And so it goes throughout life, except that as our roles proliferate we identify more with certain ones than others.

Attachment to roles.   As we know, people have varying degrees of commitment and attachment to the roles they play. Commitment is the degree of *felt obligation* to perform a role. Attachment refers to one's cathectic or *emotional* feelings about it. Individuals learn to retain some detachment or develop distance from roles that they do not embrace, particularly so for roles that detract from their image of self. In the extreme case, one can be almost totally alienated from a role (such as mental patient) into which one has been thrust, and develop a personal story to explain the errors or treachery that forced one into that state (see Goffman, 1961). Long-time political prisoners may survive by mentally remaining in the private world of their previous identities. More casually, we often partially remove ourselves from roles by daydreaming or being less attentive than our external appearance might indicate. Students who habitually sit in the back rows seem to signal their less than full absorption into the classroom role. In contrast, a person can embrace a role to such an extreme that it is embarrassing, as in the case of the overconforming new military recruit whose excessive saluting proves annoying rather than ingratiating.

Participation in different types of groups may range from involuntary to fully self-chosen, from ascribed membership in racial, religious, and gender groups to achieved participation in educational or occupational organizations. Organizations, too, as we have seen, can select, in varying degrees, the people who pass through them.

Because the individual may resist placement into negatively valued roles or may lack commitment to others, the organization must create psychological mechanisms that will sufficiently overcome people's resistance to roles. An organization intent on drastic modification of behavior or major switches in identity often deems it necessary to extinguish previous identities and resocialize individuals to new values and new self-concepts.

Graphically portrayed by Goffman is the stripping process in total institutions such as mental hospitals and prisons, the degradation rituals that are gone through in order to make previously distinctive individuals into anonymously, standardly debased patients or convicts. The term *brainwashing* has been used to describe how organizations go about such drastic reorganizations of the self. One example used by Goffman was the ritualized, highly institutionalized debasement of religious order novitiates. But recently certain new religious groups have been accused of brainwashing young people to make them total and devoted converts, raising the question of how far an organization—especially one considered a cult—may be allowed to go (see Bromley & Shupe, 1979).

As discussed earlier (see chapter 3) the total institution can be understood as a polar concept, with other organizations forming a continuum from more to less totally encompassing of the individual. Less drastic transformations of self are required by organizations that are less than total, that incorporate only a portion of the individual's total waking time under their direction. A temporary or segmental role may be shed.

For example, the ordinary patient in a hospital may be resocialized from prepatient outsider to the patient role, learning to say "fine" when asked how he or she feels (all patients are sick but they are supposed to act cheery), to fall asleep with the light on, to accept being poked and prodded by numerous strangers in a variety of uniforms. But later this temporary patient status can be left behind. An individual taking one course "for fun" is unlikely to undergo the changes in identity of a full-time, career-oriented student.

The higher one's general status, the greater the possibility of maintaining the self intact in new situations. The upper-class private patient in a fancy hospital gets more individualized treatment than the public patient in a charity ward. A famous professor, taking on a new university post, can usually make his or her own terms, teaching what and how much he or she wishes. Such professors have power to influence the organization and its definition of their role. The title "doctor," with its built-in prestige value, can be manipulated to afford oneself better service in other roles, such as a client or a parent. In my role as mother in conferences with a school principal, the principal seemed to be much influenced by the knowledge of my Ph.D. status. A Ph.D. calling herself "doctor" in a medical situation is apt to confuse many role players, who—uncorrected—accord her the privileges of a medical doctor.

Persistence of the status-conferring quality of roles.   Obviously, statuses and their accompanying roles are ranked into hierarchies of prestige, into "highers" and "lowers." Crucial roles tend to confer lasting prestige or degradation on the individual; many of them are very fateful for the individual's self. For example, the military cadet hopes to acquire the qualities of an officer and to have that role incorporated into his or her personality. The polished product is a "type." Note that the first American woman astronaut maintained a strictly astronaut image, showing the usual eagerness to be off on the mission and reporting the usual exhilaration and fun experienced after it was over. No astronaut is supposed to mention the motion sickness with which a rather large proportion of them are afflicted, and of course astronaut Sally Ride was mute on this subject. The first black American astronaut was exposed to the press in 1983 and presented a carefully designed blend of the usual modesty, matter-of-factness, and loyalty to the program.

As a less dramatic example of how statuses become incorporated into our identities and self, take the simple case of marital status. Once married, this status becomes part of one's life and social history. Or take the Hollywood starlet who is glamorized and recast into the look of the day. The innocence of her "before" pictures will never return.

For many reasons, and because of the tendency of conferred status to remain with the individual, most organizations make careful distinctions between people in different roles. It was pointed out in chapter 6 that hierarchical levels of workers and managers frequently coincide with race, ethnicity, or gender divisions, reinforcing organizational status by way of ascribed societal status.

Official concepts, justifications, and ideologies are developed in order to explain the different kinds of people that inhabit the organization. Typical role players are found to have the qualities appropriate to their roles—managers and secretaries, teachers and students being very different types of people. Numerous jobs are sex-typed, as suitable only for men or only for women. Advancements in the electronic industry have been technologically modern but have followed the older patterns of job segregation. Very precise, eye-straining, repetitive, and low-paid work in this industry is most frequently allocated to young, docile, third-world women (Lim, 1983:70-91).

Kinds of Careers

The concept of career. The notion of career is most commonly applied to the individual's mobility or lack of it, over time, in a desirable profession or field. But work career needs to be looked at much more generally as an individual's progression through various types of jobs, career changes, mishaps, unemployment, and the like. Work careers will be examined more closely when we consider the impact of organizations on participants.

The term *career* can also be used to refer to any major involvement over time that helps shape individual identity, rather than limiting it to paid work (Becker & Strauss, 1970). A career involves a sequence of related stages that are passed through over the life course; however, one person may have a number of interlocking careers. Women frequently have two important careers, their family career and their work career, each contingent on the other. That is, a woman's work career, if she marries or has elderly relatives to care for, tends to be influenced greatly by stages in her family career, and vice versa. The family career used to consist, most typically, of being unmarried, then probably married, then possibly a mother, then possibly a grandmother, and if these previous statuses have been achieved, very likely a widow or divorcee.[2] During these stages the woman is accorded different degrees of respect, faces varying demands on her time from the various role players in her family, and must integrate work outside the home with her family career.

Figure 8-2 depicts the double day, so characteristic of working married women all over the world. Studies show that these women are generally expected to perform most household duties in addition to their outside paid work (Malos, 1980). The man also has a family career consisting of many of the same stages, but being married affects him differently. As we have already noted, his lesser responsibilities in the home plus the support that he receives from a wife tend to affect his work career positively, as measured in salary (Pfeffer & Ross, 1982). To the extent that a man attempts a more egalitarian role in the home (e.g., does more housework, takes more time off for child care), he stands to reduce the present gender advantage.

In addition to family and work careers, people may have other important careers that help define their lives, for example in crime (the "professional thief"), in health (periods of illness, recovery, or debilitation), in voluntary or social movement work. The last type of career often provides a satisfying substitute for persons lacking absorbing or prestigeful paid jobs. Parent-Teacher Associations, Leagues of Women Voters, and numerous church organizations have profited from the long devoted service of numerous homemakers. Persons have given up the usual work

---

[2] In the United States, more unmarried women are becoming mothers, a modification in the traditional family career pattern.

FIGURE 8–2   A Woman's Dual Careers and the Double Day

careers for total commitment to political, social, or religious movements, defining their inner selves in terms of movement roles.

Roles and moral careers.   The concept of *moral career* was used by Goffman (1961) to describe the changes in self-concept and concepts of others that developed in the process of becoming a mental patient. Such changes similarly accompany other major career landmarks, such as becoming a parent. As their children develop, the mothers judge themselves according to their cultural "good mother" image. The good mother and good worker roles are frequently juggled. Mature women who return to college often find that their new schedules, time needed for self, and anxiety over grades is incongruous with the previously developed mother role.

But combinations of career, looked at this way, are not so unusual. The man who holds a relatively uninteresting job may be king of the bowling league, playing in increasingly more prestigeful tournaments as he rises in his after-hours career. In sponsoring recreational activities such as a bowling league, companies provide alternative sources of rewards for persons destined to remain low in the work hierarchy.

Given the combinations of roles and types of careers that most people engage in, there is an integrating process that must go on. Individuals need to fit their developing selves into their previous concepts of self and to make sense out of their lives (Berger & Luckmann, 1967).

The moral career parallels an individual's transitions through important statuses. That is, something happens to the self-conception as individuals proceed through various group contexts. The contrast is stark between those voluntarily entering status-enhancing groups and those consigned to status-debasing ones. In the first case the individual is transformed into someone with a higher or loftier status, is presumed to have been resocialized to be that kind of person. In the second the individual has been publicly defined as inferior in some way and will bear a stigma such as that of an ex-con or an ex-mental patient, which creates, whenever known, a permanently lower status. Not only that, but people meeting the ex-con or the former mental patient are likely to interpret present behavior in terms of the past stigma. This tendency is so strong that concentration camp victims were haunted by a sense of shame, and many were unwilling to discuss the dehumanizing process they had gone through.

Individual construction of reality.   Faced with the status-defining aspects of organizations as well as specific objective conditions (e.g., deprivation of one's usual diet, an office that lacks windows), the acting individual tries to build a world of meaning that leaves the self somewhat intact (Berger & Luckmann, 1967). And when many people are in the same objective position, they collectively create their symbolic world, as we saw in the case study of the women's prison.

The socially constructed reality of adults is passed on to children as they are socialized. Yet the child in turn filters this social reality through the lens of his or her own experiences. Each acting individual understands reality subjectively and enters into dialectical interaction with his or her social world, continually recreating society and groups. A familiar example is the tendency to make sense out of or rationalize events after they have happened, such as saying "It turned out to be all for the best." Another frequent practice is that of discovering the problems for which solutions have appeared, such as claiming, "When Bob dragged me off to a movie, I realized that I had been working too hard."

Given these basic facts about roles, the self, careers, moral careers and the individual construction of reality, we can proceed to examine more closely the impact of organizations on role players in different organizational positions. The image of the individual–organization relationship that underlies our discussion is well-expressed in these three statements by Kanter (1977):

> Each position in an organization carries with it a set of constraints and limits on the possibilities for occupants to achieve recognition and autonomy. (p. 250)

What people do, how they come to feel and behave, reflects what they can make of their situation, limited though it might be, and still gather material rewards and preserve a modicum of human dignity. (p. 251)

People's choices reflect strategic approaches to managing a situation. (p. 252)

THE IMPACT OF ORGANIZATIONS ON PARTICIPANTS: WORKERS

Structural Determinants of Behavior in Organizations

In examining the impact of organizations on participants, we will emphasize the lower or rank-and-file participants, the ones who do the day-by-day work. The sources of their behavior lie in the way they interact with the organizational structure and their position in it. Miller and Form (1980:125) emphasize the two-way interaction between acting individuals, with their own personal aims, and an organization that is trying to use them for its purposes. Workers try to meet their needs by, for example, bargaining for job changes or special conditions. On the job, persons emphasize the functions they like to perform and, when possible, minimize those they do not like. They will develop self-conceptions about the nature of the work and the status it entails.

From this perspective worker behavior is not dependent on inherent human nature or on a single device such as job enrichment. Workers' perceptions of what their jobs offer will help determine their behavior as they seek to maintain individual integrity and satisfactory self-images. This should not suggest that behavior is entirely dependent on psychological factors; a satisfactory self-image may be very contingent on making what one considers a decent living. Job conditions affect personality and, in turn, personality influences work behavior.

A series of studies examined this interactive effect of job conditions and personality (Kohn & Schooler, 1981; J. Miller et al., 1979). Among the job conditions included by Kohn and his associates were those that identified "a man's place in the organizational structure, his opportunities for occupational self-direction, the principal job pressures to which he is subject, and the principal extrinsic risks and rewards built into his job" (Kohn & Schooler, 1981:1259). Elements that defined occupational self-direction were the complexity of the work, the closeness of supervision, and the degree of routinization. Opportunities for self-direction in the job tended to increase ideational flexibility (a form of intellectual flexibility) and to promote a "self-directed orientation to self and society" (Kohn & Schooler, 1981: 1281). Jobs that limited occupational self-direction (e.g., those that were simple, repetitive, and closely supervised) tended to promote a conformist orientation to self and society. Apparently, when given the opportunity to use judgment, persons develop this facility.

But personality, in turn, was found to have important consequences for work. Intellectual flexibility and a self-directed orientation tended to lead the individual, in time, toward jobs that allowed greater freedom for occupational self-direction.

Work roles and identity. Work organizations tend to absorb a good part of a man's day, and increasingly of a woman's day, and to form an important element in the individual's self-concept and feelings of worth. Traditionally and still, the "good provider" element is basic to a family man's role set (Bernard, 1984). That is why unemployment can be so devastating in more than a monetary sense. Failure in a work role, not meeting one's own expectations or those of others, or being frustrated by one's job raises the possibility of alienation from work. Contrary to views that suggest women are not involved in their work roles, recent studies show that occupational conditions have a decided psychological impact on women as well as men (Miller et al., 1979:66) The disappointed or disillusioned individual may not give his or her all or might even sabotage the work process in the many ways that are possible.

Among the adaptive acts of frustrated employees, Argyris (1959) includes the following:

> Leave the situation (absenteeism and turnover); climb the organizational ladder; become defensive (daydreaming, aggression grievances, regressions, projection, feelings of low sense of social worth); become apathetic, disinterested, non-ego involved in the organization and its formal goals; create informal groups to sanction the defense reaction (above); formalize the informal groups in forms such as trade unions; deemphasize the importance of self-growth and emphasize the importance of money and other material rewards. (pp. 119–120)

Motivation and productivity. Given the array of behaviors itemized above, it is no wonder that major attention has been directed to the questions of increasing workers' motivation and productivity. Casting aside notions such as laziness or ambition being personal qualities, much research has examined the *structural determinants* of behavior in organizations, that is, how the way that organizations are set up affect people. The human relations school as a major research orientation in the 1930s (see chapter 2) sought to discover which organizational variables were most potent in achieving desired worker behavior. This school focused on the interpersonal relations of work—styles of leadership, norms and culture of the face-to-face work group, participation. The quality of work performed was to be improved through more democratic participation offered by the firm; unions were ignored.

Perrow (1979:98) and others have questioned the direct relationships between human relations factors and productivity, based on numerous studies showing how complex and variable these are. Looking only at interpersonal relations omits some important factors in the situation, such as the nature of the tasks or remuneration. The success of Japanese factories in producing high-quality outputs has restimulated American research into the human factors in management (Ouchi, 1981). Ouchi even makes the statement that "productivity may be dependent upon trust, subtlety, and intimacy" (1981:9).

Another major series of theories, which Kanter dubs the "cognitive-motivational school," were concerned with work satisfaction and motivation based on incentives, with how people weighed the various factors that entered into their attitudes and decisions about how effectively to perform in their work (1977:254).

This position focused attention on the role of the manager in fostering work satisfaction. McGregor's Theory X and Theory Y contrasted two opposing conceptions of human nature, which were said to lay behind less effective and more effective managerial styles (McGregor, 1960:33–34, 47–48). Theory X presumed the worker to be lazy and unambitious, needing to be coerced into responsibility or hard work. Theory Y presented a much more favorable picture of human nature, assuming that people do not dislike work and can be motivated to direct their best efforts toward organizational purposes. McGregor wrote at a time when workers were enjoying relatively high employment and comfortable living conditions. He accepted the psychologist Maslow's theories about the existence of a hierarchy of needs and believed that once basic needs were satisfied, people would look for greater satisfaction and self-fulfillment in work. In a similar vein, natural systems analysts argued that "highly centralized and formalized structures are doomed to be ineffective and irrational in that they waste the organization's most precious resource: the intelligence and initiative of its participants" (Scott, 1981).

Participation. Kanter suggests that behavior in organizations depends on three elements—participation, power, and opportunity—and that attempts to motivate employees need to take each of these into account. Recent research has examined many elements involved in participation, such as increasing the variety of tasks; autonomy, or the chance to make decisions and act on one's own; job rotation, where workers move around among several related jobs; and employee participation in decision making (see, e.g., Fischer & Sirianni, 1984, part 5).

The image of workers as the scientific management era saw them in the early part of this century—unthinking cogs in a machine—resulted in the breakdown of work into mechanically defined, boring, and routine rasks that involved no mental activity on the part of the worker. In the 1970s and 1980s, analysts have reopened the question, claiming that more worker input into decisions improves satisfaction and productivity and that different styles of work organization need to be created. Others maintain that the technology of the operations, the task at hand, largely determines whether or not work can be varied and whether or not decision making can be built into jobs (Perrow 1980:118–130). It is claimed that certain types of mass production are by their nature repetitive and uninteresting. In contrast, the production of a highly specialized unit, such as a custom car, can involve much more intelligence and autonomy. Because of concern with worker dissatisfaction and the related lower productivity, many modifications in the organization of work have been put forward. Miller and Form (1980) believe the following hold promise:

1. Job enlargement or enrichment. This reverses the practice of scientific management of breaking jobs down into minuscule units; it puts some of these units back together again and thereby gives the employee a chance to use more of his or her abilities.

2. Job rotation. This system, used in Japanese industry, rotates workers among different jobs, giving them the opportunity to broaden their knowledge and become less bored. It also provides management with a more flexible labor force that can be moved around easily.

3. Employee-centered supervision. This has to do with management practice that is congruent with the Theory Y view of human behavior. The subordinates are given increased control over their work environment, and the supervisor attends to their human relations needs.

4. Employee participation in the plant community. This can take place in several ways, from recreational activities to profit sharing. Through participation the employee gains more of a stake in his or her work. Some firms, for example, offer employees stock options, which gives them a chance to own part of the business.

5. Training for mobility into new occupations and new types of work situations. Miller and Form acknowledge that not all jobs can be enriched. But firms can offer training so that employees' skills are upgraded and they can be moved into other occupations.

The issue of mobility and blocked mobility is an important one to which we shall return.

Some critics of the job enrichment schemes see them as mere window dressing for management's true objectives. A group of Marxist scholars, following the lead of Braverman (1974), discuss the process of deskilling and disempowering workers that exists in many industries, in jobs as diverse as police work and computer programming (Zimbalist, 1979). Rather than accept the premise that some kinds of work are basically repetitive and monotonous and that other types lend themselves to greater worker involvement, these scholars maintain that technology can be manipulated. They see capitalism as involved in a constant process of inhibiting worker power and breaking down skills. So, for example, computer programmers were put to work to break down various skilled jobs into mechanical ones, but they themselves are now finding their work simplified and made less skilled (Kraft, 1979:1-17).

Zimbalist views job enrichment programs as a response to the results of job fragmentation. He maintains:

> This ongoing tendency toward job impoverishment and "worker alienation" is confronted by another tendency—a labor force with higher educational levels and higher expectations for rewarding work. The outcome of this confrontation is often high labor turnover, high absenteeism, and lackadaisical work which, in turn, imply low productivity and low quality. In recent years the job impoverishers have responded to this dilemma with programs of "job enrichment" and "work humanization." (1979:xvii)

The significance of mobility. While the nature of the job at one point of time is important, those who focus only on that ignore the weight of long-run career prospects and aspirations. Plans that try to motivate all workers may ignore the fact that certain career lines are blocked while others afford ample upward movement.

Kanter found that people with high mobility prospects behave quite differently than those with low prospects within the corporation. As a parallel, students frequently begin to assess their chances of success in a particular class and gauge their behavior according to the expected outcome.

Opportunities for advancement vary tremendously. Opportunity refers to "expectations and future prospects," and it has a structure. Such things as promotion rates and ability to acquire new skills and advance systematically differ according to where one is in the structure. Another factor affecting job performance that has been mentioned before is proportions—"the social composition of people in approximately the same situation" (Kanter, 1977:248.) People whose type (e.g., women, blacks, elderly) is represented in small proportion in a job tend to be more visible, feel more varied pressures, and find it harder to gain credibility. That is, as tokens they have a harder time doing their job well and have special constraints on their role performance (see chapter 7).

Within Indsco, the corporation Kanter studied, employees are divided into "exempt" and "nonexempt" categories, terms absolutely understood in corporation culture. The exempt are those in the managerial track who receive salaries rather than wages. Mobility is their most important motivating force.

The nonexempts, mainly secretaries, have little hope of entering more prestigeful, remunerative, or responsible positions except by accompanying a boss who is on the rise. Length of service means very little. Under these conditions motivation to rise would be a waste of energy. Most of the women selected as secretaries were not types who would challenge this system. Hence, when the firm posted some nonsecretarial job openings for which the secretaries were newly eligible, few of them dared to take their option to apply. They were encouraged to maintain female behavior, loyalty, and service to a particular boss.

In contrast, the exempt employees define their success as movement upward, a change in title, a better salary, and more authority. Particular spots in the organization were known to be either dead ends or stepping stones, and people behaved toward them accordingly, regardless of the content of the particular job. A tremendous amount of informal knowledge was necessary in order to avoid pitfalls and grasp opportunities on the way up the career ladder. Certain people were identified as possible officer material and exposed to more top officers who were in a position to help them. Those who were given these opportunities increased their aspirations and commitment. But not all could rise in this high-pressure atmosphere. Others became "stuck," recognizably so after upward movement had stopped for a long enough time.

Certain functions carried more prestige and power than others in Indsco. That is also true elsewhere, as a woman who had risen to become manager of the word processing division in an advertising firm recently discovered. She had successfully built the size and reputation of her department. Yet when she requested a transfer to a managerial post in another part of the structure, she was turned down. Presumably, she was still being treated as the head of a typing pool, her high status in this department was not transferrable, and her managerial ability was overlooked.

She also felt that she could not accept a turndown and quit to form her own firm—proper managerial behavior!

Consequences of high and low mobility.   The behavior of the organizational participants at Indsco depended greatly on how they were "making out" in this corporation structure. Unlike the more successful exempt employees, individuals who were blocked tended to exhibit distance or disengagement from their work roles. Blocked mobility led to a solidarity with peers and those lower down. Such persons might be more likely to join a union. On the other hand, one of the reasons given for the reticence of many American workers to become solid union members is the American myth that everyone can rise. The employees who were truly moving up were more oriented to top persons in the structure who might act as sources of support. The finding that the less mobile are more friendly to peers and to those below them in the structure is probably widely applicable. In the academic setting, instructors who are "stuck" may find more rewards in associating with their low-level peers or with students than with "the big shots." This adaptation may also occur because they are not included in the informal system of the "in" group.

Work satisfaction and alienation.   The aspirations of workers depend not only on the particular work organization but also on their total life chances. Two typically female jobs have been mentioned frequently—secretaries and factory workers in the electronics industry. In both cases, the work, while not affording mobility, may represent a better opportunity than the women had elsewhere. A secretarial job tends to mean a great deal to a black woman because of the traditional barriers that have kept her out of white-collar work. The young Asian woman working in an electronics factory may consider herself lucky to have urban employment so that she can help out her family or save for a wedding. Illegal aliens, coming from a disadvantaged position, take on jobs that the native-born disdain. A nurse I interviewed told me that nursing was far superior to a life in the mines such as his father and uncles had experienced. On the other hand, a foreman neighbor used to conceal his lunchbox when he arrived home from work, embarrassed that he, the son of a doctor, had not made it to a professional career. Thus, a particular job may represent either upward or downward mobility in life to different people, depending on their own expectations, the definitions of "success" they bring with them.

While alienation frequently occurs among those who cannot make it up the organizational ladder, it also arises for other reasons. Persons in situations where they cannot do the jobs for which they were trained, where they are overburdened or not provided with the necessary equipment, may withdraw from commitment. Distance is needed when one cannot meet the obligations of one's role due to external circumstances.

A now classic study that looked at occupational differences in work satisfaction came up with findings that mesh well with Kanter's case study of Indsco (Blauner, 1969:223-249). Blauner found the highest percentages of satisfied workers among professionals and businessmen—those on the top of the occupational ladder. In a given plant, satisfaction was higher among clerical than factory workers. Skilled workers were more satisfied than unskilled ones. Statistically, work satisfaction correlated closely with the prestige of the job as measured by the public's appraisal of the relative prestige of various occupations.

Occupational prestige is the best general index of satisfaction since it includes within it many factors that are correlated with differences in satisfaction. The most prestigious jobs are also those that involve higher levels of education or skill, more control and responsibility, and better remuneration. Control is said to include "control over the use of one's *time* and physical *movement*, which is fundamentally control over the *pace* of the work process, control over the *environment*, both technical and social, and control as the *freedom* from *hierarchical authority*" (Blauner, 1969:234). These other advantages are in addition to the higher status that upper-level jobs carry with them.

Besides occupational prestige, Blauner found two other features that enhance worker satisfaction, which he calls on-the-job social relations and occupational communities. Because of their technology certain types of work, such as steel production and mining, have to be done in teams. The greater the extent to which people work together in integrated teams, the greater the job satisfaction appears to be. Occupational communities are ones where workers not only work in an integrated way but live in communities made up mainly of fellow workers. Miners, for example, tend to live in mining communities and share a special culture with their peers. Isolation from other types of work gives them the opportunity to develop pride and avoid invidious distinctions. They do not experience a sharp split between their work lives and home lives.

Job satisfaction is often assumed to increase productivity, but studies have failed to show a clear relationship between the two (Schwab & Cummings, 1970; Scott, 1981:90). Nonetheless, the interest in work satisfaction and alienation remains high on the agenda of those managing others or teaching others to manage, especially during a period of decline in American industry (see chapter 11). Now we turn to another very general aspect of organizations that shape participants' behavior—the effect of bureaucracy on the personality of the bureaucrat.

The Creation of Occupational Types
and Bureaucratic Personalities

Much of our discussion shows the adjustment of participants to the positions in which they find themselves. But bureaucratic organizations are also said to produce a certain personality type. This is the kind of service-providing bureaucratic worker about whom most of us complain when frustrated in our quest for some service. According to Merton (1952:361–371), bureaucracies do tend to spawn a certain exasperating type of personality. White-collar work, such as that done in government agencies, best fits his caricature.

Bureaucratic personality. Merton calls the bureaucratic personality a dysfunction of bureaucracy. Using Weber's model, he points out that Weber was preoccupied with the precision, reliability, and efficiency that bureaucratic structures could attain. These aims are responsible for the tendency to make rules, establish procedures, define statuses. Merton also accepts as obvious the Marxian tenet that people are largely controlled by their relations to the instruments of production—in this case, the bureaucracy. As they are shaped by their roles in these structures, workers become less adaptable. Merton (1952) compares his notion of the dysfunctions of bureaucracy to Veblen's concept of "trained incapacity":

> Trained incapacity refers to that state of affairs in which one's abilities function as inadequacies or blind spots. Actions based upon training and skills which have been successfully applied in the past may result in inappropriate responses *under changed conditions.* (p. 364)

The person with trained incapacity is typically one fairly low in the hierarchy who is hemmed in by rules and regulations. He or she has a circumscribed role to play or function to perform in the division of labor and a good deal of paperwork to complete—filling out forms, reports, and the like. The day-to-day demands of the occupational role require uniform behavior patterns. Merton was concerned with the rigidities that set in under such circumstances.

The bureaucratic personality is preoccupied with following the highly specialized, detailed rules and procedures, "dotting the *i*'s and crossing the *t*'s" in more familiar parlance. Any originality or creativity has been reduced by supervisors who insist on things being done "by the book," that is, strictly according to the rules. The person is fearful and timid, afraid that any deviations from the rules will cost the job. Such an individual is totally at a loss when there is any change in routine, for he or she has not been allowed to learn how to exercise discretion. The emphasis on methodical performance of routine duties has created a personality who is more concerned with the means rather than the ends of action. So, for example, the caseworker may spend a great deal of time filling out forms and writing reports and forget the aim of seeing that the client gets his or her needs attended to in the best way possible. Failure to get satisfaction from such a functionary is often described in terms of "red tape," shorthand for the rules, paperwork, and rigidity that complicates the giving of service.

This, however, presumes that the organization intends that its workers provide good service. As pointed out elsewhere in this book, all of these complications are dysfunctional only from the viewpoint of providing good individual service. From another point of view, bureaucratic behavior may serve to reduce the huge, seemingly insatiable demand for public services such as welfare and food stamps. A certain number of potential applicants are discouraged by the procedure; were it totally pleasant, the agency might be swamped with clients. The bureaucrat's behavior in slowing down and limiting services may reflect the public's ambiguity about giving aid: the notion of helping the truly needy combined with the suspicion that some people do not want to work or are out-and-out cheats. Observe that in commenting on organizational participants we inevitably get into a discussion of the organization's impact on publics-in-contact, the clients of the agency in this case.

Here is another case in which role players seem to have lost sight of the service element of their jobs. When workers must punch in to work very promptly or suffer consequences, they will tend to do so—but they will not necessarily start their work immediately. This is easily observable in an urban U.S. post office or a bank, where clerks and tellers arrive at their posts and then rather slowly take care of their housekeeping—such as arranging their stamps or cash before facing the public. Looking at this behavior another way, the employees are combating rigid supervision of their working hours by conforming to the letter rather than the spirit of the time-clock routine.

Another use of bureaucracy is to replace individual judgment by contractual obligation. That is, the individual is required to do his or her duty, not to exercise moral judgment. Officers in concentration camps used this rationale to exonerate themselves from responsibility for their part in the torture and murder of 6 million European Jews and many others during the Nazi era (Rubenstein, 1978). The Nazi chief, Heinrich Himmler, is reported to have

> praised the SS for exercising an obedience so total that they overcame the feelings men would normally have when engaged in mass murder. The honor of the SS, he held, involved the ability to overcome feelings of compassion and achieve what was in fact perfect bureaucratic objectivity. (1978:24)

The worker who struggles against bureaucracy may suffer. The film, *The Coming Asunder of Jimmy Bright*, dealt in part with the conflicts of the public case worker in a social agency providing services to the poor. Jimmy was an overloaded social caseworker who wanted to do his best. But the regulations for giving out public welfare hemmed him in; money could only be allocated for specific purposes and not for others, and he became increasingly frustrated. Jimmy's supervisor was the essential bureaucrat. In a crisis situation—Jimmy going beserk on the job—the supervisor was unable to modify his behavior. He kept asking Jimmy to finish his paperwork and straighten his files. With regard to his own superiors, the supervisor was a total conformist.

Role types within occupations. Using the example of nurses again, a study of registered nurses in three hospitals found variations on the bureaucratic personality model among them. The most bureaucratic would only "go by the book," take no initiative, and call doctors numerous times in order to ask instructions. Others, particularly at night when the doctor in residence might be sleeping, took more initiative (and risk) in treating patients, with the understanding that the doctor would back them up and write out the instructions. One might say that the first type was more bureaucratic, the second more professional. Or that the first nurse went by the formal structure and did not acknowledge the informal structure that mediates and facilitates interaction between frequent role partners.

Different personalities selected what was most comfortable in the available role; a person working as a professional in a bureaucracy has both professional and bureaucratic models from which to choose. The essence of professional training is to develop judgment and flexibility; it can be easily seen how this sometimes conflicts with bureaucratic norms. Professionals may resist the power of the bureaucracy in attempting to adhere to their professional norms. A study of strikers and nonstrikers among a group of schoolteachers found that the most professionally oriented teachers were the ones who were most active in trying to get their union recognized, thereby hoping to increase their control over the work situation (Falk et al., 1982).

Some time ago, Gouldner (1957) defined role types in academia in terms of "cosmopolitans" and "locals." Some faculty members were oriented to their own profession in the broader society as their main reference point; others were deeply involved in their own institution, its committees, and its politics. A restudy might now be in order, which could test the survival value of these two types in various colleges or universities.

The notion of role types brings out the fact that individuals have a certain flexibility within a given status and orient themselves according to their own predispositions. We mentioned in chapter 6 that many occupational roles consist of a bundle of tasks, a term used by Everett C. Hughes (lectures, University of Chicago).

Faculty members tend to have a bundle of tasks that include teaching, doing research, writing, marking examination papers, advising students, and the like. If upward mobility is highly dependent on research and writing, as it is in major research universities, the other aspects of work may be devalued. Or highly committed teachers may find themselves looking for jobs at "teaching" colleges, lower in prestige than research universities. In times of job scarcity, the employer can more readily demand excellence in the performance of all tasks. Intensive study of other work roles will uncover the varieties of tasks among which the occupants choose.

THE TAYLORIZATION OF POLICE WORK: *A CASE STUDY IN DESKILLING*

The police are a much-criticized group, but occasionally a study examines the nature of the work itself and the problems of police officers. Harring (1984) has shown that, despite much talk about "professionalizing" police work, an opposite trend has taken place. The objective of professionalization was financed by the Law Enforcement Assistance Administration (LEAA) in the 1960s in the form of providing grants for college credits. A more educated, professionalized police force was desired. Whereas this emphasis on professionalization would seem to imply that greater control over work would result, Harring maintains that "Taylorization" has reduced such control by the police officer. Despite the rhetoric of professionalization, fiscal crises in cities brought about changes in the organization of police work. Emphasis on fiscal restraint in public services resulted in having a number of former police functions given to much lower paid civilian workers.

Whereas police unions claim that a vigorous patrol function is at the heart of good police work, patrols were reduced by reducing the size of the police force. Police were laid off and shift structures became very complicated. "Reactive" policing, much cheaper than patrolling, was increasingly used. "In this form, the patrolman becomes an 'appendage' of a communication system, summoned by citizen phone call via a radio dispatcher's message" (Harring, 1984:161). Officers no longer run their own patrol operation in their own sectors.

At the same time that the patrol function has declined, the range of other types of work open to individual officers is dropping. Certain jobs once held by older police officers, such as answering emergency phone calls, are now done by lower-paid civilians. The labor force becomes stratified by class and race into relatively well-paid white male police officers and lower-paid civilians, who are often black, Hispanic, or female.

The trend toward civilianization is great in traffic work. In large cities like New York a separate labor force of civilian traffic officers wear distinctive uniforms, direct traffic, write tickets, tow cars away, and also earn about one-third to one-half of a police officer's pay. Thus police work is broken down into specialized tasks. As the police labor force gets increasingly divided up, it gets weakened.

Highly skilled professional jobs that open up tend to go to civilians, because police officers have not been trained in such skills as computer science or business administration. Automation also enters the picture, for example, through the use of television cameras, monitored at central locations, to patrol lonely streets and subway stations. Increased computerization leads to increased management control over the police labor process.

The main point of the analysis is to show that police are not immune to the dehumanizing experiences of other workers. "Police alienation, formerly rooted in relations with the public, increasingly is generated by the organization of work in the police institution itself" (Harring, 1984:169). This consideration of changes in the structure of police work, creating a greater division of labor and specialization and a stratified work force, focuses on the "Taylorization" of the work. It does not deal with the impact of such changes on the relations of the public with the police. Our next chapter does consider the problems of organizations and their publics, particularly focusing on public service bureaucracies, of which the police department is one.

SUMMARY

Chapter 8 has explored the organization–individual relationship. Each of us interacts with the many organizations that touch our lives through specific, varied, and changing roles—as owners or managers, as rank-and-file participants, as publics-in-contact or as members of the public-at-large. The meaning of roles and their relation to identity was discussed as a prelude to considering each of these types of organizational roles.

We are all involved in many role sets. There is a role set for every status in a person's status set, required behaviors as student, worker, parent, consumer, or other status toward an assortment of partners. Roles together produce a person's ongoing, developing concept of self, his or her identity. But the self is not passive. Individuals need to integrate their various roles, lest they become—in the extreme case—split personalities. As they perceive and construct their own social reality, they attempt to explain their behavior and their careers and retain some degree of self-dignity. People create mental distance from roles that detract from their self-image, embrace others that are satisfying and self-enhancing.

Chapter 8 showed that status is frequently arranged hierarchically, with high or low amounts of prestige attached to particular statuses and their accompanying roles. The status-conferring quality of roles is persistent. It includes the official labeling of one who has earned a title or degree as well as the inescapable stigma of ex-con status. These distinctions are recognized in organizational structure, where different types of role players tend to be clearly distinguished from each other.

The concept of career, used broadly, refers to an individual's progress through related statuses over a period of time. Important careers such as work, family, and social movements enter into an individual's "moral" career—feelings and attitudes about self and others developed in the process of moving through a career line. The individual filters new experience through the lens of past ones, including subjective feelings as well as objective happenings.

Given this general knowledge about the relation of the individual to organizations, the chapter's next section proceeded to examine the impact of organizations on the general types of role players, especially certain lower, rank-and-file participants: workers. It considered how the structures of work organizations affect worker behavior. From management's point of view, alienated workers tend to be low in productivity and commitment to the organization. Hence, much attention has been devoted to the structures and practices responsible for worker productivity and motivation. Some theorists emphasize human relations factors, such as management styles, while others highlight the importance of worker participation and opportunities for mobility and power. There is a question about the degree to which technology—the nature of the tasks to be performed—determines the degree of fragmentation and routinization of jobs and to what degree technology can be manipulated in the interests of management. Some writers view suggested changes, dubbed work enlargement and work humanization, as positive attempts to affect the structure of work and opportunities; others consider these superficial gestures. Attitudes toward jobs and toward mobility are related not only to specific jobs but to the expected life chances of individuals and the meaning of work to them.

Bureaucratic personality was described as a trained incapacity, most typical of lower-level government bureaucrats who are hemmed in by rules and regulations. The danger of extreme bureaucratic behavior, the dehumanized, mechanical carrying out of orders, was illustrated by the chilling behavior of Nazi functionaries in carrying out mass killings. Finally, brief consideration was given to the role types within occupations that provide leeway for some individual choice. Many occupations consist of bundles of tasks, from which different role players choose those they care to minimize or maximize.

9

ORGANIZATION AND THE INDIVIDUAL: PUBLICS

The Public-in-Contact
    The Problem: What are Publics-in-Contact?
    Commonalities of Public-in-Contact Experiences
    Variations in Status and Power Relationships
    Constraints on Service
    Openness of Organizational Boundaries
    Adaptations of Functionaries to People Work
    Adaptations of the Public-in-Contact
    The Revolt of the Client
The Public-at-Large
    Who Is the Public-at-Large?
    Importance of Relationships between the Organization and the Public-at-Large
    Public Opinion
    Elements of the Public-at-Large
    The Public's Exercise of Power
Controlling Clients and the Work Situation: The Case of Street-Level Bureaucrats
Summary

THE PUBLIC-IN-CONTACT

The Problem: What are Publics-in-Contacts?

The term *public-in-contact* covers a wide variety of role players in direct contact with an organization who are, in a sense, outsiders. Although they may interact with the organization regularly, these role players are neither an official nor a permanent part of the structure, not workers or managers. In many cases they come to the organization voluntarily for needed goods or services, subjecting themselves, temporarily, to its norms and control. People choose to enter a retail store, buy a ticket to a play, drive into a gasoline station. In other cases the contact is forced; the individual is required by society to be changed, helped, or improved in some way. The child has little choice about submitting to the people-changing operation of the elementary school, the convicted felon to the prison.

In all cases, dealing with the public-in-contact constitutes the work of the organization; that is, "people work" is the central task to be performed by functionaries. Both the people who are the objects of work and the functionaries who process them are affected by the interaction and guided by its bureaucratic norms and special culture.

Working on people incurs special problems for such workers, such as the need to be maintain a symbolic separation from the objects of their work. In this chapter we shall look further at the special characteristics of people work and its impact on both the functionaries and their publics-in-contact. The interaction between bureaucracies and their publics-in-contact has received much less research attention then many subjects within the field or organizations (Lefton & Rosengren, 1966; Katz & Danet, 1973:3).[1]

Commonalities of Public-in-Contact Experiences

The awkward term *public-in-contact* captures the common elements present in many different situations. The individual who is a client, customer, prisoner, or such is usually part of a large group of others who are being processed, who are in a similar relationship to a bureaucracy. The individual must be classified and handled in terms of selected characteristics, for example, as a sophomore English major, a first-time misdemeanor offender, or a person opening a new account. Waiting for service at an airline counter, to see a doctor in a clinic, on a public food line or a college cafeteria all confirm to the individual that he or she is part of a large mass of people to be processed. Further, the outsider is being subjected to the organizational culture, which he or she must interpret and understand. Most of us experience some confusion when entering a new office and trying to figure out what line to stand on or which secretary to approach. As we gingerly address our question to one secretary, we may be given a cold look (for being so ignorant) and abruptly directed to another. This, however, is rather more acceptable than the experience of standing on the wrong line for half an hour without being redirected. Entering a new department store, the prospective purchaser must figure out the layout, the rules for trying on garments, whether to go to a special cashier, which credit cards

---

[1] Despite some additional studies, this observation holds as true today as when Katz and Danet made it in introducing their reader, *Bureaucracy and the Public* (1973). Much of chapter 9 is based on insights derived from study with the late Everett C. Hughes. I am indebted to Professor Hughes for sensitizing me to an understanding of organizational and occupational cultures. Too, he stressed to his students the need to view social life from the perspective of lower participants.

are acceptable, and other numerous items of local culture that the initiated take for granted. Language is a part of culture; we have learned that each organization develops its own jargon, which the outsider may struggle to understand and which surrounds the insider with an aura of superior knowledge. Given these similarities, there are also many differences in the public-in-contact experience, which we intend to explore.

Variations in Status and Power Relationships

Status of the public-in-contact. The terminology used to label publics-in-contact suggests great differences in statuses: client, consumer, customer, prisoner, patient. People of all kinds, reflecting all societal divisions of class, age, race, and gender, play various public-in-contact roles. The organization sometimes takes societal status into account formally by providing different services for different classes of customers or clients. For example, airlines offer a first-class service to those who can afford it, such as persons on expense accounts. The actual flight is the same; the difference lies in the "red carpet" treatment afforded the first-class patrons—linen napkins, deferential service, free liquor. There are those who are willing and able to pay extra hundreds of dollars to be separated from the ordinary air traveler and firms happy to provide this tax-deductible perquisite for their executives.

Frequently, different organizations are intended to serve different classes of publics, for example, private and public hospitals, community colleges and research universities, high-fashion shops and mail-order stores. There is a sifting process that goes on between members of the potential public-in-contact and various types of organizations, with each seeking organization–individual contacts that meet their needs and seem appropriate, although the two parties may not agree about this.

These needs vary. Private corporations such as banks and airlines actively seek paying customers to service, while others, such as agencies dependent on public funds, are less eager to tap their total supply of potential clients. Retail stores cater to certain types of clientele and find ways of discouraging the "undesirables." Minority students tell of being followed around in department or variety stores by security personnel, having it made clear to them that they are not the normal type of customer and might be up to no good. In fact, black faculty members may be no exception to such treatment: a university colleague was thus insulted when he was browsing in a bookstore located in a predominantly white area. And a white executive, accustomed to deferential treatment, described as unpleasant a situation in which he had to wait on line with ordinary folk.

The public service bureaucracy is a polar case for illustrating the control organizations have over relatively powerless individuals—not that such persons are totally without power. *Street-level bureaucrat* is the term Lipsky uses to describe those who work for agencies that serve the public; their special problems of controlling clientele will be presented as a case study at the end of this chapter. Street-level bureaucracies are "the schools, police and welfare departments, lower courts, legal services offices, and other agencies whose workers interact with and have wide discretion over the dispensation of benefits or the allocation of public sanctions" (Lipsky, 1980:xi). While some street-level bureaucies merely "process" people, that is, provide needed services, others are intended to change people. In either case there is a nonvoluntary aspect to the situation. The client has little alternative but to interact with the available public agency or institution (Lipsky, 1980:54).

Most clients of public agencies are of lower status than those serving them; they are, for example, clients in health clinics or public welfare and unemployment agencies. Public schools that have large minority or low-income populations tend to lose higher-income children to the private schools. Thus middle-class teachers frequently teach children from lower socioeconomic classes. Differences in culture as well as differences in status may affect the interaction: Status distinctions reinforce the power positions of the functionaries, who expect respect and deference.

Organizational monopoly.   Such organizations as public utilities and the U.S. Post Office are monopolies, which means that their customers have little individual choice about using them. In contrast, competition and the need for customers or clients tends to constrain other organizations to provide better service. Many banks advertise their care and concern for the individual customer—"you have a friend at X bank." They compete with each other for the mass base necessary to their operations. Yet once hooked, the customer must put up with the inevitable. The teller tends to act like a bureaucrat, which he or she is, rather than a friend. If I need to withdraw money from my account, I am at the mercy of the bank tellers, the length of the lines, and the speed with which transactions are completed. I cannot choose to go to another bank because my money is in this one. It has a monopoly on the service needed at the moment. Withdrawing my funds and starting another account elsewhere is a possibility if I am continually displeased, but this too takes time.

The easier it is for the public-in-contact to leave an organization, the more freedom it has to select one that is preferred. I may be able to choose either a supermarket or a small grocery, depending on whether price, quality, or service is more important to me and on what is available in my shopping area. The patient waiting to see a particular specialist after obtaining a treasured appointment has little choice but to keep on waiting. Much professional practice now takes place in groups, and in the case of medicine, in hospitals. The home visit has been largely replaced by a bureaucratic encounter, which involves nurses and receptionists, waiting in an office, filling out forms. The professional service provider may also find operating within a bureaucratic context frustrating.

Constraints on Service

Variations in work flow.   Variations in the amount of work processed by the organization are frequent. Even with the best intentions, an organization's functionaries may be unable to provide desired service. Many organizations have peak times of activity and slow times. The wary public-in-contact may try to calculate its contacts to avoid busy periods but may be unable to approach the organization during slow times. The very reason for peak activity times relates to the working hours of the full-time labor force, whose available hours for medical appointments, shopping, and recreation tend to be similar. Large department stores often advertise widely in order to reach the mass public and achieve a high volume of sales. Yet if they succeed, their labor force may not be sufficient to handle the volume. We are familiar with the cartoons showing crowd behavior during pre- or post-Christmas sales, as customers struggle with each other over the merchandise, let alone access to a salesperson. Presumably, the bargains afforded counterbalance the primitive conditions for people who make this choice.

FIGURE 9-1   Bank Tellers and the Customer: The Meshing of Time Schedules

Workers try to control their flow of work, slowing down when times are sluggish but recognizing the need, in certain circumstances, to look busy whether or not they are. Their concept of work pace may be at sharp variance with that of the public-in-contact. Control over time tends to be one-sided. At the same time that the worker is pacing his or her work, the person seeking service is trying to meet a personal time schedule. As a faculty member I can allocate a portion of my office hours to waiting students as I see fit; as an applicant for a driver's license, my role is reversed and I am dependent on the clerk, the line of other applicants, and the work pace that has been developed in that office.

Scarcity of resources.   The department store at Christmas time is an example of scarce resources in the form of available salespersons and cashiers at peak periods. For public service bureaucracies, scarcity of resources is a chronic problem, because (1) the demand for services tends to increase to meet the supply, and (2) street-level bureaucracies tend to have very high case loads relative to their responsibilities. Here are some examples (italics mine):

> *Public defenders* sometimes come to trial without having interviewed their clients, or having interviewed them only briefly. Legal service lawyers, while responsible for perhaps 80 to 100 clients whose cases they currently represent, may typically be working actively on only a dozen or so cases. . . . *Social workers* are unable to make required home visits in public welfare work and are so inundated with paperwork that they are never without a backlog. . . . *Lower-court judges* are typically inundated with cases, often causing delays of several months in providing defendants their day in court. . . . For *teachers*, overcrowded classrooms (with meager supplies) mean that they are unable to give the kind of personal attention good teaching requires. High student-teacher ratios also mean that teachers must attend to maintaining order and have less attention for learning activities. (Lipsky, 1980:29–30)

Finally, in many street-level bureaucracies there is an emphasis on "housekeeping chores" such as filling out forms and reports, which reduces the amount of time available for direct service. Even on the college level, teachers with weak support services may find themselves typing their own letters or examinations, spending professional time on secretarial work.

Openness of Organizational Boundaries

Control over boundaries.   The match between the organization and its public-in-contact is not always all that both would want. Some organizations are very selective, others designedly more open. For example, compare Harvard to an open-enrollment or community college. The Ivy League institution selects among numerous highly qualified students vying for entry and able to pay high fees. The community college is available to a broader group of high school graduates of varying capability and limited funds. The control that each institution has over who enters is quite different. Public mental hospitals and prisons are designed to accept large numbers of persons deemed deviant; the institutions have limited choice over who enters. But even those institutions differentiate between categories or appropriate and inappropriate persons, such as prisons limited to serious offenders. Publicly supported institutions such as prisons or mental hospitals are frequently overcrowded, dependent as they are on public financing.

Role of gatekeepers. The bureaucrat facing the public-in-contact may be relatively low in status or remuneration but high in power to block service. Small towns are typically thought of as being friendlier than cities. Yet the case comes to mind of a postmaster in a small New Jersey town who seemed to be a sadist. People approached him with fear and trembling, their wrapping and tying of packages subjected to minute scrutiny. More often than not he would find them unacceptable and insist they be repackaged. Sticking to bureaucratic rules is one way of exercising power in a relatively powerless position. That postmaster, a minor civil servant who had limited power, managed to become a gatekeeper who could withhold vital services. He was clearly in charge of the office, and his authority could not be questioned. He showed his power by refusing to accept packages the first time around.

Such gatekeepers, with high power, relatively low status, and low material rewards, are sometimes vulnerable to bribery by more affluent favor seekers. The briber wants to gain a competitive advantage rather than accept routine treatment, and key individuals such as the police officer, court clerk, or member of a local planning board are in the position to make exceptions. Zoning and land-use rules, if applied strictly, may prevent developers from building commercial centers, but developers know that variances are obtainable.

Adaptations of Functionaries to People Work

Moral limits on people work. Special problems arise for functionaries who deal with live, conscious human beings. Some workers would prefer to avoid or minimize such contacts, even in institutions that typically deal with people. The surgical nurse may prefer a technical task on an unconscious patient to one requiring conversation with a conscious one. Other nurses who want to minimize interpersonal contact may choose the night shift, when things are generally slower.

Work on human beings evokes moral and ethical issues. For example, to what extent may experimentation be allowed? Voices are being raised over animal experimentation, questioning the apparent cruelty imposed on innocent animals used for medical research. Nazi experimentation on Jews was not different and was performed in a bureaucratic, impersonal manner by medical professionals (see Rubenstein, 1978). Prisoners are sometimes offered a chance to volunteer for scientific experiments in exchange for a shortening of sentence (*Time*, March 19, 1973, p. 61). Indeed, it is frequently the less valued members of society that suffer such experimentation, as in a United States case condemned after the fact. In this infamous study, which occurred at the Tuskegee, Alabama, Veterans' Administration

Hospital, syphilis patients went untreated over a period of many years in order to compare them with others who were given medication (Slater, 1972). Subsequent to the revelation about Tuskegee, scientific investigators at universities were required to file reports and meet guidelines for human subject research.

In a more everyday way, questions arise as to how far a functionary may go in dealing with the physical or mental condition of the public-in-contact. Should physical punishment be allowed in schools? Should mental patients be placed in restraints or drugged excessively? Should instructors publicize student grades? The justification for questionable procedures rests in the assertion that the professional knows best, better than the lay person, what is good for the client. It is not unlike parents who discipline their children "for their own good." Because judgment is involved, it is difficult to prove other than altruistic intent. Nonetheless, society does set legal and official limits, such as that between normal parental discipline and child abuse. Because the functionary often has official power over the public-in-contact member being treated, safeguards may have to be built into the contact. Police officers, for example, are enjoined not to use "excessive force" and not to shoot unless threatened. The awesome power of the small bureaucrat is revealed in cases where it has been abused, such as the unexplained bruises on and occasional deaths of patients or prisoners who are in restraints.

Maintaining distance.   There are several reasons why people workers find it necessary to maintain the social and symbolic distance that distinguishes them from those they serve. One is to keep clear the difference in status between them, as pointed out in chapter 6. Especially if the subjects are stigmatized in some way, the worker seeks to avoid the contamination of close association. (In relatively less hierarchical societies such as the United States, these attitudes are often masked by more egalitarian pretensions.) The functionary protects his or her status as a law maintainer rather than a law breaker, as a sane attendant rather than an insane patient, as a professional rather than an impoverished client. When there are visible status differences, such as the age differences between public schoolteachers and their charges, the distinction is obvious. But the young college teacher creates a contrast by dressing differently than her students and carrying a briefcase. Incidentally, the status distinctions also help to protect the public-in-contact members; there is less danger of sharing peer group secrets with someone who is clearly not a peer.

Another reason for maintaining distance is the threat of emotional involvement, which could prejudice or interfere with rational role performance. Doctors usually do not treat close members of their own families for this reason; their feelings might interfere with judgment or calculated responses. The teacher is enjoined not to show favoritism but to maintain the universalism required of one who must continually pass judgment on many others. These are role prescriptions or requirements; real-life deviations are frequent, simply because the lower-participant functionaries are often in close contact with the people they are working on. The very tendency to form human attachments is part of the reason for rules to minimize favoritism or emotional involvement.

Maintaining control. People workers, just as much as those who work with paper or things, try to maintain some control over their work. When the raw material is other human beings, it means keeping them in line with the organization's rules, orderly and untroublesome. Especially if the public-in-contact is recalcitrant, suspicious of the organization, or in forced contact, this issue looms large. The case study at the end of this chapter enlarges on the techniques by which street-level bureaucrats attempt to maintain control.

Adaptations of the Public-in-Contact

Typical problems of the public-in-contact. Some of the problems of publics-in-contact have already been suggested: the need to cope with demeaning, physically or mentally harmful treatment, limited knowledge of the organizational culture one is confronting, losing control over one's time and waiting a lot, competing with others for scarce resources, being treated impersonally. In chapter 7 we also discussed some of the conflict that arises from the differing viewpoints of publics-in-contact and functionaries.

The bureaucracy routinizes individual dilemmas, and exceptional cases are difficult to handle. Mistakes are made in human services as well as in other types of work, yet their consequences may be tragic. When the mistake is a matter of paperwork, it often appears unbelievably difficult to correct. Since the coming of the computer age, a convenient scapegoat has been added to the arsenal in the command of functionaries. The computer is blamed for mistakes, as if it had a mind and a will. Human intervention to correct the computer error is viewed as intervening with the Divine. College students probably need no reminder of such occurrences as being deregistered from courses or receiving payment notices after having already paid a bill. Anyone with a soft heart who has answered the appeal of a charitable organization finds it is impossible to get off computerized solicitation lists, which have been sold to other related charities. An inventor who discovers a way of eliminating names from these lists might make a fortune.

Secondary adjustments. Goffman (1961) used his own term, *secondary adjustments*, to refer to the ways that inmates or patients adapt to the available resources and treatment, ways that were not intended by the institution. A familiar example is use of any available physical materials for one's own purposes: institutional food may be personalized by adding odd combinations of condiments or hoarded by saving nonperishable items for later consumption. These are individual, sometimes covert ways of getting the most out of a difficult situation. In situations that are less than total, clients may still try to "beat the system" by developing knowledge of the organizational culture and its possible loopholes, and by role playing the kind of correct behavior that will maximize their advantages. Clients may maintain personal distance from the role, seeing themselves as merely "acting out" the expected behavior in order to get the desired result from workers. For example, they may appear to be polite and deferential without internalizing the deference as valid. This is personal behavior adaptive to a situation of low power.

Sometimes, however, people who are part of the same group, the same public-in-contact, may be able to band together for group action.

Informal organization. Just as workers who are peers develop informal systems of self-help, of work pace norms, of filling in for or covering each other, some client groups manage to do the same. Needed information may be offered to relative strangers who are new to a setting. Students may share crucial facts about teachers, classes, and tests with one another, depending on how competitive the situation is. The inmate organization has already been described. In addition to informal organizing, members of a public-in-contact may create a formal group to put forth their claims and grievances.

The Revolt of the Client

Publics-in-contact also band together openly to seek redress of group grievances when they are convinced that their problems are social, not individual, and that something can be done about them. Those who must deal with public service bureaucracies are often the poor, minorities, or people with little individual power. It is only through collective action that they feel they can make their voices heard.

In times of social unrest societal institutions and their leaders are questioned. A "revolt of the client" took place in the 1960s, a decade of social movements. Some movements, such as the welfare rights movement were directed against inadequate or demeaning public services. Writing at the end of the 1960s, Haug and Sussman (1969) compared the revolt of clients within schools, among the poor, and in the black community. They saw publics-in-contact increasingly questioning both the expertise and the humanitarian motives of professionals who served them.

These characteristics, expertise and concern for the client, have been touted as the very hallmarks of professionalism. But they are norms, inculcated in training, and not necessarily fulfilled by those to whom they are taught. The professional service ethic can be muddied to suit the convenience of the practitioners or by the wish to acquire wealth. After all, the profession is also the practitioner's livelihood and road to comfort. But equally important, the bureaucratic settings in which professional services increasingly take place create pressures that constrict professional behavior. Elsewhere we have suggested that bureaucratic needs (such as having to process large numbers of cases efficiently and keep numerous records) conflict with individualization of care and limit professional discretion.

As citizens become more knowledgeable about matters that affect their lives, they call into question the expertise of the practitioners. How can white, middle-class social workers presume to know best how the welfare budget of a poor black family should be divided up? Why can't college students have a say in the curricula being offered, or have their judgment of teaching ability taken into account? Revolts of college students against the impersonal multiuniversity included the demand for more power. The urban unrest of the late 1960s brought out the dissatisfaction of black communities with white-run urban institutions. The thrust of many of the complaints was that the professionals were too far removed in knowledge and experience to really "know best." In addition to questioning the professionals' knowledge, the clients in revolt questioned their altruism—their desire to really work in the best interests of their clients.

One of the consequences of the client revolt was increased community participation on the boards of such institutions as schools and hospitals, at least for a period. Another was the creation of federal poverty programs that gave local community leaders jobs and resources to distribute.

In a phenomenon whose long-run effects are yet to be analyzed, the women's movement has promoted skepticism about male-dominated institutions, such as those providing obstetrical and gynecological care. The Boston Women's Health Collective produced a widely read book, *Our Bodies, Ourselves* (1971, 1984), encouraging self-examination, self-knowledge about the body, and self-help. One of the results of the women's health movement has been exploration of alternative methods of handling the birth experience, such as home birth and use of midwives instead of hospital births. According to Peterson (1983), childbirth at home is a striking example of the current demedicalization of U.S. society. The vast structure of obstetrical care is challenged in at least two ways: the necessity of a physician at normal births is questioned, and both mothers and fathers are involved as responsible participants in the birth process. The use of lay as well as professional midwives is seen as a grass-roots development opposing the definition of normal childbirth as a medical experience that must be presided over by medical doctors. The birthing experience is redefined as a family event.

As is true in the home birth movement, the client revolt often attempted to reestablish the competence, worth, and self-esteem of people being treated by superior-acting professionals and bureaucrats. Some of the practices and attitudes that led to this revolt are revealed in the case study that concludes this chapter. The many ways that functionaries try to control their clients are described. But for now, let us turn to consideration of another type of public—the public-at-large.

THE PUBLIC-AT-LARGE

Who Is the Public-at-Large?

The public-at-large corresponds closely to what the average person thinks of as "the public." Unlike those in direct contact with an organization, the general public consists of all the people who do not have regular, direct contact with it. This does not mean that members of the general public might not ever cross the line and develop ongoing relationships with a particular organization. Indeed, social movement organizations spend much time trying to convince the general public that their cause is worthy and that people should join. A high school graduate may have little to do with colleges or universities—unless and until he or she decides to apply for admission. At that point, contacts may start, and the student eventually chooses one institution and becomes one of its public-in-contact.

Importance of Relationships between the Organization and its Public-at-Large

All of us know about and are affected by a great number of organizations with which we may never have direct contact. Major corporations, governmental agencies, the huge foundations—all have an impact on us, and indeed on the future of the world. In addition, *commonweal* organizations are a special type intended to protect the welfare of the public-at-large (Blau & Scott, 1962). The military services, police and fire departments, and certain government agencies are examples. Although Blau and Scott included only public organizations within this type, we can broaden it to take in social movement organizations such as peace groups that aim to benefit the general public.

Public Opinion

Let us relate the concept of the public-at-large to the familiar public opinion polls. These surveys attempt to find out what the statistical average of different population groups thinks about various issues. A sample of members of these groups, stratified by such things as age, sex, social class, race, and ethnicity, may be queried about issues ranging from their preference for a particular political candidate to their fears about nuclear war or environmental protection. These polls are frequently published and generalizations are made, such as "people over the age of forty-five tend to favor the policies of the present political administration," or the reverse. The very fact that there are so many polls, especially around election time, alerts us to the fact that organizations and their leaders want to know if they are in public favor and what they might be doing wrong. Their dependence, in varying degrees, on the good will of the public is also evident in various books on public relations that advise business firms, schools, libraries, professions, and other groups on how to develop and keep a good public image. Citizenship activities of corporation executives in serving on various community boards helps project the desired image of public-mindedness.

Organizations may engage in publicity campaigns to explain the constraints they are under. For example, "a concern will spend many thousands of dollars to inform the public through advertising that it cannot reduce or must raise prices because of union demands for higher wages or because of the high taxes imposed by the government" (Blau & Scott, 1962:196). Social movement organizations try to rouse the public to become involved in their objectives through mass mailings, sometimes offering a check list of concerns for the recipient to respond to (see figure 9–2).

Interestingly enough, despite the millions of advertising dollars that go into building positive public images, little scholarly attention has been directed to the relationship between organizations and the public-at-large The image of benevolence and civic-mindedness emerges from literature sympathetic to management, while those critical of the status quo and "the corporations" convey a totally opposite image. Perhaps because the views are strongly partisan there is little scien-

FIGURE 9-2 A Social Movement Organization's Check List of Concerns

ACTION NOW TO STOP ACID RAIN!

YES! I want to help the Environmental Defense Fund win a strong national acid rain law such as the one EDF helped pass in New York State. I am returning my Acid Raid Initiative Ballot with a message to the President and Congress.

I want to do more! To help the Environmental Defense Fund lead campaigns vital to the health of our environment, I am enclosing a tax-deductible contribution of :

| $100 | $50 | $25 | $20 | Other: $_____ |

... Your gift at this level would really help.

NSAR98
KHODA BLUMBERG
_____

Please make your check payable to the **Environmental Defense Fund** and return it with this card in the enclosed envelope.

(do not detach)

National Acid Rain Initiative Ballot

Do you favor strong legislation to control acid rain by reducing our nation's annual emission of 26 million tons of sulfur dioxide?	☐ YES	☐ NO
Do you urge the President to act now on acid rain and recommend strong action to Congress?	☐ YES	☐ NO

Please verify your name and address above and return this ballot in the enclosed postage-paid envelope within two weeks from date of receipt.

Environmental Defense Fund 444 Park Avenue South, New York, New York 10016

Source: Environmental Defense Fund. Used with permission.

tific analysis of how the relationship between organizations and the public-at-large actually works. However, given the currently strong interest in the general topic of organizational environment, the public as part of that environment is bound to gain attention.

Elements of the Public-at-Large

As the discussion of public opinion polls suggested, the public is made up of a vast number of collectivities—women, minority groups, persons of different class levels, different occupations, different religions. There are myriad interest groups composed of persons who share a particular orientation about the things that affect them as a group. Some are, of course, more powerful than others. We hear of agricultural interests, business interests, medical interests, consumer interests. We know that religious groups sometimes take positions on public issues, such as the legality of abortion or the morality of capital punishment.

When an issue gains attention, such as proposed legislation raising the drinking age to twenty-one, the various relevant interest groups react either openly or secretly. Those between age eighteen and twenty-one may criticize such legislation on the basis of the fact that their age group is allowed to vote and serve in the Armed Forces. Liquor interests may find the proposed law unpalatable, inasmuch as it will cut down on profits and also require checking the age of immature-looking patrons. Colleges and universities will have to give up a source of revenue that some of them get from on-campus "pubs." They may also have to take on an additional policing function. A new interest group, mothers, some of whose children were traffic fatalities, formed an organization (Mothers Against Drunk Driving) to speak publicly in support of raising the drinking age. This was related to a public campaign, which got underway in 1984, focusing on the fatal results of drunken driving, a problem that has been around a long time. Thus at certain times, public consensus can be built up to support types of intervention that might not have been attained earlier.

From this example one can see that a given issue has many publics, such as various agencies of government, other organized groups, interested individuals, and incipient groups (based on interests that have the potential for future organization). A work on school public relations defined the publics of a school system as shown in figure 9–3.

Like the school system, most organizations have publics that are part of their specific environments, that is, which affect them especially. These publics are oriented to and interested in how the organization functions, have ideas about what

FIGURE 9–3   The Publics of a School System

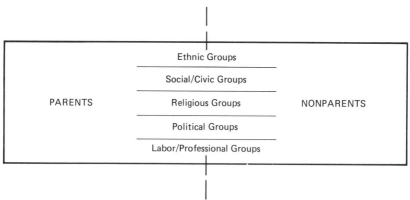

Source: *The Complete Book of School Public Relations: An Administrator's Manual and Guide* by Donavan R. Walling. Copyright © 1982 by Parker Publishing Company, Inc. Reprinted by permission of the publisher.

it should accomplish, and interact with it more intensely than does the general public. The case study at the end of this chapter begins with an examination of the "multiple constituencies," or publics, of human service organizations (Martin, 1980a). These constituencies, or interest groups, may hold conflicting and even incompatible expectations about what the output of a particular human service agency should be.

The Public's Exercise of Power

In addition to acting as interest groups, the public sometimes has a chance to express its opinions through voting. When political parties take opposing positions about regulating organizations, or about how much federal agencies should do, the consequences can be tremendous. Natural resources may be protected or turned over to private interests. Home markets may or may not be insulated from competition by high tariffs on imports. Banks may be regulated or deregulated. It is no wonder then that powerful organizations have their own lobbies in Washington, paid advocates who try to convince lawmakers to act sympathetically towards the interests of their clients. At the same time the lawmakers' constitutents are pressing their interests and the lawmaker must balance the views of these varied groups in order to get reelected. Organizational interest groups, of course, contribute to the political candidates and campaigns whose actions are likely to help them. They also influence government policy through interlocking relationships among community power groups. The connections between government, corporations, and the military were described by C. Wright Mills in *The Power Elite* (1956) and observed in various community studies. The influence of private organizations can be direct or indirect. Proposed federal legislation that would have required the withholding of tax on interest, much as it is withheld on salaries, was defeated by a successful campaign in which banks enlisted their customers in a blitz show of enraged public opinion.

In the case of international issues, too, governments make strong efforts to gain the backing of major interest groups. In extreme cases of disunity, members of armies may desert or refuse to fight in unpopular wars. Or they may refuse to take action against a publicly defined enemy with which they have ties. In 1984 Sikh soldiers, members of a religio-ethnic group from the Punjab region, deserted the Indian Army in large numbers. This occurred during a conflict between the constituted government of India and Sikh activists who sought more autonomy, possibly even an independent Sikh state between India and Pakistan. In the United States the National Guard has been brought in to quell riots when it was felt that local police were too allied with lawbreakers by ties of race and region to act in the public good.

The government is often a mediating agency between organizations and the public-at-large. If a public regulatory agency is not protecting the people, public interest groups may raise a strong outcry that causes it to be investigated or to perform more effectively.

Advertising has been mentioned as a way that organizations influence the public, not only about products, but also about ideas. Organizations and industries, as well as trade unions, may take out ads explaining their position. For many years the American Federation of Teachers has had a weekly paid "column" in the *New York Times*.

On its part, the public tries to make its wishes known in ways other than voting. Letters to the editors of newspapers are one such way that opinion gets expressed, even though the representativeness of the ones that get printed is open to question. One tactic of social movement organizations seeking major change has been the organized boycott. The civil rights movement of the 1950s and the 1960s provides one of the best examples. In 1955 black people in Montgomery, Alabama, decided to protest the discriminatory and rude practices of bus segregation and vowed not to ride the buses. Since they made up a good share of people using public transportation in that city, the boycott caused the bus companies large financial losses. While those who boycotted the buses were the public-in-contact, many other individuals helped in the boycott, and donations came in from all parts of the country. Publicity about the boycott engendered much support from the general public, mostly from persons outside of Montgomery. Some of these protest methods were used by the black people of South Africa in 1985—internal boycotting of white businesses and seeking the moral and economic support of the international community.

CONTROLLING CLIENTS AND THE WORK SITUATION: THE CASE OF STREET-LEVEL BUREAUCRATS

Street-level bureaucrats develop ways to control their clients and their work situation. To put that behavior into perspective, we need to examine the special dilemmas they face in dealing with the multiple constituencies that are involved in their operation. Patricia Yancey Martin (1980a) has identified twelve distinctive interest groups whose preferences regarding organizational goals and objectives can be expected to differ (see figure 9–4). Based on their own goal preferences, these groups will judge the organization's effectiveness differently.

From the perspective of the resource-dependence model, however, an organization's effectiveness is based on its ability to get what it needs in the way of resources. Human service organizations often exist in volatile economic and political climates; in order to survive, their members must pay a great deal of attention to external constituencies. There is competition for funds, for qualified staff, and for valued clients.

Who are these constituencies? As shown in figure 9–4, Martin identifies the following groups in the public—external to the organization but in interaction with it: (1) the general public, including the media, civic groups, churches, ordinary citizens, and so on; (2) legislative and regulatory bodies, including federal, regional, and state agencies; (3) local funding and regulatory bodies; (4) employee unions, professional associations, licensing and accreditation bodies; (5) client referral sources and targets, such as other human service

FIGURE 9-4   A Multiple Constituencies Model of Human Service Organizations

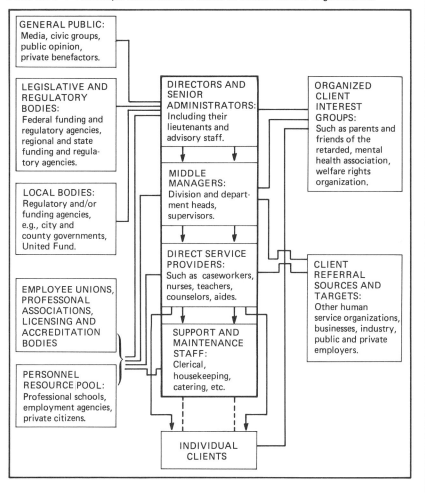

Source: Patricia Yancey Martin, "Multiple Constituencies, Differential Power and the Question of Effectiveness in Human Service Organizations," *Journal of Sociology and Social Welfare* 7 (1980):804. Used with permission.

organizations, private and public employers; (6) the personnel resource pool, including education and professional schools; and (7) organized client-interest groups (pp. 805–806).

Martin also portrays the bureaucratic hierarchy within such agencies as consisting of role players with different degrees of power and, frequently, different interests. Top administrators who have the most influence on the organization are obliged to please external resource controllers and elites. The latter tend to value quantity of clients served or number of services provided, which will then be emphasized by the top administrators (1980a:809). Quality of service is harder to measure and runs counter to "quantity related values (e.g., productivity, efficiency, growth, size)," which "tend to dominate Western thought in general and views of organizational success in particular" (p. 809).

This outline of Martin's provocative analysis provides a useful background for understanding how public service bureaucrats, the lower participants, cope with their tasks. For, regardless of official rhetoric about service, street-level bureaucrats must translate the actual constraints and dilemmas under which they work into operating policies. Michael Lipsky's book *Street-Level Bureaucracy* (1980) shows how they do so. (The remainder of this case study will be based on Lipsky's book.)

As part of public policy, the rules and objectives of public agencies are created and recreated through the interaction of their various internal and external constituencies. In this sense, street-level bureaucrats actually create public policy in the day-to-day working out of the problems and conflicts inherent in their work. Teachers, social workers, public interest lawyers, and other such professionals may go to work in such agencies with high ideals based on publicly proclaimed policy goals. In practice, however, they are effectively prevented from implementing those ideals by the constraints of time, money, limited power, and the rules themselves. The messages they receive from the official fund-givers can be taken in two ways: help the poor—but not enough to make them too comfortable, and be sure to weed out the lazy; be fair in administering justice—but be tough to lawbreakers and put them away forever; be humane to prisoners—but do not coddle them.

Although there may be vague general agreement on the need for humane treatment and the responsibility to keep citizens from starving, the weak underlying consensus masks shifting ideologies. The public-in-contact is vulnerable to changing definitions: When a new federal administration drastically reduced spending on social programs, many children were cut from the school lunch program. Persons may be eligible for food stamps one day and not eligible the next. Social security payments may be tax-free one year, taxable the next. A local branch office of an agency or a particular hospital emergency room may close down, making access to services more difficult. The functionary, a rank-and-file participant, must put the ever-shifting policies into practice in determining eligibility and services.

Starting with the basic premise mentioned earlier in this chapter, that "street-level bureaucrats work with inadequate resources in circumstances where the demand will always increase to meet the supply of services" (1980:81), Lipsky shows how it affects the patterns of practice of street-level bureaucrats. Many feel they are performing well, given the constraints under which they operate. He studies "the routines and subjective responses street-level bureaucrats develop in order to cope with the difficulties and ambiguities of their jobs" (p. 82).

How do street-level bureaucrats attempt to control their work? According to Lipsky, these are some of the mechanisms they develop:

1. "Street-level bureaucrats interact with clients in settings that symbolize, reinforce, and limit their relationship" (p. 117). The physical setting is arranged to emphasize the status distinctions between the workers and

those they serve, perhaps best exemplified by the exalted position of the judge in the courtroom, indicative of the exaggerated deference he or she must be shown. Welfare clients may be interviewed in large offices lacking privacy, or they may be made to wait in crowded, unventilated rooms.

2. "Clients are isolated from one another" (p. 118). They tend to know little about others in the same position or may be encouraged to think of themselves as in competition for the available resources. Students may be told not to reveal to others privileges obtained, such as being allowed to take exams at special times. If publics-in-contact band to- gether, forming client groups, the bureaucracy may select out the most innocuous of these organizations to favor with official relationships, providing a semblance of more access to power.

3. "The services and procedures of street-level bureaucrats are presented as benign. Actions affecting clients are always taken in their best interest" (p. 119). Professionals, with their greater education and expertise, are presumed to know better than their clients what is best for them. In the case of action against criminals, the public-at-large or the victim, rather than the public-in-contact, is being protected, but still action is presented as altruistic professionalism.

4. "Clients must come in for service" (p. 119). While this is most econom- ical, it also serves to protect the functionary from venturing out into what might be dangerous turf. It is also easier to control the physical and symbolic aspects of the status distinctions described earlier. Police officers are, of course, exceptions to this rule, and minimizing personal danger becomes a most important aspect of their job. They customarily operate in pairs. Similarly, if other workers have to make site visits, they tend to do so in teams, for protection.

5. "Interactions with clients are ordinarily structured so that street-level bureaucrats control their content, timing, and pace" (p. 120). For ex- ample, the client may immediately be presented with a form to be filled out, which then guides the interaction. A study of legal service lawyers found that clients were discouraged from presenting their stories in their own way, with questions shut off and redirected according to the law- yer's own perception. The interaction becomes structured and routinized. It is more than possible to come away from a visit to a lawyer or physi- cian without having asked one's questions, let alone had them answered clearly.

6. "When control of clients is problematic yet critical to task performance or personal safety, interactions between citizens and street-level bureau- crats are dominated by control routines" (p. 122). For example, both the schoolteacher and the police officer must establish authority imme- diately to maintain their own safety as well as that of others. Control routines refer to keeping students or suspects "in line" and preventing confrontations. Police officers are taught to position themselves in ways that will prevent surprise attack and to present themselves as tough and willing to use violence. Lipsky sees this behavior as paradoxical in that it may engender the very reactions that are feared. A person unjustly stopped on suspicion may act hostile in response to police behavior and not because he or she is guilty. Yet those most familiar with police pro- cedures may not take such behavior personally when they are stopped, recognizing that this is how police officers routinely behave.

7. "Street-level bureaucrats develop sanctions to punish disrespect to routines of order" (p. 124). Clients who do not adhere to the bureaucratic routines are seen as potential troublemakers who have to be punished. For example, children may be suspended for not having a pass or smoking in the bathroom, though these acts have nothing to do with their educational behavior.

Lipsky concludes his analysis of the problems of street-level bureaucrats in the following way:

> We can now restate the problem of street-level bureaucracy as follows. Street-level bureaucrats attempt to do a good job in some way. The job, however, is in a sense impossible to do in ideal terms. How is the job to be accomplished with inadequate resources, few controls, indeterminate objectives, and discouraging circumstances? (p. 82)

One way that they try to manage their situation is through the control measures enumerated above.

SUMMARY

Many books on organizations start by reviewing the truism that organizations powerfully affect the lives of people in modern society, then go on to focus solely on organizational issues. In this chapter we continued our exploration of organizations and the individual, analyzing the interaction of types of publics with organizations. Included in the concept of public-in-contact were such groups as clients, students, prisoners, and customers, all of whom have an ongoing contact with organizations although they are neither members of nor workers in those organizations. The public-in-contact constitutes the "people work" of an organization, even though there are great variations in the statuses of various publics-in-contact. We looked at how these differences in status affect relationships with the organization. Various constraints or limits on service to publics-in-contact were discussed, related to the intent of the organization, its variations in work flow, and the degree of competition it faces.

Organizational gatekeepers often control access to the organization or its services. Both the functionaries who work on people and the people being worked on develop adaptations to the situation of contact. Among such adaptations of functionaries are those related to the approved moral limits on people work, the need to maintain distance, and the need to maintain control. Typical problems of the public-in-contact were described, as well as some of the adjustments they make, including secondary adjustments, informal organization, and outright "revolt."

The second part of the chapter dealt with the concept of the public-at-large, that part of the public that does not have regular direct contact with an organization but that nonetheless affects and is affected by major organizations. Public opinion was discussed as the expression of the attitude of the public-at-large, some-times reflected in polls. The importance attached to positive images is seen in such things as the large amount of money organizations spend in advertising and the service of their leaders on community boards. Some of the ways in which members of the public-at-large try to exert power are by writing letters to newspapers, voting, and supporting social movement organizations. Further research is needed on this important topic of the mutual interaction between organizations and the public-at-large.

We concluded the chapter with a case study that showed how workers—street-level bureaucrats—in public service organizations attempt to control their work.

10

ORGANIZATIONS AND THEIR ENVIRONMENTS

The Nature of Organization—Environment Interaction
    The Problem: How Do Organizations and Their Environments Influence Each Other?
    Why the Focus on Environments?
Interorganizational Relations
    The Environment of Related Organizations
    Populations and Organizational Forms
    The Interorganizational Network
    Resources
    Bases of Power within Networks
    Effects of Interorganizational Power
    Network Environments
The General Environment
    The Specific versus the General Environment
    Natural Selection Models versus the Resource Dependence Model
    Criticism of the Population Ecology Model
    Types of Environmental Conditions
    How Powerful Organizations Mold Their Environments
The Underworld
    The Underworld as Part of Organizational Society
    What Is Organized Crime?
    Differences between Legal and Illegal Organizations
    The Borderline between Legal and Illegal Activity
    The Effects of Demand and Supply
    The Corruption of Officials
    The Effects of Changing Technology

Social Movements and Institutionalized Organizations
    Voluntary Associations
    Social Movements
Corporate Fraud. A Case Study
Summary

THE NATURE OF ORGANIZATION-ENVIRONMENT INTERACTION

The Problem: How Do Organizations and Their Environments Influence Each Other?

The topic of organizational environments should be a familiar one by now, since our approach has presupposed a continuing organization-environment interaction. Chapter 1 introduced this framework, placing organizations within their general context of other types of collectivities and describing them as intermediary groups between individuals, nation-states, and the international community. Chapter 4 defined goals as being set and modified by environmental as well as internal influences. That chapter initiated discussion of some of the current models for understanding the environment, such as the population ecology model, to be readdressed here. Chapter 9 examined, as part of the environment, the public-in-contact and the public-at-large. Now we bring together these insights and present some of the latest thinking on organizational environments.

Why the Focus on Environments?

A great deal of research is currently being focused on the organization-environment relationship. Many of us wonder why. You may recall the discussion in chapter 2 of the social roots of knowledge and the kinds of factors that help determine which topics are chosen for research. Some guesses can be made about the surge of interest in the crucial role of organizational environments. It was in the late 1960s and the 1970s that research in this area burgeoned. One hypothesis might be that the turbulence and instability of the 1960s, the social movement decade, heightened awareness of general environmental forces. Writing in that decade, Terreberry (1968) credits the increasing complexity and turbulence of society as having such an effect. Another hypothesis could be that major changes in technology, such as the advances in electronics, in weaponry, and in medicine, have required important readjustments on the part of the organizations they affect, highlighting their vulnerability to environmental change.

Certain structural features of organizations including size, centralization, degree of formalization, and complexity were at one time thought manipulable—if managers could figure out the right or most efficient mix. They are now seen as at least partly determined by changing environments.[1] Environmental uncertainty has been recognized as an influential ingredient that may require a looser, more decentralized structure than the traditional hierarchical bureaucracy of Weber's model. The organization must be flexible and loosely coupled enough to adapt.

INTERORGANIZATIONAL RELATIONS

The Environment of Related Organizations

Other organizations form only one part of a given organization's environment. For this reason, many writers analyze the general environment and then consider the specific case of relations between and among organizations. Benson (1980) approaches the topics the other way round, by first describing interorganizational networks. The key concepts he develops then enable him to perceive and portray the general environment in a systematic, structured way. Following this lead we will begin by examining interorganizational relationships and move from there to consider the impact of other types of forces in the environment.

How are organizations grouped together? What patterns can we see in their relationships? Three concepts widely used in pursuing this task are *populations, organizational forms*, and *networks*.

Populations and Organizational Forms

The term *population* refers to organizations in much the same way that it refers to people. People who are members of a human population do not necessarily interact with each other, but they coexist as part of the same society. Just as human populations vary over time in their composition—for example, in size and in the proportions of different age groups, sexes, and races—so populations of organizations vary. At any one time they include a particular mix of organizations.

The population ecology perspective maintains that certain types of organizations survive more successfully than others under particular environmental conditions, that is, that certain *forms* of organizations are selected for survival. Thus, some forms of organizations die out, some new ones appear and proliferate. For example, many new social movement organizations were formed in the 1960s. Given the

[1]For example, Hage and Aiken have tested the relationship of structural characteristics to each other and to such variables as productivity, efficiency, and morale (Hage, 1965; Hage & Aiken, 1967). Another author describes the shift in viewpoint that has led to more emphasis on the determining role of the environment in organizational structure in this way: "The early theorists . . . saw the importance of structure for effectiveness and efficiency and assumed without the slightest question that whatever structure was needed, people could fashion accordingly. Organizational structure was considered a matter of choice. . . . Suddenly in the 1960s a different view arose. . . . This view maintains that to some important extent, organizational structure is an externally caused phenomenon, an outcome rather than an artifact. Human choice may surely play a role, but one that is almost passive, that consists in bending to the demands of the forces that always put spontaneous pressure on organizational structuring: the organization's technology, environment, and size" (Mohr, 1982:102–103).

large population of such groups, a change-oriented individual would have had little difficulty in finding one or more civil rights, peace, environmental, or feminist organizations to join. In the 1970s such organizations became much less active on a mass basis and many disappeared. The atmosphere was no longer conducive to the flourishing of change-oriented social movement organizations. Similarly, for a short period in the 1960s, communes—antibureaucratic, countercultural groupings—were popular among teen-age youth and college dropouts. These, too, have lessened in number as the national atmosphere turned increasingly conservative. In the field of agriculture the small family farm appears to be moving toward extinction, replaced by big-business agriculture. This continues the trend in which giant corporations proliferated in the late nineteenth century as a result of mergers. Giant corporations as an organizational form became more common, and they too became subject to mergers and takeovers. While small businesses continue to be created, their rate of demise is much greater than that of the very large ones.

Some might assume that the large ones are more efficient. The fact is that many of these corporations have been ailing. But there is a greater tendency for the U.S. government to come to the aid of sick giants since their failure might have severe repercussions on the economy.

The "environment" of the 1980s favors the large business as an organizational form. Or, put more dynamically, the political environment and political decision makers favor big business. Taken by itself, use of the term *environment* tends to transform decision making and use of power into natural, rather bland, impersonal processes. What is at least in part the result of social processes, including the use of power, comes to be seen as the result of natural processes (see Perrow, 1985:283, who cautions, "Beware of unspecified 'environments'"). Strategic choice theorists maintain that continual decision making occurs as powerful role players actively scan and attempt to manipulate the environment on behalf of the organization (Beer, 1980:106).

Much literature discusses populations of organizations in terms of *organizational forms*, but examples of them are easier to give than clear definitions of what is meant by the concept. Here is how it is presented by the population ecology model:

> Organizational *forms*—specific configurations of goals, boundaries, and activities—are the elements selected by environmental criteria, and change may occur either through new forms eliminating old ones or through the modification of existing forms. . . .
> Selection pressures may favor or eliminate entire groups of organizations, such as industries, and the changing population distribution of organizations in a society reflects the operation of such selection pressures. (Aldrich, 1979:28)

It can be seen from these quotes that the population ecology approach, which utilizes biological concepts and a modified evolutionary framework, gives great weight to the seemingly impersonal power of the environment. Another major approach to the study of organization–environment relations, *resource dependence*, allows organizations a larger role in modifying and manipulating the environment. The two frameworks will be contrasted later in this chapter.

In addition to being favored or eliminated as a whole, a given organization may respond to pressures by changing certain of its activities or parts. Chapter 4 described how organizations changed goals, formed coalitions, co-opted other organizations, and engaged in other changes in order to survive. In the business world, firms drop certain of their product lines or introduce new ones in an effort to maintain profitability.

Aldrich recognizes the problems in being precise about what constitutes an organizational form. In his book, *Organizations and Environments*, he states: "Examples presented throughout this book will indicate just how difficult it is to unambiguously identify a unique 'organizational form' " (Aldrich, 1979:28).

This difficulty has not stopped organizational researchers from trying to document the rise and fall of organizational forms. They look for what is similar in organizations that succeed and fail at a particular time. They have shown the tendency for new organizational forms to appear in waves, related to particular historical periods and the conditions they reflect. Table 10-1 illustrates patterns of organizational creation—waves of similar kinds of organizations created during

TABLE 10-1   Patterns of Organizational Creation: Waves of New Forms

TYPE	DATE OF EMERGENCE
Men's national social fraternities	
a. Northern liberal arts colleges	1840–1850
b. Southern colleges	1865–1870
c. "Anti-fraternities" for Jews, blacks, Catholics, teacher's	
colleges	1900–1920
Savings banks	1830s
Textile factories (imported to the U.S. from England)	1800–1830
Railroads and steel companies	1850s & 1870s
New universities in the U.S.	1870–1900
National craft unions	1860–1900
Streetcar companies and electricity producing companies	1887–1910
Reorganization of retail trade:	1858–1900
department stores, chain stores, mail-order houses	
Mass communication industries	1920s
New federal agencies: Securities and Exchange Commission,	
Federal Communications Commission, Federal Housing	
Authority, National Labor Relations Board, Social Security	
Administration, Rural Electrification Administration	1934–1935
Air transportation	1945–1950
Record producing and distributing companies	1955–1970
"Pure" conglomerate corporations	1960s
Junior colleges	1960s

Source: Adapted from Arthur L. Stinchcombe, "Social Structure and Organizations," in James G. March (ed.), *Handbook of Organizations* (New York: Rand McNally, 1965). Reprinted with additions, by permission of James G. March.

particular periods. Thus, men's national social fraternities were started at northern liberal arts colleges in the years 1840–1850, at southern colleges a decade and a half later, and fraternities for minority racial and religious groups from 1900 to 1920. These are called "antifraternities," probably because they were a response to exclusion from the existing ones (see table 10-1). Because fraternities have survived they have a history as a form.

The Interorganizational Network

The next important term, the *interorganizational network*, is easier to conceptualize but more difficult to uncover in the real world. Networks are sometimes defined as groups of related *organizations* but at other times the term is used to refer to the *relationships* themselves, the links between organizations. Here are two contrasting definitions. The interorganizational network "consists of *a number of distinguishable organizations* having a significant amount of interaction with each other" whether positive or negative (Benson, 1980:350; italics mine).

Or, instead, networks are "the total *pattern of interrelationships* among a cluster of organizations that are meshed together in a social system to attain collective and self-interest goals or to resolve specific problems in a target population" (Van de Ven & Ferry, 1980:299; italics mine). From this point of view, a network is a relationship, an abstraction that has to be inferred from other information. (Bob and Sue exchange warm glances in class; others infer they have a particular kind of relationship.) However, even those who prefer to define interorganizational networks as groups of interrelated organizations still recognize as a major task the need to describe the *nature* of their relationships. Study in this field must therefore be concerned with *both* the related organizations and the nature of their relationships. Serious research must be done to uncover all but the most open and formal networks. For, just as in the case of individual organizations, the relationships between organizations may develop informally to supplement formal relationships. Such relationships may be both legal and illegal.

Resources

The term *resource* is used very broadly to include human resources such as workers and customers, power in its varied forms, money and material supplies, esteem, and legitimacy. That resource acquisition is a central task of organizations would not be debated by any of the schools of thought concerned with organizational environments.

Resource is a key word in the formulations of the resource dependence model of organization–environment relations. This framework also includes what is sometimes called a political economy model (Zald, 1970) or a dependence exchange approach (Aldrich & Pfeffer, 1979).

The resource dependence model "argues for greater attention to internal organizational political decision-making processes and also for the perspective that organizations seek to manage or strategically adapt to their environments" (Aldrich & Pfeffer, 1979:3). Resource dependence means that organizations seek to acquire an adequate supply of varied resources from the environment in order to maintain themselves.

Key resources. But what resources are most crucial? Benson emphasizes political and economic forces and their connections, describing the interorganizational network as a "political economy" (1980:349-368). Each organization has an internal polity or political economy, with major decision makers being those in positions of dominance within the organization. The dominant (most powerful) coalition at any one point of time may be able to make strategic choices in selecting appropriate environments or modifying given ones. As examples, decision makers may relocate a plant, drop a product line for which raw materials are expensive or scarce, or import foreign workers for seasonal work. They may join trade associations to push for a favorable tax structure or add to the campaign coffers of sympathetic legislators.

From the political economy perspective, money and authority are basic needs, the resources most sought by organizations. In this case, "Authority refers to the legitimation of activities, the right and responsibility to carry out programs of a certain kind, dealing with a broad problem area or focus. Legitimated claims of this kind are termed domains" (Benson, 1980:351).

Domains. An organization's *domain* reflects its accepted right, its legitimated claim, to operate in a given area and to seek support for its activities. The various colleges and universities in a state may specialize in preparing certain types of students, requesting funds and support on this basis. Different social welfare agencies usually have recognized purposes and refer clients to the proper agency in their network. This is not to say that there is not rivalry over domains. Indeed, network relationships may be both cooperative and conflicting. Organizations struggle to acquire legitimacy and significant domains, that is, domains of high social importance. Many social agencies compete for a share of community united funds, which may be allocated by a central board. Each has to justify its functions as being important enough to receive a desired share of these funds. Actions of other organizations that prevent an organization from carrying out its established program are resisted.

Bases of Power within Networks

Organizations are linked to others within the same network and also to forces external to the network, such as racial, ethnic, or gender groups, political parties, or social movements. In a study of networks of human service agencies Benson and his colleagues observed two sources of power deriving from these two types of relationships (1973).

Power derived from position in the network. Within a network some organizations hold more central, strategic locations than others. A state's employment security agency is one such example in that many other community agencies must refer clients to it for job placement. The community action agency is dependent on the state employment agency, but the latter, receiving referrals from many sources, is not mutually dependent on the community action agency. Patterns of dependence can shift, depending on external environmental forces. When the number of potential college students is plentiful, due to an earlier "baby boom," colleges can be selective and turn down many students referred by various high schools. The high schools are then in a position of low power. If enrollments drop, the colleges may send out recruiting teams to convince high schools of what they have to offer potential students.

Power derived from external sources.   This brings us to the second source of power suggested by Benson, the other forces in the environment that impinge on organizations in a network. If community groups can be rallied to support an agency, the agency thereby gains in power, even if its clients are relatively low in social rank. Of course, the more prestigious an organization's sources of support in the community, the more clout that support carries. Hence, organizations may seek the support of the clergy, politicians, and celebrities.

Effects of Interorganizational Power

The control of network resources is very much affected by the more powerful organizations. Administrators in such agencies are able to defend their flow of resources, claim new domains, resist the claims of less powerful agencies, and prevent the creation of competitive organizations (Benson, 1980:353).

When cooperative programs are being attempted or disputes being settled, the more powerful organizations will have more influence in the negotiations. At times, organizations are closer to equality in power, making the results of negotiation less predictable.

An interesting case to examine is the rivalry among the major civil rights organizations in the 1960s. These groups formed a national network. Although all were engaged in seeking equal rights for black Americans, they did not always agree on strategies and tactics. The major national organizations were the Southern Christian Leadership Conference, the Congress on Racial Equality (CORE), the Student Non-Violent Coordinating Committee (SNCC), and the National Association for the Advancement of Colored People (NAACP). They developed domains, which were sometimes territorial. Thus if SNCC was engaging in a voter registration campaign in Mississippi, CORE was likely to confine its similar activities to Louisiana. The NAACP was generally recognized as the legal arm of the movement. Although each organization engaged in separate activity, there were times when they needed the power of numbers and of joint cooperative action.

A great deal of negotiation regarding tactics to be used, who would be the spokespersons, and so forth might have to take place prior to joint public action. Sometimes the disagreements would surface in public. On one symbolic Mississippi march, Stokely Carmichael forced a public debate between himself and Martin Luther King, Jr., about the relative merits of the new "Black Power" movement and King's philosophy of nonviolent resistance (R. Blumberg, 1984, chap. 8).

Among the sources of power in a social movement are commitment and militancy. Organizations that are not committed and militant may be accused of "selling out" to the enemy. On the other hand, the less militant organizations are often more successful in gaining financial resources from the less committed public, thereby gaining leverage.

The network of civil rights groups also illustrates the concept of interorganizational equilibrium. An interorganizational network is considered to be "equilibrated" when its participating groups cooperate and coordinate their efforts on the basis of "normative consensus and mutual respect" (Benson, 1980:354). The civil rights coalition, or network of cooperating organizations, became more and more strained, until finally severe conflicts precluded further large-scale cooperative actions between some of them. The original equilibrium that had been worked out through continual negotiation and the pressure of a common enemy was broken.

Network Environments

We have followed Benson's analysis at length partly because it provides direction for seeking out the essential part of the environment that affects particular networks. The relevant environment affects the supply of both money and authority to organizations within a network and the distribution of power within it. This environment consists of many elements: other organizations, officials, publics, and nonorganizational collectivities such as communities, ethnic groups, families, and masses. Research is necessary in order to discover the crucial and significant environmental elements influencing any specific network.

There is variation in the structure of the environment. Resources may flow from many or only one source. For example, public agencies depend on being funded by a branch of government, while colleges are funded by endowment funds, new donations, research grants, tuitions, athletic events, and sometimes government. Certain environmental forces have more power than others, and the amount of power varies at different times.

Some networks are more open to environmental influences than others. The junior college is more dependent on short-term enrollments than some other types of colleges, and hence curricula tend to be adjusted to meet fluctuating demands. Industries that obtain their flow of raw material for production mainly from within their own country are obviously less dependent on world politics than are those that are highly dependent on foreign imports.

Some networks have more resources available to them than others. National budgets can be surveyed to note where most of a nation's resources are being allocated. In the United States networks concerned with research on and production of military goods receive a much richer resource flow than do social service agencies. Such agencies, dependent on public funding, face scrutiny from many parts of the public, some of whom have little sympathy with the clientele being served. The funding of public mental hospitals is seen as a duty, but so is conservation of public funds, as has been pointed out before. Families who can afford it will send their sick members to private mental hospitals, thus providing financial resources for those hospitals. Countries vary in the amount of resources put into the public and private sectors, so these observations cannot be generalized to all countries. In India, college teachers prefer to work for public rather than most private universities because there is an extensive nationwide system of public universities, affording a greater possibility of permanent employment.

THE GENERAL ENVIRONMENT

The Specific versus the General Environment

Organizational networks have both specific and general environments. Depending on their domains, their accepted areas of functioning, particular networks have more intense relationships with certain parts of the environment than others (see the case study on human service organizations in chapter 9). The producers of toxic materials will experience more governmental regulation and surveillance than those who deal with nonhazardous products. While many people and groups in a society are affected by warfare, munitions industries are affected more intensely and directly. During a time of student revolt, colleges and universities faced very distinctive pressures from the environment; other organizations were affected in lesser ways. Laws are made regulating many facets of societal life, yet some areas are relatively unregulated and thereby less affected by changes in law.

In addition to the specific environmental forces affecting interorganizational networks, general trends and conditions in the society may affect virtually all organizations. Turbulent or uncertain times, such as periods of warfare, economic depression, or natural disaster may create conditions that even the strongest of organizations cannot modify. Revolutionary technological developments may force their attention on many sectors of the economy and their related organizations.

The extent to which organizations can actively intervene to resist or transform environmental factors is viewed differently by the natural selection and resource dependence perspectives mentioned earlier. How do they differ?

Natural Selection Models versus the Resource Dependence Model

Natural selection models, including the population ecology model, and resource dependence models both deal with the interaction between organizations and their environments. An important summary of the two theoretical positions appears in the 1976 *Annual Review of Sociology* (2:79–105) and has been reprinted in Zey-Ferrell (1979:3–27). In this article Aldrich and Pfeffer discuss the strengths and limitations of each position. Summarizing the main distinction between the two, they state:

> A critical distinction between the resource dependence and natural selection models of organizational change is the relative importance of environmental selection as opposed to strategic decision making by organizational members. (1979:10)

The resource dependence model allows the organization to play a greater role in actively responding to environmental pressures. Decisions are made by dominant coalitions in the organization, and choices are available. Organizations vary in the amount and kinds of power they have, in how much they can select from and modify their environments.

Natural selection models include several stages. In the first stage variations occur, not through genetic mutation as in organic evolution, but as "exploratory responses made to stimuli" (Aldrich & Pfeffer, 1979:5). Sometimes this is called the trial-and-error stage. A retail store might try several approaches to gaining more customers: carrying very cheap products, carrying expensive, esoteric products, staying open longer hours, providing credit, giving out prizes. These are possible variations—responses to a highly competitive market. From these variations, the environmental selection process picks out what works best or is most suitable.

The second stage is "the operation of consistent selection criteria that differentially select some variations over others or selectively eliminate certain variations" (Aldrich & Pfeffer, 1979:5). If the retail store is operating in a neighborhood that features expensive boutiques and attracts wealthy purchasers, carrying cheap products is unlikely to prove successful. Stores that generally survive in that particular neighborhood are the ones that offer unique, exclusive, and esoteric products. Bargain or discount stores are "selected out"; they do not survive.

The third stage in the natural selection or ecological process is "the operation of a retention mechanism for the selective retention of the positively selected variations" (Aldrich & Pfeffer, 1979:5). Organizational forms need to find niches in the environment that will support them. "Environmental *niches* are distinct combinations of resources and other constraints that are sufficient to support an organizational form" (Aldrich, 1979:28).

The stores that fit the environment prosper and open up branches, while those that do not fit the neighborhood fail. That example describes the theoretically perfect operation of the natural selection model, but just as in the economic sphere, pure competition and pure selection do not exist. Government agencies that are not functioning well do not necessarily go out of existence. National governments protect private enterprises, especially large firms that would have gone into bankruptcy or some other form of demise. As Aldrich and Pfeffer point out, "the population of business organizations is bifurcated into a segment of very large organizations with a very low mortality rate and another segment of small organizations with high variation and turnover" (1979:11). Going back to the example of our retail store, if the store is part of a large chain, it can continue to operate in the red, supported by other branches and a large amount of capital, until it hits the proper variation. The small entrepreneur may put all of his or her capital into one venture and be unable to withstand a long period of experimentation.

Hence, it becomes clear that "environmental selection of entire organizations exists mainly for small businesses, organizations not linked to or subsidized by governmental units, and voluntary associations" (Aldrich & Pfeffer, 1979:11). The position that less absolute forms of selection operate for all organizations is more tenable. Environments do force the modification of parts or aspects of organizations and by responding, organizations may be able to maintain themselves over time.

Criticism of the Population Ecology Model

The notion of environmental "niche" sounds more precise than it is. The world is not made up so simply of fixed niches. More than one kind of organization can fit into a niche, meet an unmet need. Organizations can also experiment with fitting into new niches. If the use of marihuana were legalized, various new niches would open up and others would close. Natural disasters, such as floods and fires, change the environment dramatically—providing "niches" for looters, Red Cross workers, and government relief agencies, while destroying business-as-usual niches. The term *niche* is a rather passive and colorless word that obscures the dynamic, interacting nature of organizations and environment. In correcting the previous neglect of the environment, the population ecology model may go too far in the other direction, making organizations and their decision makers seem less autonomous than they actually are. Organizations do try to alter their environments as well as seek to fit in.

In trying to incorporate this truth, McKelvey and Aldrich have expanded the concept of niche (1983). Recall Aldrich's 1979 definition: "Environmental *niches* are distinct combinations of resources and other constraints that are sufficient to support an organizational form," first quoted in the previous section. McKelvey and Aldrich (1983) now define niche as:

> the activity space of an organization or population or community of organizational forms that reflects the sum total of both its adaptation *to* environmental forces that are not subject to its influence and adaptation *of* environmental forces that are subject to its influence. . . . Organizational environments are not composed of pockets or niches, but rather are best seen as broad resource pools, which may be drawn upon in return for goods and services. (p. 111)

This later definition answers some of our criticisms but is a lot to bear in mind when we hear the simple word *niche*. Of value is the increased attention to organizational interaction with forces in the environment, which has corrected previous models that examined single organizations as almost self-contained, goal-directed units.

Types of Environmental Conditions

Richard Hall provides this simple and useful list of the broad types of conditions that impinge on organizations: technological, legal, political, economic, demographic, ecological, and cultural (1982:227-233). Many of them have been discussed in examples, but let us review them.

Technology. While certain technological innovations affect particular networks more than others, major developments have impact on the society in general. The advent of the computer age has been mentioned many times as a technological innovation that, within our lifetime, has required response from all kinds of organizations. Recent changes in manners of intervening in human reproduction have potential for altering the world ratio of men to women, just as contraceptive devices have made conceivable new ways of limiting the world population. A major perspective, the contingency or technology approach, has developed around the importance of technology in affecting the internal structures of organizations (see chapter 3).

Legal conditions. The effect of laws on organizations has been discussed many times. A topic that is frequently ignored or glossed over is the presence of networks of illegal organizations that exist alongside legal ones and interact with them. The section of this chapter on the underworld will consider this neglected topic in more detail.

Political conditions. Each nation's political ideology is translated into its economic system, creating different mixes of public and private organizations. And United States history has seen periods of more and less regulation, periods of greater and fewer governmental social programs, and the rise and demise of various federal and state agencies that generate and/or regulate organizations.

Workers' organizations such as unions at times may have to struggle for recognition; they may be permitted in one period and severely restricted in another. Similarly, social movement organizations may sometimes be tolerated and sometimes outlawed. The enforcement of laws may be relatively stringent or relatively weak. Obviously, elections bringing in new officeholders may have widespread impact on organizations. In their turn, organizations lobby to influence government to act favorably on issues of major interest to them. As we know, in the United States the Supreme Court's interpretations of various laws has fluctuated, reflecting changes in public opinion and the political climate. Political conditions also include the relative power of particular organizations to affect the environment.

Economic conditions. Economic fluctuations, ranging from depression to prosperity, affect the availability of resources, the national mood, the nature of buying and saving, budget allocations, the failure or success of small businesses, marriage and divorce rates, and just about all the other interrelated elements of a society. They may even result in the creation of new types of organizations, such as those set up to house the homeless during the recession of the 1980s. Economic development has transformed some countries from essentially agricultural nations to ones based on manufacturing, service industries, and large-scale organizations. Economic competition for resources is a major force determining the behavior of organizations.

Demographic conditions. Demography refers to population distribution in terms of age, sex, race, ethnicity. Different population groups reproduce at different rates, creating a changing demographic mix. Advances in medicine have enabled people to live longer, creating a drastic shift towards an older population in the United States, one in which the proportion of older people is expected to increase still further in the future. One dramatic response to this age shift is the rise of gerontology, the study of aging; another is concern with the ability of the social security system to provide the promised benefits to the retired. The social movements to gain women, black Americans, and other minorities freer entry into jobs for which they are qualified has somewhat decreased the domination of white males in the top occupations and professions. As an exercise, consider some possible effects of a rise or decline in birthrates on various organizations.

Ecological conditions. Ecology includes both physical and social environments. Climate and geography may influence where firms will locate: the cost of heating and air-conditioning as well as the ability of persons to get to work during severe weather are factors to be considered. A location's distance from sources of supply and demand is also important. The social environment varies in terms both of publics and other organizations. A fast-food outlet located in a changing neighborhood may experience waves of very different kinds of customers at different times of the day.

Cultural conditions. The apparent efficiency of Japanese auto makers prompted American producers to study the differences in organizational structure and style between Japan and the United States. Ouchi's findings emphasized traditional Japanese cultural values as they were translated into organizational settings (1981). Culture and cultural conditioning also seem to be factors in the choice of overseas locations of multinational firms. And some electronics firms on the West Coast are hiring immigrant Asian workers who are culturally similar to the overseas work force in this field (Green, 1983).

The concept of culture, usually applied by anthropologists to societies, has been given a new use in the notion of internal "organizational cultures" (see chapter 7). The manipulation of organizational culture was described as one way of creating a more positive internal environment in various businesses.

Now let us look at a much less studied topic, the issue of how powerful organizations mold their environments.

How Powerful Organizations Mold Their Environments

Acknowledging the dynamic interaction between the organization and its environment, Perrow pointedly inquires about why we do not worry more about how powerful organizations shape and modify the environment, rather than only the reverse (1979:196). Corporations may be targets of public policy, but they often implement and determine public policy as well (R. Hall, 1983). Hall points out that many public policies are designed to be implemented in the private sector and are dependent on the degree to which such directives are resisted or found acceptable. While the influence of corporations on public policy is generally accepted, he suggests that this influence is not totally predictable. It would be false to say, for example, that corporations resist federal intervention in their affairs. There are times when such intervention—for example, the regulation of foreign trade—may be welcome.

By *environment* we have meant the whole environing society and the world. Yet the actual physical environment—nature—provides one of the best and most troubling illustrations of the impact of large corporations, the government, and the military on the world around them. Protecting and preserving the physical environment, for example, maintaining clean water supplies and uncontaminated soil and air, has now become crucial to the current health of large segments of our population and to the genetic safety of future generations.

The value of protecting the physical environment is perceived differently by different role players, who act from the vantage point of their own background and group affiliations. Strategic choices about any part of the environment depend on how it is perceived (R. Hall, 1982:319–320). Example: Democrats and Republicans are typically concerned with the problems of different interest groups. This affects the way in which they intervene, when in power, with forces in the environment. The first Republican administration of Ronald Reagan was committed to making sweeping changes in the operation of government agencies. Reagan and the functionaries he selected believed that close government scrutiny and regulation cost large companies too much money and harmed the economy. They maintained that enforcement of environmental controls should be eased to promote economic growth. Reagan appointed persons who agreed with his philosophy of lesser regulation to head various agencies, thus changing the government's posture toward many aspects of the environment.

There had already been major environmental disasters; for example, in Times Beach, Missouri, $33 million had to be spent to buy out an entire town stricken by floods and dioxin contamination. (Dioxin is a byproduct in the manufacture of the disinfectant hexachlorophene and other products used in soaps and cosmetics.)

While directing their concerns to the problems of business, Reagan and his appointees were less geared to the worries of the general public, for according to a 1981 survey, two-thirds of the public supported strong environmental laws (*New York Times*, February 27, 1983, p. E1). A federal regulatory agency, the Environmental Protection Agency (EPA), had been charged with cleaning up hazardous wastes. The years 1982 and 1983 brought increasing disclosures that many more dangerous chemical dump sites existed than had been publicized. Extremely toxic wastes had been discarded in casual fashion. A hunt went on in Missouri for more than forty pounds of dioxin that had not been accounted for. Mysterious deaths of horses and other farm animals signaled possible sites of contamination. In the process of disclosure it was found that the government had known about the existence of some of the contamination for ten years, which implies that earlier Democratic administrations had also been lax in enforcement.

In the early 1980s, as more and more sites of hazardous wastes were uncovered, the EPA was accused of complicity in minimizing their dangers. It was revealed that Rita Lavelle, the agency person in charge of allocating funds for cleaning up hazardous dumps, was a former official of various chemical companies. She appeared to have maintained close ties with her former colleagues and to have been lax in allocating funds for the execution of the stated purpose of her agency.

Congressional investigating committees started to make inquiries and a complicated legal battle ensued over the release of agency files. Lavelle resigned under a cloud, as did the head of her agency, Ann McGill Burford. Congress seemed to be stepping in to try to reguide the agency back toward efforts at protecting the environment. In this it was prodded by various voluntary organizations dedicated to environmental protection as well as by the legal actions of citizens who alleged that they had been exposed to contamination.

Many competing interest groups try to influence public policy regarding the physical environment in which we live. Ranged against those concerned with maximizing environmental protection are those concerned with the increased costs to business of complying with governmental regulations. Given the difficulties and costliness of disposing of hazardous wastes, deviance from these regulations has frequently occurred. These business crimes, not always thought of as such, lead us into a relatively uninvestigated part of the organizational world. We turn now to a little researched environmental force—the vast network of illegal organizations that are often examined in criminology texts but rarely find their way into organization texts.

THE UNDERWORLD

The Underworld as Part of Organizational Society

Organized networks of groups engaged in illegal activities are part of highly organized modern societies and hence are elements in the environment with which legal organizations interact.

Most writing about formal organizations deals with organizations that are set up according to the laws of the society and considered legitimate by it. Of course deviance—individual misbehavior within these organizations—is acknowledged, and a great deal of attention is placed on gaining compliance, getting people to do what they should do. Just as rules are frequently broken within organizations, so the laws of societies are frequently broken, necessitating huge criminal justice systems. If the profit motive influences the creation and persistence of legitimate business, so it also motivates the creation of illicit businesses. Nonetheless, little attention is paid to organized deviance as part of the study of organizations. One exception is Vaughan's research (1983) on corporate Medicaid fraud, reported on as a case study at the end of this chapter.[2]

If we are aware of group processes, of the fact that much legal, official be-

[2] Also see Gerald Mars, *Cheats at Work: An Anthropology of Workplace Crime* (1982) and Ermann and Lundman (eds.), *Corporate and Governmental Deviance* (1978).

havior is organized and systematized, why should the same not be true of illegal behavior? In fact, illegal enterprises, existing in the bureaucratized, mass society, face problems of organizing similar to those of legitimate organizations and do in fact become highly organized.

The interconnectedness of various organizations in the environment means that legal and illegal organizations are often linked in the same network. The criminal underworld needs lawyers, accountants, banks, lobbies, supplies, customers, and the favor of politicians. The study of interorganizational relations has only just begun to investigate these links between legal and illegal organizational activity (see Ermann & Lundman, 1978). The borderline between legal and illegal activity is both difficult to locate and constantly open to redefinition. So we will start with the polar case, familiar to all movie-goers and viewers of television—organized crime.

What Is Organized Crime?

Organized crime, the underworld, is often thought of in terms of criminal rackets, as in this description:

> Organized crime has the unique distinction of being unlike any other criminal activity. There is no question of impulse or insanity, nor ignorance of law or negligence. In organized enterprises each activity is pre-planned and carefully prepared so as to avoid direct confrontation with law enforcement. Because of this nonconfrontation policy the public is not reminded of the millions of dollars that change hands as a part of illegal activities.
>
> No one actually knows the extent of crime that results from these illegal activities. There is no barometer to measure corruption, legal inconsistencies, and police deceptions that result from the covert activities of organized criminal action. (Pace & Styles, 1975:15)

The concept of organized crime is not restricted to the Cosa Nostra, "Godfather," or Mafia; it also includes the polite (usually nonviolent) acts of fraud, bribery, forgery, juggling of books and bank accounts, and theft of secrets that is planned and executed by groups in the white-collar world. Individual acts of deviance, such as pilfering pencils from the office or making unauthorized long-distance calls, may occur with or without the sanction of informal group norms. But when such acts involve the participation of others, it is, in some sense at least, "organized" crime. Such office crime involves the cooperation of a number of role players who have expertise and play specialized roles, although they may not be tied into the criminal syndicates that control illegal rackets generally described as "vice." In many cases, however, the criminal syndicates have expanded into the world of legitimate business.

Differences between Legal and Illegal Organizations

The criminal syndicates engage in supplying illicit vice activities—prostitution, drugs, gambling, "protection"—as well as the associated bribery of public officials, white-collar crime, and the infiltration of legitimate businesses. They also use coercive force—killings, beatings, and threats—since they do not have the bureaucratic-legal authority of legitimate organizations. Competition among syndicates may be played out along violent lines. The syndicates are dependent on both coercion and the charismatic appeal of gang leaders. The greater need for loyalty because of the dangerous nature of their activities makes reliance on blood ties frequent; hence, the gangs are often based on and known as families.

Several of these features militate against truly bureaucratic forms of organization, yet size, scale, and complexity require organizational efficiency. Scope and size require that tasks be organized and allocated, that specialists be developed. The complexity of much organized crime requires there to be several strata of workers—from the street-corner pusher to the international drug trader-tycoon, with intermediaries in between. Accounting and legal talent are needed. Rewards and punishments for performance must be meted out. The term *contract* used for killings by hire suggests the businesslike nature of such transactions. The resultant hybrid structure has not yet received definitive analysis.[3]

Making a human activity illegal may either increase or decrease demand for it, often depending on how the consequences of illegality are managed. For example, there is the question of how information about illegal activities or products is to be spread. Sales must be organized. Since danger of prosecution makes open advertising difficult, the need for personal contact and promotion is made greater. Coupons cannot be offered to entice purchasers to buy. But in the illegal drug business, free samples can be given to "hook" potential users. Rank-and-file workers, "pushers," are needed. Illegal products and services are advertised through the use of code words and in publications known to cater to particular interests such as pornography. Thus, massage parlors may front for sexual services. The need for protection from prosecution makes attempted bribery of police officers and public officials part of organizing to do illicit business.

The Borderline between Legal and Illegal Activity

Laws make a given type of behavior legal or illegal. Hence, the same behavior—gambling, for example—may be legal in one place and illegal in another. Legality also varies over time. A statute may be repealed, legitimizing what was once illegal behavior. We can compare the smoking of marihuana and that of cigarettes, one illegal and one legal. Both are said to be injurious to health. Campaigns have been waged, thus far unsuccessfully, to make the smoking of marihuana legal. Were cigarettes made of tobacco to be outlawed, there is every reason to believe that they would still be available through illegal sources. Problems of obtaining and distributing supplies would continue, although new problems would be added if the cigarette industry had to go underground, into the criminal underworld. There it would join a number of other long-existing rackets such as gambling, drugs, prostitution, and adoption schemes.

---

[3] Because the problems of conducting illicit enterprises do not have societal approval, there are few books or articles instructing people on how to do so successfully—unlike the thousands of management books. Here is an uncultivated area for applied organizational sociologists—or less legitimate entrepreneurs.

In addition to changes in laws, changes in enforcement policies affect the amount of illegal behavior that can occur. Obviously if penalities are reduced and the government only half-heartedly enforces a particular statute, there is less chance that the illegal behavior will be adequately controlled. The same behavior that would be tolerated under one administration might be prohibited under another, even if the laws remained the same. For example, strict enforcement of narcotics violations appears to get in the way of positive international relations. Sam Billbrough, the Drug Enforcement Administration official in Miami who is responsible for the U.S. ally, Jamaica, a main source of drugs, is quoted as saying,

> Some analysts believe that if you came in with a severe narcotics program you could affect the existence of the present Government [in Jamaica]. The issue is should we press them to do things which could result in the election and installation of a leftist government, as they've had in the previous administration. Drugs are a serious problem. But Communism is a greater problem. (*New York Times*, September 10, 1984, p. A1)

Jamaican marijuana exports are estimated at over 1,900 tons a year with a wholesale value in Miami of about $1.4 billion, "more than twice the country's earnings from all other exports" (*New York Times*, September 10, 1984, p. A12).

The line between good business practice and fraud is clearer in theory than in practice. Take the case of advertising. Major firms have been forced to modify advertising that is misleading or downright erroneous or that makes claims that cannot be proven. In response, advertisers develop terminology that makes their claims sound authoritative yet contains necessary hedges: for example, manufacturers of cold remedies claim to relieve *symptoms*; they have had to cease claiming to cure colds.

The question of conflict of interest on the part of public officials is continually being raised in the newspapers and in assessing qualifications for public office. The issue is whether or not particular officials are influenced in their official actions by their private interests; do they, for example, give government contracts to former business associates or firms in which their relatives own stock? Illegal as well as legal organizations have their lobbying activities. Government regulation of various products tends to raise costs. Attempts to evade regulation may be coupled with lobbying efforts to repeal them. Lobbies are paid to influence legislators. Legislators need campaign funds and may be susceptible to undue influence.

Another hazy area involves taxes and tax shelters. Clever manipulation of private and organizational finances can result in greatly reduced taxes for highly paid executives, legally. Yet, the borderline between legal and illegal deductions is constantly being argued in cases before the Internal Revenue Service. And tax evasion cases abound. It is perhaps not surprising that this borderline between legal and illegal activity is often crossed. Many white-collar crimes are executed by seemingly respectable executives, government officeholders, accountants, and other professionals.

The Effects of Demand and Supply

Opportunities for deviance are great within a legitimate business enterprise. But the laws of supply and demand also invite entrepreneurs to provide new goods or services not available legitimately. Our assumption that cigarette smoking would continue even if outlawed takes into account that demand does not disappear simply because a product is decreed illegal.

Some people will be deterred from *some* illicit activities by the law. But for others, their need for a product weighs more heavily than their need to be law-abiding. Besides, there is an unwritten law or custom that the otherwise respectable citizen who patronizes illegal establishments is not punishable for the illegality of the activity. The prostitute is periodically arrested or forced to move her place of operation; the "john" who uses her services is not prosecuted.

One case of severe need is that of immigrants whose desperation forces them to flee their homelands and attempt to enter other countries, legally or illegally. Given the large numbers of persons in this plight in an unstable world of poverty, dictators, and military coups, the pressure to bypass restrictive immigration regulations is great. Bribery of immigration officials occurs in many countries, regardless of their politics. Such official gatekeepers are crucial to the individual seeking a special privilege or dispensation that lies on the borderline between legality and illegality.

Once inside a country the illegal immigrant needs forged documents for many purposes, perhaps to obtain a driver's license or social services. A black market system of forgeries, hideouts, and transportation services develops to meet this need. The client, unprotected by fair business regulations, is powerless against exploitation by the purveyors of such services. Nor is satisfaction guaranteed.

Since profit making is an idealized goal in a free enterprise society, entrepreneurs will be found willing to take the necessary chances to make a profit by providing illegal services or products. There are always needy persons available for rank-and-file participation in illegal work, especially when it is the only available alternative to legitimate unskilled labor or unemployment. Under the conditions of scarcity and restrictions in Communist societies, black markets furnishing illegal goods at high prices also flourish.

The Corruption of Officials

The need for "protection"—the assurance that the purveyors of illicit products and services will not be arrested too frequently or with too dire consequences—feeds into a system of payoffs and the corruption of public officials. Those in close contact with the criminal world, such as police officers and judges, are exposed to the temptation of bribes larger than what they could earn in years. Political pressure often mandates periodic crackdowns, which the underworld expects and learns how to manage. Then the system of legal–illegal organizational relationships goes back to business as usual.

The Effects of Changing Technology

In recent years the tremendous value of technological secrets in the world of computers has tempted many persons attached to the industry to pass on information illegally. Obtaining or manipulating privileged information is a major element in organized crime as well as business. Automated information gathering has expanded with the computerization of modern society. Most Americans have their "profile" recorded in several computer banks (Pace & Styles, 1975), the end result of all types of automated data gathering. Private industry and government put millions of dollars into computerized information, and all of their systems of information can be combined. Criminal conspiracies also gain access to these sources, and computer generated information is widely used by organized crime. In providing examples, Pace and Styles (1975) maintain:

> Consumer fraud practices are so common as to defy individual identity. For example, price fixing, securities manipulation and other forms of theft are dependent upon the flow of massive amounts of information. Cooperative wholesale grocery associations, for example, frequently do not rely upon supply and demand, but upon monopolies in fixing food prices. . . .
> Credit information such as financial status, assets, etc., are for sale to criminal organizations through some credit reporting associations. This same information is available to extortionists, promoters, and others. No laws presently in use or proposed can stop or slow this practice. . . .
> The use of information obtained by the surveillance of criminal elements may be used for bribery, extortion, and shakedowns in a large number of ways. This type of activity is extremely effective when dealing with political figures and those who hold positions of trust. (p. 84)

Obviously, the underworld needs its computer experts, hardware, and sophisticated programs. The international underworld now engages in a highly lucrative type of thievery—that of computer ideas and computer chips. The ease of thievery is aided by the extremely small size of the valuable computer chips—no trucks are needed to haul away the loot. Computer chips drive a wide range of modern products from missile guidance systems to the newest data processing systems.

In April 1983, the *New York Times* reported that the nation's first "high tech" criminal task force had been activated "to combat the booming illicit business of selling trade secrets and stolen microchips" (April 30, 1983, p. 9). Illegal trafficking in the tiny microchips was said to run into millions of dollars annually. And it is being done by highly educated criminals—engineers, technicians, and corporate executives.

The U.S. government has tried to restrict the export of sophisticated American technology. However, the attempts of other countries, including the Soviet Union, France, Japan, China, and Israel, to obtain American technology are pervasive. Safeguards for protecting industrial secrets are so imperfect that the United States is said to be losing its technological edge through "espionage, legitimate sales and American greed. . ." (p. 9).

Some of the information is being stolen by intelligence officers from other countries who pose as businesspersons or students. But much of the technology is being passed along by "profit-motivated" Americans. In 1985 a major spy case was uncovered that involved several members of an American family who had passed on secrets to the Soviet Union.

Our consideration of the organized underworld and white-collar crime was intended to be exploratory and suggestive, in the hopes of stimulating more careful research into the connections between legal and illegal organizational networks. It should also demonstrate that to restrict the study of organizations to legitimate ones, honestly administered, is to cast an unwarranted aura of morality on the world of organizations.

Another connection that requires greater attention is that between social movements and the institutionalized, accepted organizations that they hope to change.

SOCIAL MOVEMENTS AND INSTITUTIONALIZED ORGANIZATIONS

Voluntary Associations

Voluntary associations vary tremendously, from small, locally based social or fraternal clubs to nationwide networks of federated organizations that employ paid personnel. Voluntary associations "are a means of uniting both spatially distant individuals and individuals with some common goal or concern" (Lieberson & Allen, 1962:317). The members may share an aspect of identity, such as race or ethnicity. These associations are often linked to accepted, institutionalized organizations such as churches and businesses and function to maintain and support institutional goals in less bureaucratic settings. They may also be the vehicle through which change-oriented movements mobilize supporters.

The Encyclopedia of Associations (1985) lists the following types of associations: trade, business, and commercial; agricultural and commodity; legal, governmental, public administration, and military; scientific, engineering, and technical; educational; cultural; social welfare; health and medical; public affairs; fraternal, foreign interest, nationality, and ethnic; religious; veteran, hereditary, and patriotic; hobby and avocational; athletic and sports; labor unions, associations, and federations; chambers of commerce; and Greek letter and related organizations.

Such organizations are said to have integrative functions for individuals, linking them to the larger structures of society through networks of interpersonal ties. But these organizations often provide important informal links between and among larger ones. Many also serve as interest groups, maintaining lobbies in Washington to push desired legislation and appointments. Service clubs such as Lions, Elks, Kiwanis, Jaycees, fraternities, and sororities have numerous functions. In addition to their most publicly stated purposes, such as aiding charities or providing social events for members, they constitute networks of sponsorship and connections. Trade unions are more openly designed to protect and increase the benefits of their members.

It is commonplace to note the prevalance of "joining" in the United States and our tendencies to set up committees and organizations for every purpose. This means that voluntary associations range from being ultraconservative to ultraliberal and radical. Some are supportive of the status quo, others want to turn the clock back, and still others see the need for changes in organizations and institutions. Our discussion of environmental protection noted that there are voluntary associations such as the Sierra Club and the Natural Resources Defense Council that seek safeguards for the physical environment. Business and trade associations that are affected may lobby in the other direction, for the easing of standards. The interplay of these organizations with conflicting viewpoints can be acted out in many ways: pressure for the passage or repeal of legislation; donations to favored politicians; attempts to woo public opinion. But sometimes the usual methods do not work satisfactorily and the organization may seek innovative ways of pushing their concerns. When strong emotions are involved, as in the case of pro- and anti-abortion groups, the members may use the tactics of social movements.

Social movements are unconventional collectivities that grow out of felt concerns, dissatisfaction with progress through official channels, and attempts to create quicker or more drastic change. People in a small church discussion group, a legitimated voluntary association, may present speakers and discussions to deal with an issue such as abortion. If some of the group feel that more drastic action is needed, they may split off to form a social movement organization. Thus, preexisting group relations often lead to social movements. The social movement organization is itself a form of voluntary association.

Social Movements

Social movements often have spearheading organizations to which people belong, but they also involve mass action such as rallies, boycotts, and picketing, which draw sympathizers. Many more people participate in and are influenced by social movements than join social movement organizations. Movements try to mobilize people, power, and resources to bring about desired change—whether toward some new state of affairs or back to an older one. There was a pro-Prohibition movement and then a countermovement for repeal of the Prohibition amendment. Particular institutions, such as churches, may experience movements for change within them, sometimes resulting in internal change but at other times resulting in split-offs into new sects. The student movements of the 1960s, directed against bureaucratic features of the multiuniversity, brought about considerable disruption and reevaluation at the time. The civil rights and women's movements directed attention to discriminatory employment policies. These movements were the force behind the government-instituted affirmative action mandates.

Social movements are directed at numerous issues, and their strength and saliency vary at different times. The labor movement was one of the major social movements of the first half of the twentieth century; in the second half labor has moved towards institutionalization. *Institutionalization* means that the goals and purposes of the movement have been accepted as legitimate and that it need no longer struggle through unconventional means for acceptance. If outlawed, trade unionism would again take on more characteristics of a movement. Obviously, social movements are a source of change and disruption, militating against the inertia of established bureaucracies.

CORPORATE FRAUD: *A CASE STUDY*

INTRODUCTION

Sometimes individuals try to defraud the government by receiving benefits to which they are not entitled, such as welfare payments or food stamps. Such cases of "welfare cheats" are generally well publicized, evoking the righteous indignation of the public. The extent to which organizations also pursue illegal claims from government agencies and the amounts of money involved is difficult to assess. This excerpt is about a well-publicized case that *was* discovered.

A large drug chain in Ohio was found to have engaged in computer-created false Medicaid billings over a twenty-one-month period, thus cheating the state public welfare department of more than half a million dollars. When the matter made headlines, the drug chain responded by painting itself as victim rather than perpetrator. Fortunately, an alert graduate student in sociology was looking for such a case of business fraud on which to base her Ph.D. dissertation. The result was the book, *Controlling Unlawful Organizational Behavior; Social Structure and Corporate Misconduct*, by Diane Vaughan (1983). This summary, and all quotations, are drawn from Vaughan's analysis of how a network of governmental organizations investigated suspected fraud by Revco Drug Stores, succeeded in uncovering it, and worked out a particular settlement to close the case.

Organizational deviance in the field of health services, such as that being described, is made more possible precisely because of the complexity of current delivery systems for such services. For many,

> Obtaining goods and services related to health is no longer an exchange between the seeker and provider of services; the encounter has now expanded to include the government, which formulates the rules for the exchange. Nursing homes, pharmacies, hospitals, dentists, physicians, and ambulance services sign contracts with federal, state, or local government program sponsoring agencies to deliver their specialized goods and services to the public. These providers are then reimbursed in accordance with established guidelines and regulations. (p. xi)

Aware of the possibilities for fraud and abuse of government benefit programs, federal, state, and local governments have evolved various inspection procedures to prevent such crime. Nonetheless, on July 28, 1977, Revco Drug Stores, Inc., a large retail drug chain, was found guilty of a computer-generated double-billing scheme. Through false Medicaid claims it had defrauded the Ohio Department of Public Welfare of over half a million dollars. It turned out that two top executives, one a computer expert and the other an expert in pharmaceuticals, had engineered a double-billing scheme that operated automatically through the computer system.

The falsified prescription claims were discovered "serendipitously"—by accident. The Ohio State Board of Pharmacy had been called in to investigate the prescriptions of a podiatrist, which included large quantities of narcotics and tranquilizers, unusual in that medical specialty. These records could be found by tracing the route taken by all prescriptions reimbursed by Medicaid. Records of such prescriptions filled at Revco's 159 pharmacies in the state were routinely sent to corporate headquarters in Cleveland, where they were then entered on tape and submitted to the welfare department as claims for reimbursement. The Ohio Department of Public Welfare, therefore, had computer tape records of the prescriptions filled at the Revco store used most frequently by the podiatrist in question. It became the second governmental organization drawn into the investigation, agreeing to generate the computerized claims records for Medicaid prescriptions written by the podiatrist and filled in the key store.

The welfare department's investigative unit, the Bureau of Surveillance and Utilization Review (SUR), examined computer output of the prescriptions of the podiatrist. It was here that patterns of irregularities in prescription numbers and dates were discovered. A major one was that the last three digits of certain six-digit numbers were being transposed. A prescription would be recorded as a claim and three days later the identical prescription was recorded again with the last three digits transposed.

The investigation then shifted away from the particular podiatrist towards finding out if such irregularities were more widespread. Several months of work uncovered the fact that transposed prescription numbers appeared in each of the store's computerized records, no matter who the prescribing physician was. The suspicion increased that certain prescriptions were the basis of false billing to the welfare department, submitted for payment a second time with numbers transposed and dates changed. Computer records had to be verified against original prescriptions held in individual pharmacies. The work would have to proceed with a great deal of secrecy to prevent the stores from "losing" the needed verifying data.

Another agency was brought into the network, the Ohio State Highway Patrol, which had jurisdiction to investigate any criminal act involving state property interests. This agency had certain powers that the others involved did not, but it lacked the legal expertise that would be necessary to pursue an airtight case. It reached out for further assistance to the Economic Crime Unit of the Franklin County Prosecutor's Office—the county in which all welfare billing for the state originates. The Economic Crime Unit then assumed direction of the rest of the investigation. One more subunit of the welfare department would be needed—its Division of Data Services. This division had the expertise to develop special computer programs that could examine past claims paid to all Revco stores in the state. Thus, what Vaughan calls a social control network of five investigative agencies became involved in uncovering and prosecuting this corporate "misconduct."

The rest of the story involves exciting detective work: serving search warrants simultaneously at pharmacies in five locations in four counties, maintaining secrecy, outwitting the press so that Revco would not be forewarned, and setting up command posts to coordinate action, and highway patrol communications to keep all informed. Original prescriptions were seized at all of the locations.

The corporation responded immediately, as soon as it was notified by its pharmacists of the raid. Revco executives called the Economic Crime Unit and arranged a meeting at corporate headquarters, and the story broke in the press.

Two highly trained Revco executives admitted that they worked out the system for modifying dates and transposing the last three digits of legitimate claims to create the fraudulent ones. Their explanation was that they had done it to make up for the losses involved in a large number of claims rejected by Medicaid's system of screening them. Medicaid, through a prepayment editing scheme routinely screened out claims that contained errors, sent them back to the provider, and withheld reimbursement until the claim was corrected and successfully resubmitted. Revco had not kept up with correcting its rejected claims and had a much higher rejection rate than other such firms. The two executives decided to cut corners by setting up this scheme to compensate for losses due to the screening process.

The disposition of the case was also complex and dramatic. Revco "was under pressure for an early, quiet settlement and hoped to avoid a trial" (p. 13). The scandal was affecting its position in the stock market. The prosecutor's office "also was interested in avoiding a trial and obtaining an early settlement" (p. 13). A trial would be lengthy and costly and was seen as not serving the public's interest. Because of the intricacy of the case, some of the facts would be hard to prove. Other political reasons also entered into the Economic Crime Unit's desire for a speedy resolution.

Both parties entered into negotiation for a plea. Legal technicalities made it more advantageous for both sides to choose the charge of a first-degree misdemeanor rather than the alternative, a fourth-degree felony charge that actually carried lesser penalties. In looking at available statutes to use, it was found that various charges either did not offer an accurate description of the act committed or carried penalities that were inadequate. For example, tampering with records, one type of first-degree misdemeanor, did not describe the case accurately. Theft by deception, usually used for cases of fraud, did not offer penalties that were serious enough. Engaging in organized crime, a first-degree felony charge, could not be made because it required the collusion of five or more persons and only two officials had been involved. This dilemma—the ineffectiveness of existing laws to cover the creative varieties of computer crime—has been recognized, and in 1984 legislation was proposed to Congress that would make computer trespassing, theft, and fraud clear-cut federal offenses (*Fortune*, 1984:141–142).

The charge that fit the present case best was called "falsification," which, while a misdemeanor, provided the largest penalty. Revco agreed to plead "no contest" to ten counts of falsification and would be fined $5,000 per count. It also would make restitution to the Ohio Department of Public Welfare of approximately half a million dollars. The two erring executives were fined

$2,000 each. The welfare department could have terminated Revco as a Medicaid provider but decided this would greatly inconvenience many customers who were in poor health and lacked transportation facilities to take their prescriptions elsewhere.

Revco had grossed approximately $650 million in total sales for their then most recent fiscal year. "The sanctions imposed amounted to less than .001 percent of gross" (p. 50). While some of the agencies involved were disappointed in the settlement, discussion among them brought out the reasoning of the Economic Crime Unit. The negative effect on Revco was temporary, but the firm did revise its internal edit system, reducing the size of its Medicaid rejection rates, the source of the original deviance.

Vaughan concludes: "The investigation led to a remedy for the specific problem that generated the unlawful behavior and close surveillance was initiated as a preventive mechanism" (p. 53).

SUMMARY

This chapter has considered the relationship between organizations and their environments, including not only established organizations but also those that are part of the criminal underworld and those that are part of change-oriented social movements. The growing focus on environment has nurtured attempts to classify organizations into populations of similar forms of organization and to study the problem of organizational survival in terms of fit with the environment. Organizations have been grouped into networks of related organizations and their interlocked domains and relative influence and power studied. Attention is also paid to resources and how various organizations obtain the needed resources from their environment.

Networks have their own specific environments, which must be discovered through research; some are more open to environmental influence than others. General events in societies, such as periods of warfare, economic depressions, or natural disasters, create broad environmental conditions that affect most organizations.

Natural selection models stress the selection process of the environment, adapting biological models of natural selection and suggesting that certain forms of organizations fit into available niches better than others. However, pure competition and pure selection for survival do not exist; moreover, other organizations such as government may bail out failing organizations. Resource dependence models place greater emphasis on the way organizations select and modify their environments, for example, by relocating to more favorable areas or changing sources of supply. The variety of environmental factors that affect and interact with organizations were classified as technological, legal, political, economic, demographic, ecological, and cultural conditions.

An overlooked aspect of organizational environment is the underworld. A number of the special features of the underworld make it unlike Weber's model of bureaucracy. But the underworld is organized, forms an interlocked part of international networks of legal and illegal organizations, is characterized by specialization and division of labor, and has many of the problems of legitimate business, such as obtaining raw materials and personnel, distributing goods and services, and responding to environmental pressures. Its special nature makes it a hybrid combination of bureaucracy, family, and autocracy. Lacking legal-rational power and the official support of government structures, the underworld builds its own system of authority. The danger of discovery and of defection has life-threatening consequences; hence, coercive power is organized and used. Leadership is often charismatic, with loyalty and fear substituting for the protection legitimate organizations can expect from law enforcement agencies. The criminal gang is like a prison in that the individual cannot choose to leave at will. The openness of illegal activity varies, depending on the nature of law enforcement in a particular locale. When many officials are bought off, vice can operate rather openly. At times of crackdown it must go under cover. Just as universities and businesses may have official counsel and other professionals on their payroll, so does the illegal organization. Legal businesses may be forced to take "protection" from a mob by the regular payment of money. The division between law-abiding and illicit behavior is often blurred; so-called upright citizens do business with the underworld, and finally, white-collar criminals clearly cross the line, using their expertise for illegal purposes.

Social movements and social movement organizations were described as related to and growing out of voluntary associations. Unconventional movements for change, they sometimes attack established bureaucracies or split off from them. Unfortunately, the study of social movements is usually seen as a separate field and not linked with analysis of change in established organizations.

11

CURRENT ISSUES IN THE ORGANIZATIONAL SOCIETY

Public Issues in Advanced Industrial Society
    The Problem: What Kinds of Public Issues Characterize Our Times?
High-Risk Technologies and Normal Accidents
    Creating Risk
    Normal Accidents
Problems of American Business and Labor
    Decline in Industry
    Worker Participation
    Community Labor–Management Committees
    Worker and Worker–Community Ownership
    The Role of Unions
    White-Collar Crime and Corporate Deviance
Issues of Equality
    The Thrust for Equality
    Women and Labor Markets
    Affirmative Action and Equal Opportunity
    Human Service Issues
Bureaucracy and Democracy
    The Relationship between Bureaucracy and Democracy
    Internal Democracy
    The Power of Bureaucracies
    The Dangers of Bureaucratic Impersonality
Summary

PUBLIC ISSUES IN ADVANCED INDUSTRIAL SOCIETY

The Problem: What Kinds of Public Issues Characterize Our Times?

The interdependence of nations. This book began by contrasting a model of modern industrial society with its polar opposite, the traditional society. Modern societies are dominated by science, advanced technology, and large complex organizations. The nations of the world are at various stages in their industrialization, with the United States and some of its Western allies as well as the Soviet Union and Japan far along in the process. Countries that may have ancient cultures are nonetheless called "less developed" or "developing," based on the extent to which they have advanced industrially and technologically. Their development is hastened or retarded by their relationships to wealthier industrialized nations. A land of bullock carts and "coolie" labor can also have an international airline and receive advanced military weapons from its allies. Life in the industrialized countries is also affected by international ties.

Technological inventions in transportation and communications increase the ability of firms in countries like the United States to transfer production from one region to another or to dependent countries. With satellite communications, central managements can oversee worldwide operations at close to the speed of light and physical commodities can be moved by speedy air transport (Bluestone, 1982:55).

The relocation of plants abroad has had an important impact on American labor and labor-management relations. Hazards involved in producing dangerous chemicals are also exported, as the people of Bhopal, India, discovered. Whatever their stage of industrialization, the countries of the world are interdependent and problems they face affect all of them.

Key issues to be considered. In this chapter we review some crucial current issues in this interdependent organizational world. Those selected are among the obvious preoccupations of thoughtful persons in highly industrialized parts of the world. Some have been discussed in other chapters of the book, and others were dealt with less explicitly.

Deciding which issues are crucial depends at least partly on what the observer considers important. But there are other sources that reflect the concerns of average people. Responses to public opinion polls specifically reveal their fears and worries. Problems are highlighted by the news media, especially when a troubling event occurs, such as a chemical explosion or an airplane highjacking. Demonstrations by citizens over nuclear energy plants, environmental pollution, military spending, and the like reflect the concerns of organized groups about what they consider dangerous or undesirable directions in modern life.

The problems we have been concerned with in various chapters are those related to modern bureaucratic organization rather than other human or social problems. They include such issues as the need for internal reorganization of American industry, white-collar and corporate crime, efforts to achieve equality and equity for minority and women workers, government's role in safeguarding the natural environment, and dilemmas of human service organizations. Another writer might have selected different aspects of modern life as equally troublesome; the list is not put forth as definitive.

We shall look at two other important issues in this chapter, the multiplication of high-risk technologies and the relationship of bureaucracy to freedom. We start with the first of these, stimulated by the work of Perrow, *Normal Accidents* (1984). High-risk technologies are used by varied organizations in interaction with each other; they pose serious problems for the preservation of human life and the natural environment. The ways in which they are regulated or not regulated become important political decisions of the state.

HIGH-RISK TECHNOLOGIES AND NORMAL ACCIDENTS

Creating Risk

Advanced industrial societies still have to cope with the natural environment, as did their predecessors. We are only partially able to protect ourselves better through the ability to predict major weather patterns and thus to react earlier to potential natural emergencies such as floods, earthquakes, and typhoons. At the same time, we have created new systems, "man"-made ones that affect nature itself and increase the possibility of disasters.

The growing interest in "risk management" attests to the fact that risk is a normal part of industrialized societies. A special issue of the journal *Management Science* (30, no. 4 [1984]) is devoted to research on the topic, the editor maintaining:

Our society seems to be gaining an increased awareness of the environmental, technological, and occupational risks associated with an industrialized world. The challenge of effective risk management is to act rationally in the face of complex emotional concerns where over-reaction and over-regulation can be costly, but where the cost associated with the occurrence of a risky event is disastrous. (Sarin: 395)

This comment might be translated as follows: "The risks involved in running our businesses are being publicized. Our problem is to avoid the costs of regulation without risking the costs of a Three Mile Island or a Bhopal disaster." The risk management statement reflects recognition of the possibility and probability that accidental harm will occur to people, animals, property, and nature as a result of systems designed by human beings rather than as a result of natural occurrences. The risk assessor tries to balance the harm that may occur against the possible benefits, stressing the organizational concept of cost-effective rationality over against "emotional concerns." Human emotional concerns have their own rationality, one not based purely on numbers, according to Perrow (1984). He asserts that high-risk technologies are multiplying:

As our technology expands, as our wars multiply, and as we invade more and more of nature, we create systems—organizations, and the organization of organizations—that increase the risks for the operators, passengers, innocent bystanders, and for future generations. (p. 3)

Normal Accidents

Accidents are normal in the sense that they are bound to occur, given the features of some of our most advanced technology. Unexpected interactions of complex elements occur through sometimes simple mistakes that set off others or are misinterpreted. Different elements may be physically placed so that they come into unplanned contact and interaction. What kinds of simple mistakes occur? Well, of the numerous valves that have to be kept in "on" or "off" positions (in nuclear and other plants), one can inadvertently be left in the wrong position. Gauges for measuring temperature or humidity or pressure can malfunction, leading to wrong conclusions. Even safety devices are sometimes set off erroneously, bringing about automatic processes that are unwarranted.

In the famous accident at Pennsylvania's Three Mile Island nuclear plant, which occurred in 1979, a valve in each of two pipes had been accidentally left in a closed position. There were two indicators on a gigantic control panel that showed that the valves were closed instead of open, one obscured by a repair tag hanging on the switch above it. Since the problem that was occurring seemed unrelated to these valves, the error was not immediately noted.

The intricate and often unexpected mutual effects of certain technical interactions lead to puzzling accidents. The human element enters in, as those involved try to figure out what is happening. Operators and managers construct plausible interpretations for unexpected or little-known reactions in the processes with which they are dealing. So, for example, a gauge that has been sticking or in need of repair can be assumed to be wrong rather than to be accurately measuring an abnormal occurrence.

The high-risk technologies examined by Perrow include those used in nuclear plants; chemical industries; aircraft and airways; marine transport; dams, lakes, and mines; and recombinant DNA technology—gene-splicing. Many accidents have already occurred in these systems; the potential of some of them for catastrophe on a large scale is real. Of those in charge of these systems, some have worked harder than others at minimizing risk, with the amount of effort related partially to public visibility and also to whom the potential victims are. The airlines are a case in point. Airline mishaps are highly visible and watched by the public, poor safety records affect profits, and important executives fly. Efforts at minimizing risk have been greater than in the marine system. When accidents occur in marine transport of crude oil and other dangerous substances, the costs are less obvious. Collisions at sea involve loss of life, but often that of lower participants such as seamen. Oil spills affect the environment and anonymous individuals. Production pressures are great, and ship captains are encouraged not to lose time in port, even though repairs may be needed. Efforts at international regulation of the seas have not been effective, and some waters, such as canals, are crowded with a variety of ships.

Perrow believes that certain organizational systems can be modified to make them safer but others have necessary structural features that contain the seed of potential error and disaster. The two features or dimensions used in his analysis are (1) complex interactions and linearity and (2) loose and tight coupling.

Complex interactions. Interactive complexity in the presence of tight coupling increases risk, the possibility of accidents. Linear interactions, the ones consciously created, are less dangerous—lever A is designed to set off a certain reaction in B. One component is supposed to interact with one other component that precedes or follows it. But additional, "redundant" components may be added as one way of reducing failures—say, adding a secondary source of oxygen to a primary supply or creating an automatic shut-off device. The more components a system has, the more complexity is introduced, and the more that can go wrong. One might assume, for example, that when a primary source of oxygen fails, the secondary source will be there to take its place. But both may be affected by the same unpredicted occurrence, such as leaks or interference by outside objects. Table 11-1 illustrates the characteristics of complex and linear systems.

TABLE 11-1   Characteristics of Complex and Linear Systems

COMPLEX SYSTEMS	LINEAR SYSTEMS
Tight spacing of equipment	Equipment spread out
Proximate production steps	Segregated production steps
Many common-mode connections of components not in production sequence	Common-mode connections limited to power supply and environment
Limited isolation of failed components	Easy isolation of failed components
Personnel specialization limits awareness of interdependencies	Less personnel specialization
Limited substitution of supplies and materials	Extensive substitution of supplies and materials
Unfamiliar or unintended feedback loops	Few unfamiliar or unintended feedback loops
Many control parameters with potential interactions	Control parameters few, direct, and segregated
Indirect or inferential information sources	Direct, on-line information sources
Limited understanding of some processes (associated with transformation processes)	Extensive understanding of all processes (typically fabrication or assembly processes)

SUMMARY TERMS	
COMPLEX SYSTEMS	LINEAR SYSTEMS
Proximity	Spacial segregation
Common-mode connections	Dedicated connections
Interconnected subsystems	Segregated subsystems
Limited substitutions	Easy substititions
Feedback loops	Few feedback loops
Multiple and interacting controls	Single purpose, segregated controls
Indirect information	Direct information
Limited understanding	Extensive understanding

Source: From *Normal Accidents* by Charles Perrow. Copyright © 1984 by Basic Books, Inc., Publishers. Reprinted by permission of the publisher.

"*Complex interactions* are those of unfamiliar sequences, or unplanned and unexpected sequences, and are either not visible or not immediately comprehensible" (Perrow, 1984:78). One component can interact with another outside the normal, expected sequence. There can be an unanticipated connection between two independent, unrelated systems that are in close proximity, causing an interaction that was not planned. Each organization can be thought of as a system, but there are also internal systems—for example, an aircraft has a food preparation and storage system and also an oxygen system, a fuel system, and so on. An electrical short in a coffee pot can set off other unexpected accidents if the same electrical system serves other functions.

The case is given of a tanker, the *Dauntless Colocotronis*, which was traveling up the Mississippi River and accidentally grazed the top of a submerged wreck. The wreck sliced a hole in the bottom of the tanker, and the oil began to seep out. This was the first accident, but it set off other unforeseen problems. The hole occurred at the point where the tank adjoined the pump room; some of the oil seeped into the pump room. From there it leaked into the engine room, eventually causing an explosion and fire. Such complex interactions were not anticipated in locating these various rooms in the tanker. The environment is also a source of complex interactions that can cause accidents. Even though one drives a car carefully or pilots a ship carefully, weather and other vehicles (part of the environment) can intervene to cause "freak" accidents.

Tight and loose coupling. We have come across the terms *tight and loose coupling* before. Here is how Perrow uses them: "*Tight coupling* is a mechanical term meaning there is no slack or buffer or give between two items. What happens in one directly affects what happens in the other" (pp. 89-90). With loose coupling there is more opportunity for independent action. Shocks and failures can be incorporated without affecting the whole system. In the "freak" car accidents mentioned above, which sometimes occur during foggy weather, one collision brings about a chain or pile-up of others when cars have been closely following each other and alternate lanes are blocked. The cars are tightly coupled. Greater distance between each car, fewer of them in line, and more lanes would have made for looser coupling and greater possibility of preventing chain accidents. Working with hazardous materials can be worse than driving in a fog; one cannot directly observe the chemical reactions taking place in a sealed tank, and the materials being processed often cannot be approached closely because of possible contamination. Table 11-2 contrasts the characteristic features of tendencies that produce tight and loose coupling.

Normal responses to normal accidents. The industries involved most frequently react to an accident in patterned ways. First, they try to minimize its severity, cheerfully reporting that it could have been worse and lauding what was learned from the experience. Second, there is a strong tendency to conclude that the accident was due to operator error. Large investments in such systems as nuclear plants

TABLE 11-2 Tight and Loose Coupling Tendencies

TIGHT COUPLING	LOOSE COUPLING
Delays in processing not possible	Processing delays possible
Invariant sequences	Order of sequences can be changed
Only one method to achieve goal	Alternative methods available
Little slack possible in supplies, equipment, personnel	Slack in resources possible
Buffers and redundancies are designed-in, deliberate	Buffers and redundancies fortuitously available
Substitutions of supplies, equipment, personnel limited and designed-in	Substitutions fortuitously available

Source: From *Normal Accidents* by Charles Perrow. Copyright © 1984 by Basic Books, Inc., Publishers. Reprinted by permission of the publisher.

plus fear of public disapproval encourage the playing down of their inherent dangers. "Blaming the victim" is a popular device for shifting blame from organized entities to individuals. Perrow shows that operators—lower participants—are often put in the position of having to ignore safety standards in order to get their quotas of work out. Later they can be blamed if something goes wrong.

Must we live with high-risk systems? Every organized human endeavor, whether it be the practice of medicine or the production of a telephone bill, is bound to incur some mistakes. But when complex systems are involved, such as those in high-technology production, the possibilities for error are greater. Even if potentially dangerous industries have no more errors than others, this is not good enough. The nuclear energy industry is not worth the high risks it entails, according to Perrow. Showing the frequency of serious accidents or near accidents that take place in nuclear plants, he states:

> The catastrophic potential of nuclear plant accidents is acknowledged by all, but defense in depth is held by experts to reduce accident probabilities to near zero. Yet core containment, emergency cooling systems, and isolated siting all appear to be inadequate; all have been threatened. Nor can we have any confidence whatsoever that quality control in construction and maintenance is near the heroic levels necessary to make these dangerous systems safe. A long list of construction failures, cover-ups, threats, and sheer ineptitude plagues the industry. (p. 60). . . .
> The potential for unexpected interactions of small failures in that system. . . makes it prone to the system accident. (p. 61)

Unhappily, a major nuclear accident did occur at the Chernobyl nuclear power plant in the Soviet Union in 1986, bearing out these fears and predictions. A timely response and warning to other nations was imperative in this situation of potential world catastrophe, yet several important delays transpired. According to the Soviet government, local authorities at first underestimated the accident's seriousness, delaying the evacuation of residents in nearby areas. Nor were affected nations warned of potential fallout until one of them, Sweden, detected such abnormal levels of radiation that the accident was revealed.

Figure 11-1 presents Perrow's policy recommendations, based on his own judgment, regarding which high-risk systems should be abandoned, which restricted, and which tolerated and improved. The cost of alternatives is measured against the net catastrophic potential of such systems as nuclear weapons and nuclear power, marine transport, and DNA research (see figure 11-1).

Perrow considers recombinant DNA—gene splicing—very dangerous but too valuable to totally abandon. Scientists using this technique are able to graft genetic information from one organism into the cell nucleus of another, designing new life forms for accomplishing specific tasks. Possible accidents could result in such disasters as a cancer epidemic. How such techniques might be used in biological warfare is best left undiscussed. After initial debate regarding the dangers of gene splicing and international conferences held by concerned scientists, a reaction has set in against governmental regulation and control. Extreme competitiveness in the field has created this resistance and perhaps contributed to unwarranted optimism that there will not be a disaster. On the other hand, the potential benefits of dis-

FIGURE 11-1 Policy Recommendations about High-Risk Systems

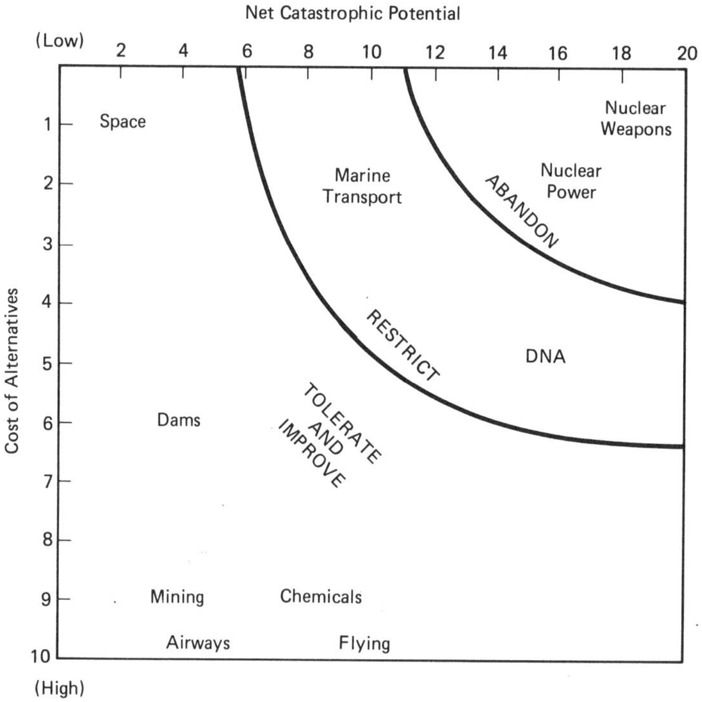

Source: From *Normal Accidents* by Charles Perrow. Copyright 1984 by Basic Books, Inc., Publishers. Reprinted by permission of the publisher.

coveries in this field leads Perrow to recommend restricting but not abandoning such research. Those who are either skeptical of Perrow's thesis or eager to know more should consult the original source, which has been presented in an extremely abbreviated fashion here.

PROBLEMS OF AMERICAN BUSINESS AND LABOR

For every book in the field of organizations that is written from the perspective of world survival, probably ten more deal with the survival of American business. Where Perrow puts forth the thesis that the potential for catastrophic accidents makes certain industries dispensable, the managerial perspective tends to take for granted the value of business survival and success. Such survival need not mean that every plant is considered indispensable; indeed, those with small profit margins may be deliberately closed.

Many plant closings are due not to bankruptcy but to the transfer of installations—to another region where labor is cheaper and less unionized or to another country, which offers tax advantages as well as cheaper labor (Bluestone, 1982, chap. 2). The export of advanced technology sometimes has repercussions on the originating nation, since it can lead to new sources of competition. It is widely acknowledged that the United States is now struggling to regain its competitive edge in a number of industries. The investment strategy of corporations since the early 1970s has been described as due to three conditions in the United States: a great increase in the degree of international competition, a post-World War II series of labor victories that placed limitations on management, and the transportation and communications revolution referred to earlier (Bluestone, 1982:51).

Decline in Industry

While management and labor have often had an adverserial or conflict relationship, their interdependence can hardly be questioned. A decline in industry means a decline in jobs. A profitable plant may be phased out, especially if it is part of a conglomerate that has varied interests, but plant closings are more readily justified when times are bad. A recession in 1969 and the severe 1973-1975 business downturn, with their increased unemployment, initiated a good deal of rethinking about American industry. The United States economy was losing its dominant position internationally (Gunn, 1984:22). William Foote Whyte and his colleagues provide a typical commentary:

> In the face of a severe recession and ballooning unemployment, there is a growing recognition that there are basic problems in our industrial relations and economic development strategies and that mere tinkering with the industrial machine will not recapture for the United States the industrial leadership we have been rapidly losing to Western Europe and particularly to Japan. (1983a:1)

Worker Participation

Both management and labor have been involved in trying to find solutions to the problems of American industry. Management has responded mainly by modifying what are thought to be demoralizing conditions of work, seeking favorable federal policies, or seeking a cheaper and more docile source of labor abroad. Chapter 7 dealt with recent approaches to rehabilitating sick firms by reorganizing management practices and creating "strong" organizational cultures. As we looked at organizations and the individual in chapter 8, we examined some of the ideas circulating about how to improve worker satisfaction and productivity—job enlargement or enrichment, job rotation, employee-centered supervision, employee participation in the plant community, and retraining for other or better jobs.

Mechanical types of organization have been going out of style, at least in public statements. The Taylorean practice of breaking jobs down into small mechanical parts, the deskilling of work, may not be efficient if it leads to low morale, absenteeism, and poor quality. Some claim it is still going on (recall our discussion of the deskilling of police work). However, belief appears to be growing that human beings of normal intelligence need to have some areas of discretion, that workers sometimes understand the work they are doing better than the managers, and that an extreme division of labor may be self-defeating. Changing perceptions of their own best interests cause some firms to institute employee participation schemes as a way of improving morale and productivity. While the contingency approach suggests that different technologies set limits to restructuring attempts, critical theory holds that managerial power and objectives can crucially influence structure.

We have repeatedly brought out the fact that many ideas about worker participation derive from observations of practices in Japanese industry, practices that are sometimes reified or misinterpreted. Of particular interest has been Japan's use of quality circles—small, temporary groups of workers organized in each work unit and led by a supervisor or senior worker who meet to solve job-related quality problems. Quality control becomes the duty of the workers rather than engineers, inspectors, or other outside personnel. One of the consequences is that in Toyota Auto Company, for example, there is a ratio of about one inspector for every twenty-five production workers, while General Motors requires about one inspector for every ten production workers. The large number of inspectors in U.S. auto firms also suggests that many items will be rejected. At Ford Motor Company there has been a 10 percent repair average; 10 percent of its labor is engaged in repairing items that do not meet specifications (Cole, 1979).

The participation of workers in helping to eliminate shoddy work and raise the quality of what they are producing does not mean that Japanese plants are run democratically. Quality control circles are coordinated and regulated by the company. The aim is to increase the responsibility of each individual employee, not to increase employee participation in management (Cole, 1979). Nonetheless, in Japanese industry the practice of small-group discussion and input is widespread and apparently successful.

Japan's success in improving the quality of its products, a post-World War II development, has drawn the jealous admiration of U.S. firms, but the latter are finding that differences in national culture make sheer imitation unwise. The blatant subordination of women in the labor force in Japan is often overlooked in lauding its industrial accomplishments, possibly because it is congruent with the "good old days" of American business when such subordination could go unnoticed. Further, unions tend to be skeptical about various plans that would increase production through new managerial techniques while not improving the economic position of workers.

Community Labor-Management Committees

Another effort, more cooperative than the management-based programs described above, is the formation of community labor-management committees. The normal suspicion and distrust between unions and management are taken for granted, but as third-party consultants, experienced labor professors such as William Foote Whyte, with the cooperation of local government officials, are able to act as facilitating agents in community or area labor-management committees. These committees encourage in-plant joint committees as well.

Cornell professors and graduate students have had much input in the Jamestown (New York) Area Labor Management Committee (JALMC). Industry in Jamestown was heavily concentrated in furniture and metal shops; the furniture industry had been going downhill. The labor force in Jamestown was highly unionized—so much so that the city had been unable to attract new industry for years because of its reputation for having a "bad" labor climate. Strikes had been severe and there was a shift to outside, absentee ownership. Previously, most American unions, in Jamestown as elsewhere, were of the "business" union type, "run by a staff whose primary function is to increase the economic well-being of the members" (Miller & Form, 1980:424). Now organized labor is increasingly concerned with larger issues: the impending loss of jobs, the image of the community, and a possible role in ownership and management.

In 1971 the largest employer in Jamestown, the Art Metal Plant, announced that it was closing. The plant had been in the area for seventy years and had employed as many as 1,700 persons. Other plants were likely to close soon.

The mayor, Stanley Lundine, was anxious to meet this crisis and improve the economic situation of the city. Community members, including a labor lawyer, were familiar with the success of joint labor-management committees in other locales. Lundine met first with key leaders of labor and management separately and then brought them together. Slowly they evolved a working committee and developed cooperative policies to prevent further industries from shutting down. The joint committee (JALMC) agreed on four objectives: "improvement of area labor relations, manpower development, assistance to local industrial development, and improving productivity through cooperative effort" (Meek et al., 1983a:11). Labor members insisted on a number of safeguards so that the last goal, improving productivity, would not be used to engineer speed-ups or eliminate jobs. The mayor and committee members used personal contacts, persuasion, and assistance in securing financing. In a two-year period, 1972-1974, JALMC was able to forestall shutdowns in five out of six efforts, saving over 700 jobs. In June 1974 a new company announced that it would take over the abandoned Art Metal plant.

With the advice of experienced consultants and a professional staff, JALMC was able to identify other problems—such as the impending loss of the base of skilled workers in the furniture industry. Training programs were begun to increase this supply. Worker participation schemes developed, with their successes and failures duly studied by the social scientists involved.

Worker and Worker–Community Ownership

A dreaded, all-too-frequent event in the 1970s was a corporate headquarters announcement of the impending shutdown of a local plant. In the past, management would be urged to reconsider; this failing, financial provisions for laid-off workers would be requested. Something different happened in the 1970s—an increase in locally organized campaigns to save the jobs by buying the plant. The threat of losing a major source of employment united church, labor, and other groups in the quest for communitywide solutions. Positive models could be found in a number of European countries where employee ownership had worked. In a number of American cases employees, or employees joined by the community, successfully bought out plants.

Employee- and employee–community-owned enterprises increased in the 1970s and gained momentum in the 1980s. By 1979 U.S. workers owned a majority interest in at least ninety companies (Squires, 1982, p. 85). Cornell and other universities have pioneered in assisting the transition to worker ownership through committees of community, labor, and management representatives. Whyte explains that Cornell University's New Systems of Work and Participation Program, has focused on "labor-management cooperative problem-solving programs and the emergence of employee ownership as a means of saving jobs in the face of impending plant shutdowns" (1983a:4-5).

Impending shutdowns do not mean that a plant is doomed to failure under any type of ownership. Even if a plant has been a steady moneymaker, its conglomerate owner may decide that profits have not been high enough. When workers or workers plus community attempt to buy it out, their first thought is to maintain jobs rather than increase the rate of profit (Hammer et al., 1983:56-57). The conglomerate has a wide diversity of interests; it can bolster a plant, for example, by investing in new machinery or phase it out in favor of some other enterprise.

Management does not automatically support worker-community efforts to buy a plant out rather than have it shut down and sometimes fails to cooperate. The parent firm might consider employee ownership inimical to its own interests for various reasons—for example, as a source of competition. Nonetheless, the success of worker ownership has encouraged more positive attitudes on the part of corporate managements in the 1980s (Hammer et al., 1983:61).

High-level union officials have also come to look more favorably on employee ownership, for two reasons: employee ownership's proven ability to prevent plant shutdowns, with "favorable consequences" for both employees and unions, and the unions' loss of faith in the ability of management to maintain profitable and productive enterprises (Whyte, 1983b:121). Leading companies seem preoccupied with buying and selling businesses in order to prevent takeovers. The shifting abroad of American investment seeking cheaper labor and tax advantages is understood to be an important factor in eliminating profitable domestic plants. U.S. investment overseas grew at a rate twice as great as its private domestic investment during 1950–1974 (Bluestone, Harrison, & Baker, 1981:16). The international or multinational perspective of many corporations conflicts with local needs of American communities to maintain their economic viability.

The Role of Unions

We characterized American unions as tending to be of the "business type"— that is, as seeking to ensure that labor receives its proper share of the fruits of American capitalism. In contrast, the "welfare type" of union, exemplified by the former Congress of Industrial Organizations (CIO) unions (now merged with the American Federation of Labor, AFL) is concerned with increasing welfare services, such as social security and fringe benefits, as well as wages. A third type is the "life-embracing" union (Dubin, 1958), found in one-industry communities and among work groups that tend to be isolated, such as miners and longshoremen. Here the union becomes the central institution in the worker's life, concerned with all facets of it. Ideological unions, concerned with achieving social goals related to particular political philosophies, are more characteristic of Europe than the United States.

A growth in the number of union members here has not kept up, proportionately, with the increased size of the labor force. Union membership reached a high of 23 percent of workers in 1968 and has declined slowly since then. The number of unionized governmental employees has increased, as has the number of professionals and white-collar workers, but these gains have been offset by a loss of union members in manufacturing and mining (Miller & Form, 1980:434–438). The newer, more middle-class unions are less militant than the more clearly working-class ones are. Oppenheimer (1985) considers American unions to be weak and in a state of crisis, but Miller and Form are more optimistic, claiming that unionism will continue to grow in absolute numbers and will make up losses in the declining manual occupations with increased unionization of service sector workers (1980:440).

Naturally, one's point of view about the desirability of unions and what their role should be influences such judgments. Their role appears to be undergoing change. The decline in production industries with its accompanying plant closings and unemployment has stimulated American union leaders to expand their concept of their responsibilities. They now envision a more active role in job creation and protection and are concerned with the workers' quality of life; some are cooperating in the transition to employee ownership. This development, seen as positive by many, is not without its own pitfalls. As more plants become employee-owned, their experiences demonstrate emergent problems and the solutions that work best (see Whyte et al., 1983). The value of true worker participation in managing, rather than mere ownership, is emphasized by writers who view workplace democracy as a cornerstone of a healthier national democracy (Mason, 1982).

White-Collar Crime and Corporate Deviance

In the previous chapter we dealt with white-collar crime and corporate deviance, with how new technologies, such as that of the computer, increase opportunities for dishonesty. Here we simply remind the reader of this growing problem that has no simple solution. Corporations found guilty of white-collar crimes are now being fined and an occasional executive is jailed; whether penalties fit the magnitude of the crime is another question. Such once-venerable names as General Dynamics, E.F. Hutton, and Bank of Boston have been accused of criminal practices. Extreme mismanagement may be the verdict in other cases. The Long Island Lighting Company (LILCO) was penalized $1.35 billion for "mismanaging the construction of its Shoreham nuclear power station," a decision made by the State Public Service Commission (*New York Times*, June 7, 1985, p. A1). Construction of the plant is more than ten years behind schedule and more than ten times over its originally projected cost.

Those who discuss corporate deviance in public generally propose harsher sentences as a means of deterrence—reflecting the same mentality that assumes harsher punishments will reduce street crime. While harsher penalties satisfy the desire for vengeance, there is little evidence that they lessen the incidence of either type of crime. The interorganizational relationships of businesses, government regulatory agencies, political and economic factors, and the multiple values that guide behavior are all involved. The stakes in corporate crime may be very high, the behavior hard to detect, and the temptations great. The extreme international competition in high-tech industries increases the possibilities for spying and the sale of technological secrets.

ISSUES OF EQUALITY

Among the most persistent inequalities in heterogenous societies are those based on race, ethnicity, sex, and age, as we have indicated. Significant movement towards greater equality requires a redistribution of privileges and liabilities and some shaking up of the existing order. Elite groups and preferred types are forced to give up their advantages or pressured to share them with the previously deprived. Such changes are viewed positively or negatively, depending on one's place in the pecking order. Resort to reform rather than revolutionary movements is more likely in a relatively open society, where protest is allowed. To gain access to the important organizations of the society—those that affect life chances—minority group movements seek public attention and governmental support for the legitimacy of their claims.

The Thrust for Equality

Such was the case in the 1960s and 1970s when black Americans spearheaded a nonviolent protest movement—the civil rights movement (R. L. Blumberg, 1984). Chicanos, Puerto Ricans, Native Americans, and women were all deeply affected by this example, and their own movements for greater justice and improved opportunities took off. Gay people and handicapped people, who had always suffered discrimination and stigma, also proclaimed their rights. These minority movements affected many institutions of American society—starting with public accommodations such as schools, buses, and lunch counters. Formal removal of segregation between blacks and whites in restaurants, hotels, parks, libraries, and the like was a dramatic achievement, but it soon became obvious that economic discrimination persisted. A difficult goal, the achievement of equal access to jobs and advanced education is one that is still being pursued.

The suffering and sacrifices of blacks and whites who joined the nonviolent civil rights struggle culminated in various pieces of legislation and executive orders that were to affect almost all work and educational organizations. These gains accrued not only to African-Americans but also to other minority groups and to women, all of whom rode in on the coattails of the black movement. In 1964 a Civil Rights Act was passed, the famous Title VII of which stated that it was unlawful to discriminate because of race, color, religion, or national origin in hiring or firing, wages, promotion, and other conditions of employment. Discrimination because of sex had been added to the bill at the last moment in an attempt to thwart its passage, but the maneuver led to a wider victory. This historic bill set up an enforcement agency, the Equal Opportunity Commission, which at first had relatively weak powers.

Later federal efforts built on this foundation. A series of executive orders followed, which spelled out and strengthened enforcement provisions. President John F. Kennedy had used the term *affirmative action* as early as 1963, but it was Lyndon Baines Johnson who expanded on the concept. In 1965 Johnson set up an Office of Contract Compliance to supervise and coordinate the compliance activities of the contracting agencies of the government. Employers holding federal contracts had to agree not to discriminate and to undertake "affirmative action" programs to rectify the effects of past discrimination. Eventually, firms were required to estimate the availability of potential minority and female workers, set up reasonable goals and timetables for hiring them, and make good-faith efforts to do so. All this was to be accompanied by appropriate documentation—paper work.

Black studies and women's studies became the source of varied research on the origins and patterning of inequality. Both of these interdisciplinary fields undertook to reveal the hidden history of their groups and their continuing invisibility in standard textbooks. In chapter 6 we quoted Alvin Gouldner's 1957 comment on the inattention to sexual identity found in so much sociology. The field of organizations continued to be a prime example of this criticism until the advent of the women's movement brought about slight modifications. Women's studies and black studies pay a great deal of attention to inequality, but their findings are circulated mostly within these specialized fields rather than entering the mainstream of academic attention.

Strangely enough, in spite of women's increasing participation in the paid labor force in the United States and elsewhere—here more than half of all mothers of young children now work outside the home—women continue to be thought of as an unimportant or peripheral element in the labor force. This is perfectly compatible with the ideology that women are only auxiliary workers, that they do not support families, and that paid work is not or should not be a central activity for them.

Such assumptions often lie behind the pronouncements of public officials. In June 1985 Treasury Secretary James A. Baker, 3rd, stated that the median income family in every state would be better off under the Reagan Administration's proposed tax plan. This "was based on the premise that a family with median income . . . had only one wage-earner" (*New York Times*, June 17, 1985, p. D1). In actuality, according to Internal Revenue statistics, about two-thirds of median-income families had two wage earners at that time.

There are at least three strands of thought about governmental efforts to further equal employment opportunity for women and minorities. One sees inequality as rooted in all of society's structures, including the patriarchal family, with each sphere reinforcing the other (Martin, 1980b:128–150). A dual labor market, where women are relegated to the less important, poorly paid, peripheral kinds of work is said to be a structural feature of capitalist societies. Massive change in the family, culture, socialization, and so on is required as a condition of changing their position in the world of work. Martin's critical analysis of women, labor markets, and employing organizations summarizes this point of view.

A second strand of thought is positive about the promise of affirmative action and equal opportunity measures while acknowledging and exposing its current problems. Some feminist writers take what might be termed a liberal position in also advocating government and industry policies to facilitate women's participation in the paid labor force, such as improved day-care facilities and flexible working hours ("flextime"). Through improving her position in the work world, it is thought, a woman will gain greater respect and more equality at home (Adams & Winston, 1980). Others, many men and some women, oppose changing the status quo in the relation of the two sexes, finding it threatening. This is reflected in the third perspective towards affirmative action, which brands it reverse discrimination and tries to water down or eliminate it. Although affirmative action laws remain on the books, the federal executive branch has reversed its earlier support for these measures. Opponents also stand against comparable worth principles—the goal of equal pay for comparable work, an effort to increase wage equality in the still sex-segregated labor force. Typically, jobs traditionally held by women pay less than ones requiring equivalent education, training, and responsibility but traditionally held by men.

Women and Labor Markets

According to Martin, the exclusion of women from certain sectors of the economy, the powerful labor unions, and high-level organizational positions is an example of the subordination of women in society generally (1980b:129). Without claiming a cause-and-effect relationship between these different inequalities, their interconnections must be seen.

The patriarchal family form supports capitalism by providing men with domestic servants (wives) who will reproduce the male labor force. Men have a vested interest in women's subordination because of all the free services they get at home and because women's home duties prevent them from competing for the better jobs in the labor market. Educational institutions, culture, and ideology, as well as the family, promote and buttress role definitions that make paid work less valued for women. Females are not reared to expect or desire serious commitment to a career or advancement in an organization.

Low opportunities tend to depress female ambition, as Kanter showed. Many women believe the ideologies that relegate them to lesser positions in the work world and socialize their male and female children to perpetuate gender roles. We have mentioned the notion of the dual labor market earlier. It suggests that labor is not homogeneous but rather is divided into higher-paying and lower-paying sectors. The latter jobs lack opportunities for mobility and are unstable. Once established, this division into labor markets is perpetuated, and sexual segregation in jobs is maintained. Workers in secondary-sector, low-paid jobs may act out a self-fulfilling prophecy by lacking commitment and changing jobs frequently. One factor increasing this latter tendency is the expectation that a family will relocate for the husband's but not for the wife's job. Dual-career families are beginning to question this assumption (Fox & Hesse-Biber, 1984, chap. 8).

Powerful unions protect white male interests by excluding women and members of racial minorities from apprenticeships (Bonacich, 1972), preventing the acquisition of skills that would qualify them for desirable jobs. In fact, the term *qualifications* often covers over with a veil of objectivity requirements that are actually tailor-made to ensure continued monopolization of good positions by the group already in power. Take the criterion of minimum height for police or military positions. Height norms are based on ranges for white males, effectively barring women and certain racial minorities of typically shorter stature.

This analysis of the interlocking effects of institutionalized subordination helps us to understand why solutions are so difficult. Paradoxically, a seemingly deep and radical critique of the roots of sexism and racism could lead to inaction in the economic sphere, to programs that would "educate," socialize children differently, or frontally combat stereotypes. An alternative is what was actually done— the federal government's response to the pressure for equal rights. It is remarkable that the liberal government of the United States (as opposed to a revolutionary one) was forced by women and racial minorities to attempt to address directly the long-standing and pervasive discrimination in jobs and education through legal methods. Let us examine more closely the impact of affirmative action and equal opportunity on corporations.

Affirmative Action and Equal Opportunity

Fernandez's study of male and female, majority and minority managers in twelve large corporations reveals how members of these different groups perceive their experiences with equal economic opportunity and affirmative action programs (EEO/AAP). Fernandez believes EEO/AAP can be made to work, abetted by some broader organizational changes that would benefit all workers.

The increased entrance of minorities and women into managerial ranks has been relatively modest. Black men filled 2.6 percent of all management and administrative jobs in 1972, and only slightly more, 3 to 4 percent in 1982 (Schaefer, 1984:259). The proportion of female managers and administrators rose from 17.6 percent in 1972 to 27.5 percent in 1981, largely due to an increase in women managers in banks and offices. This greater heterogeneity has been felt. Women and members of the minority groups often bring cultural backgrounds and value systems that differ from those of the white males who dominate organizations.

The viewpoints of women and minorities diverge especially on issues of equality and discrimination. In the past, white men formed 95 percent of corporate management, although they represented only 37 percent of the population (Fernandez, 1981:7). Many of them now claim they are being discriminated against. In contrast, many minority people and women believe that white men are still the preferred race/sex group. Their difference in viewpoint is explained as follows:

> This phenomenon of perception can be attributed largely to the differences between the people who have been accustomed to having almost all of the power in the corporate hierarchy and the people who have had almost none. Any loss from exclusivity is viewed as great, while small gains from exclusion are not viewed as being important. (Fernandez, 1981:7)

Fernandez analyzed the views and attitudes of Native Americans, Asians, blacks, Hispanics, and whites—both male and female—at all levels of management. His work shows the fallacy of lumping all minorities and women together into one category. Interviews revealed the special problems faced by black Americans, the least preferred minority group and uncovered the competition among women and other minorities for available openings and promotions. In this study, nonblack minorities and whites "see blacks as the least-desirable minority with whom to interact" (p. 55). The greatest burden of racism falls on black people—partly because of the legacy of slavery, their darker color, larger numbers, and dispersal throughout the country. Whites tend to feel more threatened by blacks because they are the largest minority and have been competing in the labor market for a long period of time.

It is not surprising that black managers prove to be the most "sensitive and empathetic to the plight of minority managers and the most outraged at the racist treatment they observe in the environs of American corporations today" (p. 19). Perhaps because of their sensitivity to discrimination, black males are also more sympathetic to the problems of women managers than are other males.

On a number of specific measures black men and black women are the group most critical of corporate treatment of minorities. For example, asked to agree or disagree with the statement that minority managers are penalized more for mistakes than are white managers, more blacks than any other group agreed (see table 11-3).

Managers were asked the extent to which they agreed or disagreed with these three statements:

Minority managers are excluded from informal work networks by whites.

Minority managers are often excluded from social activities that are beneficial to advancement in corporations.

Many minority managers have a harder time finding someone who is particularly interested in their careers. (Fernandez, 1981:29)

Responses of Asians proved to be more favorable than those of Hispanics and much more favorable than those of blacks. Thirteen percent of black male managers as opposed to 49 percent of the Hispanic male managers and 56 percent of the Asian male managers believe that minority managers face no problems in these areas (p. 29). History, culture, and experiences with discrimination are used to explain these variations in attitude among minorities. The rate for white males is the same as that of the Asian males. Thus, a little less than half of the white males studied do acknowledge the continuing problems faced by minorities.

Blacks at higher managerial levels still find themselves not quite acceptable to their white peers and somewhat isolated from blacks at lower levels. Black men and white women at higher levels are much more critical of the situation of women in their companies than are those at lower levels. Such women are much more likely to be tokens, isolated because of their small numbers, and seen as threats by some men. Higher-level minority men and women interact with high-level white managers "and are not optimistic about what they see or hear" (p. 79).

It is interesting that when asked about the effects of EEO/AAP on personal career opportunities, "every race/sex group claims that one or more of the other groups are getting all the advantages" (p. 117).

Such findings may make one pessimistic about the achievements of EEO/AAP; one wonders why the social movement organizations of women and minority groups struggle so hard to maintain these policies. The fact is, many of these minority and female managers—even though qualified—would not hold their positions if past discrimination had been allowed to continue unchecked. Any kind of social change meets opposition, cannot be built overnight, and requires continuing adjustments. Fernandez suggests broad policies that are more equitable and systematic to improve life in the corporation for everyone, similar to the ideas of others about worker participation, career planning, work design, and training and development programs.

TABLE 11-3 Are Minority Managers Penalized More for Mistakes than White Managers? (percent)

To What Extent Do You Agree or Disagree that Minority Managers Are Penalized More for Mistakes than White Managers?	NATIVE-AMERICAN		ASIAN		BLACK		HISPANIC		WHITE		Total
	Men (N = 143)	Women (N = 101)	Men (N = 121)	Women (N = 135)	Men (N = 474)	Women (N = 429)	Men (N = 384)	Women (N = 285)	Men (N = 1,306)	Women (N = 754)	(N = 4,132)
Strongly agree	0.7	3	3.3	3	19	14.7	3.4	4.9	0.3	3.3	5.3
Agree	2.8	8.9	12.4	21.5	35.9	34.7	19	18.6	4.7	12.2	15.8
Disagree	74.8	82.2	74.4	73.3	43.7	49	68.5	69.8	76.3	72.4	67.8
Strongly disagree	21.7	5.9	9.9	2.2	1.5	1.6	9.1	6.7	18.8	12.1	11

Source: Reprinted by permission of the publisher, from *Racism and Sexism in Corporate Life: Changing Value in American Business* by John P. Fernandez (Lexington, Mass.: D. C. Heath and Company, 1981), p. 41. Copyright 1981, D. C. Heath and Company.

Federal intervention on a large scale took place in response to the movements of the mid-1960s and has been in place only a short time. With the decline of minority movements and a change in political administration, enforcement efforts have slackened and key governmental officials have taken the "reverse discrimination" position. The issue of equality of opportunity for women and racial minorities is by no means resolved.

Human Service Issues

How public bureaucracies provide service to clients was the subject of chapter 9. A number of factors combine to increase impersonal and arbitrary treatment in street-level bureaucracies: a shaky commitment to individuals who need government aid, critical scrutiny of expenditures for human services such as welfare, and uncompetitive monetary rewards for professionals in government compared with those in industry. Ongoing debates occur over once taken-for-granted issues such as the right to social security and who is deserving of free school lunches. The government's role and responsibilities in many areas fluctuate, and the government lessens its activities in some spheres and increases them in others. As an example, there is a move on in many states to get government more involved in regulating potential plant closings. Some feel that the workers and the public are entitled to prior notification of such action.

Relationships between private professionals and their clients have become more turbulent, and some consumers have become increasingly cautious. The highly educated member of the public-in-contact tends to read labels, seek two medical opinions, or think it reasonable for teachers to pass proficiency tests. Malpractice suits and the costs of malpractice insurance have led to defensive practices by physicians. In some fields, such as maternity care, women have been part of a movement to make giving birth more natural and more a family event. The use of nurse-midwives for normal deliveries now has greater acceptance than twenty years ago. As some mothers- and fathers-to-be "shop" for the most comfortable, satisfactory, and psychologically beneficial maternity care, they are, in a sense, rejecting the sterile efficiency of the large bureaucratic hospital and its specialists. They challenge the typical birth position required in the hospital as convenient and comfortable mainly for the physician. The revolt against experts is part of a debureaucratizing tendency found in other areas of life. Such behavior is one of the safeguards against the potentially dehumanizing effects of bureaucracy and is related to our next topic—bureaucracy and democracy.

BUREAUCRACY AND DEMOCRACY

The Relationship between Bureaucracy and Democracy

Early writers on bureaucracy—Marx, Weber, and Michels—were concerned with the relationship between bureaucracy and democracy. For Marx, bureaucracy was linked to captalism and the rule of the bourgeoisie; a proletarian revolution would create the conditions necessary for the elimination of bureaucracy (Abrahamsson, 1977:47). While Weber explained capitalism as one cause for the rise of bureaucracy, he felt it was indispensable in all industrially developed societies (Abrahamsson, 1977:60). The specialized knowledge embedded in bureaucracies gave them power; how the power would be used was questioned by Weber. Michels went further, developing his "iron law of oligarchy" (1966). He believed that "the conflicts between the demands of efficiency and democracy are always solved to the advantage of those forces acting on behalf of efficiency, and therefore at the cost of democracy" (quoted in Abrahamsson, 1977:66). According to Michels, there is an inevitable tendency for power to become concentrated in the hands of elites within bureaucratic organizations. Michels was dealing with the issue of internal democracy as well as the concentration of power within societies. Breaking down the concerns voiced by theorists, there are at least three ways in which democracy and bureaucracy have been counterposed.

Internal Democracy

First is the issue of internal democracy versus bureaucratic efficiency as a principle by which organizations should and can be run. Weber's bureaucratic model, most clearly characteristic of armies, large production organizations, and government civil services certainly presupposes the existence of a hierarchy of authority and does not envision widespread participation in decision making. But according to Michels, even voluntary associations such as trade unions and clubs have a tendency toward oligarchy, rule by the few. Only opposition parties or factions stimulate participation and, to the extent that they exist, they encourage more democracy. Our section on worker participation in management and worker ownership is relevant here. The crisis in American industry has had varied results, but one of them has been experimentation with greater democracy in participation and in ownership. Workers and their union leaders recognize that pension funds provide an important source of investment and that the judicious use of these funds gives them leverage. The financial power of workers, collectively, may be a source of countervailing power to the large organization.

The Power of Bureaucracies

The second issue in the relationship between bureaucracy and democracy has to do with the distribution of power in the society at large. Is our society run by a "military-industrial complex," in which the giants in government, the military, and industry work out national policy together? Does the power of the experts dwarf the role of the ordinary citizen? Is the public interest always served, or are the vested interests of these leaders most crucial?

Those placing renewed emphasis on organizational environments claim that there are limits on any organization's autonomy, that all must respond to external forces in order to survive. Still in question is the extent to which powerful organizations can modify their environments. With advanced technologies that can greatly affect life on this earth and the growing possibility of accidents, the U.S. government—under pressure from citizen groups—has increasingly found it necessary to set up regulatory agencies. Their very rules and their willingness to enforce these rules are subject to power struggles between the organizations so regulated and those "bureaus" of the government who take responsibility for safeguarding the public. Because this issue is current and important, we have had many occasions to refer to it throughout this book.

The Dangers of Bureaucratic Impersonality

Finally, there is the question of the potentially dehumanizing effects of impersonal bureaucracy, in which private or public values are subordinated to norms of efficiency and obedience.

One of the best analyses of the perversion of bureaucracy for inhuman purposes is Rubenstein's study of the Nazi regime (1978), to which we have referred earlier. By making the deportation, incarceration, and forced labor of Jews into a bureaucratic task, the Nazis removed all feeling from the process. Those who cooperated in the rationalized, systematized killing, pseudomedical experiments, and deprivations did so as obedient servants of their official leaders. Science was put to the task of determining the cheapest, most expedient way of exterminating one entire ethnic group as well as other selected groups such as gypsies and homosexuals. Bureaucratization undoubtedly facilitated the carrying out of Hitler's aims, although it did not create the Fascist ideology.

Perhaps the lesson, if one is to be drawn, is that revolt against the impersonality of organizations, though sometimes disruptive in the short run, is healthy. To repeat, complex organizations in the United States exist within an environment that contains other types of active collectivities—families, communities, ethnic groups, social movements. As long as such collectivities continue their efforts to monitor powerful organizations, the latter cannot monopolize power.

The educated consumer who questions the experts is, from the point of view of democracy, a positive force. Even poor persons, such as welfare mothers, have stood up for their right to be treated fairly and with dignity. As we have said, the movements for employee participation in management and employee ownership reflect debureaucratizing tendencies. A mechanical organizational system with a strict power hierarchy and mindless lower participants is no longer accepted as a positive model for modern organizations, although many such organizations exist.

If any of the issues discussed in this chapter have been provocative, rest assured that numerous others related to organizational society could have been included. We leave it to the reader, now well-informed about organizations, to formulate his or her own list.

SUMMARY

The problem of how to run large organizations successfully in modern, technologically advanced society is one that preoccupies those in charge of them. Of broader concern are how these organizations mold and influence human life and the natural environment, and whether the desirability of organizational survival should be taken for granted. The nations of the world, developed and developing, are interdependent; they are affected by many issues relating to the prevalence of large, bureaucratically run organizations. In this chapter we reviewed issues that have come up throughout the book and added two more: the problem of normal accidents in high-technology industries and the compatibility of bureaucracy with democracy.

Accidents are inevitable in high-risk industries, according to Perrow, because of their very complexity and the frequent tight coupling of component parts. The more components there are in a system, the greater the complexity. Unexpected or unplanned interactions of seemingly unrelated elements can cause accidents in such industries as nuclear energy, chemical processing, air and marine transport, and biological engineering. Tight coupling means that elements in a system are closely linked, with no slack or buffer between them. Thus a failure or error in one part of the system immediately affects other parts. A field of risk management has developed that attempts to treat such disastrous occurrences as oil spills, ship collisions, and nuclear plant malfunctions in terms of rational assessment of the costs involved. A pattern of response to such accidents has developed in which the owners or managers of involved organizations minimize the damage, report that it could have been worse, and refashion the disaster into a learning experience. In contrast, human values dictate a willingness to consider the abandonment of certain industries that are prone to potentially catastrophic accidents—such as nuclear energy production, according to Perrow.

A more familiar theme, the problems of American business and labor, was reviewed. We pointed out before that a decline in American industry in the face of foreign competition has led to a rethinking of management strategies. Attention has been focused on creating positive company cultures and on ways of increasing worker satisfaction and hence productivity. Techniques of involving workers in some phases of decision making have been borrowed from Japan and other countries. Labor, too, has responded to the industrial crisis by expanding its role from limited concern with financial gains to helping to organize communities on labor issues. In some cases it has entered communitywide joint labor-management committees. In others it has sought to stop impending plant closings and even to buy out such plants. Plants may be capable of survival even where a conglomerate owner has decided the profit rate is not high enough for the conglomerate. The preservation of jobs is, of course, the prime motive for labor's becoming involved. Worker and worker–community ownership is a new trend in the United States, which blossomed in the 1970s and gained momentum in the 1980s. Universities such as Cornell have provided expert assistance in bringing labor, management, and community together.

Union membership has increased in numbers but has not kept up, proportionately, with the larger number of people in the labor force. Where production workers were once the backbone of the labor movement, their decreased numbers, coupled with an increase in professional and white-collar workers who are becoming unionized has changed the composition of union membership. Some see unions as becoming too much like management in their perspective, while others envision greater worker participation in management as a democratizing trend.

The prevalence of white-collar crime and corporate deviance, analyzed in chapter 10, was recalled as another major issue of advanced industrial societies. Doubt was raised about whether concentration on stiffer penalties could eliminate vulnerability to crime fostered by extreme competition and made possible by expertise.

Issues of equality for women and minorities also impinge on the organizational field. The position of women in the world of work is closely related to their general role in the family and in society, according to Martin. The patriarchal family enforces women's subordination and their inability to compete in the paid labor force. Institutionalized subordination in many areas of life are interlocked, making solutions difficult. Nonetheless, women have been helped by their inclusion in government policies aimed at eliminating discrimination.

The movements of the 1960s pressured the federal government to intervene and push forward equal economic opportunity and affirmative action programs. This attempt at reform has evoked varied reactions from the affected groups. A study by Fernandez of minority, female, and white managers in twelve large corporations revealed their differing views on how women and minority group members fare in management.

Finally, we briefly discussed the longstanding issue of the relationship between bureaucracy and democracy. Questions have been raised about the lack of internal democracy within organizations both because of the tendency toward oligarchy and because the bureaucratic model presupposes the hierarchical authority structure. Further concern focuses on the domination of societies by powerful organizations, which not only respond to their environments but actively modify them. The depersonalizing tendencies of bureaucracy were illustrated by reference to Rubenstein's work on the Nazi regime. Norms of bureaucratic efficiency and obedience to authority made genocide appear rational and impersonal.

Without providing solutions, it was suggested that revolts against bureaucracy and the active presence of nonbureaucratic collectivities in society—families, communities, ethnic groups, social movements—help reduce some of bureaucracy's threat to democracy.

REFERENCES

ABRAHAMSSON, BENGT. 1977. *Bureaucracy or Participation: The Logic of Organization.* Beverly Hills, Calif.: Sage Publications.

ADAMS, CAROLYN TEICH, and KATHRYN TEICH WINSTON. 1980. *Mothers at Work: Public Policies in the United States, Sweden and China.* New York: Longman.

Administrative Science Quarterly. 1983. 28 (September): 331–502. Issue on Organizational Culture, eds. Mariann Jelinek, Linda Smircich, and Paul Hirsch.

ALBERT, JUNE, RHODA L. GOLDSTEIN, and THOMAS F. SLAUGHTER, JR. 1974. "The Status of Black Studies Programs at American Colleges and Universities," in *The Black Studies Debate*, pp. 111–160, eds. Jacob U. Gordon and James M. Rosser. Lawrence: University of Kansas Press.

ALDRICH, HOWARD E. 1979. *Organizations and Environments.* Englewood Cliffs, N.J.: Prentice-Hall.

ALDRICH, HOWARD E., and JEFFREY PFEFFER. 1979. "Environments of Organizations," in *Readings on Dimensions of Organizations*, pp. 3–27, ed. Mary Zey-Ferrell, Santa Monica, Calif.: Goodyear Publishing.

ALVAREZ, RODOLFO. 1979. "Institutional Discrimination in Organizations and Their Environments," in *Discrimination in Organizations*, pp. 1–49, eds. Rodolfo Alvarez, Kenneth G. Lutterman, and Associates. San Francisco: Jossey Bass.

ARGYRIS, CHRIS. 1959. "Understanding Human Behavior in Organizations," in *Modern Organization Theory*, ed. Mason Haire. New York: John Wiley.

ASTLEY, W. GRAHAM, and ANDREW H. VAN DE VEN. 1983. "Central Perspectives and Debates in Organizational Theory," *Administrative Science Quarterly* 28 (June): 245–273.

BARITZ, LOREN. 1960. *The Servants of Power: A History of the Use of Social Science in American Industry.* Middletown, Conn.: Wesleyan University Press.

BARNARD, CHESTER I. 1938. *The Functions of the Executive.* Cambridge, Mass.: Harvard University Press.

——. 1946. "Functions and Pathologies of Status Systems in Formal Organizations," in *Industry and Society*, chap. 4, ed. William F. Whyte. New York: McGraw-Hill.

——. 1952. "A Definition of Authority," in *Reader in Bureaucracy*, pp. 180–185, eds. Robert K. Merton, Ailsa P. Gray, Barbara Hockey, and Hanan C. Selvin. Glencoe, Ill.: Free Press.

275

BAYLEY, DAVID H., and HAROLD MENDELSOHN. 1969. *Minorities and the Police: Confrontation in America*. New York: Free Press.

BECKER, HOWARD S., and ANSELM STRAUSS. 1970. "Careers, Personality, and Adult Socialization," in *Sociological Work*, ed. Howard S. Becker. Chicago: Aldine.

BEER, MICHAEL. 1980. "A Social Systems Model for Organizational Development," in *Systems Theory for Organization Development*, pp. 73–114, ed. T.G. Cummings. New York: John Wiley.

BENNIS, WARREN G., ed. 1970. *American Bureaucracy*. Chicago: Aldine.

BENSON, J. KENNETH. 1977. "Organizations: A Dialectical View," *Administrative Science Quarterly* 22 (September): 1–21.

——. 1980. "The Interorganizational Network as a Political Economy," in *A Sociological Reader in Complex Organizations*, 3rd ed., pp. 349–368, eds. Amitai Etzioni and Edward W. Lehman. New York: Holt, Rinehart & Winston.

BENSON, J. KENNETH, JOSEPH T. KUNCE, CHARLES A. THOMPSON, and DAVID L. ALLEN. 1973. *Coordinating Human Services, A Sociological Study of an Interorganizational Network*. Columbia, Mo.: Regional Rehabilitation Research Institute Monograph Series, No. 6.

BENSTON, MARGARET. 1977. "The Political Economy of Women's Liberation," in *Women in a Man-Made World*, pp. 216–225, eds. Nona Glazer and Helen Y. Waehrer. Boston: Houghton Mifflin.

BERGER, PETER L., and THOMAS LUCKMANN. 1967. *The Social Construction of Reality*. Garden City, N.Y.: Anchor Books.

BERNARD, JESSIE. 1984. "The Good Provider Role: Its Rise and Fall," in *Work and Family: Changing Roles of Men and Women*, pp. 43–60, ed. Patricia Voydanoff. Palo Alto, Calif.: Mayfield Publishing.

BETZ, MICHAEL, and LENAHAN O'CONNELL. 1983. "Changing Doctor–Patient Relationships and the Rise in Concern for Accountability," *Social Problems* 31 (October): 84–95.

BLAU, PETER. 1973. *The Organization of Academic Work*. New York: John Wiley.

BLAU, PETER, and MARSHALL MEYER. 1971. *Bureaucracy in Modern Society*, 2nd ed. New York: Random House.

BLAU, PETER, and W. RICHARD SCOTT. 1962. *Formal Organizations*. San Francisco: Chandler Publishing.

BLAUNER, ROBERT. 1969. "Work Satisfaction and Industrial Trends," in *A Sociological Reader on Complex Organizations*, 2nd ed., pp. 223–249, ed. Amitai Etzioni. New York: Holt, Rinehart & Winston.

BLUESTONE, BARRY. 1982. "Deindustrialization and the Abandonment of Community," in *Community and Capital in Conflict: Plant Closings and Job Loss*, pp. 38–61, eds. John C. Raines, Lenora E. Berson, and David McI. Gracie. Philadelphia: Temple University Press.

BLUESTONE, BARRY, DENNETT HARRISON, and LAWRENCE BAKER. 1981. *Corporate Flight: The Causes and Consequences of Economic Dislocation*. Washington, D.C.: Progressive Alliance.

BLUMBERG, PAUL. 1969. *Industrial Democracy*. New York: Schocken Books.

——. 1980. *Inequality in an Age of Decline*. New York: Oxford University Press.

BLUMBERG, RHODA LOIS (also published as Goldstein). 1980a. *India's Educated Women: Options and Constraints*. New Delhi: Hindustan Publishing Corp.

——. 1980b. "White Mothers in the American Civil Rights Movement," in *Research in the Interweave of Social Roles: Women and Men*, Vol. 1, pp. 33–50, ed. Helena Z. Lopata. Greenwich, Conn.: JAI Press.

——. 1984. *Civil Rights: The 1960s Freedom Struggle*. Boston: G.K. Hall, Twayne Series.

BONACICH, EDNA. 1972. "A Theory of Ethnic Antagonism: The Split Labor Market," *American Sociological Review* 37 (October): 547–559.

BOSERUP, ESTER. 1970. *Women's Role in Economic Development*. New York: St. Martin's Press.

BOSTON WOMEN'S HEALTH BOOK COLLECTIVE. 1971, 1984. *Our Bodies, Ourselves*. New York: Simon & Schuster.

BRAVERMAN, HARRY. 1974. *Labor and Monopoly Capital: The Degradation of Work in the Twentieth Century*. New York: Monthly Review Press.

BREDEMEIER, HARRY C., and RICHARD M. STEPHENSON. 1965. *Analysis of Social Systems.* New York: Holt, Rinehart & Winston.
BROMLEY, DAVID G., and ANSON D. SHUPE, JR. 1979. *"Moonies" in America: Cult, Church, and Crusade.* Beverly Hills, Calif.: Sage Publications.
BROWN, SHIRLEY VINING. 1979. "Race and Parole Hearing Outcomes," in *Discrimination in Organizations*, pp. 355–374, eds. Rodolfo Alvarez, Kenneth Lutterman, and Associates. San Francisco: Jossey-Bass.
BYRNES, ELEANOR. 1983. "Dual Career Couples: How the Company Can Help," in *The Woman in Management: Career and Family Issues*, pp. 49–53, ed. Jennie Farley. Ithaca, N.Y.: ILR Press.
CALAVITA, KITTY. 1983. "The Demise of the Occupational Safety and Health Administration: A Case Study in Symbolic Action," *Social Problems* 30 (April): 437–448.
CARSON, CLAYBORNE. 1981. *In Struggle: SNCC and the Black Awakening of the 1960s.* Cambridge, Mass.: Harvard University Press.
CHILD, JOHN. 1972. "Organizational Structure, Environment, and Performance: The Role of Strategic Choice," *Sociology* 6 (no. 1): 1–22.
———. 1973. "Strategies of Control and Organizational Behavior," *Administrative Science Quarterly* 18 (March): 1–17.
CLINARD, MARSHALL B., and PETER C. YEAGER. 1980. *Corporate Crime.* New York: Free Press.
COHEN, MICHAEL D., JAMES G. MARCH, and JOHAN P. OLSEN. 1972. "A Garbage Can Model of Organizational Choice," *Administrative Science Quarterly* 17 (March): 1–25.
COLE, ROBERT E. 1979. *Work, Mobility, and Participation: A Comparative Study of American and Japanese Industry.* Berkeley and Los Angeles: University of California Press.
COLLINS, RANDALL. 1979. *The Credential Society.* New York: Academic Press.
COOLEY, CHARLES H. 1909. *Social Organization.* New York: Charles Scribner's Sons.
CORWIN, RONALD G. 1961. "The Professional Employee: A Study of Conflict in Nursing Roles" *American Journal of Sociology* 66 (May): 604–615.
COSER, LEWIS. 1956. *The Functions of Social Conflict.* New York: Free Press.
CRESSEY, DONALD R., ed. 1961. *The Prison: Studies in Institutional Organization and Change.* New York: Holt.
CROZIER, MICHAEL. 1964. *The Bureaucratic Phenomena.* Chicago: University of Chicago Press.
DAHL, ROBERT. 1961. *Who Governs?* New Haven, Conn.: Yale University Press.
DALTON, MELVILLE. 1959. *Men Who Manage.* New York: John Wiley.
DAVIS, WARREN E., and DARYL G. HATANO. 1985. "The American Semiconductor Industry and the Ascendancy of East Asia," *California Management Review* 27 (Summer): 128–143.
DEAL, TERRENCE E., and ALLAN A. KENNEDY. 1982. *Corporation Cultures: The Rites and Rituals of Corporate Life.* Reading, Mass.: Addison-Wesley.
DUBIN, ROBERT. 1958. *Working Union-Management Relations.* Englewood Cliffs, N.J.: Prentice-Hall.
DUNCAN, GRAEME, ed. 1983. *Democratic Theory and Practice.* Cambridge: Cambridge University Press.
DURKHEIM, ÉMILE. 1933. *On the Division of Labor in Society*, trans. by George Simpson. New York: Macmillan.
ELDRIDGE, J.E.T., and A.D. CROMBIE. 1975. *A Sociology of Organizations.* New York: International Publishers.
Encyclopedia of Associations, 19th ed. 1985. Detroit: Gale Research Co.
ERMANN, M. DAVID, and RICHARD J. LUNDMAN, eds. 1978. *Corporate and Governmental Deviance: Problems of Organizational Behavior in Contemporary Society.* New York: Oxford University Press.
ETZIONI, AMITAI. 1961. *A Comparative Analysis of Complex Organizations.* Glencoe, Ill.: Free Press (rev. 1975).
———. 1964. *Modern Organizations.* Englewood Cliffs, N.J.: Prentice-Hall.
———. 1980. "Compliance Structures," in *A Sociological Reader On Complex Organizations*, 3rd ed., pp. 87–100, eds. Amitai Etzioni and Edward W. Lehman. New York: Holt, Rinehart & Winston.

FALK, WILLIAM W., MICHAEL D. GRIMES, and GEORGE F. LORD III. 1982. "Professionalism and Conflict in a Bureaucratic Setting: The Case of a Teachers' Strike," *Social Problems* 29 (June): 551–560.

FARLEY, JENNIE, ed. 1983. *The Woman in Management: Career and Family Issues*. Ithaca, N.Y.: ILR Press.

FELDMAN, MARTHA S., and JAMES G. MARCH. 1981. "Information in Organizations as Signal and Symbol," *Administrative Science Quarterly* 26 (June): 171–186.

FERNANDEZ, JOHN P. 1981. *Racism and Sexism in Corporate Life*. Lexington, Mass.: D.C. Heath.

FIEDLER, FRED E. 1972. "The Effects of Leadership Training And Experience: A Contingency Model Explanation," *Administrative Science Quarterly* 17 (December): 453–470.

FISCHER, FRANK, and CARMEN SIRIANNI, eds. 1984. *Critical Studies in Organization and Bureaucracy*. Philadelphia: Temple University Press.

Fortune. 1984. "Computer Crackdown," 110 (September): 141–142.

FOX, MARY, and SHARLENE HESSE-BIBER. 1984. *Women at Work*. Palo Alto, Calif.: Mayfield Publishing.

FREEMAN, JO. 1975. *The Politics of Women's Liberation*. New York: David McKay.

FREIDSON, ELLIOT. 1980. "Patterns of Practice in the Hospital," in *A Sociological Reader on Complex Organizations*, 3rd ed., pp. 176–193, eds. Amitai Etzioni and Edward W. Lehman. New York: Holt, Rinehart & Winston.

GAMSON, WILLIAM. 1975. *The Strategy of Social Protest*. Homewood, Ill.: Dorsey.

GANS, HERBERT J. 1962. *The Urban Villagers*. New York: Free Press.

GEIS, GILBERT, and EZRA STOTLAND, eds. 1980. *White Collar Crime: Theory and Research*. Beverly Hills, Calif.: Sage Publications.

GERTH, HANS and C. WRIGHT MILLS. 1953. *Character and Social Structure; The Psychology of Social Institutions*. New York: Harcourt, Brace.

GIALLOMBARDO, ROSE. 1966. "Social Roles in a Prison for Women," *Social Problems* 13 (Winter): 268–288.

GOFFMAN, ERVING. 1961. *Asylums*. New York: Doubleday, Anchor Books.

GOLDMAN, PAUL, and DONALD R. VAN HOUTEN. 1981a. "Managerial Strategies and the Worker: A Marxist Analysis of Bureaucracy," in *Complex Organizations: Critical Perspectives*, pp. 89–99, eds. Mary Zey-Ferrell and Michael Aiken. Glenview, Ill.: Scott, Foresman.

———. 1981b. "Bureaucracy and Domination in Turn-of-the-Century American Industry," in *Complex Organizations: Critical Perspectives*, pp. 189–216, eds. Mary Zey-Ferrell and Michael Aiken. Glenview, Ill.: Scott, Foresman.

GOLDSTEIN, RHODA L. 1952. "Interracial Professional Practices and Attitudes of Negro Dentists in a Southern City," in *The Growth and Development of the Negro in Dentistry in the United States*, chap. 5, ed. C.O. Dummett. Chicago: National Dental Association.

———. 1954. *The Professional Nurse in the Hospital Bureaucracy*. Unpublished Ph.D. dissertation, University of Chicago.

GORDON, C. WAYNE, and NICHOLAS BABCHUK. 1959. "A Typology of Voluntary Associations," *American Sociological Review* 24 (no. 1): 22–29.

GOULDNER, ALVIN. 1954a. *Patterns of Industrial Bureaucracy*. Glencoe, Ill.: Free Press.

———. 1954b. *Wildcat Strike*. Yellow Springs, Ohio: Antioch Press.

———. 1957. "Cosmopolitans and Locals: Toward an Analysis of Latent Social Roles," *Administrative Science Quarterly* 2:281–306.

GREEN, SUSAN S. 1983. "Silicon Valley's Women Workers: A Theoretical Analysis of Sex-Segregation in the Electronics Industry Labor Market," in *Women, Men and the International Division of Labor*, pp. 273–331, eds. June Nash and Maria Patricia Fernandez-Kelly. Albany: State University of New York Press.

GROSS, EDWARD. 1968. "Universities as Organizations: A Research Approach," *American Sociological Review* 33 (August): 518–540.

GROSS, EDWARD, and AMITAI ETZIONI. 1985. *Organizations in Society*. Englewood Cliffs, N.J.: Prentice-Hall.

GROSS, NEAL, WARD S. MASON, and ALEXANDER W. McEACHERN. 1958. *Explorations in Role Analysis: Studies of the School Superintendency Role*. New York: John Wiley.

GRUSKY, OSCAR. 1963. "Managerial Succession and Organizational Effectiveness," *American Journal of Sociology* 69 (July): 21–31.

GRUSKY, OSCAR, and GEORGE MILLER, eds. 1981. *The Sociology of Organizations: Basic Studies*, 2nd ed. New York: Free Press.

GUNN, CHRISTOPHER EATON. 1984. *Workers' Self-Management in the United States*. Ithaca and London: Cornell University Press.

HAAS, J. EUGENE, RICHARD H. HALL, and NORMAN J. JOHNSON. 1966. "Towards an Empirically Derived Taxonomy of Organizations," in *Studies on Behavior in Organizations*, pp. 157–180, ed. Raymond V. Bowers. Athens, Ga.: University of Georgia Press.

HABENSTEIN, ROBERT A., and EDWIN A. CHRIST. 1955. *Professionalizer, Traditionalizer, and Utilizer*. Columbia: University of Missouri Press.

HABERMAS, JURGEN. 1970. *Toward a Rational Society: Student Protest, Science and Politics*. Boston: Beacon Press.

HAGE, JERALD. 1965. "An Axiomatic Theory of Organizations," *Administrative Science Quarterly* 10 (December): 289–320.

HAGE, JERALD, and MICHAEL AIKEN. 1967. "Relationship of Centralization to Other Structural Properties," *Administrative Science Quarterly* 12 (June): 72–91.

HALL, JOHN. 1978. *The Ways Out*. London: Routledge & Kegan Paul.

HALL, RICHARD H., ed. 1972. *The Formal Organization*. New York: Basic Books.

———. 1977. *Organizations: Structure and Process,* 2nd ed. Englewood Cliffs, N.J.: Prentice-Hall.

———. 1982. *Organizations: Structure and Process,* 3rd ed. Englewood Cliffs, N.J.: Prentice-Hall.

———. 1983. "Corporations and Public Policy," paper presented at 78th Annual Meeting of the American Sociological Association, September 3, Detroit, Michigan.

HALL, RICHARD H., J.E. HAAS, and N.J. JOHNSON. 1967. "An Examination of the Blau-Scott and Etzioni Typologies," *Administrative Science Quarterly* 12:118–139.

HALL, RICHARD H., and ROBERT E. QUINN, eds. 1983. *Organizational Theory and Public Policy*. Beverly Hills, Calif.: Sage Publications.

HAMMER, TOVE HELLAND, ROBERT N. STERN, and WILLIAM FOOTE WHYTE. 1983. "Can You Buy Your Job?" in William F. Whyte et al., *Worker Participation and Ownership: Cooperative Strategies for Strengthening Local Economies*, pp. 55–80. Ithaca, N.Y.: ILR Press.

HARRAGAN, BETTY LEHAN. 1983. "Women and Men at Work: Jockeying for Position," in *The Woman in Management: Career and Family Issues*, pp. 12–19, ed. Jennie Farley. Ithaca, N.Y.: ILR Press.

HARRING, SID. 1984. "The Taylorization of Police Work," in *Critical Studies in Organization and Bureaucracy*, pp. 151–171, eds. Frank Fischer and Carmen Sirianni. Philadelphia: Temple University Press.

HASENFELD, YEHESKEL. 1983. *Human Service Organizations*. Englewood Cliffs, N.J.: Prentice-Hall.

HAUG, MARIE, and JACQUES DOFNY, eds. 1977. *Work and Technology*. Beverly Hills, Calif.: Sage Publications.

HAUG, MARIE R., and MARVIN P. SUSSMAN. 1969. "Professional Autonomy and the Revolt of the Client," *Social Problems* 17:153–161.

HELLRIEGEL, DON, and JOHN W. SLOCUM, JR. 1982. *Management*, 3rd ed. Reading, Mass.: Addison-Wesley.

HESS, BETH B., ELIZABETH W. MARKSON, and PETER J. STEIN. 1985. *Sociology*, 2nd ed. New York: Macmillan.

HEYDEBRAND, WOLF V., ed. 1973. *Comparative Organizations: The Results of Empirical Research*. Englewood Cliffs, N.J.: Prentice-Hall.

———. 1984. Discussant, "Recent Trends in Organizations," Session 146, 79th Annual Meeting of the American Sociological Association, August 29, San Antonio, Texas.

HIRSCH, PAUL M. 1972. "Processing Fads and Fashions: An Organization-Set Analysis of Cultural Industry Systems," *American Journal of Sociology* 77 (January): 639–659.

HODGETTS, RICHARD M., and STEVEN ALTMAN. 1979, *Organizational Behavior*. Philadelphia: W.B. Saunders.

HUGHES, CHARLES L. 1976. *Making Unions Unnecessary*. New York: Executive Enterprises Publications.

HUGHES, EVERETT C. 1945. "Dilemmas and Contradictions of Status," *American Journal of Sociology* 50 (March): 353–359.

———. 1958. *Men and Their Work*. Glencoe, Ill.: Free Press.

HUNTER, FLOYD. 1953. *Community Power Structure.* Chapel Hill: University of North Carolina Press.

IANNI, FRANCES A.J., with ELIZABETH REUSS-IANNI. 1972. *A Family Business: Kinship and Social Control in Organized Crime.* New York: Russell Sage.

IZRAELI, DAFNA. 1977. "'Settling-In': An Interactionist Perspective on the Entry of the New Manager," *Pacific Sociological Review* 20 (January): 135–160.

JELINEK, MARIANN, LINDA SMIRCICH, and PAUL HIRSCH. 1983. "Introduction: A Code of Many Colors," *Administrative Science Quarterly* 28 (September): 331–338.

KANTER, ROSABETH MOSS. 1977. *Men and Women of the Corporation.* New York: Basic Books.

KATZ, DANIEL, and ROBERT L. KAHN. 1978. *The Social Psychology of Organizations,* 2nd ed. New York: John Wiley.

KATZ, DANIEL, ROBERT L. KAHN, and J. STACEY ADAMS, eds. 1980. *The Study of Organizations.* San Francisco: Jossey-Bass.

KATZ, ELIHU, and BRENDA DANET, eds. 1973. *Bureaucracy and the Public: A Reader in Official-Client Relations.* New York: Basic Books.

KESSLER, FELIX. 1985. "Executive Perks Under Fire," *Fortune,* July 22, pp. 26–31.

KIMBERLY, JOHN R., FREDERICK NORLING, and JANET A. WEISS. 1983. "Pondering the Performance Puzzle: Effectiveness in Interorganizational Settings," in *Organization Theory and Public Policy,* pp. 249–264, eds. Richard H. Hall and Robert E. Quinn. Beverly Hills, Calif.: Sage Publications.

KOHN, MELVIN L. 1971. "Bureaucratic Man: A Portrait and an Interpretation," *American Sociological Review* 36 (June): 461–474.

KOHN, MELVIN L., and CARMI SCHOOLER. 1981. "Job Conditions and Personality: A Longitudinal Assessment of their Reciprocal Effects," *American Journal of Sociology* 87 (May): 1257–1286.

KOZOL, JONATHAN. 1967. *Death at an Early Age.* Boston: Houghton Mifflin.

KRAFT, PHILIP. 1979. "The Industrialization of Computer Programming: From Programming to 'Software Production,' " in *Case Studies in the Labor Process,* pp. 1–17, ed. Andrew Zimbalist. New York: Monthly Review Press.

KRAUSE, ELLIOT A. 1968. "Functions of a Bureaucratic Ideology: 'Citizen Participation,' " *Social Problems* 16 (Fall): 129–143.

LAUER, ROBERT H. 1973. *Perspectives on Social Change.* Boston: Allyn & Bacon.

LAWRENCE, PAUL R., and DAVIS DYER. 1983. *Renewing American Industry.* New York: Free Press.

LAWRENCE, PAUL R., and JAY W. LORSCH. 1969. *Organization and Environment; Managing Differentiation and Integration.* Cambridge, Mass.: Harvard University Press.

LEFTON, MARK, and WILLIAM R. ROSENGREN. 1966. "Organizations and Clients: Lateral and Longitudinal Dimensions," *American Sociological Review* 31 (December): 802–810.

LEGER, ROBERT G., and JOHN R. STRATTON. 1977. *The Sociology of Corrections.* New York: John Wiley.

LIEBERSON, STANLEY, and IRVING L. ALLEN, JR. 1973. "Location of National Headquarters of Voluntary Associations," in *Comparative Organizations: The Results of Empirical Research,* pp. 322–337, ed. Wolf V. Heydebrand. Englewood Cliffs, N.J.: Prentice-Hall.

LIGHT, IVAN. 1972. *Ethnic Enterprise in America.* Berkeley and Los Angeles: University of California Press.

LIM, LINDA Y.C. 1983. "Capitalism, Imperialism, Patriarchy: The Dilemma of Third-World Women Workers in Multinational Factories," in *Women, Men and the International Division of Labor,* pp. 70–91, eds. June Nash and Maria Patricia Fernandez-Kelly. Albany: State University of New York Press.

LINDBLOM, CHARLES E. 1977. *Politics and Markets.* New York: Basic Books.

LIPSKY, MICHAEL. 1980. *Street-Level Bureaucracy: Dilemmas of the Individual in Public Services.* New York: Russell Sage.

LOCKE, EDWIN A., and DAVID M. SCHWEIGER. 1979. "Participating in Decision-Making: One More Look," in *Research in Organizational Behavior,* pp. 265–339, ed. B. Staw. Greenwich, Conn.: JAI Press.

McCARTHY, JOHN D., and MEYER N. ZALD. 1977. "Resource Mobilization and Social Movements: A Partial Theory," *American Journal of Sociology* 82 (May): 1212–1241.

McGREGOR, DOUGLAS. 1960. *The Human Side of Enterprise: Theory X and Theory Y*. New York: McGraw Hill.

McKELVEY, BILL. 1975. "Guidelines for the Empirical Classification of Organizations," *Administrative Science Quarterly* 20 (December): 509–525.

——. 1982. *Organizational Systematics: Taxonomy, Evolution, Classification*. Berkeley and Los Angeles: University of California Press.

McKELVEY, BILL, and HOWARD ALDRICH. 1983. "Populations, Natural Selection, and Applied Organizational Science," *Administrative Science Quarterly* 28 (March): 101–128.

MACOBY, MICHAEL. 1976. *The Gamesman*. New York: Simon & Schuster.

MALOS, ELLEN. 1980. *The Politics of Housework*. London: Allison and Busby (Schocken Books, distributor).

Management Science. 1984. Special Issue on Risk, 30 (April): 395–531.

MARCH, JAMES G., and MARTHA S. FELDMAN. 1981. "Information in Organizations as Signal and Symbol," *Administrative Science Quarterly* 26 (June): 171–186.

MARCH, JAMES G., and JOHAN P. OLSEN, eds. 1976. *Ambiguity and Choice in Organizations*. Bergen, Norway: Universitetsforlaget.

MARGOLIS, DIANE ROTHBARD. 1979. *The Managers: Corporate Life in America*. New York: William Morrow.

MARS, GERALD. 1982. *Cheats at Work: An Anthropology of Workplace Crime*. London: George Allen and Unwin.

MARTIN, PATRICIA YANCEY. 1980a. "Multiple Constituencies, Differential Power and the Question of Effectiveness in Human Service Organizations," *Journal of Sociology and Social Welfare* 7 (November): 801–816.

——. 1980b. "Women, Labour Markets and Employing Organizations: A Critical Analysis," *The International Yearbook of Organization Studies*. London: Routledge & Kegan Paul.

MASON, RONALD. 1982. *Participatory and Workplace Democracy*. Carbondale and Edwardsville: Southern Illinois University Press.

MEAD, GEORGE HERBERT. 1934. *Mind, Self, and Society*. Chicago: University of Chicago Press.

MECHANIC, DAVID 1962. "Sources of Power of Lower Participants in Complex Organizations," *Administrative Sciences Quarterly* 7 (December): 349–364.

MEEK, CHRISTOPHER, REED NELSON, and WILLIAM FOOTE WHYTE. 1983a. "Cooperative Problem Solving in Jamestown," in *Worker Participation and Ownership*, pp. 6–32, eds. William F. Whyte et al. Ithaca, N.Y.: ILR Press.

——. 1983b, "Lessons from the Jamestown Experience," in *Worker Participation and Ownership*, pp. 33–54, eds. William F. Whyte et al. Ithaca, N.Y.: ILR Press.

MERTON, ROBERT K. 1952. "Bureaucratic Structure and Personality," in *Reader in Bureaucracy*, pp. 361–371, eds. Robert K. Merton et al. Glencoe, Ill.: Free Press.

MEYER, MARSHALL W. 1971. *Structures, Symbols, and Systems: Readings on Organizational Behavior*. Boston: Little, Brown.

MICHELS, ROBERT. 1966 (first published 1915). *Political Parties*. Glencoe, Ill.: Free Press.

MILLER, DELBERT C., and WILLIAM H. FORM. 1980. *Industrial Sociology: Work in Organizational Life*, 3rd ed. New York: Harper & Row.

MILLER, GALE. 1980. "The Interpretation of Nonoccupational Work in Modern Society: A Preliminary Discussion and Typology," *Social Problems* 27 (April): 381–391.

MILLER, JOANNE, CARMI SCHOOLER, MELVIN L. KOHN, and KAREN A. MILLER. 1979. "Women and Work: The Psychological Effects of Occupational Conditions," *American Journal of Sociology* 85 (July): 66–94.

MILLS, C. WRIGHT. 1956. *The Power Elite*. New York: Oxford University Press.

MOHR, LAWRENCE B. 1971. "Organizational Technology and Organizational Structure," *Administrative Science Quarterly* 16 (December): 444–451.

——. 1973. "The Concept of Organizational Goal," *American Political Science Review* 67 (June): 470–481.

——. 1982. *Explaining Organizational Behavior: The Limits and Possibilities of Theory and Research*. San Francisco: Jossey-Bass.

MOUZELIS, NICOS P. 1967. *Organization and Bureaucracy*. Chicago: Aldine.

NAISBITT, JOHN. 1984. "Reinventing the American Corporation," *New York Times*, December 23, Section 3, p. 2.

NEUGEBOREN, BERNARD. 1985. *Organization, Policy, and Practice in the Human Services*. New York: Longman.

OPPENHEIMER, MARTIN. 1985. *White Collar Politics*. New York: Monthly Review Press.

OUCHI, WILLIAM G. 1980. "Markets, Bureaucracies and Clans," *Administrative Science Quarterly* 25 (March): 129–141.

_____. 1981. *Theory Z: How American Business Can Meet the Japanese Challenge*. Reading, Mass.: Addison-Wesley; New York: Avon, 1982.

OUCHI, WILLIAM G., and ALAN L. WILKINS. 1985. "Organizational Culture," *Annual Review of Sociology* 11: 457–483.

PACE, DENNY F., and JIMMIE C. STYLES. 1975. *Organized Crime: Concepts and Control*. Englewood Cliffs, N.J.: Prentice-Hall.

PARSONS, TALCOTT. 1951. *The Social System*. New York: Free Press.

_____. 1981. "Social Systems," in *The Sociology of Organizations: Basic Studies*, pp. 98–109, eds. Oscar Grusky and George A. Miller. New York: Free Press.

PERROW, CHARLES. 1961. "The Analysis of Goals in Complex Organizations," *American Sociological Review* 26 (December): 854–866.

_____. 1967. "A Framework for the Comparative Analysis of Organizations," *American Sociological Review* 32 (April): 194–204.

_____. 1970. *Organizational Analysis: A Sociological View*. Belmont, Calif.: Wadsworth.

_____. 1979. *Complex Organizations: A Critical Essay*, 2nd ed. Glenview, Ill.: Scott, Foresman.

_____. 1980. "Technology," in *A Sociological Reader on Complex Organizations*, 3rd ed., pp. 118–130, eds. Amitai Etzioni and Edward W. Lehman. New York: Holt, Rinehart & Winston.

_____. 1984. *Normal Accidents: Living with High-Risk Technologies*. New York: Basic Books.

_____. 1985. "Comment on Langton's 'Ecological Theory of Bureaucracy,' " *Administrative Science Quarterly* 30 (June): 278–283.

_____. 1986. *Complex Organizations: A Critical Essay*, 3rd ed. rev. New York: Random House.

PERRUCCI, ROBERT, ROBERT M. ANDERSON, DANIEL E. SCHENDEL, and LEON E. TRACHTMAN. 1980. "Whistle-Blowing: Professionals' Resistance to Organizational Authority," *Social Problems* 28 (December): 149–164.

PETERS, THOMAS J., and ROBERT H. WATERMAN, JR. 1982. *In Search of Excellence: Lessons from America's Best-Run Companies*. New York: Harper & Row.

PETERSON, KAREN J. 1983. "Technology as a Last Resort in Home Birth: The Work of Lay Midwives," *Social Problems* 30 (February): 272–283.

PFEFFER, JEFFREY. 1981a. *Power in Organizations*. Marshfield, Mass.: Pitman Publishing.

_____. 1981b. "Who Governs?" in *The Sociology of Organizations: Basic Studies*, rev. ed., pp. 228–247, eds. Oscar Grusky and George A. Miller. New York: Free Press.

_____. 1982. *Organizations and Organization Theory*. Marshfield, Mass: Pitman Publishing.

PFEFFER, JEFFREY, and JERRY ROSS. 1982. "The Effects of Marriage and a Working Wife on Occupational and Wage Attainment," *Administrative Science Quarterly* 27 (March): 66–80.

PFEFFER, JEFFREY, and GERALD R. SALANCIK. 1974. "Organizational Decision Making as a Political Process: The Case of a University Budget," *Administrative Science Quarterly* 19 (June): 135–151.

_____. 1978. *The External Control of Organizations: A Resource Dependence Perspective*. New York: Harper & Row.

_____. 1980. "Determinants of Supervisory Behavior: A Role-Set Analysis," in *The Study of Organizations*, pp. 126–156, eds. Daniel Katz, Robert L. Kahn, and J. Stacey Adams. San Francisco: Jossey-Bass.

PHILLIPS, W.M., JR., and RHODA LOIS BLUMBERG. 1982. "Tokenism and Organizational Change," *Integrateducation* 20 (January-April): 34–39.

PIVEN, FRANCES FOX, and RICHARD A. CLOWARD. 1971. *Regulating the Poor: The Functions of Public Welfare*. New York: Pantheon.

PUGH, D.S., D.J. HICKSON, and C.R. HININGS. 1969. "An Empirical Taxonomy of Structures of Work Organizations," *Administrative Science Quarterly* 14 (March): 115–126.

PUGH, D.S., D.J. HICKSON, C.R. HININGS, and C. TURNER. 1968. "Dimensions of Organizational Structure," *Administrative Science Quarterly* 13 (June): 65–105.
RAINES, JOHN C., LENORA BERSON, and DAVID McI. GRACIE, eds. 1982. *Community and Capital in Conflict: Plant Closings and Job Loss*. Philadelphia: Temple University Press.
REDFIELD, ROBERT. 1947. "The Folk Society," *American Journal of Sociology* 52 (January): 293–308.
REISSMAN, LEONARD G. 1949. "A Study of Role Conceptions in Bureaucracy," *Social Forces* 27 (March): 305–310.
ROBERTS, RON E., and ROBERT MARSH KLOSS. 1979. *Social Movements: Between the Balcony and the Barricade*. St. Louis: C.V. Mosby.
ROESTHLISBERGER, F.J., and WILLIAM J. DICKSON. 1939. *Management and the Worker*. Cambridge, Mass.: Harvard University Press.
ROSALDO, MICHELLE ZIMBALIST. 1974. "Women, Culture and Society: A Theoretical Overview," in *Women, Culture and Society*, pp. 17–42, eds. M.Z. Rosaldo and Louise Lamphere. Stanford, Calif.: Stanford University Press.
ROTHMAN, BARBARA KATZ. 1983. "Midwives in Transition: The Structure of a Clinical Revolution," *Social Problems* 30 (February): 262–271.
ROWBOTHAM, SHEILA. 1973. *Women, Resistance and Revolution*. New York: Pantheon.
ROY, DONALD F. 1952. "Quota Restriction and Goldbricking in a Machine Shop," *American Journal of Sociology* 56 (March): 427–442.
_____ . 1959-60. "'Banana Time,' Job Satisfaction and Informal Interaction," *Human Organization* 18 (Winter): 158–168
RUBENSTEIN, RICHARD L. 1978. *The Cunning of History: The Holocaust and the American Future*. New York: Harper, Colophon Books.
RUSHING, WILLIAM A., and MEYER N. ZALD, eds. 1976. *Organizations and Beyond: Selected Essays of James D. Thompson*. Lexington, Mass.: Lexington Books.
SARIN, RAKESH, ed. 1984. *Management Science* 30 (April): 395–531 (Special issue on risk).
SCHAEFER, RICHARD. 1979. *Racial and Ethnic Groups*, 1st ed. Boston: Little, Brown.
_____ . 1984. *Racial and Ethnic Groups*, 2nd ed. Boston: Little, Brown.
SCHEIN, EDGAR A. 1970. *Organizational Psychology*. Englewood Cliffs, N.J.: Prentice-Hall.
SCHEIN, VIRGINIA ELLON. 1975. "Relationships between Sex Role Stereotypes and Management Characteristics among Female Managers," *Journal of Applied Psychology* 60 (June): 340–344.
SCHWAB, DONALD P., and LARRY CUMMINGS. 1970. "Theories of Performance and Satisfaction: A Review," *Industrial Relations* 9 (October): 408–430.
SCOTT, W. RICHARD. 1981. *Organizations: Rational, Natural and Open Systems*. Englewood Cliffs, N.J.: Prentice-Hall.
SCOTT, WILLIAM G., and DAVID K. HART. 1979. *Organizational America*. Boston: Houghton Mifflin.
SEEMAN, MELVIN. 1959. "On the Meaning of Alienation," *American Sociological Review* 24 (December): 783–791.
SELZNICK, PHILIP. 1969. "Foundations of the Theory of Organization," in *A Sociological Reader on Complex Organizaions*, 2nd ed., pp. 19–32, ed. Amitai Etzioni. New York: Holt, Rinehart & Winston.
SHIBUTANI, TAMOTSU, and KIAN M. KWAN. 1965. *Ethnic Stratification*. New York: Macmillan.
SILLS, DAVID L. 1957. *The Volunteers*. New York: Free Press.
SLATER, JACK. 1972. "Condemned to Die for Science: Tuskegee Study," *Ebony* 28 (November): 177 passim.
SMITH, TOM W., and D. GARTH TAYLOR, with NANCY A. MATHIOWETZ. 1979. "Public Opinion and Public Regard for the Federal Government," in *Making Bureaucracies Work*, pp. 37–63, eds. Carol H. Weiss and Allen H. Barton. Beverly Hills, Calif.: Sage Publications.
Society Today. 1973. Del Mar, Calif.: CRM Books.
SQUIRES, GREGORY D. 1982. "'Runaway Plants,' Capital Mobility and Black Economic Rights," in *Community and Capital in Conflict*, pp. 62–97, eds. John Raines et al. Philadelphia: Temple University Press.

STEERS, RICHARD M. 1975. "Problems in the Measurement of Organizational Effectiveness," *Administrative Science Quarterly* 20 (December): 546–558.

SYKES, GRESHAM M., and SHELDON L. MESSENGER. 1960. "The Inmate Social System," pp. 5–48, in *Theoretical Studies in Social Organization of the Prison*. New York: Social Science Research Council.

TAUSKY, CURT. 1978. *Work Organizations: Major Theoretical Perspectives*, 2nd ed. Itasca, Ill.: F.E. Peacock.

TAYLOR, FREDERICK W. 1911. *The Principles of Scientific Management*. New York: Harper Brothers.

_____. 1947. *Scientific Management*. New York: Harper & Brothers.

TERREBERRY, SHIRLEY. 1968. "The Evolution of Organizational Environments," *Administrative Science Quarterly* 12 (March): 590–613.

THOMPSON, DENNIS F. 1983. "Bureaucracy and Democracy," in *Democratic Theory and Practice*, pp. 235–250, ed. Graeme Duncan. Cambridge: Cambridge University Press.

THOMPSON, JAMES D. 1967. *Organizations in Action*. New York McGraw-Hill.

_____. 1976. "Organizational Management of Conflict," in *Organizations and Beyond: Selected Essays of James D. Thompson*, pp. 23–29, eds. William A. Rushing and Mayer N. Zald. Lexington, Mass.: Lexington Books.

THOMPSON, JAMES D., and WILLIAM J. McEWEN. 1969. "Organizational Goals and Environment," in *A Sociological Reader on Complex Organizations*, 2nd ed., pp. 187–196, ed. Amitai Etzioni. New York: Holt, Rinehart & Winston.

Time. 1973. "Convicts as Guinea Pigs," March 19, p. 61.

UNGSON, GERARDO RIVERA, DANIEL N. BRAUNSTEIN, and PHILLIP D. HALL. 1981. "Managerial Information Processing: A Research Review," *Administrative Science Quarterly* 26 (March): 116–134.

Union of Concerned Scientists. 1984. Letter (no date).

U.S. Department of Labor, Bureau of Labor Statistics. 1979. "Employment in Perspective: Working Women," Report 565, No. 1.

_____. 1983. *Women at Work: A Chartbook*. Bulletin 2168.

USEEM, MICHAEL. 1979. "The Social Organization of the American Business Elite and Participation of Corporate Directors in the Governance of American Institutions," *American Sociological Review* 44 (August): 553–572.

VAN DE VEN, ANDREW H., and DIANE L. FERRY. 1980. *Measuring and Assessing Organizations*. New York: John Wiley.

VAUGHAN, DIANE. 1983. *Controlling Unlawful Organizational Behavior: Social Structure and Corporate Misconduct*. Chicago: University of Chicago Press.

VERBA, SIDNEY, and NORMAN H. NIE. 1972. *Participation in America: Political Democracy and Social Equality*. New York: Harper & Row.

VOGEL, DAVID. 1978. *Lobbying the Corporation: Citizen Challenges to Business Authority*. New York: Basic Books.

VOYDANOFF, PATRICIA, ed. 1984. *Work and Family: Changing Roles of Men and Women*. Palo Alto, Calif.: Mayfield Publishing.

WALDINGER, ROGER. 1984. "Immigrant Enterprise in the New York Garment Industry," *Social Problems* 32 (October): 60–71.

WALLACE, PHYLLIS A., ed. 1976. *Equal Employment Opportunity and the AT&T Case*. Cambridge, Mass.: MIT Press.

WALLING, DONOVAN R. 1982. *Complete Book of School Public Relations: An Administrator's Manual and Guide*. Englewood Cliffs, N.J.: Prentice-Hall.

WAMSLEY, GARY L., and MAYER N. ZALD. 1973. *The Political Economy of Public Organizations*. Lexington, Mass.: Heath.

WEBER, MAX. 1952. "The Essentials of Bureaucratic Organization: An Ideal-Type Construction," in *Reader in Bureaucracy*, pp. 18–27, ed. Robert K. Merton et al. Glencoe, Ill.: Free Press.

_____. 1958. *From Max Weber: Essays in Sociology*. New York: Oxford University Press. Trans., edited, and with an introduction by H.H. Gerth and C. Wright Mills.

_____. 1980. "The Three Types of Legitimate Rule," in *A Sociological Reader on Complex Organization*, 3rd ed., pp. 4–10, eds. Amitai Etzioni and Edward W. Lehman. New York: Holt, Rinehart & Winston.

Webster's New Collegiate Dictionary, 7th ed. 1970. Springfield, Mass.: G. & C. Merriam.

WEICK, KARL E. 1969. *The Social Psychology of Organizing.* Reading, Mass.: Addison-Wesley.

WEINSTEIN, DEENA. 1979. *Bureaucratic Opposition.* Elmsford, N.Y.: Pergamon Press.

WESTHUES, KENNETH. 1980. "Class and Organization as Paradigms in Social Science," in *A Sociological Reader on Complex Organizations,* 3rd ed., pp. 74–84, eds. Amitai Etzioni and Edward W. Lehman. New York: Holt, Rinehart & Winston.

WESTRUM, RON, and KHALIL SAMAHA. 1984. *Complex Organizations: Growth, Struggle, and Change.* Englewood Cliffs, N.J.: Prentice-Hall.

WHEELER, STANTON. 1961. "Socialization in Correctional Communities," *American Sociological Review* 26 (October): 696–712.

WHYTE, WILLIAM FOOTE, ed. 1946. *Industry and Society.* New York: McGraw-Hill.

_____ . 1948. *Human Relations in the Restaurant Industry.* New York: McGraw-Hill.

_____ . 1983a. "On the Need for New Strategies," in *Worker Participation and Ownership: Cooperative Strategies for Strengthening Local Economies,* pp. 1–5, eds. William F. Whyte et al. Ithaca, N.Y.: ILR Press.

_____ . 1983b. "Policy Options for Unions, Management and Government," in *Worker Participation and Ownership: Cooperative Strategies for Strengthening Local Economies,* pp. 118–142, eds. William F. Whyte et al. Ithaca, N.Y.: ILR Press.

WHYTE, WILLIAM FOOTE, TOVE HELLAND HAMMER, CHRISTOPHER B. MEEK, REED NELSON, and ROBERT N. STERN. 1983. *Worker Participation and Ownership: Cooperative Strategies for Strengthening Local Economies.* Ithaca, N.Y.: ILR Press.

WILSON, JAMES Q. 1978. *The Investigators: Managing FBI and Narcotics Agents.* New York: Basic Books.

WITTE, JOHN F. 1980. *Democracy, Authority and Alienation in Work: Workers' Participation in an American Corporation.* Chicago: University of Chicago Press.

WOOD, JAMES R. 1972. "Unanticipated Consequences of Organizational Coalitions: Ecumenical Cooperation and Civil Rights Policy," *Social Forces* 50 (June): 512–521.

WOODWARD, JOAN. 1965. *Industrial Organization: Theory and Practice.* London: Oxford University Press.

YUCHTMAN, EPHRAIM, and STANLEY SEASHORE. 1967. "A System Resource Approach to Organizational Effectiveness," *American Sociological Review* 32 (December): 891–903.

ZALD, MAYER N. 1970. "Political Economy: A Framework for Comparative Analysis," in *Power in Organizations,* pp. 221–261, ed. Mayer N. Zald. Nashville, Tenn.: Vanderbilt University Press.

ZEY-FERRELL, MARY, and MICHAEL AIKEN, eds. 1981. *Complex Organizations: Critical Perspectives.* Glenview, Ill.: Scott, Foresman.

ZIMBALIST, ANDREW, ed. 1979. *Case Studies on the Labor Process.* New York: Monthly Review Press.

ZURCHER, LOUIS A., and DAVID SNOW. 1980. "Collective Behavior: Social Movements," in *Sociological Contributions to Social Psychology,* eds. Morris Rosenberg and Ralph Turner. New York: Basic Books.

ZWERDLING, DANIEL. 1980. *Workplace Democracy.* New York: Harper & Row.

INDEX

Page numbers followed by *n* or *t* refer to *footnotes* or *tables*.

abortion groups, 243
Abrahamsson, Bengt, 270
academic freedom, 90, 91, 92
accidents, 2, 63, 251, 252–57, 270
accountability, 67, 78–79, 80
achieved status, 126
Acquired Immune Deficiency Syndrome (AIDS), 28
Adams, Carolyn Teich, 264
Adams, J. Stacey, 49–50
address, language of, 99, 134
Administrative Science Quarterly, 35, 43, 44, 52
advertising, 9–10, 20, 114, 210, 214, 238, 239
AFL–CIO, 261
affirmative action programs, 19, 130, 131, 158, 243, 263, 264, 266–69
Africa, 126–27
age, ageism, 126, 127
agriculture, 7, 126–27, 224
Aiken, Michael, 50, 51, 223*n*
airlines industry, 27, 201, 250, 252
Albert, June, 37
Aldrich, Howard E., 13 *fig.*, 16, 49, 63–64, 79, 86, 225, 226, 230, 231
  on environmental niches, 231, 232
  on organizational forms, 224
  on population ecology theory, 84
alienation, 60, 107, 112
  and involvement, 106, 107 *fig.*
  in power relationships, 58, 59, 60, 103
  in the workplace, 187, 189, 191–92, 196

Allen, Irving L., Jr., 242
Altman, Steven, 116, 154, 158
Alvarez, Rodolfo, 128
Annual Review of Sociology (1976), 230
apartheid, 18, 41
Argyris, Chris, 187
ascribed status, 11, 126, 127, 128, 130
Astley, W. Graham, 17*n*
astronauts, 182
Asylums (Goffman), 18
attitudes, 82, 169–70
authoritarian leadership, 155
authority
  bureaucratic-legal, 8, 12
  charismatic, 8–9
  and communication patterns, 99–100, 114–15
  and compliance, 100–103
  definitions of, 8, 97–98
  institutionalization of, 114
  limitations of concept, 103–5
  and managers, socialization of, 36
  norms vs. rules in, 9
  opposition to (whistle-blowing), 119–22
  political economy theory of, 227
  vs. power, 96, 106, 154–55
  rational-systems theory of, 12–13
  traditional, 8
  see also power
automation, 29, 196, 241
automobile industry, 27, 154, 156, 234, 258

287

Babchuk, Nicholas, 73
Baker, James A., III, 264
Baker, Lawrence, 261
"Banana Game, The" (Roy), 160
Bank of Boston, 262
banks, 201, 202, 213
bargaining
    collective, 87, 111, 136–37, 164
    and managerial role-shaping, 166
    negotiation, 85, 110–11, 164
    plea, 270–71
    and strategic leniency, 162
Baritz, Loren, 32–33, 38, 39, 40
Barnard, Chester I., 98, 100, 101–3, 104,
    115, 133–34
Bayley, David H., 139
Becker, Howard S., 183
Beer, Michael, 82, 83, 224
Bennis, Warren G., 135
Benson, Kenneth, 35, 44, 62, 226, 227–28,
    229
Benston, Margaret, 127
Berger, Peter L., 185
Bernard, Jessie, 187
Betz, Michael, 65–67
Bhopal disaster, 165, 250
Billbrough, Sam, 239
Black History (film), 37
black managers, 266–67, 268 *fig.*
black markets, 240
Black Power movement, 228
black studies, 37, 263–64. *See also* minority
    groups; racial groups
Blau, Peter, 49, 50, 52–56, 57, 64, 65, 67,
    143, 176, 210
Blauner, Robert, 191–92
Bluestone, Barry, 250, 257, 261
Blumberg, Rhoda L., 6, 58, 82, 143, 173,
    228. *See also* Rhoda L. Goldstein
Bonacich, Edna, 265
Boserup, Ester, 126–27
Boston Women's Health Collective, 209
boundary controls, 204–5
boycotts, 214, 243
brainwashing, 181
Braunstein, Daniel N., 163
Braverman, Harry, 35, 189
Bredemeier, Harry C., 11, 124, 179
bribery, 205, 237, 238, 240, 241
Bromley, David G., 181
Brown, Shirley V., 129
Bulgaria, 135–36
bundle of tasks concept (Hughes), 144, 195
bureaucracies, 4–5, 67, 119, 192–94, 223
    client relationships, 55, 178, 193–94. *See
        also* main entry
    contractual obligations in, 194
    definitions of, 4–5
    and democracy, 269–71
    and goal displacement, 78
    impersonality of, 205–6, 269, 271
    individual responsibility in, 102, 193, 194
    and nonbureaucratic collectivities, 17–21
    norm conflicts in, 102
    theories, 11–17, 56–58, 150, 192–93

Bureaucracy and the Public (Katz & Danet),
    200*n*
bureaucratic-legal authority (Weber), 8, 97,
    98
bureaucratic personality (Merton), 78,
    192–95
bureaucratic societies, 5–11
Burford, Ann McGill, 236
businesses
    as bureaucracies, 5
    cui bono analysis of, 54
    demise of small, 79, 85, 224, 231
    employee and community ownership,
        260–62, 270, 271
    environmental influences on, 79, 83–85
    family enterprises, 18, 21–22
    natural selection theory of, 231
    1980s environment, 224
    and organized crime, 237
    see also corporations; management
business schools, 26 & *n*, 32, 34, 38, 150,
    151, 167
Business Week, 27
Byrnes, Eleanor, 172

calculative involvement (Etzioni), 106, 107
    fig., 108
capitalism, 11, 30, 31, 42, 135, 136, 261
    and democracy, 269–70
    and deskilling, 189
    and the patriarchal family, 265
careers, 167–70, 183–86
    combinations of, 184–85
    definitions of, 183
    and mobility, 167, 169–70, 189–91
    moral, 184–85
    substitute, 183–84
Carmichael, Stokely, 228
Carson, Clayborne, 86
case studies
    corporate fraud, 244–47
    corporations and university research,
        44–45
    deskilling, 195–96
    family and ethnic business, 21–22
    physician-patient relationships, 65–67
    street-level bureaucrats, 214–18
    university goals, 88–93
    whistle-blowing, 119–22
    women managers, 171–73
cathective-evaluative factors, in involve-
    ment, 106
centralization, of power, 104, 155, 222
Challenger disaster, 28
charismatic authority, 8–9, 17, 97, 157
charities, 77, 86, 207
cheating, and peer-group acceptance, 105
chemical industry, 63. *See* hazardous chem-
    icals
Chernobyl disaster, 2, 255–56
child abuse, 121, 206
childhood
    nuclear war fears, 2
    self-concept in, 179–80

China, 241
Christ, Edwin A., 138
citizen movements, 37, 41, 250. *See also*
    consumer movements; social move-
    ment organizations
Civil Rights Act (1964), 263
Civil Rights Commission, 151
civil rights movement, 40, 86, 152, 214,
    228-29, 243, 263
civil service positions, 10, 12
Civil War, 29
clans, 158-59, 168
clients, 53, 54, 55, 65-66, 178, 193-94,
    201-2, 204-6, 214-18
  informal organization of, 208
  and latent status, 132
  revolt by, 208-9
  role playing by, 207-8
  time and space dimensions with, 59 & *n*
  see also consumer movement; publics-in-
    contact
cliques, 14-15, 17, 54, 100, 160, 161
  communication patterns, 118-19
  and latent identities, 130-31
Cloward, Richard A., 81, 87
clubs, 5, 54, 56, 72-73, 242-43, 270
cluster chains, 118-19
coalitions, 82, 85, 88, 104, 227, 229, 231
coercive power, 58, 105, 237
cognitive-motivation theories, 187-88
cold war ideology, 30-31
Cole, Robert E., 258
collective bargaining, 87, 111, 136-37, 177
collective behavior, 37, 41-42
collectivities, 3, 17-18, 41, 72, 211-13,
    229
colonialism, 113
Coming Asunder of Jimmy Bright, The
    (film), 139-40, 194
commitment, testing of, 160-61
committees, labor-management, 259-60
common-sense typologies, 3, 48-49
commonweal organizations, 54 *fig.*, 55, 56,
    210
communes, 5, 224
communication
  authority and power relations in, 96, 99-
    101, 114-19
  patterns and modes, 114-19
    formal, 116-17
    horizontal, 116-17
    informal, 99-100, 117-18
  and language of address, 99, 134
communications revolution, 2, 250, 257
communism, communistic societies, 11, 30,
    239, 240
communities, 17, 18, 66, 229
  citizen control of public services, 178, 209
  conflict with organizations, 140-41
  labor-management committees and, 259-
    60
  managerial involvement in, 170
  occupational, 192
  ownership of enterprises, 260-61
  power structures, 108-9

company culture, 156. *See also* organiza-
    tional culture
comparable worth principle, 264
competition, 85, 86-87, 256, 257
  between criminal syndicates, 237-38
  and information complexity, 164
  and secrecy, 119
  sexual, 265
complexity
  in the division of labor, 7-8
  of information, 164
  of organizational structure, 222, 253-54
complex organizations, 4, 5
compliance, 97, 100-105, 125, 150
  defined, 98
  and legitimate power, 154-55
  types of, 58-59, 103, 105
  zone of indifference in, 103
computer analysis, 16*n*
computer chips, 241
computer industry
  secrets, export of, 241-42
  women in, 168, 182-83, 191
computer programming, 189
computers, computerization, 55, 163, 196,
    233, 241
  crime and fraud with, 80, 244-47
  in education, 79-80
  errors, 55, 207
concentration camps, 102, 194
conflict, 96
  in bargaining, negotiation, 136-37
  in goals, 80-81, 82, 113
  interorganizational, 228-29
  Marxist analyses of, 43, 44
  in orders and compliance, 101
  and power, exercise of, 112-13
  in role relationships, 137-40
  and status systems, 135-36
  worker-manager, 35
conflict of interest, 31-32, 44-45, 88, 99
conformity, 186
Congress on Racial Equality, 228
congruent involvement, 107, 108
congruent power, 58, 108
constituencies, 213, 214-15
consumer movement, 5, 41, 66, 140-141,
    178, 269
contingencies, 141
contingency theory, 3, 60, 155-56, 162,
    233
contracts, 9, 238
contractual obligation, 194
control
  in complex systems, 253 & *fig.*
  with publics-in-contact, 204-5, 207, 216-
    18
  and work satisfaction, 192
*Controlling Unlawful Organizational Behav-
    ior* (Vaughn), 244-47
Cooley, Charles, 6
cooperative systems, 124, 133-35, 258-60
co-optation, 85, 87-88, 176
Cornell University, 259, 260
Corporate Cultures (Deal & Kennedy), 158

corporations, 2, 18, 19, 21, 104
    and business schools, 34, 150–51
    and capitalist economies, 30
    vs. citizens' groups, 41
    crime and fraud in, 244–47, 250, 262
    foreign manufacturing and labor, 15 & *n*,
        109, 234, 250, 261
    government ties, 57, 154, 213, 224
    international dominance of, 30, 109
    in Japan, 9, 12, 157, 187, 189
    mergers, takeovers, 109, 151, 224
    minority managers, 266–67, 268 *fig.*
    and nonbusiness institutions, directorships
        of, 27 & *n*
    and public policy, 234–35
    public relations, 210
    research and development by, 27–29, 31–
        32, 44–45, 110
    survival and success factors, 50–51, 64
    see also businesses; management
corruption, 112, 240
Corwin, Ronald G., 138
Cosby, Bill, 37
Coser, Lewis, 136
coupling, loose vs. tight, 16, 253, 254, 255*t*
courts, 201, 204, 217, 233
Cressey, Donald R., 146
crime. *See* bribery; corruption; organized
    crime; white-collar crime
Crombie, A.D., 59, 60
Crozier, Michael, 135, 136, 137
cui bono typologies, 52–56, 65–67
culture, 155–56, 168, 234. *See also* organi-
    zational culture
Cummings, Larry, 192
customers, 132, 145. *See also* clients; pub-
    lics-in-contact

Dahl, Robert, 108
Dalton, Melville, 159–160
Danet, Brenda, 140, 200 & *n*
Darrow, Clarence, 29
Darwin, Charles, 30
Davis, Warren E., 15*n*
Deal, Terrence, E., 155, 157, 158, 159–60,
    161
decision making
    by employees, 135, 188, 270
    environmental factors in, 224, 227, 231
    and information seeking, 76
    by managers, 150, 162–65
    rationality factors in, 82
deductive theories, 64
democracy, democratic values, 262, 269–71
demographic conditions, 234
dependence-exchange theory, 226
dependency, and power relations, 109–10
deskilling, 175, 189, 195–96, 258
developing societies, 6, 8, 126–27, 250
deviance, 7, 102, 160, 236, 240, 262
dialectics, 7, 43–44
Dickson, William J., 33
dioxin contamination, 235

dirty work 138, 144–45
distance maintenance, 206
division of labor, 6, 113, 124–28, 135, 175–
    76
    age and, 127
    and cultural values, 168
    in ideal bureaucracies, 11
    informal, 141–45
        dirty work, sloughing off of, 144–45
        mutual aid patterns, 143–44
        obligations, adding or eliminating, 142–
            43
        voluntary action in emergencies, 145
    and power, 109–10
    racial and ethnic, 127
    sexual, 126–27
    simple vs. complex, 7–8
    status, role, and 124–25, 132–33
    see also deskilling; scientific management
        studies
Dofny, Jacques, 136
domains, 227
dress customs, 114, 157, 169
drinking age, raising of the, 212
drug addiction, 28, 73,103
drug trafficking, 237, 238–39
dual labor market, 264, 265
Dubin, Robert, 261
Durkheim, Émile, 127
Dyer, Davis, 151, 154, 156, 164

ecological change, 21, 234
economic conditions, 230, 233
economic incentives, 103–4
effectiveness, 51, 52 *fig.*, 72
efficiency, in organizational societies, 9
E. F. Hutton Inc., 262
Eldridge, J. E. T., 59, 60
elites, 11, 27, 34, 43, 54, 105, 270
emergency situations, 140, 145
employees
    behavior, 77–78, 80, 186–92
    and information processing, 163
    ownership of enterprises, 260–62, 270,
        271
    participation in management, 181, 187–
        89, 258–59, 260, 270
    regular vs. temporary, 131
    shift workers, interdependence of, 137–38
    see also lower participants; work behavior
employment
    latent identity vs. technical requirements
        in, 131, 132
    lifetime, in Japan, 12
    of minorities, 18–19, 234, 263–66. *See
        also* affirmative action; equal opportu-
        nity programs
    permanent vs. temporary, 80
    primary and secondary fields of, 18–19
    public vs. private sector, 57
    racial and sexual bias in, 130, 263–66
    and remunerative power, 103–4, 105, 106
    spouse employment networks, 172

employment agencies, 227-28
enterprises, 5
  employee ownership of, 260-62, 270, 271
  types of, 56-58, 150
environmental factors, 15, 16, 17n, 43, 49,
    156, 222-36, 270-71
  and accidents, 252, 254
  conditions, types of, 232-34
  and goal formation, 73, 79, 83-88, 89
  interorganizational relations, 223-30
  physical environment, organizations'
    impact on, 234-36
  research focus on, 222-23
  specific vs. general, 230
  structural effects of, 222-23, 233n, 229
  theories, 230-32
environmental niches, 231, 232
Environmental Protection Agency (EPA),
    235-36
environmental protection groups, 140-41,
    151, 178, 236, 243
epidemic diseases, 28-29
equality, issues of, 262-69
equal opportunity policies, 130, 131, 263,
    264, 266-69
equilibrium, in interorganizational relations,
    229
Ermann, M. David, 237
espionage, 241-42. *See also* industrial
    spying
ethnic groups, 18-19, 229
  business enterprises, 21, 79
  and the division of labor, 127, 196
  managers, selection of, 167
  see also minority groups; racial groups
Etzioni, Amitai, 49, 53, 64, 125
  on goals, 74, 75, 76
  involvement continuum, 106-7
  power and compliance theory, 58-59,
    103, 104, 105-6
evolution, 29-30, 63-64, 224, 231
exceptional cases, in work procedures, 61-62
experimentation, human and animal, 205-6
expressive goals, 72-73, 74, 89, 92

Fairchild Semiconductor, 15n
Falk, William W., 195
families, 5, 17, 224, 229
  businesses, 18, 21-22
  and careers, 183, 184
  criminal syndicates, 238
  farming, 224
  in Japan, 6. 9
  vs. loyalty to corporations, 169, 170
  median incomes, 264
  patriarchal, 264, 265
  and prison roles, 146, 147
  two-career, 170, 172, 183, 265
Farley, Jennie, 169
farm workers, 111
fashion industry, 114
Fayol, Henri, 116
Feldman, Martha S., 76, 163-64

Fernandez, John P., 19, 171-72, 266-69
Ferry, Diane L., 226
firemen, fire departments, 3, 55, 107,
    210
Fischer, Frank, 188
folk societies, 5, 6-7
force, as a source of power, 103, 104
Ford Motor Company, 258
Form, William H., 161, 186, 188-89, 259,
    261
formal organizations, 4, 5
Fortune (magazine), 134, 246
Fox, Mary, 126, 171, 173, 265
France, 241
fraternities, 225t, 226, 242
fraud, 74, 239, 241, 244-47
Freeman, Jo, 58
Friedson, Elliott, 138, 140

games, in the workplace, 160
gangplank principle, of communication, 116
Gans, Herbert J., 6
gatekeeper roles, 176, 205, 240
gender groups, 19, 167, 171-72. *See also*
    sex; sexual discrimination; women
General Dynamics, 262
General Motors, 29, 258
gene splicing techniques, 252, 256-57
gerontology, 234
Gerth, Hans C., 176
Giallombardo, Rose, 131, 146-47
goal displacement, 17, 78, 86
goals, of organizations, 14, 71-93
  case study (universities), 88-93
  conflict, ambivalence in, 113
  and environment, 73, 79, 83-88
  institutionalization of, 244
  nature of, 71-75
  operative, 76-83
goal succession, 85-86
Goffman, Erving, 18, 34, 59-60, 65, 80, 81,
    136, 159, 179, 184-85, 207. *See also*
    total institutions
Goldman, Paul, 35, 42-43
Goldstein, Rhoda L., 37, 138, 140, 144,
    145
Gordon, C. Wayne, 73
gossip, 118 *fig.*, 119. *See also* grapevine
Gouldner, Alvin, 128, 131, 155, 263
  academic role types, 195
  on managerial succession, 164-65
government
  bureaucracies, 5, 151
  co-optation of minority leaders, 87
  corporate ties, 57, 154, 213, 224
  employment, 57
  equal rights policies, 263-66, 269
  and public-at-large, 213
  regulation of organizations, 27, 28, 73-74,
    83, 88, 178
  see also public service agencies; regulatory
    agencies; welfare agencies
Grace, J. Peter, 167

grapevine, communication by, 14, 99, 117–19
Green, Susan S., 234
Gross, Edward, 76, 88–93
groups, group relations, 6–7, 124, 181
Grusky, Oscar, 137, 166

Habenstein, Robert A., 138
Hage, Jerald, 223*n*
Hall, John, 132
Hall, Phillip D., 163
Hall, Richard, 16, 48, 49, 63, 124, 131, 136, 140, 150, 154, 164, 177, 232–33, 234–35
Hammer, Tove Helland, 260
handicapped persons, 130, 131, 176, 263
Harring, Sid, 195–96
Harrison, Dennett, 261
Hart, David K., 135
Hatano, Daryl G., 15*n*
Haug, Marie R., 133, 136, 178, 208
Hawthorne studies, 33, 38–40
hazardous chemicals, wastes, 165, 235–36, 250, 254
Hellriegel, Don, 152, 153–54, 155, 162
"helping out," in the workplace, 143–44
Hess, Beth B., 130
Hesse-Biber, Sharlene, 126, 171, 173, 265
Heydebrand, Wolf V., 159
hierarchies
chain of command in, 101–2, 104, 124
and communication patterns, 99, 115–17
of needs (Maslow), 188
power relationships in, 97, 98, 100, 105
see also authority; status
Himmler, Heinrich, 194
Hirsch, Paul, 35, 110
Hitler, Adolf, 271
Hodgetts, Richard M., 116, 154, 158
home birth movement, 209, 269
"homeys," in women's prisons, 130–31, 146–47
homosexuals, homosexuality, 28, 146, 147, 263, 271
hospitals, 81, 202, 209
Emergency Rooms, 140
foreign interns in, 132
patient socialization in, 181–82
reciprocity and cooperation in, 144
role conflict in, 138, 140
workers' strikes, 107–8
housing discrimination, 129–30
Huelga (film), 111
Hughes, Charles L., 111, 115
Hughes, Everett C., 127, 129, 140, 144–45, 195, 200*n*
human nature, theories of, 188
human relations theory, 33–34, 40, 187
human service organizations, 213, 214–18, 251, 269. *See also* public service organizations

Ianni, Frances A. J., 18
ideal type (Weber)
of bureaucracy, 11–12, 16
of society, 5
identity, 179–80, 182
ideology, 26–27, 261
defined, 26–27
managerial, 31, 34, 36–37
and research, 30–31
illegal aliens, 191, 240
illegal organizations, 233, 236–39
illicit goals, 74–75
immigrant groups, 19, 21–22, 79, 191, 234, 240
impersonality, bureaucratic, 7, 205–6, 269, 271
India, 6, 57, 165, 213, 230
individuals
and cultural change, 157
high-mobility attitudes, values, 169–70
power of, in organizations, 97, 105, 177
and reality, construction of, 185–86
responsibility of, in bureaucracies, 102, 193, 194
Indsco, 37, 117, 167, 169, 190–91
inductive theories, 64–65
industrial accidents, 251, 252–57
industrialization, 6, 7–8, 11
industrial psychology, 32–33, 38
industrial sociology, 32, 38
industrial spying, 29, 119, 241–42, 262
industry, industries, 229
employee ownership, 260–62, 270
public issues, 250–51, 269
research activities, 31–32
U.S. leadership loss, 153, 257–60, 270
see also manufacturing; technology
influence, 154–55
informal norms, 112, 142, 159
informal structures
in company cultures, 159–62, 172
natural systems theory, 13–15
in peer groups, 136, 141–42, 145
in the workplace, 33, 40, 138–39, 141–45, 159
information, 76, 163–64, 241–42. *See also* knowledge
information complexity (IC), 164
information processing, 163
initiation rituals, 160–61
innovation, 114, 159
institutionalization
of goals, 244
of power, 113–14
institutionalized organizations, 242–43. *See also* total institutions
instrumental goals, 72–73, 74, 89, 92
interdependence
of nations, 250
of organizations, 112–13, 137–39, 226
interest groups, 211–12, 214, 235, 236
international relations, 104–5, 239, 250
interorganizational relationships, 15, 16, 43, 86–88, 109, 223–30

equilibrium, 229
illegal and legal organizations, 237–38,
    262
networks, 226, 227–28
power in, 227–29
interpersonal relations, and productivity,
    187
intimacy, in modern life, 7
involvement, 106–8
Israel, 241
Izraeli, Dafna, 155, 166

Jamaica, 239
Jamestown (N.Y.) Area Labor Management
    Committee (JALMC), 259–60
Japan, 153, 241, 257
    cultural values and business success, 6, 9,
        157, 187, 234, 259
    job rotation in, 189
    lifetime employment, 12
    quality-control circles, 258–59
    women, status, of, 12, 259
jargon, 3–4, 117, 201
Jelinek, Mariann, 35
Jews, Nazi persecution of, 102, 194, 205,
    271
job enrichment, 188, 189
job rotation, 188, 189
job satisfaction, 191–92
job security, 12
Johnson, Pres. Lyndon B., 263
junior colleges, 225*t*, 229

Kahn, Robert L., 49–50
Kanter, Rosabeth Moss, 19, 30, 37, 38, 40,
    131, 132, 151, 158, 187–88, 190, 265
    on individuals' relationships in organiza-
        tions, 185–86
    on power, 96–97
    on selection and promotion of managers,
        167–68, 169
    on status systems, 134–35
Katz, Daniel, 49–50
Katz, Elihu, 140, 200 & *n*
Kay, Mary, 167
Kennedy, Allan A., 155, 157, 158, 159–60,
    161
Kennedy, Pres. John F., 263
Kessler, Felix, 134
Kimberly, John R., 51
King, Martin Luther Jr., 228
kinship groups, 6, 18. *See also* clans
knowledge
    and influence, 155
    and secrecy, 119, 241
    social roots of, 25–26, 43
    as source of power, 105, 110–11
Koch, Mayor Edward, 121–22
Kohn, Melvin L., 78, 186
Korean immigrants, 79

Kozol, Jonathan, 139
Kraft, Philip, 189
Krauskopf, James A., 121
Kroc, Ray A., 167
Kwan, Kian M., 127

labor
    definitions of, 7, 127–28
    and foreign manufacturing, 15 & *n*, 109,
        234, 250, 261
    household, 127, 144, 170, 183
    and immigrant groups, 19, 21–22
    paid vs. unpaid, 127
    social science research on, 32–33, 40
    specialization in, 11, 66, 78, 127, 132–33
    supply and demand factors, 132
    and technology, variations in, 61–62
    and the U.S. industrial decline, 257–58
    voluntary, 127, 142–43, 145
    see also division of labor; employment;
        management
Labor Department, 38
labor-management committees, 259
labor markets, women in, 264, 265–66
labor unions, 32, 34, 40, 43, 53, 115, 142,
    214, 215 *fig.*, 225*t*, 233, 243, 244,
    259
    "business" vs. "welfare" types, 259, 261
    collective bargaining in, 87, 111, 136–37,
        177
    and employee ownership of enterprises,
        261
    membership
        declines, 261
        and job mobility, 187, 191
        minorities and women, exclusion of,
            265
    pension funds, power of, 270
    role changes of, 261–62
    in socialistic countries, 135–36
language, linguistic usage, 156, 158
    of address, 99, 134
    jargon, 3–4, 117, 201
    public vs. private, 117
    sexism and racism in, 38–40
latent identity, 128–31
latent status, 126, 132
Lavelle, Rita, 236
Lawrence, Paul R., 151, 154, 155–56, 164,
    168
laws, legislation, 83, 131, 212, 213, 230,
    233, 236
    legality and enforcement policies, varia-
        tions in, 238–39
    and minority rights, 262, 263
    as public policy, 27
    rule by, 97–98
leadership, 152, 154–62, 164–65
Lefton, Mark, 59*n*, 200
legal authority (Weber), 8, 97, 98
legal services agencies, 201–2, 204, 217
Leger, Robert C., 136, 146

legitimacy
  of authority and orders, 8, 97, 103, 104,
    106, 115
  facades of, 74–75
  and interorganizational relations, 227
Levin, Irwin, 121
Lewin, Tamar, 77
Lieberson, Stanley, 242
Light, Ivan, 19, 21
Likert, Rensis, 116 *fig.*
linear interactions, in organizational sys-
    tems, 253 & *fig.*
line positions, in hierarchies, 124, 172
Lipsky, Michael, 34, 78, 81, 178, 201–2,
    204, 216–18
lobbies, lobbyists, 80, 213, 239, 243
Long Island Lighting Company (LILCO),
    262
Lorsch, Jay W., 155–56, 168
Love Canal homeowners, 141
Lowell (Mass.) workers' strike (1812), 111
lower participants
  and industrial accidents, 255
  power of, 97, 112
  roles, 176–77
  work behavior, 186–92
loyalty, 9–10, 18, 106, 117, 154, 157, 158,
    165–66, 167, 169, 170, 238
Luckmann, Thomas, 185
Lundine, Stanley, 259, 260
Lundman, Richard J., 237

Mafia, 237
magic, 10
maintenance goals, 74, 81
"making out," 80, 136
Making Unions Unnecessary (Hughes), 111,
    115
Malos, Ellen, 183
malpractice suits, 269
management, 82, 90, 149–73, 177–78
  and communication skills, 115–16
  decision making, 162–65
  functions and duties, 149–50, 153–54
  ideologies of, 31, 34, 36–40
  and labor
    employee ownership of enterprises,
      260–62
    joint committees with, 259–60
    see also collective bargaining
  and leadership, 154–62
  levels of, in business, 152–53
  mobility and promotions, 169–70, 190
  and organizational culture, 154, 156–62
  of risks, 251
  and social science research, use of, 32–34,
    50–51
  status symbols of, 133–34
  succession, 155, 156–66
  and technology, variations in, 61–62, 164,
    165
  theories of, 33, 155–56
  and U.S. industrial decline, 257–59

Management Science (journal), 251
managers
  minority group, 167, 173, 266–67, 268 *fig.*
  selection of, 167–68
  socialization of, 36, 150, 168–69
  training of. *See* business schools
  wives of, 170
  women, 130, 167–69, 171–73
manufacturing, 8, 20
  offshore plants and labor, 15 & *n*, 109,
    234, 250, 261
  production, types of, 49, 60, 188
March, James G., 76, 163–64
Margolis, Diane R., 154, 160–61, 168, 169,
    170
marihuana use, 232, 238, 239
marine transport systems, 252, 254, 256
Markson, Elizabeth W., 130
marriage, 48, 170, 182, 183
Martin, Patricia Yancey, 19, 213, 214–16,
    264, 265
Marx, Karl, 30, 42, 269–70
Marxist analyses, 30, 35, 136, 177, 193
  bureaucracy and capitalism, 269–70
  dialectics, 43–44
  labor and means of production, 136, 193
  organizational theory, 41–44
  social construction-production, 62
  technology and social structures, 63
  work impoverishment, 189
Maslow, Abraham, 188
masses, mass societies, 18, 19–20
mass production methods, 49, 60, 164,
    188
master status-determining traits, 129–30
McEwen, William J., 73, 79, 86–88
McGregor, Douglas, 155, 188
McKelvey, Bill, 49, 63–64, 232
Mead, George Herbert, 179
mechanistic organizations, 155, 164, 258,
    271
Medicaid fraud, 236, 244–47
medicine, 28–29, 65–67. *See also* physicians
Meek, Christopher, 259
Men and Women of the Corporation
    (Kanter), 40
Mendelsohn, Harold, 139
mental institutions, 55, 59, 60, 62, 80, 159,
    184, 204–5, 229–30
Merton, Robert K., 78, 134, 192–93
Messinger, Sheldon L., 146
Meyer, Marshall, 143
Michels, Robert, 54, 269, 270
microanalysis, 43, 51
middleman, -woman roles, 138–39
middle management, 152–53, 168, 171
midwives, 86, 209, 269
military-industrial complex, 270
military groups, institutions, 55, 59–60,
    117–18, 182, 210
Miller, Delbert C., 161, 186, 188–89, 259,
    261
Miller, Gale, 127
Miller, Joanne, 186, 187
Mills, C. Wright, 108, 176, 213

minority groups, 21, 41, 158
  college fraternities for, 225*t*, 226
  co-optation and, 87
  employment of, 18-19, 234, 250-51, 263
  informal power techniques, 112
  job mobility, 190
  in labor unions, 265
  in management, 167-68, 173, 266-67,
    268 *fig.*
  1960s-70s activism, 263
  token representatives, 139, 168, 190, 267
  universalistic treatment of, 11
mixed organizations, 5-6, 55-56, 67
mobility, 167, 178, 183, 195
  high vs. low, 169-70, 189-91
  of populations, 66
  of women and minorities, 265
modernization, 2, 7
modern societies, 5, 6, 7, 127-28, 250-51
Mohr, Lawrence B., 74, 223*n*
Mondale, Walter, 165
monopolies, 202, 241
Montgomery bus boycott, 214
Monthly Review, 43
moral careers (Goffman), 184-85
morale, 112, 158, 258. *See also* alienation
moral involvement (Etzioni), 107-8
moral issues, with publics-in-contact, 205-6
motivation, 187-88
Ms. Magazine, 39
multiple constituencies, 213, 214, 215 *fig.*
miltiple goals, 80-81, 88
multivariate analysis, 16*n*, 51, 52 *fig.*
mutual aid patterns, 141, 142, 143-44
mutual benefit associations, 53-54, 57

Naisbitt, John, 163
National Aeronautics and Space Agency
  (NASA), 28
National Association for the Advancement
  of Colored People (NAACP), 20, 228
natural selection theory, 230, 231-32
natural systems theory, 13-15, 16, 188
Nazi Germany, 102, 194, 205, 271
need-dispositions (Etzioni), 104
negotiation, 136-37. *See also* bargaining
nepotism, 10, 18
networks, 223, 226-30
  environmental, 229-30
  "old boy," 172
  power bases within, 227-28
  resources and domains, 226-27
  spouse employment, 172
news media, 250
New York City
  ethnic enterprises, 21-22
  Human Resources Administration, 121-22
  police department, 196
New York Times, 27, 29, 30, 44-45, 77, 84,
  121, 141, 235, 239, 241, 262, 264
nonprofit organizations, 74, 77
Norling, Frederick, 51

Normal Accidents (Perrow), 63, 251, 255*t*,
  256 *fig.*
normative power, 58, 59, 106
norms, 9, 112, 142, 159
nuclear power industry, 2, 63, 250, 251,
  252, 254-56, 262
nuclear weapons, 2
nurses, 138, 140, 144, 194-95. *See also*
  midwives

obligations, in the workplace, 142-43
occupational communities, 192
occupations
  feminization of, 132
  racial distribution, 18-19, 127
  roles, role types, 138-39, 194-95
  see also employment; professionals; work
    behavior
O'Connell, Lanahan, 65-67
oligarchy, 270
open systems theory, 15-16, 57, 83
operative goals, 76-83
Oppenheimer, Martin, 261
organic organizations 155, 160
organizational climate, 148*n*
organizational culture, 35, 36-37, 49, 154,
  156-62, 234
  creation of, 158-59
  defined, 157
  in informal organizations, 159-62
  institutionalization of, 114
  language usages, 158
  managerial role, 157, 158
  and publics-in-contact, 200-201
  "strong," 159-60, 258
organizational forms, 64 & *n*, 223-26
  defined, 224
  waves of new, 225*t*, 225-26
organizational politics, 35, 36, 104
organizational roles, 175-76
Organizational Systematics (McKelvey), 49,
  63
organization charts, 12-13, 13 *fig.*
organization perspective (Westhues), 42
organizations (formal)
  classification of. *See* typologies (ch. 3)
  debates on, 16-17, 17*n*, 35
  defined, 2, 4
  informal and nonrational factors, 13-15,
    17
  learning about, 2-4
  role of, in modern life, 1-2
  terminology of, 3-4
  theories, 11-17, 34-35, 42-43
  ubiquity of, 2
"Organizations: A Dialectical View"
  (Benson), 44
Organizations and Environments (Aldrich),
  225
organized crime, 18, 236-37, 240, 241, 246
Ouchi, William G., 9, 12, 16*n*, 26*n*, 157,
  158, 187
Our Bodies, Ourselves (BWHC), 209
output goals, 74, 88-89, 91

Pace, Denny F., 237, 241
paradigms, 42
Parsons, Talcott, 11, 73
participation, employee, 181, 187, 188–89,
    258–59, 260, 270
particularism, 10
patriarchal authority (Weber), 8, 97
patriarchal family, 264, 265
pattern variables (Parsons), 11
peer groups, 13–14, 66, 101, 179
    horizontal communication between, 116–
    17
    and low mobility, 169–70, 191
    occupational teams, 192
    power relationships in, 105, 106
    work output, regulation of, 136, 141–42,
    160, 203–4
peer pressure, 142
performance, defining people by, 11
perquisites, 133–34
Perrow, Charles, 27, 33, 35, 43, 49, 80, 87,
    108, 151, 187, 188, 224, 251
    on goal displacement, 78
    on high-risk technologies, 251–57
    managerial ideologies, 34
    on operative goals, 76
    on prisons and coercion, 58–59
    technology typology, 60–63
Perrucci, Robert, 120–21
personality
    bureaucratic, 78, 192–95
    and job conditions, 186
    and work behavior, 187–88
Peterson, Karen J., 209
Pfeffer, Jeffrey, 35–37, 43, 82, 104, 113,
    114, 164, 170, 179n, 183, 226, 230,
    231
    on conflict and power, use of, 112
    on organizational politics, culture, 36–37
    on sources of power, 109–10
Phillips, W. M., Jr., 143, 173
physicians
    and calculative involvement, 108
    communication with nurses, 99
    vs. nurse-midwives, 86, 209, 269
    patient relationships, 54, 65–67, 202, 206,
    269
    see also hospital workers
Piven, Frances Fox, 81, 87
plea bargaining, 87, 246
police, police departments, 55, 107, 112,
    201, 206, 210, 217
    deskilling study, 195–96
    minority-group officers, 139
    women, exclusion of, 265
poliomyelitis, 29, 85
political economy theory, 226, 227
political ideologies, 233
political parties, 235
politics. *See* organizational politics
population ecology theory, 49, 63–64, 230
    critique of, 232
    survival, selection of organizations for,
    84–85, 223–24
populations, 21, 66, 223, 234

post offices, 202, 205
poverty programs, 87, 208, 209
power, 35–37, 103–19, 224, 270–71
    vs. authority, 96
    communication as vehicle of, 96, 99–101,
    114–19
    definitions of, 36, 96–97, 105–6
    vs. influence, 154–55
    institutionalization of, 113–14
    interorganizational, 227–29
    and involvement, 106–8
    of managers, 149–50
    and organizational politics, 36–37
    and the public-at-large, 213–14
    sources of, 108–12
    of subgroups, subordinates, 97, 104–5,
    112, 205
    types of, 58–59, 103, 104, 105–6
    use of, conditions determining, 112–13
    see also authority
power elite theory (Mills), 108–9, 213
Power in Organizations (Pfeffer), 109–10
preliterate societies, 9, 10
Preservation of American Free Enterprise,
    Inc., 77
presidency
    and government agencies, 151
    incumbent powers of, 113
    limits and constraints on, 164–65
prestige, occupational, 192
price fixing, 241
primary groups, 6–7
prisons, prisoners, 55, 56, 58–60, 80, 81,
    102, 118, 200, 204–5
    communication patterns, 118, 119
    racial minorities, in, 129
    rehabilitative vs. punitive goals, 81
    status and privilege in, 136
    women in, 130–31, 145–47
probability channel, in communication,
    118, 119
productivity, of workers, 187–88, 192, 258–
    59
professionals
    vs. bureaucratic norms, 195
    client distrust of, 65–66, 269
    and publics-in-contact, 65–66, 202, 208–
    9, 217, 269
    work satisfaction, 191–92
profit motive, 74, 75, 113, 136, 236, 240,
    242
Prohibition movement, 243
promotion, of managers, 167, 169–70. *See
    also* mobility
prostitution, 237, 240
psychological counseling, of workers, 40
psychological testing, 32
public-at-large (Blau), 55, 178, 209–14
    collectivities, constituencies, 211–13
    defined, 53, 177, 209
    power, exercise of, 213–14
    and public opinion polls, 210
publics-in-contact (Blau), 54, 55, 178, 199–
    209
    adaptations of, 207–8

and boundary controls, 204–5
case study, 214–18
client revolts, 208–9, 269
defined, 53, 176–77, 199–200
distance maintenance, 206
informal organization, 208
moral limitations, 205–6
and organizational culture, 200–201
service constraints, 202–4
status issues, 201–2, 206, 216–17
typical problems, 207
public officers, corruption of, 240
public opinion, 178, 210–11, 214, 250
public policy, 27–28, 216, 234–35, 236
public relations, 74, 83, 86–87, 210
public schools, 80, 201, 202, 269
accountability, 78–79
evolution vs. creationism dispute in,
20–30
punishment in, 206, 218
publics of, 212 & *fig.*
sexual stereotyping in, 38
see also schoolteachers
public service agencies
bureaucracies, 77–81, 200–202, 205, 206,
214–18
domains of, 227
management of, 151
monopolies, 202
objectives of, 150*n*
and publics-in-contact, 201–2, 214–18
and resources, 204, 229
see also welfare agencies
Pugh, D. S., 132

qualities, defining people by, 11
quality control circles, 258–59

racial groups, 11, 145, 129–30
cohesiveness and power of, 111
managerial study, 266–67, 268 *fig.*
occupational distribution, 18–19, 127
prison populations, 129
as publics-in-contact, 201, 208–9
role conflict of police personnel, 139
stereotyping of, 37, 40, 117
urban revolt, 208–9
see also minority groups
racism, in language, 40
rank-and-file participants, 176–77
rationality, 10, 102–3
and decision making, 162, 164, 251–52
and goal formation, 82
rational-systems theory, 12–13, 34, 36, 100
Reagan, Pres. Ronald, 151, 165, 235, 264
reality, individual construction of, 185–86
Rebecca Myth (Gouldner), 166
recalcitrance, toward authority, 100–101
recessions, 257
reciprocity, in the workplace, 143–44

recombinant DNA technology, 252,
256–57
Redfield, Robert, 5
reflexive goals, 74
regulatory agencies, 27, 88, 213, 214, 215
fig., 235, 239, 271
Reissman, Leonard, 125
religion, religious institutions, 10, 20, 59,
60, 212, 243
remunerative power, 58, 105–6
research, 26, 27
by business schools, 26*n*
on classification, typologies, 49–51, 64,
65
by corporations, 27, 28, 29, 31–32, 44–45
dissemination of findings, 29–30
human and animal experimentation,
205–6
and ideological conflicts, 30–31
Marxist critique of, 42–44
organizational environments and, 222–23,
223*n*
and public policy, 27–28
social science, 31, 32–37
topic selection, 28–29
in universities
and academic job mobility, 195
corporate influences on, 31–32, 44–45
goal setting, 89
resocialization, in institutions, 59
resource dependence theory, 110, 214, 224–
25, 226–27, 230, 231
resources, 204, 226, 229–30, 233
retail stores, 201, 203, 204, 225*t*, 231
Revco Drug Stores, 244–47
reverse discrimination, 264, 269
rewards
in company cultures, 159–60
and status factors, 135
of voluntary service, 107–8
Ride, Sally, 182
risk management, 251
rites, rituals, 156–57, 158, 160–61
of passage, 127
in total institutions, 181
Roesthlisberger, F. J., 33
role overload, 139–40, 194
role partners, 125
role performances, 126, 207–8
roles, 124–25, 126, 128, 175–86
attachment to, 180–82
as bridge between individuals and groups,
176
conflict, sources of, 137–40
decisional, 162
and the division of labor, 132–33
and identity, 179–80
informal, in occupations, 138–39
in prisons, 146–47
and status, conferrment of, 182–83
and status sets, 125
types, 138–39, 177–78, 195
see also sex-role stereotypes
role set, 179
role strain, 137

Roosevelt, Pres. Franklin D., 29, 85
Rosaldo, Michelle Z., 126
Rosengren, William R., 59n, 200
Ross, Jerry, 170, 183
Rowbotham, Sheila, 111
Roy, Donald F., 160
Rubenstein, Richard L., 194, 205, 271
rules
  and authority, 8, 98
  and bureaucratic power, 205
  in company cultures, 159-60
  defined, 9
  in ideal bureaucracies, 12, 97-98
  vs. informal behavior norms, 14, 137
  negotiation and bargaining over, 136-37
rumors. *See* grapevine

Salancik, Gerald R., 82, 104, 179n
Samaha, Khalil, 5, 49, 56-58, 60, 150
San Francisco Bay Area Rapid Transit system, 120, 121
Sarin, Rakesh, 251
scapegoats, of management, 165
Schaefer, Richard, 132, 266
Schein, Edgar A., 51
Schein, Virginia Ellon, 171
Schlein, Miriam, 30
Schooler, Carmi, 186
schoolteachers, 79-80, 139, 195, 202, 204, 206, 214, 217, 269
Schwab, Donald P., 192
science, scientific knowledge, 10, 26, 27-30, 48, 241-42, 250. *See also* research; technology
scientific management studies, 33, 136, 160, 188, 258
scientific revolutions, 42
Scopes trial (1925), 29
Scott, W. Richard, 4, 15, 49, 50, 52-56, 57, 58, 63, 64, 65, 67, 73, 143, 176, 188, 192, 210
Scott, William G., 135
search process, in work procedures, 61-62
Seashore, Stanley, 51, 72
secondary adjustments (Goffman), 159, 207-8
secondary group relations, 6, 7
secrecy, 99, 117, 119
secretaries, 103, 117, 130, 190, 191
secrets, technological, 241-42, 257, 262
self-direction, in the workplace, 78, 186, 192
self-identity, 179-80, 182, 185, 186, 187
Selznick, Philip, 14, 100-101, 160
Servants of Power, The (Baritz), 32-33
service economies, 8, 54, 261
service organizations, 54-55, 65
sex
  and the division of labor, 126-27, 168, 170, 171, 182-83, 191
  as a master status-determining trait, 130
sex-role stereotypes, 38-40, 117, 167, 171-72, 190, 265
sexual discrimination, 263-64

sexual harassment, in offices, 110, 172
Shibutani, Tamotsu, 127
shift workers, 137-38
Shoreham nuclear power plant, 262
Shupe, Anson D., Jr., 181
Sikh activism, 213
Silkwood, Karen, 120-21
Sills, David L., 85
single strands, in grapevine communication, 118 *fig.*, 119
Sirianni, Carmen, 188
Slater, Jack, 206
Slaughter, Thomas F., Jr., 37
Slocum, John W., Jr., 152, 153-54, 155, 162
Smircich, Linda, 35
social class, 42, 43
socialism, 11, 135-36
socialization
  of hospital patients, 181-82
  of managers, 36, 150, 168-69
  to sex roles, 265
  in total institutions, 59
social movement organizations, 18, 20-21, 27, 41, 58, 87, 106, 110, 178, 209, 233, 243-44, 267
  defined, 243
  and goal succession, 86
  leadership of, 152
  1960s-70s turbulence, 208, 222, 223-24
  and numbers, power of, 111
  and the public-at-large, 209, 210, 211 *fig.*
  and substitute careers, 183-84
social security system, 269
social workers, 208
societies
  bureaucratic vs. traditional, 5-11
  modern, 5, 6, 7, 127-28, 250-51
Society Today, 19
soldiering (Taylor), 117
Solidarity movement, 40-41
South Africa, 18, 41, 214
Southern Christian Leadership Conference, 228
Soviet Union, 11, 30, 241, 242, 255-56
space weapons, 2
specialization
  of knowledge, 7
  of labor, 11, 66, 78, 127, 132-33
  see also deskilling
sponsors, of management trainees, 169, 172
sports industry, 20
spouse employment networks, 172
Squires, Gregory, D., 260
staff-inmate split (Goffman), 136, 143
staff positions, in hierarchies, 124, 172
Stake, Joan, 121, 122
status, 124-37, 176
  conflict perspective, 135-37
  cooperative perspective, 133-35
  and the division of labor, 124-26, 132-33
  and dress customs, 157
  and latent identity, 128-31, 132
  and moral careers, 185
  of publics-in-contact, 201-2, 206, 216-17
  roles, self-identity, and 179, 182-83

and work obligations, 143
see also hierarchies
status set, 125 *fig.*, 126, 179
status symbols, 133–34
Steers, Richard M., 51, 52
Stein, Peter J., 130
Stephenson, Richard M., 11, 124, 179
stereotypes
racial, 37, 40, 117
sex-role, 38–40, 117, 171–72, 265
Stinchcombe, Arthur L., 225*t*
Stratton, John R., 136, 146
Strauss, Anselm, 183
street-level bureaucracies, 178, 201–2, 204, 214–18, 269
stripping process, in total institutions, 181
structural determinants, of behavior, 187
structural features, of organizations
complexity, 222, 253–54
computer analysis of, 16*n*
coupling, loose vs. tight, 16, 253, 254, 255*t*
dual labor market and, 264
environment factors and, 222–23, 223*n*, 229
technology vs. management, influences of, 164, 165
Student Nonviolent Coordinating Committee (SNCC), 86, 228
students, 80, 81, 84, 114, 128, 181, 217, 230
cheating, 105
division of labor and, 128
faculty committees and dissertations, 119
mutual aid among, 141, 142
output goals, 89, 91–93
revolt (1960s), 208, 243
role set of, 179, 180 *fig.*
status and rewards, 128
Styles, Jimmie C., 237, 241
subcultures, 157–58
subgroups, power of, 104
subordinates
job problems questionnaire, 116 & *fig.*
power of, 97, 105, 112
supervision, 186, 189
survival, of organizations, 83–85, 257
and environmental threats, 83–84, 270
and goal modification, 79
population ecology model, 79, 84–85, 223–24
research studies on, 50–51
survival of the fittest doctrine, 34, 64
Sussman, Marvin P., 133, 178, 208
Sykes, Gresham M., 146
symbols, symbolism, 115, 117, 156–57
in information gathering, 164
status, 133–34
syphilis experimentation, 205–6
systems, complex and linear, 253–54
systems, resource theory, 72

task environments, 139
Tausky, Curt, 135
taxes, taxation, 74, 134, 239, 264

taxonomy (McKelvey), 63
Taylor, Frederick, 33, 117, 160
Taylorization, 195–96, 258. *See also* scientific management studies
teams, occupational, 192
technology, 2, 7, 10, 230, 250
high-risk, and accidents, 251–57, 270
and organizational structure, 164, 165, 223, 233
secrets, export of, 241–42, 257, 262
and skills, changing demand for, 8
and social structure, 63
typologies, 49, 60–63
and work structure, 61–62
see also computers; science
Terreberry, Shirley, 222
Texas public schools, textbook selection in, 30
Theory X, Theory Y (McGregor), 155, 188, 189
Thompson, James D., 73, 79, 86–88, 130, 131, 139
Three Mile Island nuclear accident, 251, 252
time and motion studies, 33, 40
time and space dimensions, in client relationships, 59 & *n*
Times Beach toxic waste cleanup, 235
token minority representation, 139, 168, 190, 267
total institutions (Goffman), 18, 34, 59–60, 65, 81, 136, 178
and clients, impact on, 178
staff-inmate split in, 136, 143
stripping process in, 181
toxic waste dumping, 235–36
Toyota Corporation, 258
trade secrets, 241–42
traditional societies, 5, 6–7, 250
authority in, 8
characteristics, 6*t*
division of labor in, 7
particularism in, 10
religion and magic in, 10
trained incapacity (Veblen), 193
transitive goals, 74
Tuskegee syphilis experiments, 205–6
Tylenol poisoning cases, 83–84
typologies, 47–67
bureaucracy, enterprise, voluntary association (Westrum-Samaha), 56–58
common-sense, 48–49
cui bono (Blau & Scott), 52–56, 65
intentional, 49
neglect of, 49–50
population and taxonomy (McKelvey), 63–64
power and compliance (Etzioni), 58–59
survival and effectiveness models, 50–51, 52 *fig.*, 64
technological (Perrow), 60–63
total institutions (Goffmann), 59–60

uncertainty
managerial ability to cope with, 109, 110–11, 153

and organizational structure, 223
underworld crime. *See* organized crime
unemployment, 187, 202, 256, 260, 261
Ungson, Gerardo R., 163
Union Carbide, 165
Union of Concerned Scientists, 2, 33
universalism, 10
universities, colleges, 81, 110-11, 114
   academic roles and status, 182, 195
   boundary controls in, 204
   career promotion, 110-11, 167
   goals, 76-77, 88-93
   management of, 90
   power relationships, 104, 110-11
   research programs, and corporate inter-
      ests, 31-32, 44-45, 110
   resource flows, 229, 230
University of California, 44-45
urbanization, 7, 20
Useem, Michael, 27 & *n*

Van de Ven, Andrew H., 17*n*, 226
Van Houten, Donald R., 35, 42-43
Vaughn, Diane, 236, 244-47
Veblen, Thorstein, 193
vice activities, 237
violence, and power concessions, 111-12
voluntary organizations, 98, 242-43, 270
   as bureaucracies, 5
   functions, 242-43
   and goal succession, 85-86
   and institutionalized organizations,
      242-43
   and involvement, 107-8
   leadership of, 152
   substitute careers in, 183-84
   typologies, 56-58, 150, 242
Volunteers, The (Sills), 85
volunteer work, 127, 142-43, 145
voting behavior, 178, 213
Voydanoff, Patricia, 170

waiters, waitresses, 117, 128, 138-39, 144
Waldinger, Roger, 21-22
Walling, Donovan R., 212 *fig.*
Wamsley, Gary L., 150*n*
wars, warfare, 55, 117-18, 127, 132, 230
Weber, Max, 42, 99, 100, 150, 157, 223,
      269, 270
   on authority, 8, 97, 98, 106
   on bureaucracies, 4-5, 11-12, 16 & *n*,
      193, 223, 269, 270
   on charismatic leaders, 9
   on power, 96, 97
Weick, Karl E., 16, 82
Weinstein, Deena, 112, 121
Weiss, Janet A., 51
welfare agencies, 77-78, 81, 132, 151, 193-
      94, 201, 217, 218, 227, 244-45

"welfare" labor unions, 261
Westhues, Kenneth, 42
Westrum, Ron, 5, 49, 56-58, 60, 150
Wheeler, Stanton, 146
whistle-blowing, in the workplace, 119-22
white-collar crime, 112, 119-22, 237, 239,
      241-42, 250, 262
Whyte, William Foote, 135, 138-39, 257,
      259, 260, 261, 262
Wilkins, Alan L., 16*n*, 26*n*
Winston, Kathryn Teich, 264
women, 1-2, 11, 12, 19, 259
   in Japan, 12, 259
   mothers, motherhood, 12, 183 & *n*, 184,
      209, 212, 264, 269
   occupations, 3, 19, 58, 182-83
      division of labor and, 126-27, 130
      family responsibilities and, 170, 172,
         183, 264, 265
      and job conditions, 187, 191
      and job mobility, 190-191, 265
      labor force participation, 264, 265-66
      labor unions, exclusion from 265
      as managers, executives, 130, 167, 168,
         169, 171-73, 266, 267
   in prison, 130-31, 145-47
   wives of managers, 170
Women and Work (Fox & Hesse-Biber), 171
Women's Christian Temperance Union
   (WCTU), 85
women's movement, 21, 37, 58, 86, 147,
      209, 243, 251
women's studies, 19, 37-40, 263-64
Woodward, Joan, 49, 60, 65
work behavior, 186-92
   bureaucrats, 202-3, 207, 216-18
   "making out," 81, 136
   and mobility, 189-91
   motivation and productivity, 187-88
   and organizational goals, 77-78
   participation and autonomy in, 188-89,
      258, 270
   personality factors, 186-87
   and productivity, 187-88, 192, 258-59
   research on, 32-33, 38
   and work flow, regulation of, 117, 136,
      141-42, 160, 203-4
   and working conditions, 186
   work satisfaction, alienation, 191-92
workers. *See* employees; labor; lower partic-
      ipants

Yuchtman, Ephraim, 51, 72

Zald, Mayer N., 150*n*, 226
Zey-Ferrell, Mary, 50, 51, 230
Zimbalist, Andrew, 177, 189
zone of indifference, in compliance, 103
zoning, land-use rules, 205